Houghton Mifflin

Reading

Triumphs

Senior Authors
J. David Cooper
John J. Pikulski

Authors
Kathryn Au
David J. Chard
Gilbert Garcia
Claude Goldenberg
Phyllis Hunter
Marjorie Y. Lipson
Shane Templeton
Sheila Valencia
MaryEllen Vogt

Consultants
Linda H. Butler
Linnea C. Ehri
Carla Ford

 HOUGHTON MIFFLIN

BOSTON

Acknowledgments begin on page 656.

Printed in the U.S.A.

ISBN: 0-618-24151-5

3 4 5 6 7 8 9 VH 09 08 07 06 05 04

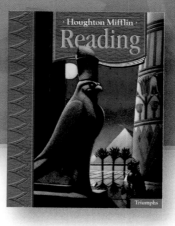

Triumphs

Theme 1: **Courage** **20**

Focus on *Poetry* **118**

Theme 2: **What Really Happened?** **136**

Focus on *Plays* **216**

Theme 3: **Growing Up** **238**

Theme 4: **Discovering Ancient Cultures** . . . **354**

Focus on *Myths* **430**

Theme 5: **Doers and Dreamers** **448**

Focus on *Speeches* **520**

Theme 6: **New Frontiers:**
Oceans and Space **542**

Glossary **642**

COURAGE

Theme Connections

Courage with Avi **20**

Background and Vocabulary **26**

Hatchet **28**
by Gary Paulsen, illustrated by Michael Steirnagle
Strategy Focus: Summarize

Media Link: Courage in the News **46**
Skill: How to Read a News Article

Fiction

Student Writing Model ▶ **A Personal Narrative** **48**

Background and Vocabulary **50**

Passage to Freedom **52**
by Ken Mochizuki, illustrated by Dom Lee
Strategy Focus: Evaluate

Primary Source Link: A Mother's Courage **68**
Skill: How to Read Primary Sources

Nonfiction

Background and Vocabulary **72**

Climb or Die **74**
by Edward Myers, illustrated by Bill Farnsworth
Strategy Focus: Predict and Infer

Social Studies Link: Battling Everest **90**
Skill: How to Read a Social Studies Article

Fiction

Historical Fiction

Background and Vocabulary......................... 94

The True Confessions of Charlotte Doyle 96

by Avi, illustrated by Scott McKowen
Strategy Focus: Monitor and Clarify

Social Studies Link: Alone Against the Sea.............. 112
Skill: How to Take Notes

Theme Wrap-Up
Check Your Progress

Nonfiction

Read and Compare 116A

Rosa Parks: My Story 116B

*by Rosa Parks
with Jim Haskins*

Realistic Fiction

Making a Difference 116H

by Catherine Nichols, illustrated by Robert Rodriguez

Think and Compare 116M

Taking Tests Choosing the Best Answer.......... 116N

Focus on Genre

POETRY

Poetry 118

Friends

Good Hotdogs 121
by Sandra Cisneros
Losing Livie from *Out of the Dust* 123
by Karen Hesse
Poem 124
by Langston Hughes
The Pasture 125
by Robert Frost
Oranges 126
by Gary Soto

Family

Family Style 128
by Janet Wong
Sundays 129
by Paul Janeczko
My Own Man 130
by Nikki Grimes
From **The People, Yes** 131
by Carl Sandburg
Child Rest 132
by Phil George
Family Photo 133
by Ralph Fletcher

What Really Happened?

Theme Connections

What Really Happened? with Shelley Tanaka **136**

Background and Vocabulary **142**

Biography

**Amelia Earhart:
First Lady of Flight** **144**
by Jan Parr
Strategy Focus: Question

Social Studies Link: Barnstorming Bessie Coleman **160**
Skill: How to Outline an Article

Student Writing Model ➤ A Story **164**

Background and Vocabulary **168**

Legend

The Girl Who Married the Moon **170**
by Joseph Bruchac, illustrated by Lisa Desimini
Strategy Focus: Summarize

Poetry Link: Images of the Moon **184**
Skill: How to Read a Poem

What Really Happened?

Nonfiction

Background and Vocabulary **188**

Dinosaur Ghosts **190**
by J. Lynett Gillette, illustrated by Douglas Henderson
Strategy Focus: Monitor and Clarify

Career Link: Doctor Dinosaur **210**
Skill: How to Categorize Information

Theme Wrap-Up
Check Your Progress

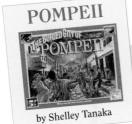

Historical Fiction

Read and Compare **214A**

Pompeii **214B**
by Shelley Tanaka
illustrated by Bleu Turrell

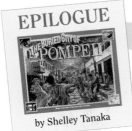

Nonfiction

Epilogue **214G**
by Shelley Tanaka

Think and Compare **214M**

Taking Tests   Filling in the Blank **214N**

PLAYS

Plays.. **216**

The Diary of Anne Frank **218**
by Frances Goodrich and Albert Hackett

A Better Mousetrap **226**
by Colleen Neuman

A Better Mousetrap
by Colleen Neuman
Wanted: state-of-the-art pest control
for clever rodent...

Theme 3

Growing Up

Theme Connections

Growing Up with E.L. Konigsburg **238**

Background and Vocabulary **244**

Where the Red Fern Grows **246**
by Wilson Rawls, illustrated by Joel Spector
Strategy Focus: Predict and Infer

Social Studies Link: Puppy Love **268**
Skill: How to Skim and Scan

Fiction

Student Writing Model ▶ A Description **272**

Background and Vocabulary **274**

Last Summer with Maizon **276**
by Jacqueline Woodson, illustrated by Eric Velasquez
Strategy Focus: Evaluate

Poetry Link: Poetic Power **294**
Skill: How to Read an Interview

Fiction

Background and Vocabulary **298**

The Challenge **300**
by Gary Soto, illustrated by David Diaz
Strategy Focus: Question

Health Link: How to Be a Good Sport **316**
Skill: How to Read a Persuasive Article

Short Story

Fiction

Background and Vocabulary **320**

The View from Saturday **322**
by E.L. Konigsburg, illustrated by Kevin Beilfuss
Strategy Focus: Monitor and Clarify

Science Link: Home-Grown Butterflies **348**
Skill: How to Read a Science Article

Theme Wrap-Up
Check Your Progress

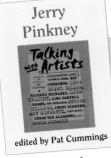

Realistic Fiction

Read and Compare **352A**

The Ink-Keeper's Apprentice **352B**
written and illustrated by Allen Say

Biography

Jerry Pinkney **352H**
by Jerry Pinkney with Pat Cummings, illustrated by Jerry Pinkney

Think and Compare **352O**

Taking Tests Writing a Personal Response **352P**

Theme 4

Discovering Ancient Cultures

Theme Connections

Discovering Ancient Cultures with Patricia and Fredrick McKissack **354**

Nonfiction

Background and Vocabulary **360**

Lost Temple of the Aztecs **362**
by Shelley Tanaka, illustrated by Greg Ruhl
Strategy Focus: Evaluate

Science Link: Raising Royal Treasures **380**
Skill: How to Adjust Your Rate of Reading

Student Writing Model ▶ A Research Report **384**

Background and Vocabulary **388**

The Great Wall **390**
by Elizabeth Mann, illustrated by Alan Witschonke
Strategy Focus: Summarize

Nonfiction

Technology Link: Building Ancient Rome **404**
Skill: How to Read a Timeline

Nonfiction

Background and Vocabulary **408**

The Royal Kingdoms of Ghana, Mali, and Songhay **410**

by Patricia and Fredrick McKissack, illustrated by Rob Wood
Strategy Focus: Monitor and Clarify

Social Studies Link: Daily Life in Ancient Greece **426**
Skill: How to Read a Diagram

Theme Wrap-Up
Check Your Progress

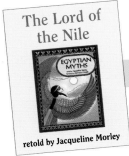

Myth

Read and Compare **428A**

The Lord of the Nile **428B**

by Jacqueline Morley
illustrated by Michael Jaroszko

Nonfiction

The Great Pyramid **428G**

by Elizabeth Mann, illustrated by Laura Lo Turco

Think and Compare **428M**

Taking Tests Vocabulary Items **428N**

Focus on Genre

MYTHS

Myths **430**

Arachne the Spinner **432**

Guitar Solo **437**

How Music Was Fetched Out of Heaven **441**

Three myths from collections by Geraldine McCaughrean

Doers and Dreamers

Theme Connections

Doers and Dreamers with Alma Flor Ada **448**

Background and Vocabulary **454**

A Kind of Grace **456**
by Jackie Joyner-Kersee
Strategy Focus: Summarize

Music Link: **A Real Jazzy Kid!** **470**
Skill: How to Read a Magazine Article

Autobiography

Student Writing Model ▶ A Personal Essay **474**

Background and Vocabulary **476**

Under the Royal Palms **478**
by Alma Flor Ada, illustrated by Stephanie Garcia
Strategy Focus: Predict and Infer

Social Studies Link: **Help Wanted** **492**
Skill: How to Skim and Scan

Autobiography

Doers
and
Dreamers

Biography

Background and Vocabulary **496**

Chuck Close, Up Close **498**
by Jan Greenberg and Sandra Jordan
Strategy Focus: Question

Fine Art Link: Different Strokes **514**
Skill: How to Look at Fine Art

Theme Wrap-Up
Check Your Progress

Realistic Fiction

Read and Compare **518A**

Yolonda's *Genius* **518B**
by Carol Fenner
illustrated by Colin Backhouse

Biography

No Ordinary Baby:
Wolfgang Amadeus Mozart **518G**
by Kathleen Krull

Think and Compare **518K**

Taking Tests   **Writing an Answer to a Question** **518L**

Focus on Genre

SPEECHES

Speeches. **520**

The Gettysburg Address. **522**
by Abraham Lincoln

**A Story of Courage, Bravery,
Strength, and Heroism** **525**
by Shao Lee

**On Accepting the
Newbery Medal**. **529**
by Jerry Spinelli

A Commencement Speech **533**
by Katherine Ortega

I Have a Dream. **536**
by Dr. Martin Luther King, Jr.

Theme 6

New Frontiers: Oceans and Space

Theme Connections

New Frontiers with Eugenie Clark. **542**

Background and Vocabulary **548**

The Adventures of Sojourner **550**
by Susi Trautmann Wunsch
Strategy Focus: Monitor and Clarify

Technology Link: Little Brother, Big Idea. **566**
Skill: How to Read a Technology Article

Nonfiction

Student Writing Model ▷ A Persuasive Essay **570**

Background and Vocabulary **572**

Franklin R. Chang-Díaz **574**
by Argentina Palacios
Strategy Focus: Evaluate

Science Link: Build and Launch a Paper Rocket! **590**
Skill: How to Follow Directions

Biography

Background and Vocabulary **594**

Beneath Blue Waters **596**
by Deborah Kovacs and Kate Madin
Strategy Focus: Question

Science Link: Sharks Under Ice **612**
Skill: How to Adjust Your Rate of Reading

Nonfiction

Short Story

Background and Vocabulary **616**

Out There **618**
by Theodore Taylor, illustrated by Rob Bolster
Strategy Focus: Predict and Infer

Career Link: Exploring the Deep **636**
Skill: How to Use the SQP3R Strategy

Theme Wrap-Up
Check Your Progress

by Tim Wynne-Jones

Realistic Fiction

Read and Compare **640A**

The Night of the Pomegranate **640B**
by Tim Wynne-Jones
illustrated by Mike Reed

Nonfiction

Eugenie Clark: Adventures of a Shark Scientist **640G**
by Ellen R. Butts and Joyce R. Schwartz

Think and Compare **640M**

Taking Tests Writing a Persuasive Essay **640N**

Glossary **642**

Theme 1

COURAGE

"You must do
the thing you think
you cannot do."

— *Eleanor Roosevelt*

COURAGE

with Avi

What qualities make a person courageous? Read this letter, and discover how author Avi defines courage. Take a chance, compare ideas, and find out what courage means to you.

THE NEWS

Firefighters to the Rescue!!!!

Dear Reader,

Courage is often used to describe larger than life actions. It might be a soldier's actions on the battlefield. It might refer to the rescue of someone from a life-threatening situation. Such actions make headlines.

I suspect, however, that most acts of courage go unnoticed by the public. Acts of courage — in my opinion — have to be noticed by *someone*, because I believe courage is *a moral action performed with the awareness that the result may well be failure.*

What do I mean by "moral action"? It is an act that is based on the desire to do good.

The soldier, for example, who acts *mindlessly* to save a comrade from harm may be acting heroically, but it is not courage if he or she isn't aware of the danger involved. If that same soldier *does* realize the danger and risk involved in saving a comrade, yes, that is courage.

It is an act of courage to speak publicly about your ideas and feelings when you *know* other people will not like what you have to say. It is an act of courage for a publisher to issue books knowing that some people might not approve. It is an act of courage to walk down a school hallway and say a big public "hello" to someone who *is* thought to be different from the majority. It is even an act of courage to cut your hair in the way you like, even though you know others might make fun of you.

In all of society there is tremendous pressure to look, act, talk, and think the same. But it is particularly hard for young people to show courage. Kids want so much to be accepted that they more often than not reject what may be different. If one breaks "the rules," kids can and will inflict extraordinary pain and rejection on those who are different.

Think about your classmates. Who struggles (often loudly) to be the same as everyone else? Who is quietly different?

Why is this important? It is important because every person alive has unique thoughts and ideas. Having a unique idea is not unusual. Acting upon those ideas is.

So, if courage is acting in a moral way that has the potential for risk and failure, ask yourself this hard question: "When did I last do a courageous thing?"

Sincerely,

It Takes Courage

Compare Avi's ideas about courage with your own. When you think of a courageous action, what comes to mind? Who, in your opinion, has performed an act of courage?

Look at the selections shown below. In what ways do you think the characters in these selections will show courage? As you read, think about each character's bravery. Compare how the characters change as they find ways to solve their problems. Discover the many different ways people learn to be courageous.

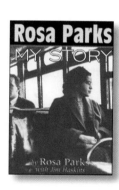

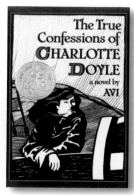

Internet

To learn about the authors in this theme, visit Education Place. **www.eduplace.com/kids**

Background and Vocabulary

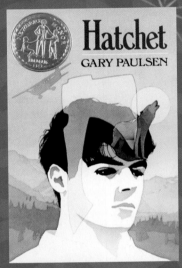

Hatchet

Read to find the meanings of these words.

e ○ Glossary

hatchet
quills
shelter
survival

In the Wild

After a plane crash in the Canadian wilderness, the boy in *Hatchet* struggles to stay alive on his own. Without shelter or human contact, he finds the wilderness beautiful but frightening. The forest is full of surprises, and many animals hide there. These animals may look harmless in their natural environment, but they can be dangerous and make survival difficult. With only a hatchet, or small ax, and the clothes on his back, how will the boy survive?

A typical view of the Canadian wilderness

Ouch! A porcupine's quills — stiff and sharp as needles — are its main defense.

An elk in the Canadian woods

A gray wolf amidst fall color

A grizzly bear causes fear in the wild.

Meet the Author
Gary Paulsen

"I simply can't not write," says Gary Paulsen. "I tried it when I ran dogs, but I ended up writing in longhand by the campfire when the dogs were sleeping. *Hatchet*, *Dogsong*, and *Woodsong* were all written while I was camping with dogs."

Besides being an award-winning author, Paulsen has also been a teacher, field engineer, magazine editor, soldier, actor, director, farmer, rancher, truck driver, trapper, professional archer, migrant farm worker, singer, sculptor, and sailor.

Meet the Illustrator
Michael Steirnagle

Growing up in El Paso, Texas, Michael Steirnagle played basket ball and baseball when he wasn't drawing and painting. Being around his mother, an artist, may have helped him decide to become an illustrator. He also teaches art at Palomar College in California. His advice to would-be artists or illustrators: "Learn to draw. Draw all the time and also use your imagination."

To find out more about Gary Paulsen and Michael Steirnagle, visit Education Place. **www.eduplace.com/kids**

Hatchet

GARY PAULSEN

Strategy Focus

How does Brian handle being alone in the wilderness? As you read the selection, **summarize** in your own words what happens.

Thirteen-year-old Brian Robeson is flying to meet his father when the pilot of the plane suffers a heart attack. When the plane crashes into a lake, Brian is stranded and alone in the Canadian wilderness. He builds a shelter near the lake and has a close encounter with a bear. As the days go by, Brian realizes that he must find food to survive.

At first he thought it was a growl. In the still darkness of the shelter in the middle of the night his eyes came open and he was awake and he thought there was a growl. But it was the wind, a medium wind in the pines had made some sound that brought him up, brought him awake. He sat up and was hit with the smell.

It terrified him. The smell was one of rot, some musty rot that made him think only of graves with cobwebs and dust and old death. His nostrils widened and he opened his eyes wider but he could see nothing. It was too dark, too hard dark with clouds covering even the small light from the stars, and he could not see. But the smell was alive, alive and full and in the shelter. He thought of the bear, thought of Bigfoot and every monster he had ever seen in every fright movie he had ever watched, and his heart hammered in his throat.

Then he heard the slithering. A brushing sound, a slithering brushing sound near his feet — and he kicked out as hard as he could, kicked out and threw the hatchet at the sound, a noise coming from his throat. But the hatchet missed, sailed into the wall where it hit the rocks with a shower of sparks, and his leg was instantly torn with pain, as if a hundred needles had been driven into it. "Unnnngh!"

Now he screamed, with the pain and fear, and skittered on his backside up into the corner of the shelter, breathing through his mouth, straining to see, to hear.

The slithering moved again, he thought toward him at first, and terror
took him, stopping his breath. He felt he could see a low dark form, a bulk
in the darkness, a shadow that lived, but now it moved away, slithering and
scraping it moved away and he saw or thought he saw it go out of the door
opening.

He lay on his side for a moment, then pulled a rasping breath and held
it, listening for the attacker to return. When it was apparent that the shadow
wasn't coming back he felt the calf of his leg, where the pain was centered
and spreading to fill the whole leg.

His fingers gingerly touched a group of needles that had been driven
through his pants and into the fleshy part of his calf. They were stiff and
very sharp on the ends that stuck out, and he knew then what the attacker
had been. A porcupine had stumbled into his shelter and when he had
kicked it the thing had slapped him with its tail of quills.

He touched each quill carefully. The pain made it seem as if dozens of
them had been slammed into his leg, but there were only eight, pinning the

cloth against his skin. He leaned back against the wall for a minute. He couldn't leave them in, they had to come out, but just touching them made the pain more intense.

So fast, he thought. So fast things change. When he'd gone to sleep he had satisfaction and in just a moment it was all different. He grasped one of the quills, held his breath, and jerked. It sent pain signals to his brain in tight waves, but he grabbed another, pulled it, then another quill. When he had pulled four of them he stopped for a moment. The pain had gone from being a pointed injury pain to spreading in a hot smear up his leg and it made him catch his breath.

Some of the quills were driven in deeper than others and they tore when they came out. He breathed deeply twice, let half of the breath out, and went back to work. Jerk, pause, jerk — and three more times before he lay back in the darkness, done. The pain filled his leg now, and with it came new waves of self-pity. Sitting alone in the dark, his leg aching, some mosquitoes finding him again, he started crying. It was all too much, just too much, and he couldn't take it. Not the way it was.

I can't take it this way, alone with no fire and in the dark, and next time it might be something worse, maybe a bear, and it wouldn't be just quills in the leg, it would be worse. I can't do this, he thought, again and again. I can't. Brian pulled himself up until he was sitting upright back in the corner of the cave. He put his head down on his arms across his knees, with stiffness taking his left leg, and cried until he was cried out.

He did not know how long it took, but later he looked back on this time of crying in the corner of the dark cave and thought of it as when he learned the most important rule of survival, which was that feeling sorry for yourself didn't work. It wasn't just that it was wrong to do, or that it was considered incorrect. It was more than that — it didn't work. When he sat alone in the darkness and cried and was done, was all done with it, nothing had changed. His leg still hurt, it was still dark, he was still alone and the self-pity had accomplished nothing.

At last he slept again, but already his patterns were changing and the sleep was light, a resting doze more than a deep sleep, with small sounds awakening him twice in the rest of the night. In the last doze period before daylight, before he awakened finally with the morning light and the clouds of new mosquitoes, he dreamed. This time it was not of his mother, but of his father at first and then of his friend Terry.

In the initial segment of the dream his father was standing at the side of a living room looking at him and it was clear from his expression that he was trying to tell Brian something. His lips moved but there was no sound, not a whisper. He waved his hands at Brian, made gestures in front of his face as if he were scratching something, and he worked to make a word with his mouth but at first Brian could not see it. Then the lips made an *mmmmm* shape but no sound came. *Mmmmm — maaaa.* Brian could not hear it, could not understand it and he wanted to so badly; it was so important to understand his father, to know what he was saying. He was trying to help, trying so hard, and when Brian couldn't understand he looked cross, the way he did when Brian asked questions more than once, and he faded. Brian's father faded into a fog place Brian could not see and the dream was almost over, or seemed to be, when Terry came.

He was not gesturing to Brian but was sitting in the park at a bench looking at a barbecue pit and for a time nothing happened. Then he got up and poured some charcoal from a bag into the cooker, then some starter fluid, and he took a flick type of lighter and lit the fluid. When it was burning and the charcoal was at last getting hot he turned, noticing Brian for the first time in the dream. He turned and smiled and pointed to the fire as if to say, see, a fire.

But it meant nothing to Brian, except that he wished he had a fire. He saw a grocery sack on the table next to Terry. Brian thought it must contain hot dogs and chips and mustard and he could think only of the food. But Terry shook his head and pointed again to the fire, and twice more he pointed to the fire, made Brian see the flames, and Brian felt his frustration and anger rise and he thought all right, all right, I see the fire but so what? I don't have a fire. I know about fire; I know I need a fire.

I know that.

His eyes opened and there was light in the cave, a grey dim light of morning. He wiped his mouth and tried to move his leg, which had stiffened like wood. There was thirst, and hunger, and he ate some raspberries from the jacket. They had spoiled a bit, seemed softer and mushier, but still had a rich sweetness. He crushed the berries against the roof of his mouth with his tongue and drank the sweet juice as it ran down his throat. A flash of metal caught his eye and he saw his hatchet in the sand where he had thrown it at the porcupine in the dark.

He scootched up, wincing a bit when he bent his stiff leg, and crawled to where the hatchet lay. He picked it up and examined it and saw a chip in the top of the head.

The nick wasn't large, but the hatchet was important to him, was his only tool, and he should not have thrown it. He should keep it in his hand, and make a tool of some kind to help push an animal away. Make a staff, he thought, or a lance, and save the hatchet. Something came then, a thought as he held the hatchet, something about the dream and his father and Terry, but he couldn't pin it down.

"Ahhh . . ." He scrambled out and stood in the morning sun and stretched his back muscles and his sore leg. The hatchet was still in his hand, and as he stretched and raised it over his head it caught the first rays of the morning sun. The first faint light hit the silver of the hatchet and it flashed a brilliant gold in the light. Like fire. That is it, he thought. What they were trying to tell me.

Fire. The hatchet was the key to it all. When he threw the hatchet at the porcupine in the cave and missed and hit the stone wall it had showered

sparks, a golden shower of sparks in the dark, as golden with fire as the sun was now.

The hatchet was the answer. That's what his father and Terry had been trying to tell him. Somehow he could get fire from the hatchet. The sparks would make fire.

Brian went back into the shelter and studied the wall. It was some form of chalky granite, or a sandstone, but imbedded in it were large pieces of a darker stone, a harder and darker stone. It only took him a moment to find where the hatchet had struck. The steel had nicked into the edge of one of the darker stone pieces. Brian turned the head backward so he would strike with the flat rear of the hatchet and hit the black rock gently. Too gently, and nothing happened. He struck harder, a glancing blow, and two or three weak sparks skipped off the rock and died immediately.

He swung harder, held the hatchet so it would hit a longer, sliding blow, and the black rock exploded in fire. Sparks flew so heavily that several of them skittered and jumped on the sand beneath the rock and he smiled and struck again and again.

There could be fire here, he thought. I will have a fire here, he thought, and struck again — I will have fire from the hatchet.

Brian found it was a long way from sparks to fire.

Clearly there had to be something for the sparks to ignite, some kind of tinder or kindling — but what? He brought some dried grass in, tapped sparks into it and watched them die. He tried small twigs, breaking them into little pieces, but that was worse than the grass. Then he tried a combination of the two, grass and twigs.

Nothing. He had no trouble getting sparks, but the tiny bits of hot stone or metal — he couldn't tell which they were — just sputtered and died.

He settled back on his haunches in exasperation, looking at the pitiful clump of grass and twigs.

He needed something finer, something soft and fine and fluffy to catch the bits of fire.

Shredded paper would be nice, but he had no paper.

"So close," he said aloud, "so close . . ."

He put the hatchet back in his belt and went out of the shelter, limping on his sore leg. There had to be something, had to be. Man had made fire. There had been fire for thousands, millions of years. There had to be a way. He dug in his pockets and found a twenty-dollar bill in his wallet. Paper. Worthless paper out here. But if he could get a fire going . . .

He ripped the twenty into tiny pieces, made a pile of pieces, and hit sparks into them. Nothing happened. They just wouldn't take the sparks. But there had to be a way — some way to do it.

Not twenty feet to his right, leaning out over the water were birches and he stood looking at them for a full half-minute before they registered on his mind. They were a beautiful white with bark like clean, slightly speckled paper.

Paper.

He moved to the trees. Where the bark was peeling from the trunks it lifted in tiny tendrils, almost fluffs. Brian plucked some of them loose, rolled them in his fingers. They seemed flammable, dry and nearly powdery. He pulled and twisted bits off the trees, packing them in one hand while he picked them with the other, picking and gathering until he had a wad close to the size of a baseball.

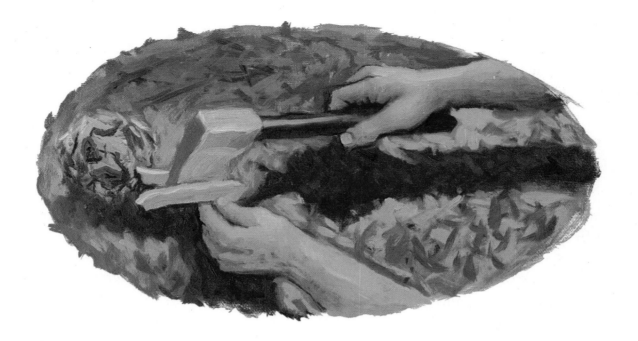

Then he went back into the shelter and arranged the ball of birchbark peelings at the base of the black rock. As an afterthought he threw in the remains of the twenty-dollar bill. He struck and a stream of sparks fell into the bark and quickly died. But this time one spark fell on one small hair of dry bark — almost a thread of bark — and seemed to glow a bit brighter before it died.

The material had to be finer. There had to be a soft and incredibly fine nest for the sparks.

I must make a home for the sparks, he thought. A perfect home or they won't stay, they won't make fire.

He started ripping the bark, using his fingernails at first, and when that didn't work he used the sharp edge of the hatchet, cutting the bark in thin slivers, hairs so fine they were almost not there. It was painstaking work, slow work, and he stayed with it for over two hours. Twice he stopped for a handful of berries and once to go to the lake for a drink. Then back to work, the sun on his back, until at last he had a ball of fluff as big as a grapefruit — dry birchbark fluff.

He positioned his spark nest — as he thought of it — at the base of the rock, used his thumb to make a small depression in the middle, and slammed the back of the hatchet down across the black rock. A cloud of sparks rained down, most of them missing the nest, but some, perhaps thirty or so, hit in the depression and of those six or seven found fuel and grew, smoldered and caused the bark to take on the red glow.

Then they went out.

Close — he was close. He repositioned the nest, made a new and smaller dent with his thumb, and struck again.

More sparks, a slight glow, then nothing.

It's me, he thought. I'm doing something wrong. I do not know this — a cave dweller would have had a fire by now, a Cro-Magnon man would have a fire by now — but I don't know this. I don't know how to make a fire.

Maybe not enough sparks. He settled the nest in place once more and hit the rock with a series of blows, as fast as he could. The sparks poured like a golden waterfall. At first they seemed to take, there were several, many sparks that found life and took briefly, but they all died.

Starved.

He leaned back. They are like me. They are starving. It wasn't quantity, there were plenty of sparks, but they needed more.

I would kill, he thought suddenly, for a book of matches. Just one book. Just one match. I would kill.

What makes fire? He thought back to school. To all those science classes. Had he ever learned what made a fire? Did a teacher ever stand up there and say, "This is what makes a fire . . ."

He shook his head, tried to focus his thoughts. What did it take? You have to have fuel, he thought — and he had that. The bark was fuel. Oxygen — there had to be air.

He needed to add air. He had to fan on it, blow on it.

He made the nest ready again, held the hatchet backward, tensed, and struck four quick blows. Sparks came down and he leaned forward as fast as he could and blew.

Too hard. There was a bright, almost intense glow, then it was gone. He had blown it out.

Another set of strikes, more sparks. He leaned and blew, but gently this time, holding back and aiming the stream of air from his mouth to hit the brightest spot. Five or six sparks had fallen in a tight mass of bark hair and Brian centered his efforts there.

The sparks grew with his gentle breath. The red glow moved from the sparks themselves into the bark, moved and grew and became worms, glow-

ing red worms that crawled up the bark hairs and caught other threads of bark and grew until there was a pocket of red as big as a quarter, a glowing red coal of heat.

And when he ran out of breath and paused to inhale, the red ball suddenly burst into flame.

"Fire!" He yelled. "I've got fire! I've got it, I've got it, I've got it . . ."

But the flames were thick and oily and burning fast, consuming the ball of bark as fast as if it were gasoline. He had to feed the flames, keep them going. Working as fast as he could he carefully placed the dried grass and wood pieces he had tried at first on top of the bark and was gratified to see them take.

But they would go fast. He needed more, and more. He could not let the flames go out.

He ran from the shelter to the pines and started breaking off the low, dead small limbs. These he threw in the shelter, went back for more, threw those in, and squatted to break and feed the hungry flames. When the small wood was going well he went out and found larger wood and did not relax until that was going. Then he leaned back against the wood brace of his door opening and smiled.

I have a friend, he thought — I have a friend now. A hungry friend, but a good one. I have a friend named fire.

Think About the Selection

1. If the porcupine hadn't entered Brian's shelter, do you think Brian would have discovered a way to make fire? Why or why not?

2. If you were Brian, would you pull the quills out of your leg? Explain.

3. Why does Brian feel sorry for himself? What does this tell you about Brian?

4. Think about the people in Brian's dream. What part do they play in his thinking of using the hatchet to make fire?

5. Brian recalls what he learned in school about what makes a fire. What have you learned in school that has helped you solve a problem or make a decision?

6. Why do you think Brian calls fire "a hungry friend"?

7. **Connecting/Comparing** Do you think Brian's actions alone in the wilderness showed courage? Why or why not?

Explaining

Write an Explanation

To Brian, the most important rule of survival is that feeling sorry for yourself doesn't work. Do you agree? If so, why? If not, what do you think is the most important rule of survival? Why? Write an explanation of your point of view or opinion.

Tips

- Begin by thinking of what you know about survival rules or skills.
- State your point of view clearly in a topic sentence. Support it with details and reasons.

Design a Poster

With a partner, review the materials Brian gathers and the steps he takes to make a fire. Then make a poster showing the materials and the steps he uses to build the fire.

Chart the Five Senses

Make a chart listing the five senses: touch, taste, smell, sight, hearing. Look back at the selection and list under each sense what Brian experiences.

Bonus Find examples of similes (comparisons using *like* or *as*) that describe what Brian feels with his senses. Add the similes to the five senses chart.

Internet

Post a Review

Write a review of *Hatchet*. Post your review on Education Place.

www.eduplace.com/kids

Skill: How to Read a News Article

1 Look first at the **head-line** to find out what the article is about.

2 Then look for answers to these questions:

Who is the article about?

What happened?

Where and **when** did the event occur?

Why did it happen?

3 Look at the **photo-graphs** and read the **captions** to help you picture the event.

COURAGE in the NEWS

Newspapers are full of stories about courage. As you read the following news article, you may wonder: "What would I do in the same situation?"

Boy Wonder; 5th-Grader Stops Bus After Driver Collapses

Carolyn Bower of the Post-Dispatch Staff

A fifth-grade student became a hero Tuesday when he took control of a runaway school bus on U.S. Highway 40 in St. Louis and stopped it before anyone was badly injured, police and the boy's principal said.

Larry Champagne III, 10, was credited with saving the lives of about 20 fellow students, including his brother, on a Mayflower bus when its driver apparently suffered a stroke.

The students from St. Louis were en route to Bellerive School in the Parkway School District when Larry felt the bus swerve back and forth and saw the driver slump and fall into the stairwell.

Larry ran to the front of the bus, grabbed the wheel and stomped on the brake. A passer-by stopped to help, and Larry opened the door.

Authorities said the driver, Ernestine Blackman, apparently suffered a stroke that temporarily paralyzed the right side of her body. Blackman was reported in serious condition late Tuesday at Barnes Hospital.

Five children suffered minor injuries. Two were treated at St. Louis Children's Hospital and released, and three at Cardinal Glennon Hospital.

Larry was fairly low-key about what had happened. But other

children chanted to Ken Russell, principal at Bellerive:

"Larry saved our lives."

Larry Champagne is a hero to his classmates.

Here's the story police and Russell pieced together:

At 8 A.M., about 20 minutes before Blackman's bus normally delivered the voluntary transfer students to Bellerive, Blackman apparently suffered a stroke driving on Highway 40 near Sarah Avenue. Police don't know how fast the bus was traveling.

The bus started swerving, passing cars honked their horns, and Blackman slid from her seat. Larry rushed forward to apply the air brake. Before he got the bus under control, it hit a guardrail, swerved and hit another guardrail, and a pickup hit the bus. Police had no indication whether the truck's driver was injured.

At some point, other students came forward to help. They included Crystal Wright and Gregory McKnight, both third-graders; and Gregory's brother, Angelo McKnight, and Imani Butler, both in fourth grade.

Crystal handed a passer-by Blackman's radio microphone to call Mayflower. Someone with a cellular phone called police.

Gregory, Angelo and Imani were unable to move Blackman. Imani and Angelo were among the children treated for minor injuries, the principal said.

Another bus took the uninjured children to Bellerive. Russell met with them and asked them how they had known what to do.

They told him the bus driver earlier had instructed them what to do in an emergency. And Larry said his grandfather, Lawrence Champagne, had given him some driving tips.

Russell said: "I'm proud our students were able to remain calm and take care of one another. I'm also proud that they listened to the instructions that the driver gave them and remembered those."

The bus company's division manager, Tim Stieber, marveled at Larry's success in stopping the bus.

"Considering how bad it could have been, it was good," Stieber said.

Larry was too nervous to talk to a reporter later Tuesday, his mother, Dawn Little, said. She praised Larry for his fast thinking and said she was especially grateful that he and his brother, Jerrick, 9, were uninjured.

A Personal Narrative

A personal narrative gives a first-person account of a true experience. Use this student's writing as a model when you write a personal narrative of your own.

Rappelling in Ocala

> **Beginning** your narrative with a question helps to hook your reader.

Have you ever gone rappelling? In case you don't know, rappelling is a way to descend from a mountain using a special kind of rope. On January 3, 1999, I went rappelling with my three cousins, my brother, and my two uncles. Wow! Did I learn a lot, and have fun at the same time. I had only been rappelling one other time before that special day. The most awesome part was the zip line. A zip line means that you tie one end of a rope to a tree and the other end of the rope to another tree down low or at a slant, and then you hook your carabiner (a long metal ring with a clip) to the rope and slide down.

> Using careful **sequencing** is essential for clarity.

One of the things I learned this time was to turn upside down while I was rappelling. It took me a couple of tries before I got the hang of it. It was especially exciting because I was given plenty of chances to rappel and also to go down the zip line.

I had a great time learning to use some equipment that I hadn't used on my last trip. The barrack and the ascender are two pieces of rappelling equipment I learned to use. The last time I went rappelling, I used an item called a figure eight instead of the barrack, but now that I have used the barrack I am more comfortable with it. A barrack is what the rope slides through to get down to the bottom. The ascender is something you hook onto a rope to help you climb. I only used the ascender when I was trying to get to the top of the cliff. My three cousins used their ascenders to get to the top of the cliff and climb the wall. They had an advantage over me because they had been rappelling more often.

On this rappelling trip, I learned a lot and enjoyed myself at the same time. Because I hope to do a lot more rappelling, I have asked for some equipment for my birthday. I am hoping to get many more opportunities to rappel with my cousins and the rest of my family.

> Using specific **details** brings your narrative to life for the reader.

> It's important to draw your narrative to a satisfactory **conclusion.**

Meet the Author

Megan M.
Grade: six
State: Florida
Hobbies: swimming and rollerblading
What she'd like to be when she grows up: an actress or a news broadcaster

Background and Vocabulary

PASSAGE TO FREEDOM
The Sugihara Story

Written by KEN MOCHIZUKI
Illustrated by DOM LEE
Afterword by HIROKI SUGIHARA

Passage to Freedom

Read to find the meanings of these words.

e ● Glossary

diplomat
government
refugees
superiors
visas

Album for a Hero

During World War II, many people had to leave their countries and become **refugees** — people fleeing the dangers of war. One escape route was the small country of Lithuania, as you will see in the story *Passage to Freedom*. The narrator's father, Chiune Sugihara, could use his powerful job to move people from Lithuania to safety.

Sugihara was a **diplomat** — someone chosen to represent his or her **government** in another country. A diplomat carries out his or her **superiors'** orders.

Kaunas, Lithuania, is the small town where Sugihara and his family lived in 1940.

Chiune Sugihara (*above*) risked the lives of his wife, Yukiko, and his children (*pictured top, right*) to save the lives of thousands of Jews. He issued **visas** — official written permission to enter and travel in another country — to Jewish refugees from Poland. The refugees (*right*) would line the gates outside of Sugihara's home hoping for freedom.

This is the official stamp that was applied to each visa.

Selection 2

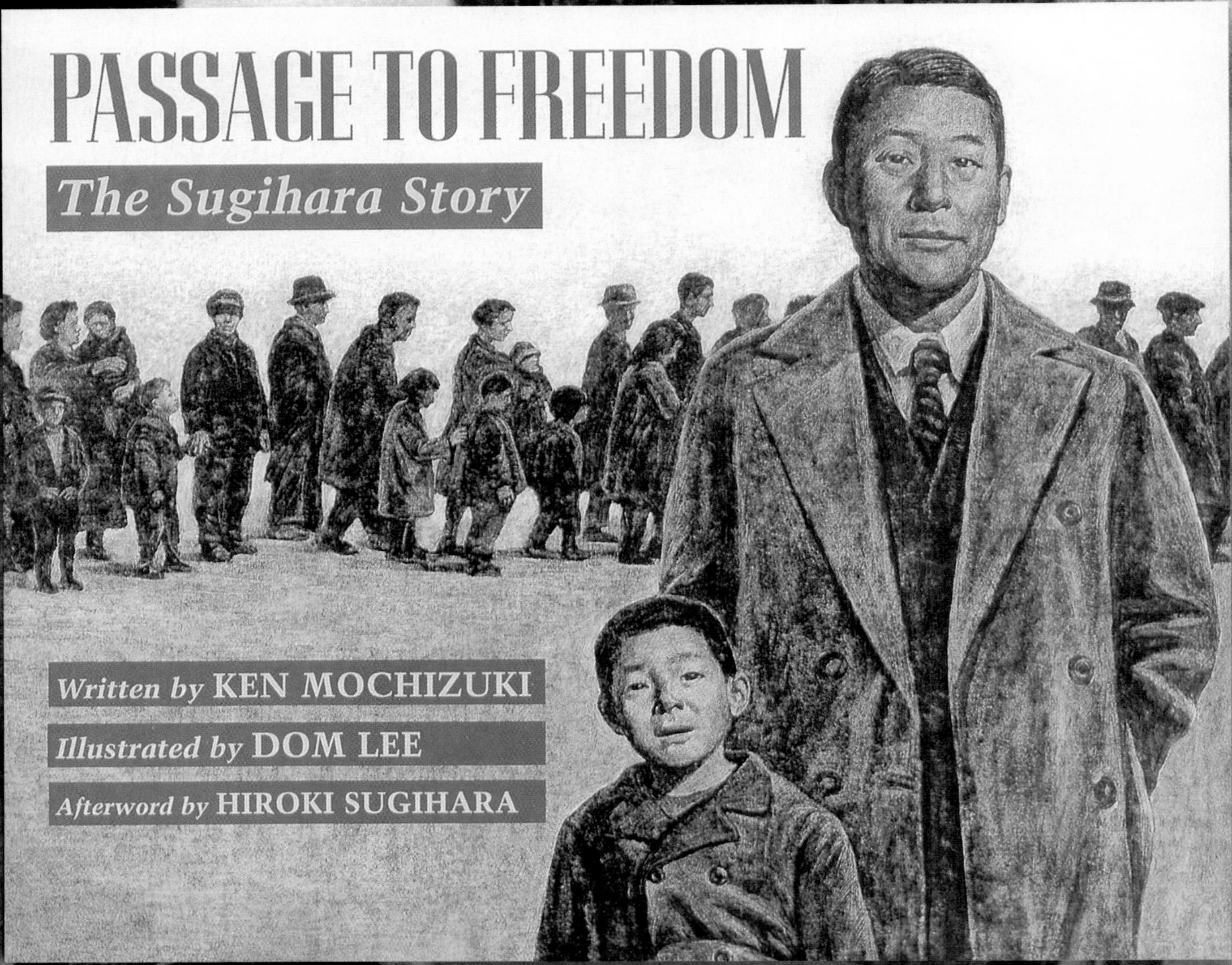
PASSAGE TO FREEDOM
The Sugihara Story
Written by KEN MOCHIZUKI
Illustrated by DOM LEE
Afterword by HIROKI SUGIHARA

Strategy Focus

Hiroki Sugihara and his family face a difficult problem involving thousands of lives. As you read, **evaluate** how well you think the author captures the difficulty of the family's decision.

There is a saying that the eyes tell everything about a person.

At a store, my father saw a young Jewish boy who didn't have enough money to buy what he wanted. So my father gave the boy some of his. That boy looked into my father's eyes and, to thank him, invited my father to his home.

That is when my family and I went to a Hanukkah celebration for the first time. I was five years old.

In 1940, my father was a diplomat, representing the country of Japan. Our family lived in a small town in the small country called Lithuania. There was my father and mother, my Auntie Setsuko, my younger brother Chiaki, and my three-month-old baby brother, Haruki. My father worked in his office downstairs.

In the mornings, birds sang in the trees. We played with girls and boys
from the neighborhood at a huge park near our home. Houses and churches
around us were hundreds of years old. In our room, Chiaki and I played with
toy German soldiers, tanks, and planes. Little did we know that the real
soldiers were coming our way.

Then one early morning in late July, my life changed forever.

My mother and Auntie Setsuko woke Chiaki and me up, telling us to get
dressed quickly. My father ran upstairs from his office.

"There are a lot of people outside," my mother said. "We don't know
what is going to happen."

In the living room, my parents told my brother and me not to let anybody see us looking through the window. So, I parted the curtains a tiny bit. Outside, I saw hundreds of people crowded around the gate in front of our house.

The grown-ups shouted in Polish, a language I did not understand. Then I saw the children. They stared at our house through the iron bars of the gate. Some of them were my age. Like the grown-ups, their eyes were red from not having slept for days. They wore heavy winter coats — some wore more than one coat, even though it was warm outside. These children looked as though they had dressed in a hurry. But if they came from somewhere else, where were their suitcases?

"What do they want?" I asked my mother.

"They have come to ask for your father's help," she replied. "Unless we help, they may be killed or taken away by some bad men."

Some of the children held on tightly to the hands of their fathers, some clung to their mothers. One little girl sat on the ground, crying.

I felt like crying, too. "Father," I said, "please help them."

My father stood quietly next to me, but I knew he saw the children. Then some of the men in the crowd began climbing over the fence. Borislav and Gudje, two young men who worked for my father, tried to keep the crowd calm.

My father walked outside. Peering through the curtains, I saw him standing on the steps. Borislav translated what my father said: He asked the crowd to choose five people to come inside and talk.

My father met downstairs with the five men. My father could speak Japanese, Chinese, Russian, German, French, and English. At this meeting, everyone spoke Russian.

I couldn't help but stare out the window and watch the crowd, while downstairs, for two hours, my father listened to frightening stories. These people were refugees — people who ran away from their homes because, if they stayed, they would be killed. They were Jews from Poland, escaping from the Nazi soldiers who had taken over their country.

The five men had heard my father could give them visas — official written permission to travel through another country. The hundreds of Jewish refugees outside hoped to travel east through the Soviet Union and end up in Japan. Once in Japan, they could go to another country. Was it true? the men asked. Could my father issue these visas? If he did not, the Nazis would soon catch up with them.

My father answered that he could issue a few, but not hundreds. To do that, he would have to ask for permission from his government in Japan.

That night, the crowd stayed outside our house. Exhausted from the day's excitement, I slept soundly. But it was one of the worst nights of my father's life. He had to make a decision. If he helped these people, would he put our family in danger? If the Nazis found out, what would they do?

But if he did not help these people, they could all die.

My mother listened to the bed squeak as my father tossed and turned all night.

The next day, my father said he was going to ask his government about the visas. My mother agreed it was the right thing to do. My father sent his message

by cable. Gudje took my father's written message down to the telegraph office.

I watched the crowd as they waited for the Japanese government's reply. The five representatives came into our house several times that day to ask if an answer had been received. Any time the gate opened, the crowd tried to charge inside.

Finally, the answer came from the Japanese government. It was "no." My father could not issue that many visas to Japan. For the next two days, he thought about what to do.

Hundreds more Jewish refugees joined the crowd. My father sent a second message to his government, and again the answer was "no." We still couldn't go outside. My little brother Haruki cried often because we were running out of milk.

I grew tired of staying indoors. I asked my father constantly, "Why are these people here? What do they want? Why do they have to be here? Who are they?"

My father always took the time to explain everything to me. He said the refugees needed his help, that they needed permission from him to go to another part of the world where they would be safe.

"I cannot help these people yet," he calmly told me. "But when the time comes, I will help them all that I can."

My father cabled his superiors yet a third time, and I knew the answer by the look in his eyes. That night, he said to my mother, "I have to do something. I may have to disobey my government, but if I don't, I will be disobeying God."

The next morning, he brought the family together and asked what he should do. This was the first time he ever asked all of us to help him with anything.

My mother and Auntie Setsuko had already made up their minds. They said we had to think about the people outside before we thought about ourselves. And that is what my parents had always told me — that I must think as if I were in someone else's place. If I were one of those children out there, what would I want someone to do for me?

I said to my father, "If we don't help them, won't they die?"

With the entire family in agreement, I could tell a huge weight was lifted off my father's shoulders. His voice was firm as he told us, "I will start helping these people."

Outside, the crowd went quiet as my father spoke, with Borislav translating.

"I will issue visas to each and every one of you to the last. So, please wait patiently."

The crowd stood frozen for a second. Then the refugees burst into cheers. Grown-ups embraced each other, and some reached to the sky. Fathers and mothers hugged their children. I was especially glad for the children.

My father opened the garage door and the crowd tried to rush in. To keep order, Borislav handed out cards with numbers. My father wrote out each visa by hand. After he finished each one, he looked into the eyes of the person receiving the visa and said, "Good luck."

Refugees camped out at our favorite park, waiting to see my father. I was finally able to go outside.

Chiaki and I played with the other children in our toy car. They pushed as we rode, and they rode as we pushed. We chased each other around the big trees. We did not speak the same language, but that didn't stop us.

For about a month, there was always a line leading to the garage. Every day, from early in the morning till late at night, my father tried to write three hundred visas. He watered down the ink to make it last. Gudje and a young Jewish man helped out by stamping my father's name on the visas.

My mother offered to help write the visas, but my father insisted he be the only one, so no one else could get into trouble. So my mother watched the crowd and told my father how many were still in line.

One day, my father pressed down so hard on his fountain pen, the tip broke off. During that month, I only saw him late at night. His eyes were always red and he could hardly talk. While he slept, my mother massaged his arm, stiff and cramped from writing all day.

Soon my father grew so tired, he wanted to quit writing the visas. But my mother encouraged him to continue. "Many people are still waiting," she said. "Let's issue some more visas and save as many lives as we can."

While the Germans approached from the west, the Soviets came from the east and took over Lithuania. They ordered my father to leave. So did the Japanese government, which reassigned him to Germany. Still, my father wrote the visas until we absolutely had to move out of our home. We stayed at a hotel for two days, where my father still wrote visas for the many refugees who followed him there.

Then it was time to leave Lithuania. Refugees who had slept at the train station crowded around my father. Some refugee men surrounded my father to protect him. He now just issued permission papers — blank pieces of paper with his signature.

As the train pulled away, refugees ran alongside. My father still handed permission papers out the window. As the train picked up speed, he threw

them out to waiting hands. The people in the front of the crowd looked into my father's eyes and cried, "We will never forget you! We will see you again!"

I gazed out the train window, watching Lithuania and the crowd of refugees fade away. I wondered if we would ever see them again.

"Where are we going?" I asked my father.

"We are going to Berlin," he replied.

Chiaki and I became very excited about going to the big city. I had so many questions for my father. But he fell asleep as soon as he settled into his seat. My mother and Auntie Setsuko looked really tired, too.

Back then, I did not fully understand what the three of them had done, or why it was so important.

I do now.

ABOUT THE AUTHOR

Ken Mochizuki

Hometown: Seattle, Washington

Roots: Grandparents born in Japan

How he got the story: By spending hours on the phone as Sugihara's son recalled what happened 50 years ago

What he thinks of Sugihara: "I consider Chiune Sugihara as one of my personal heroes."

Mochizuki's motto: Believe in what you can do, not in what someone says you can't.

ABOUT THE ILLUSTRATOR

Dom Lee

Roots: Born and raised in Seoul, Korea, but currently lives in Plainsboro, New Jersey

How he makes his art: First he puts handmade beeswax on paper, then scratches out images, and finally adds oil paint and colored pencil to complete the illustration.

Teamwork: Dom Lee and Ken Mochizuki have worked together on two previous children's books, *Baseball Saved Us* and *Heroes*.

To find out more about Ken Mochizuki and Dom Lee, visit Education Place. **www.eduplace.com/kids**

Think About the Selection

1. Why do you think Sugihara's decision to write visas for the refugees was a difficult one? Explain.

2. Do you think Sugihara did the right thing, giving his money to the boy at the store? Why or why not?

3. Why did the narrator feel especially sorry for the children of the refugees?

4. Give examples of how Sugihara used his diplomatic skills in talking to the refugees and communicating with his government.

5. At that time, the narrator didn't fully understand the importance of what his parents had done. Give an example of an event or person in your life that you understand better now than when you were younger.

6. Why didn't the Sugihara children and the children of the refugees need to speak the same language to play with each other?

7. **Connecting/Comparing** Compare Brian's courage in *Hatchet* with Sugihara's courage. How was each courageous in his own way? Explain.

 Expressing

Write from Another Point of View

Think of how a Polish refugee may have felt standing outside the Sugiharas' house. Write a few paragraphs expressing the refugee's feelings both while awaiting Mr. Sugihara's decision and after learning that he would grant the visas.

Tips

- To write from the point of view of a refugee, think about what it would be like to *be* that refugee.
- Reread the selection to find clues about how the refugees felt.

Measure Distances

Using a world map, trace the route that the refugees followed as they escaped their homeland. Use the scale on the map to measure the distances between major locations. Make a chart listing each of these distances and the total distance.

Bonus **Figure out how the total distance the refugees traveled compares to the distance from the west coast to the east coast of the United States.**

Exploring Color

Dom Lee uses a brown color palette in his illustrations for *Passage to Freedom*. This monochromatic color scheme — using different shades of one color — suggests a certain mood. Choose a color scheme that suggests a certain mood for you. Draw, paint, or describe a scene, using shades of those colors to create that mood.

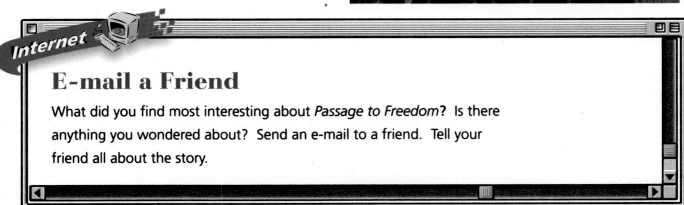

Internet

E-mail a Friend

What did you find most interesting about *Passage to Freedom*? Is there anything you wondered about? Send an e-mail to a friend. Tell your friend all about the story.

A Mother's
Courage

by Tammy Zambo

*M*onique Goodrich (*above, right, with her brother, Michel, in 1942*), who lives in Bradford, Massachusetts, was born Monique Jackson in 1937 in Paris, France. When the Germans invaded Europe in World War II, many Jewish families tried to leave or hide. Some couples, like Monique's parents, Hélène and Charles Jackson, sent their children to live with non-Jewish families until it was safe to be reunited. In this interview, Monique tells what it was like to be a hidden child during the war.

What do you remember before the war?

For me there is no "before," because in my earliest recollection, I was in the Pyrenees Mountains and it was already the war.

When the Germans invaded France in 1940 and were on their way to Paris, the authorities said, "Get out," to the women and children. My mother had a friend who suggested that we go into this little town in the Pyrenees called Saint-Laurent-de-Neste.

How did your parents know when they needed to hide you?

Someone came to my parents and said that we children should be hidden. Also, the head of the police, Monsieur Couquebert, was my mother's friend, and a help to us. He had told my mother that if the authorities came for my father, he would tell her ahead of time. (At first, the authorities arrested Jewish men only.) We had this old house with a room like a pantry, with thick walls, and my father hid there if anybody came to the house. But I was very young, and I would point and call, "Daddy, Daddy, Daddy." It became very dangerous.

So they hid me. First it was in the same courtyard, at a neighbor's, Madame Caseau. At night I would go to sleep at her house with their daughter, Renée, who was eighteen or nineteen.

Then my mother took me to stay with a sister of Madame Caseau who had a farm in a place called Labastide. People would come to Labastide by bicycle, but the road was so steep they couldn't take the bicycles down to the town, so they would leave them at our place.

Were you ever in danger there?

By then, the Germans were all over France. They would come down the steep hill and park their bicycles, and I would get very scared. I lumped the Germans and the police in the same category, and I would sit by the fireplace on a stool and just shake.

After a while, my mother was told that she should hide us under another name and in a different area where she wouldn't know where

Monsieur Couquebert, pictured with (clockwise, from upper right) his wife and two daughters, as well as Michel, Monique, and Monique's mother.

we were. So in 1943, the Red Cross placed me, my brother, and my cousins Louis and Simon in a home. The homeowners didn't give us enough to eat. About the only thing we subsisted on was bread, and water and vinegar to drink. We were so hungry, we used to go in the fields and pick wild turnips.

One day my mother dreamt that we were starving, and she woke my father and said, "We've got to go get the children, because I'm afraid." So she went to the headquarters of the Red Cross, and she insisted that they tell her where we were. She raised such a ruckus that they told her, and she came and was absolutely horrified. I was glad to be with my parents again, but it was very scary getting back to Saint-Laurent-de-Neste, as it was not safe to be on the roads.

Was your family in danger after you reunited?

They did come for my father one night. Monsieur Couquebert sent his wife to tell my mother that my father should not be there that night. As head of police, he himself had to come and knock at the door with the authorities. He had to make believe, and he sent the men through the house. My father was in a barn across the street watching the whole thing. But after that the Jewish refugees in Saint-Laurent-de-Neste had to leave the Pyrenees.

Monique and her family were sheltered in this house in Saint-Laurent-de-Neste, France.

How did they leave?

The men decided to go to Spain first. For the children and wives, it was more difficult. Many refugees, including my mother's sister Raymonde, her husband, Jacques, and their son, Marcel, hired a guide who delivered them to the Nazis. When they got on the bridge at Chaum, France, the Germans were waiting for them. When they said, "Halt!" they saw my uncle move and they shot him and killed him. They took the others to Drancy, which was an internment camp in France, and from there they ended up in Auschwitz. My cousins Louis and Simon also perished there.

What was your life like after your father left?

A few times the Nazis came, and then it wasn't safe for my mother to be there. The townspeople would come and tell her, "Hélène, leave." So she put the two of us in a stroller — my brother was two and I was six — and started walking, and she took a little bit of food with her. She would stop at night and knock at a farm and ask if she could stay. They were afraid to let her in, so they told her she could stay in the barn, but she'd have to leave before dawn. She walked like that for about two days. Then Renée came and told her that it was safe to come back.

My mother had a tremendous amount of courage. I always say I owe my life to her more than once. She stood by what she thought she needed to do, and she saved our lives.

Monique's uncle (far left), Jacques Kadinski, was shot while fleeing France for Spain. His son, Marcel, and wife, Raymonde, died in Auschwitz. At right are Monique with her parents, Charles and Hélène Jackson.

After the war ended in 1945, Monique's father was reunited with the family, and they all returned to Paris. In 1950, when Monique was thirteen, her family moved to the United States.

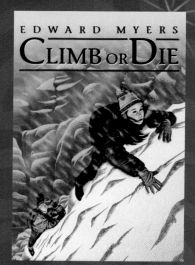

EDWARD MYERS
CLIMB OR DIE

Climb or Die

Read to find the meanings of these words.

e • Glossary

belay

carabiner

desperate

foothold

ice ax

improvising

overcome

piton

EQUIPPED TO CLIMB

Mountain climbers in winter must **overcome** the dangers of snow and ice. Special ice-climbing tools have been developed to make their climbing safer. In *Climb or Die*, the characters find themselves in a **desperate** situation where **improvising** their tools is the only solution.

A firm and secure **foothold** is always important for any type of climbing. Crampons, or iron spikes attached to boots, prevent slipping while climbing.

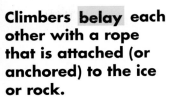

Climbers **belay** each
other with a rope
that is attached (or
anchored) to the ice
or rock.

A **piton** (*top, above*),
is a metal spike ham-
mered into rock or ice
as support for moun-
tain climbing.
A **carabiner** is a
metal ring used to
attach a rope to the
piton.

An **ice ax** is used to
support the upper
body as the climber
steps upward.

EDWARD MYERS
CLIMB OR DIE

Strategy Focus

Danielle and Jake must climb to a weather station near the top of a mountain if they hope to survive. Will they make it? As you read the selection, stop from time to time to **predict** what will happen next.

The Darcy family trip to their cabin in the mountains turns to disaster when their car crashes in a blizzard. To find help, Jake and Danielle must leave behind their injured parents and their dog, Flash. Their only hope for rescue is to reach a manned weather station at the top of Mount Remington. With Danielle's climbing experience at Camp Mountain Mastery and Jake's imagination, the two attempt the final icy cliff. Their only equipment is two hammers, two screwdrivers, and a nylon dog leash.

DANIELLE was bashing at the rock with Dad's hammer. With

each blow, chips of icy snow flew like sparks. Some of the chips sprayed toward Jake; a few even struck his face. He held out his hand, motioning for her to stop. Before he could speak, however, something caught his attention.

Danielle wasn't bashing at the rock just to let off her frustration. She was experimenting. She was trying to figure something out.

The hammer came down once, twice, three times.

Chips flew outward.

Then, without saying a word, Danielle turned the hammer around. She continued to grip its metal shaft by the rubber-clad handle, but now she struck at the icy granite with the claw, not with the head. The claw was the side you used for pulling nails out — a curved, pointed piece of forged steel.

"What are you doing?" Jake asked.

Danielle replied, "Improvising."

Jake watched in puzzlement. Then, suddenly, he understood.

"An ice ax?"

"You got it." Danielle struck the slab several times with the hammer's claw. Instead of scattering lots of chips, it sent fewer of them outward and mostly sideways; otherwise the metal dug deep into the crust. "The claw cuts in much more steeply than a regular ice ax would," she told Jake. "It's more like what climbers use for what they call vertical ice. It's not very sharp." She pulled the hammer back with her right hand, then stroked the claw with the fingers of her right. "But like you said — beggars can't be choosers."

Jake felt a surge of hope and delight. "You think it'll work?"

"There's only one way to find out." She reached out to Jake. "Here," she said. "I'll need your hammer, too."

He handed it over at once.

The hammers worked, Danielle told herself. Just as the screwdrivers functioned as crude pitons and the loops of nylon leash served as crude carabiners, the hammers worked well as crude ice axes. She couldn't quite believe it, but they worked just fine.

Something else she couldn't believe: Danielle herself had thought up half the system. Not Jake. Danielle. Even though Jake suggested the general idea of improvising hardware, Danielle was the one who figured out most of the specifics. First the fake carabiners, now the fake ice axes. And the system worked!

No wonder Jake got such a kick out of doing this, she told herself. It wasn't just coming up with a new idea. It was getting in a jam, then finding a way out. It was a great feeling — a feeling much like what she'd felt at Mountain Mastery when, stuck high on a cliff, Danielle had taken a chance, pulled herself out of danger, and discovered strength she hadn't even known she had.

Somehow he'd done it, Jake thought. He'd fallen, yet he'd pulled himself up. He'd kept going. He'd overcome the pain, the fear, the doubt that he could continue. Despite dropping two or three feet and slamming into the cliff, despite banging his shoulder and his face, he hadn't given up. Here he was now, heading up all over again.

For the first time, Jake started to understand why Danielle liked sports so much. Not because of winning — coming out ahead of everyone else. Instead, because of coming out ahead of *himself*.

He glanced at his watch. Three-thirty.

Now the biggest challenge rose right before them.

"Belay on?" Danielle called down to Jake.

"On belay," he shouted back.

"Climbing."

"Climb."

Climbing that icy trench was the hardest work Danielle had ever done. With a hammer in each hand, she struck out with the right one till it caught securely, then flexed her biceps to pull her body upward while she kicked at the slab with her boots, struggling to find some kind of foothold. Then she struck out with the left hammer and, kicking once again, pulled herself still higher. More often than not, her feet skittered around, helplessly at first. Two or three efforts let her find rough spots for the boot soles to catch on; the slab's angle was sufficiently gradual that she could get by with risky footholds. Somehow she kept going.

Danielle proceeded by exerting most of her weight on the hammers. Sometimes she felt the claws slipping, and once or twice she almost lost control. Yet she managed to keep her grip anyway. She pulled herself upward a few inches at a time. Panting, gasping, and fighting the fatigue that left her close to passing out, Danielle managed to fumble up the trench all the way to the top.

Then it was Jake's turn. Danielle didn't even stop to rest. She tied a length of Flash's nylon leash onto one of the two hammers and lowered it to Jake. After Jake untied it, Danielle pulled up the leash, tied on the second hammer, and lowered it as well. Then she assumed the belay position, told Jake what to do, and coaxed him all the way up.

The snowstorm had eased again. Snow still sifted down from above but so much more thinly now that it might as well have stopped altogether. Danielle could see the snow-covered rocks around them, the clouds massing around the mountain, and even some of the land visible below the clouds.

She could see that they were on a mountain; she could also see the contours of that particular peak. But where she expected to see the cliff above her, she saw only a low mound of snowy granite rising off to the left. Mount Remington didn't keep going higher, higher, and higher. On the contrary: it seemed to be leveling off.

Danielle felt the angle of the slope underfoot starting to ease. The mountain felt less and less steep. With each step the ground seemed more nearly level. Soon Danielle and Jake couldn't even keep going on all fours — they had to stand upright. Thick mist streaked around them, so they couldn't see much of the terrain, but within a few minutes they weren't climbing at all; they were just walking over an uneven but relatively flat surface.

"Danielle," said Jake, badly winded. "Danielle —" He stopped, leaned over, coughed, then stood upright again, heaving for breath. "I think we — I think this is —"

"The top!" Danielle exclaimed. She wanted to say more but couldn't. She wanted to shout, to scream for joy, to thank her brother for teaming up to do what they'd done — but she couldn't. She could scarcely breathe, much less talk. All she could say was, "The — *top!*"

The snowfall had stopped. Great clouds massed below them, around them, almost everywhere but above them. They were so high up now that the only vistas Danielle could remember like this were what she'd seen from airplanes. Danielle suddenly understood what people meant by a breathtaking view.

Then, abruptly, she didn't care about the view at all. She didn't care if it was beautiful or ugly. She started looking around in a different, almost desperate way.

Something was wrong. Something about the view. Something that wasn't what she saw but was what she *didn't* see.

There was no weather station in sight.

Together Jake and Danielle worked their way over the jumble of rocks. They walked about fifteen or twenty feet ahead to where the flat place they'd reached began curving downward again. Clouds swept all around them. They couldn't see very far — perhaps a few dozen yards down the mountain. But that was just the problem. They were looking down the mountain. Down the mountain's far side.

Danielle turned, took twenty paces to the right, then turned again and worked her way to Jake's left. She peered over the edge and saw nothing but rock and snow vanishing into the clouds below. The sight chilled her more than the wind needling at her.

Danielle watched her brother doing what she herself had just finished doing, except that Jake went farther and peered still more intently over the edge. They must have missed something, she told herself. They hadn't looked hard enough.

Yet she couldn't see anything like what they were looking for. There was nothing at all like a weather station.

They were at the summit.

Alone.

"We're dead," Danielle moaned. "Jake — we're dead."

Jake stumbled over to her. He had begun to shake and now shook so hard he couldn't stop. He couldn't believe all their efforts had come to this. He couldn't believe his plan hadn't worked. There was supposed to be a weather station up here. He'd seen it on TV. It had to be here. Yet the place around them looked as desolate as the moon. So Jake stood staring at his sister, at how miserable she looked with her gloved hands up against her mouth while she cried, and he felt hollow and terrible inside. "Danielle," he said. "I'm sorry —" A moment later he started crying, too. He reached out to embrace her.

They held each other a long time. He wanted to reassure Danielle, to suggest a new idea that would save them after all, but he couldn't think of anything. All he could think about was the cold. What would it feel like, freezing to death? How long would it take? Would it be peaceful, as some people said it was? Peaceful! What a joke! How could it be peaceful? Even if Jake went numb and didn't feel the pain of his fingers and toes turning to ice, of his blood thickening to slush, then surely he'd still think every last second about how he'd let down Mom, Dad, and Danielle —

She was pushing him away. That push hurt worst of all, and tears filled Jake's eyes so fast that his vision went blurry.

"This is *your* fault!" she screamed.

"Danielle, I'm sorry —"

"*Your* fault!"

"Listen —"

"You and your stupid weather station!"

"Danielle, listen —"

She took him by the shoulders and shook him.

"I'm sorry," Jake shouted back. "I'm sorry, I'm sorry, I'm sorry!"

She shook him harder and harder. She shook him so hard that Danielle almost knocked him over. But then, gradually at first, the way she shook him started to change. She wasn't punishing him now — she was trying to get his attention. Puzzled at first, Jake soon understood what his sister was doing. He pulled back from her. He wiped his eyes with the back of his glove.

"*Look!*" she cried. "Just look!"

Danielle was pointing into the clouds sweeping past from left to right.

"What is it?"

"Over there!"

Jake leaned this way and that to get a better look. At first all he saw was the soft gray-white nothingness of the clouds. Then, looking more closely, he realized that what he saw wasn't just the clouds; it was also the clouds shifting, parting, and revealing something beyond. First just textures, then shapes. Some sort of low horizontal box. Some vertical lines. He couldn't tell what it was. Something inside the clouds?

At that moment the clouds shifted and whatever he'd been seeing took on more detail. Walls. Windows. A metal roof. Some sort of shed next to the main structure. A big antenna poking up from the shed. A satellite dish mounted on the roof. The longer he looked, the more he saw. And he saw something else, too: a stony ridge that connected Danielle and Jake's summit to another summit, a pile of massive boulders topped by these ghostly buildings.

"The weather station!" Jake exclaimed.

"We're on a false summit," Danielle said. "That's the real summit over there."

Without another word they rushed over to the edge, and, scrambling as fast as possible without tumbling headfirst, they climbed down toward the ridge connecting where they were to where they wanted to be.

Danielle was shaking hard by the time she and Jake worked their way over to the weather station. Her hands shook, her knees shook, her whole body shook. She was shaking from excitement but mostly from the cold. Danielle couldn't remember having ever felt so cold. She almost felt as if she were bleeding to death, except that her blood was heat, and all the heat was leaking from her body. In a few minutes the heat would be gone.

Danielle and Jake staggered the last few feet up the slope to the weather station. Drifts lay piled on the far side of the buildings, drifts so deep that Danielle had to wallow to get anywhere. She lost her balance several times trying to push through. Twice she fell over and ended up with a faceful of snow. Yet somehow she managed, and Jake did, too, and they made it all the way to the biggest of the buildings.

"Where's the door?" Danielle asked.

"Maybe this way," Jake answered, and they worked their way around to the right.

Danielle started pounding on the door the moment she reached it. Her hands felt so numb, however, that she couldn't even make a fist. She wasn't really pounding, she was slapping. Then Jake started in, too, striking the door as hard as he could.

They both stopped and fell silent.

All they heard was the whistle of the wind and the fluttering noise it made against the weather station.

"Maybe nobody's home," Jake said.

"Don't be ridiculous," Danielle told him, but his words chilled her even more than the cold. Was it possible? Could they have come all the way here only to reach a vacant building?

She glanced around. There was a relatively flat, open area right next to the building — the sort of area someone might use to park a truck up here — but no truck in sight. Danielle saw no vehicles at all. On the other side of this area, though, was a shedlike structure, and she decided that must be a garage. But she didn't really care. She knew someone was up here. Someone *had* to be up here.

Danielle started pounding again.

Jake interrupted her: "Listen!"

She held off. She waited.

Just then she heard something. "Music!" Danielle exclaimed. Some kind of jazz.

At once she went back to pounding. "Open!" she yelled. "Open up! Please! We need help!"

Jake pounded, too.

Then they stopped, waited, listened.

Nothing happened.

Danielle could feel her excitement vanish in a moment's time. Surely they wouldn't climb all day only to discover that no one could hear them!`

Before she could start pounding again, though, Jake said, "Wait — maybe the music's too loud." He took off his pack, pulled it open, and rummaged around inside. When he couldn't find what he wanted, he dumped everything out onto the snow.

"What are you doing?" Danielle asked.

Jake picked up Dad's biggest hammer. He said, "Improvising."
At once he started banging on the door — banging so hard that each blow
dented the metal.

The music stopped a few moments later.

Danielle could almost imagine that she heard a voice.

Then Jake said, "Okay, get ready."

"Ready?" Danielle asked, unsure of what he meant. Watching, she saw
Jake reach down to his empty pack. Just then Danielle saw what he was going
to do, but she understood too late to stop him.

As the door swung open, revealing two startled men on the other side,
Jake held out his empty pack like a Halloween bag.

"Trick or treat!"

ABOUT THE AUTHOR

EDWARD MYERS

Ed Myers loves the outdoors — especially hiking and mountain climbing. Although no one should copy the characters in *Climb or Die*, Ed Myers has successfully tested all the climbing techniques himself. He lives in New Jersey with his wife Edith and two children.

ABOUT THE ILLUSTRATOR

BILL FARNSWORTH

"Draw what you see all the time and talk to illustrators. You have to be a sponge and take in all the information you can," Bill Farnsworth advises. Several times a year, he visits schools to talk with children about what he does as an illustrator. He also enjoys playing tennis, gardening, and cooking in his Sarasota, Florida, home.

To find out more about Edward Myers and Bill Farnsworth, visit Education Place. **www.eduplace.com/kids**

Responding

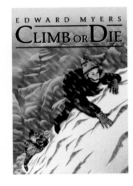

THINK ABOUT THE SELECTION

1. If you were Jake or Danielle, would you try to climb Mount Remington to get help for your parents? Explain.

2. Danielle's interest in climbing increases as she learns more about it. Give an example from your own life of something that interested you as you learned more about it.

3. Why are the people in the weather station surprised to see Jake and Danielle?

4. Why do you think the author chose to alternate the focus in the selection between Danielle and Jake?

5. When they reach the false summit, Danielle pushes Jake away and his feelings are hurt. What does this tell you about Jake?

6. What do you think Jake and Danielle learn from each other?

7. **Connecting/Comparing** Compare how Jake and Danielle improvise their tools with how Brian uses his hatchet. What qualities help them to survive? Explain.

Informing

WRITE A MESSAGE

Suppose that when Danielle and Jake reach the weather station, they find it empty. Write a message they might leave at the weather station. Explain their situation and tell what they plan to do next.

Tips

- State the message very clearly. Remember, the information it contains might lead to the characters' rescue.
- Include the date, the time, and the characters' names.

DESIGN A CLIMBING CATALOG

Make a catalog of mountaineering tools climbers use. Start with tools from the story such as an ice ax and carabiners. Draw items that you cannot find pictures of. Then label and describe each picture.

Bonus Give an oral report about your catalog. Explain how and why each item is used in climbing.

GIVE A DRAMATIC READING

With a small group, give a dramatic reading of part of the selection. Begin on page 82, at the paragraph that starts with "Jake stumbled over to her." Read through to the end of the selection. One person can read Danielle's lines, while another reads Jake's lines. Other group members can take turns reading the narrator's parts.

Tips

- Read more slowly than usual, and include pauses. Make sure that your audience can hear you.
- You do not need to move or make gestures, but do read with expression.

Internet

COMPLETE A WEB CROSSWORD PUZZLE

How much do you learn about the sport of climbing from reading *Climb or Die*? Find out by completing a crossword puzzle that can be printed from Education Place.

www.eduplace.com/kids

NATIONAL GEOGRAPHIC
world

FUTUREWORLD

Battling
EVEREST
by Michael Burgan

Could the two climbers conquer the killer mountain?

Skill: How to Read a Social Studies Article

Before you read . . .

Scan each page of the article. Read the title, subtitle, and headings.

Note the **time** and **location** of the topic.

Ask yourself what you already know about the topic. **Predict** what you will learn by turning each heading into a question.

While you read . . .

Look for answers to your questions.

Use **context clues** to help you understand unfamiliar words.

Look for **sequence words** that show the order of events.

THIS WAS IT: THE DAY THEY HAD spent years preparing for. The two men peered out of a tent and saw around them icy peaks glowing in the early morning sun. The men were perched more than five miles high on one side of Everest, the world's tallest mountain on land. The wind, which had been howling at 60 miles an hour, was calm now, but the temperature was a brutally cold *minus* 17°F. This day, May 29, 1953, Edmund Hillary and Tenzing Norgay hoped to become the first to step onto Everest's peak.

They almost hadn't made it this far. One month earlier the two climbers, linked by a rope, had been exploring an icefall, a rugged expanse of huge, jagged, shifting ice blocks. Hillary, in the lead, came upon a crevasse, or deep gap, that was much too wide to step across. As climbers sometimes do, Hillary used a chunk of ice near the opening as a step. But when he landed on the chunk, it gave way. He tumbled with the ice into the crevasse. "Everything seemed to start going slowly," said Hillary later, "even though I was free-falling into the crevasse." As he fell, Hillary twisted his body to avoid getting pinned inside the crevasse.

Watching his friend plummet into the icy hole, Tenzing acted quickly. He thrust his ice ax into the snow and wrapped the rope around it. "The rope came tight with a twang," Hillary later recalled, "and I was stopped and swung in against the wall." The ice chunk smashed into the bottom of the crevasse. Without Tenzing's fast action, Hillary would have crashed there, too.

Danger Ahead

The men came from different worlds. Edmund Hillary had worked as a beekeeper in his native New Zealand. Tenzing Norgay, his partner, was a Sherpa. (Sherpas, a people native to Nepal in the Himalaya, are famous as mountain guides.) But Hillary and Tenzing shared a passion for climbing mountains. Hillary had made two previous climbs in the Himalaya. Tenzing had already attempted to climb Everest six times. Each had the determination and skills to reach the summit as well as a deep trust in each other's talents.

Still, they knew the dangers, from frostbite to avalanches, crevasse falls, sudden blinding snowstorms, and lack of oxygen. Already 24 climbers had died trying to scale Everest. Just three days earlier, two climbers had turned back, exhausted and unable to continue. They warned Hillary and Tenzing of the risks ahead.

Nevertheless at 6:30 A.M. on May 29, Edmund Hillary looked at Tenzing Norgay and asked, "All ready?" "**Ah chah**," Tenzing replied, "ready." Just 1,100 feet higher, and they would make history.

Months of Struggle

Their quest to reach the top of Everest had begun more than two months earlier on March 10, 1953. Sir John Hunt, a British army colonel, led a team of 14 climbers, 36 Sherpa guides, and 350 porters carrying tons of supplies.

Tenzing Norgay and Edmund Hillary celebrate the first ascent of Everest over cups of tea.

Hillary, Tenzing, and the other team members set out from Kathmandu, the capital of Nepal. At first they walked along colorful hillsides dotted with small farmhouses. As they climbed higher, the landscape changed. Steep cliffs lined a rushing river. To cross it, the climbers made a rickety bridge of rocks and bamboo. Heavy rains and swarms of hornets tormented them. Progress was slow.

Moving eastward, the party finally saw Everest in the distance as if it were hovering in the sky. The climbers set up a base camp at an elevation above 12,000 feet. From there they would move higher up into the mountains, setting up new camps along the way.

The team spent a few weeks at the base camp to prepare the route upward by cutting steps in the snow. One day Hillary led a small team to explore the Khumbu Icefall, "one of the most awful and utterly forbidding scenes ever observed by man," according to George Mallory, a climber who had died in the region. Hillary and his team came up against a field of tilting, shifting giant blocks of ice pushed, pulled, and swept by glaciers and avalanches.

He guided the team through the treacherous terrain as it shifted and split into crevasses. Avalanches continually threatened to bury the team in boulders of ice. But Hillary found a route through the icefall and set up camp at 19,400 feet.

Along the route, the men named some of the more difficult spots. One they called "Hillary's Horror." Another was "Atom Bomb" for the explosive noises of shifting ice. It was at Atom Bomb that Hillary's fall into a crevasse had almost ended his climb — and his life.

That close call was only a memory now, as Hillary and Tenzing started their final climb. Once again a rope linked them. Tenzing took the lead first, then Hillary went ahead. They hiked along a ridge only a few feet wide. The soft snow made the going tough. Discouraged by the difficulty, they considered turning back. Hillary finally said to himself, "Forget it! This is Everest."

Further on the snow became more solid, allowing Hillary to cut steps into it. Still the climbers were cautious. To their right were cornices, or twisted ridges of snow. Just beyond them was an 8,000-foot drop. To their left ran a rocky ledge. Painstakingly the two men — the only members of the team to make it this far — continued up the mountain.

The Death Zone

Each man wore eight layers of clothing and three pairs of gloves. Each carried a 40-pound oxygen tank on his back. At high elevations the air is "thin," meaning it contains less oxygen. But climbers need **extra** oxygen to survive, especially at 25,000 feet, an elevation some call the beginning of "the Death Zone."

As he chipped at the snow, Hillary worried about their oxygen supply. Would they have enough? Now it was even harder to breathe because ice was forming in their oxygen tubes. Hillary and Tenzing had to keep clearing out the tubes to breathe well enough to continue their climb. Nothing, they hoped, would stop them. Yet, as Hillary later said, "We didn't know if it was humanly possible to reach the top of Everest."

The two climbers now came upon a rock wall 40 feet high. They no longer had the strength to climb straight up. Instead Hillary climbed between the rock and a nearby cornice, using his crampons, or spikes on his boots, to help him. Once he reached the top of the wall, Hillary pulled Tenzing up. Then they went back to cutting steps in the snow.

To the Top

The hours passed. Both men were slowing down. Their conquest, Hillary later said, was turning into a "grim struggle." Then the ridge they were climbing peaked, and they were on the top of Everest!

The two men hugged and shook hands. Hillary snapped some photographs. Tenzing buried candy and biscuits in the snow as presents to the gods that Sherpas believe live on Everest. After 15 minutes, the two men left the peak and its majestic view — a sight no human being had ever seen before. They had reached the roof of the world.

Hillary took this photograph of Tenzing holding a flag at the top of Everest.

Background and Vocabulary

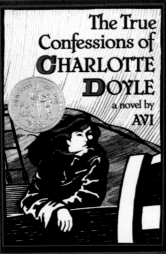

The True Confessions of Charlotte Doyle

Read to find the meanings of these words.

e • Glossary

entangled

ratlines

rigging

seasoned

treacherous

To Sail a Ship

What was it like to be on board a sailing ship in the early 1830s? In *The True Confessions of Charlotte Doyle*, a girl finds out what a sailor's life is really like.

On a brig, or two-masted ship, a **seasoned** sailor had to climb the masts or the **rigging** — the ropes that support the masts and sails — to untie the sails so the wind could move the ship. The climb itself was **treacherous**. The sailor might get **entangled** in the **ratlines** and would sometimes even fall. The highest spar, or pole, that supports the top of the highest sail was called the royal yard. It could be as high as 130 feet. During a severe storm at sea, the sails needed to be tied so that they would not be damaged. A sailor's life on a sailing ship provided many challenges.

94

Royal Yard

Rigging

Ratlines

Main Mast

Meet the Author
Avi

How he got that name: His twin sister gave it to him as a baby.

Beating the odds: Avi almost flunked out of school because his writing was so bad. He feels very fortunate to have come as far as he has.

What honed his skill: Avi played a game with his children in which they would give him a subject — "a glass of water" — and he would have to make up a story about it.

Notable books: *The Fighting Ground; Perloo the Bold; Beyond the Western Sea, Books 1 and 2*

Meet the Illustrator
Scott McKowen

What he was like as a young boy: Scott McKowen's parents always brought paper and pencils to keep him quiet in restaurants.

How he makes his art: McKowen works in scratchboard, an engraving medium. He carves white lines with a sharp blade onto an all-black board. Then he colors it with a special oil paint.

Internet

To discover more about Avi and Scott McKowen, visit Education Place. **www.eduplace.com/kids**

Selection 4

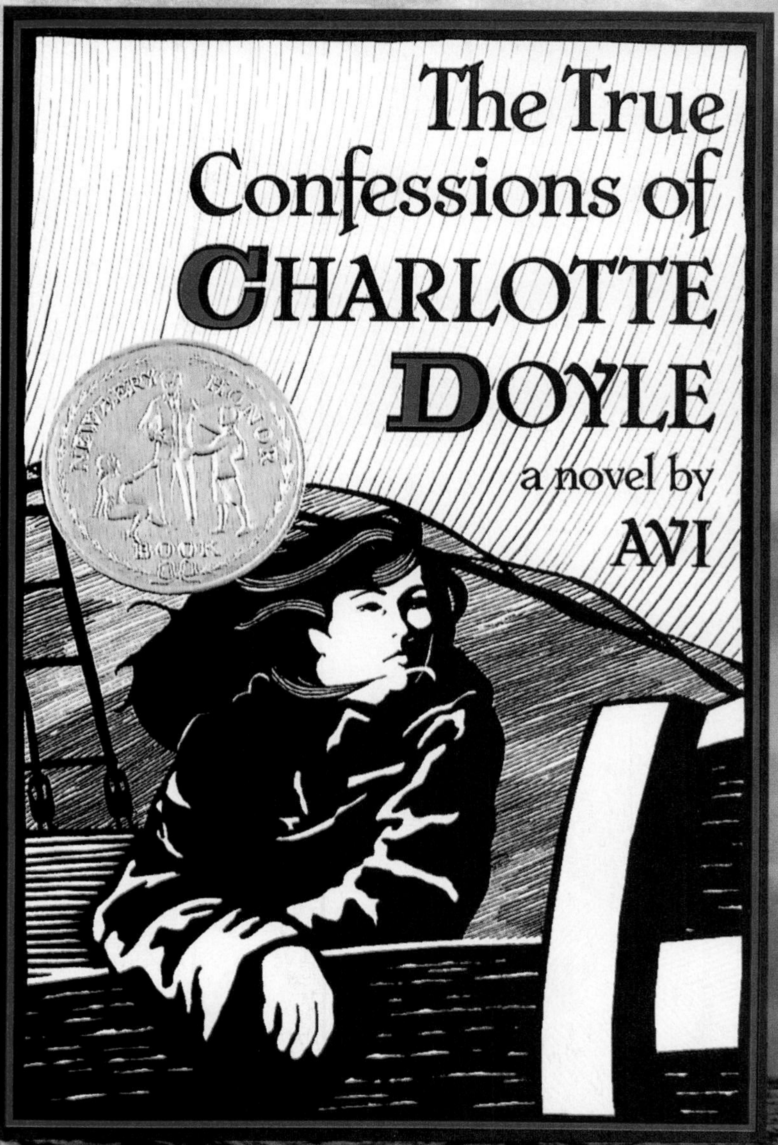

The True
Confessions of
CHARLOTTE
DOYLE
a novel by
AVI
NEWBERY HONOR BOOK

Strategy Focus

Charlotte Doyle faces the toughest challenge of her life when she joins the ship's crew. As you read, **monitor** how well you understand the selection, and **clarify** parts you don't understand by rereading or reading ahead.

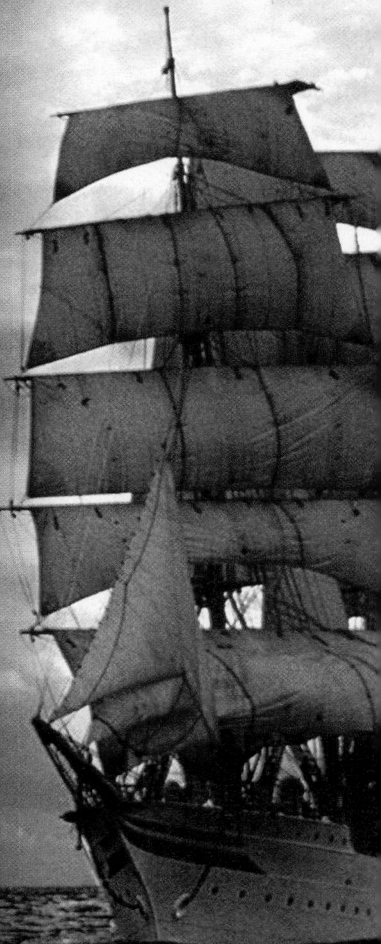

The year is 1832 and thirteen-year-old Charlotte Doyle is sailing on the *Seahawk*, a brig bound for America from England. Once on board she finds herself the only passenger and the only girl among a rough crew. When the crew needs a replacement, she boldly offers to join them. Little does she realize that as a test to prove her worth, she must climb the tallest mast of the ship.

"Miss Doyle," he pressed, "you have agreed to climb to the top of the royal yard. Do you know that's the highest sail on the main mast? One hundred and thirty feet up. You can reach it only two ways. You can shimmy up the mast itself. Or you can climb the shrouds, using the ratlines for your ladder."

I nodded as if I fully grasped what he was saying. The truth was I didn't even wish to listen. I just wanted to get past the test.

"And Miss Doyle," he went on, "if you slip and fall you'll be lucky to drop into the sea and drown quickly. No mortal could pluck you out fast enough to save you. Do you understand that?"

I swallowed hard but nodded. "Yes."

"Because if you're *not* lucky you'll crash to the deck. Fall that way and you'll either maim or kill yourself by breaking your neck. Still certain?"

"Yes," I repeated, though somewhat more softly.

"I'll give you this," he said with a look that seemed a mix of admiration and contempt, "Zachariah was right. You're as steady a girl as ever I've met."

Foley soon returned. "We're agreed," he announced. "Not a one stands in favor of your signing on, Miss Doyle. Not with what you are. We're all agreed to that. But if you climb as high as the royal yard and make it down whole, and if you still want to sign on, you can come as equal. You'll get no more from us, Miss Doyle, but no less either."

Fisk looked at me for my answer.

"I understand," I said.

"All right then," Foley said. "The captain's still in his cabin and not likely to come out till five bells. You can do it now."

"*Now*?" I quailed.

"Now before never."

So it was that the four men escorted me onto the deck. There I found that the rest of the crew had already gathered.

Having fully committed myself, I was overwhelmed by my audacity. The masts had always seemed tall, of course, but never so tall as they did at that moment. When I reached the deck and looked up my courage all but crumbled. My stomach turned. My legs grew weak.

Not that it mattered. Fisk escorted me to the mast as though I were being led to die at the stake. He seemed as grim as I.

To grasp fully what I'd undertaken to do, know again that the height of the mainmast towered one hundred and thirty feet from the deck. This mast was, in fact, three great rounded lengths of wood, trees, in truth, affixed one to the end of the other. Further, it supported four levels of sails, each of which bore a different name. In order, bottom to top, these were called the main yard, topsail, topgallant, and finally royal yard.

My task was to climb to the top of the royal yard. And come down. In one piece. If I succeeded I'd gain the opportunity of making the climb fifty times a day.

As if reading my terrified thoughts Fisk inquired gravely, "How will you go, Miss Doyle? Up the mast or

on the ratlines?"

Once again I looked up. I could not possibly climb the mast directly. The stays and shrouds with their ratlines would serve me better.

"Ratlines," I replied softly.

"Then up you go."

I will confess it, at that moment my nerves failed. I found myself unable to move. With thudding heart I looked frantically around. The members of the crew, arranged in a crescent, were standing like death's own jury.

It was Barlow who called out, "A blessing goes with you, Miss Doyle."

To which Ewing added, "And this advice, Miss Doyle. Keep your eyes steady on the ropes. Don't you look down. Or up."

For the first time I sensed that some of them at least wanted me to succeed. The realization gave me courage.

With halting steps and shallow breath, I approached the rail only to pause when I reached it. I could hear a small inner voice crying, "Don't! Don't!"

But it was also then that I heard Dillingham snicker, "She'll not have the stomach."

I reached up, grasped the lowest deadeye, and hauled myself atop the rail. That much I had done before. Now, I maneuvered to the outside so that I would be leaning *into* the rigging and could even rest on it.

Once again I looked at the crew, *down* at them, I should say. They were staring up with blank expressions.

Recollecting Ewing's advice, I shifted my eyes and focused them on the ropes before me. Then, reaching as high as I could into one of the middle shrouds, and grabbing a ratline, I began to climb.

The ratlines were set about sixteen inches one above the other, so that the steps I had to take were wide for me. I needed to pull as much with arms as climb with legs. But line by line I did go up, as if ascending an enormous ladder.

After I had risen some seventeen feet I realized I'd made a great mistake. The rigging stood in sets, each going to a different level of the mast. I could have taken one that stretched directly to the top. Instead, I had chosen a line which went only to the first trestletree, to the top of the lower mast.

For a moment I considered backing down and starting afresh. I stole a quick glance below. The crew's faces were turned up toward me. I understood that they would take the smallest movement down as retreat. I had to continue.

And so I did.

Now I was climbing inside the lank gray-white sails, ascending, as it were, into a bank of dead clouds.

103

Beyond the sails lay the sea, slate-gray and ever rolling. Though the water looked calm, I could feel the slow pitch and roll it caused in the ship. I realized suddenly how much harder this climb would be if the wind were blowing and we were well underway. The mere thought made the palms of my hands grow damp.

Up I continued till I reached the main yard. Here I snatched another glance at the sea, and was startled to see how much bigger it had grown. Indeed, the more I saw of it the *more* there was. In contrast, the *Seahawk* struck me as having suddenly grown smaller. The more I saw of *her,* the *less* she was!

I glanced aloft. To climb higher I now had to edge myself out upon the trestletree and then once again move up the next set of ratlines as I'd done before. But at twice the height!

Wrapping one arm around the mast — even up here it was too big to reach around completely — I grasped one of the stays and edged out. At the same moment the ship dipped, the world seemed to twist and tilt down. My stomach lurched. My heart pounded. My head swam. In spite of myself I closed my eyes. I all but slipped, saving myself only by a sudden grasp of a line before the ship yawed the opposite way. I felt sicker yet. With ever-waning strength I clung on for dearest life. Now the full folly of what I was attempting burst upon me with grotesque reality. It had been not only stupid, but suicidal. I would never come down alive!

And yet I had to climb. This was my restitution.

When the ship was steady again, I grasped the furthest rigging, first with one hand, then the other, and dragged myself higher. I was heading for the topsail, fifteen feet further up.

Pressing myself as close as possible into the rigging, I continued to strain upward, squeezing the ropes so tightly my hands cramped. I even tried curling my toes about the ratlines.

At last I reached the topsail spar, but discovered it was impossible to rest there. The only place to pause was three *times* higher than the distance I'd just come, at the trestletree just below the topgallant spar.

By now every muscle in my body ached. My head felt light, my heart an anvil. My hands were on fire, the soles of my feet raw. Time and again I was forced to halt, pressing my face against the rigging with eyes closed. Then, in spite of what I'd been warned not to do, I opened them and peered down. The *Seahawk* was like a wooden toy. The sea looked greater still.

I made myself glance up. Oh, so far to go! How I forced myself to move I am not sure. But the thought of backing down now was just as frightening. Knowing only that I could not stay still, I crept upward, ratline by ratline, taking what seemed to be forever with each rise until I finally reached the level just below the topgallant spar.

A seasoned sailor would have needed two minutes to reach this point. I had needed thirty!

Though I felt the constant roll of the ship, I had to rest there. What seemed like little movement on deck became, up high, wild swings and turns through treacherous air.

I gagged, forced my stomach down, drew breath, and looked out. Though I didn't think it possible, the ocean appeared to have grown greater yet. And when I looked down, the upturned faces of the crew appeared like so many tiny bugs.

There were twenty-five or so more feet to climb. Once again I grasped the rigging and hauled myself up.

This final climb was torture. With every upward pull the swaying of the ship seemed to increase. Even when not moving myself, I was flying through the air in wild, wide gyrations. The horizon kept shifting, tilting, dropping. I was increasingly dizzy, nauseous, terrified, certain that with every next moment I would slip and fall to death. I paused again and again, my eyes on the rigging inches from my face, gasping and praying as I had never prayed before. My one hope was that, nearer to heaven now, I could make my desperation heard!

Inch by inch I continued up. Half an inch! Quarter inches! But then at last with trembling fingers, I touched the spar of the royal yard. I had reached the top.

Once there I endeavored to rest again. But there the metronome motion of the mast was at its most extreme, the *Seahawk* turning, tossing, swaying as if trying to shake me off — like a dog throwing droplets of water from its back. And when I looked beyond I saw a sea that was infinity itself, ready, eager to swallow me whole.

I had to get back down.

As hard as it was to climb up, it was, to my horror, harder returning. On the ascent I could see where I was going. Edging down I had to grope blindly with my feet. Sometimes I tried to look. But when I did the sight of the void below was so sickening, I was forced to close my eyes.

Each groping step downward was a nightmare. Most times my foot found only air. Then, as if to mock my terror, a small breeze at last sprang up. Sails began to fill and snap, puffing in and out, at times smothering me. The tossing of the ship grew — if that were possible — more extreme.

Down I crept, past the topgallant where I paused briefly on the trestletree, then down along the longest stretch, toward the mainyard. It was there I fell.

I was searching with my left foot for the next ratline. When I found a hold and started to put my weight upon it, my foot, slipping on the slick tar surface, shot forward. The suddenness of it made me lose my grip. I tumbled backward, but in such a way that my legs became entangled in the lines. There I hung, *head downward*.

I screamed, tried to grab something. But I couldn't. I clutched madly at nothing, till my hand brushed against a dangling rope. I grabbed for it, missed, and grabbed again. Using all my strength, I levered myself up and, wrapping my arms into the lines, made a veritable knot of myself, mast, and rigging. Oh, how I wept! my entire body shaking and trembling as though it would break apart.

When my breathing became somewhat normal, I managed to untangle first one arm, then my legs. I was free.

I continued down. By the time I reached the mainyard I was numb and whimpering again, tears coursing from my eyes.

I moved to the shrouds I'd climbed, and edged myself past the lowest of the sails.

As I emerged from under it, the crew gave out a great "Huzzah!"

Oh, how my heart swelled with exaltation!

Finally, when I'd reached close to the very end, Barlow stepped forward, beaming, his arms uplifted. "Jump!" he called. "Jump!"

But now, determined to do it all myself, I shook my head. Indeed, in the end I dropped down on my own two India-rubber legs — and tumbled to the deck.

No sooner did I land than the crew gave me another "Huzzah!" With joyous heart I staggered to my feet. Only then did I see Captain Jaggery push through the knot of men and come to stand before me. ⚓

Responding

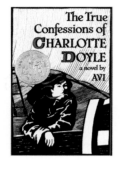

Think About the Selection

1. Why do you think none of the crew believe Charlotte is serious about becoming a crew member?

2. Why does Fisk warn Charlotte about the risks of climbing the mast? What does this tell you about Fisk?

3. Do you think that climbing the tallest mast of the ship is a good test of Charlotte's worth as a crew member? Why or why not?

4. Which word best describes Charlotte for you: *determined, steady, terrified,* or some other word? Explain why.

5. From atop the mast, the *Seahawk* was "like a dog throwing droplets of water from its back." How effective is this comparison? Explain.

6. Charlotte feels terrified when she commits herself to a test she isn't sure of passing. Describe a time when you have felt this way.

7. **Connecting/Comparing** Compare Charlotte's reasons for climbing the ship's mast with Jake and Danielle's reasons for climbing Mount Remington. How did they all show courage in their decisions?

Write a Descriptive Paragraph

Write a paragraph describing what it would be like to cling to the top of the royal yard. Include similes to make this dizzying experience vivid and dramatic.

Tips

- Remember that a simile uses *like* or *as* to compare things in an unexpected way.
- Arrange your details in spatial order or in order of importance.
- Use strong, exact words.

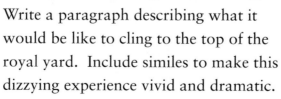

Draw a Diagram

With a partner, measure each other's height. Round each number to the nearest foot. If the main mast Charlotte climbed was 130 feet tall, how many times could you be stacked against the height of the mast? How many times could your partner? Draw a diagram to solve the problem.

Hold a Discussion

Form a group with two or three classmates and discuss this topic: Is Charlotte Doyle's climb to the top of the royal yard foolish or courageous? Try to come to a shared conclusion.

Tips

- Listen closely and politely to what others say. Don't let your attention wander.
- Take turns contributing ideas. Give reasons for your opinions.

Internet

Complete a Word Search Puzzle

You've learned a lot of vocabulary related to sailing ships in this selection. Try finding those words in a word search puzzle that can be printed from Education Place. **www.eduplace.com/kids**

How to Take Notes

As you read . . .

1 Look for the big ideas. Write headings that give the main ideas.

2 Under each heading, jot down supporting details. Keep your notes short.

3 Underline and define key terms in your notes.

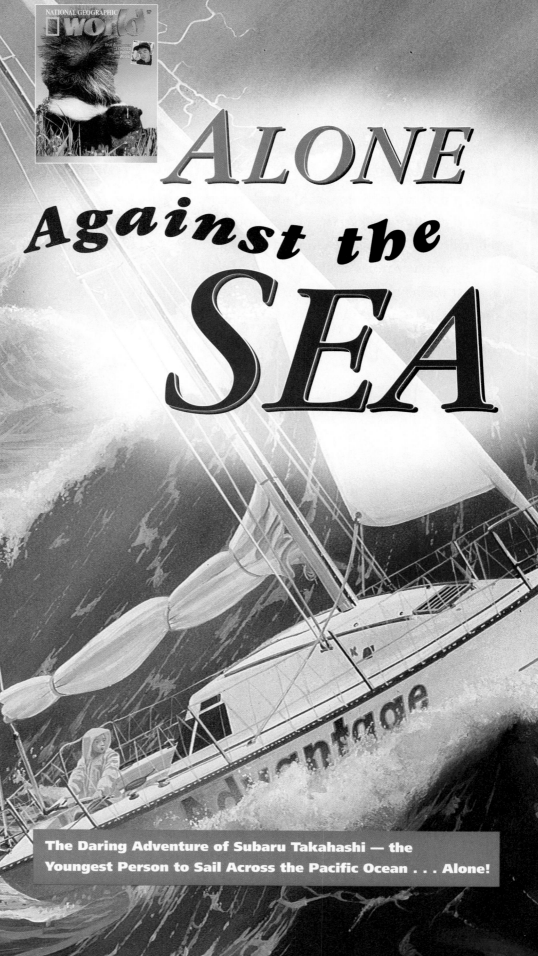

ALONE
Against the
SEA

The Daring Adventure of Subaru Takahashi — the Youngest Person to Sail Across the Pacific Ocean . . . Alone!

Lightning flashed, thunder boomed, and heavy rain pounded. A midday storm was exploding far out in the Pacific Ocean. The winds grew stronger and the waves bigger. Subaru Takahashi, then fourteen, of Shirone, in Japan, watched with widening eyes. Soon his 30-foot sailboat was being tossed about like a toy.

Suddenly huge waves began crashing over the side of the boat. As water collected on the deck, Subaru grabbed a cooking pot. Working furiously, he began bailing out the ocean water. Fortunately for him the storm's ferocity lasted only a few hours. Subaru insists today that he was never really worried.

Several weeks earlier, on July 22, 1996, Subaru had begun an ambitious journey from Tokyo Bay, in Japan. Family, friends, and reporters cheered him on. He planned to sail across the world's largest body of water, the mighty Pacific Ocean, alone. He calculated that he could make the crossing — 6,000 miles — and sail

into San Francisco Bay within seven weeks.

Aboard the *Advantage*, the sailboat he had rented from a dentist in Tokyo, was a two-month supply of water and food, including rice, noodles, and soup. His boat also was equipped with the most modern radio and navigation equipment.

Nobody who knew Subaru from his earlier childhood was surprised at his voyage. At age nine, he had paddled alone by canoe across nineteen-mile Sado Strait in the Sea of Japan. At age ten he had taken his first sailing lesson in a dinghy, or small boat. And he had not been discouraged when a sail boom hit him in the head and almost knocked him out.

Subaru began to form his plan to cross the Pacific after meeting a Japanese adventurer who had sailed solo around the world without stopping. Six months after the meeting, he began training for his daring journey. After he'd spent 200 hours sailing the *Advantage* in open water, Subaru was ready to go.

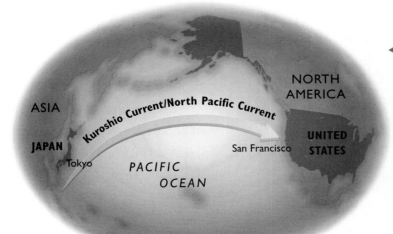

ASIA

JAPAN

Tokyo

Kuroshio Current/North Pacific Current

NORTH AMERICA

UNITED STATES

San Francisco

PACIFIC OCEAN

◀ Several currents helped Subaru on his journey across the Pacific Ocean. The Kuroshio, or Japan Current, is about sixty miles wide near Japan. Further out it merges with cooler waters and forms the North Pacific Current.

113

As he sailed away from Japan in July, his mother told reporters, "I believe that his strong will to live will bring him back, no matter what." Subaru's parents also believed their son's sailing experiences would teach him things he would never learn in school.

"I was excited when the land disappeared and I reached open ocean," Subaru recalls. "I had confidence I would succeed." Everything went smoothly at first. His occasional companions were whales and dolphins. He used a radio to keep in contact with his parents in Japan. They informed reporters of their son's progress.

To keep from getting bored, Subaru tried fishing. Just as he caught his only fish, a seabird dived and swallowed it. But the bird also swallowed the hook. Despite Subaru's rescue efforts, the bird died. So Subaru hauled it aboard, cooked it, and ate it. He says, "It tasted good."

Serious trouble arose on August 11 when an engine died, killing all power to his electric generator. That meant that with five weeks to go, Subaru had no power for the lights, radio, and automatic steering. Knocked out of action, too, was his automatic global positioning system, or GPS. This system picks up signals from satellites and locates a boat's position in the ocean.

Fortunately he had two backup systems that still worked: a hand-held GPS, and a battery-operated radio. But the radio battery failed five days later! Subaru then lost all communication with the outside world. In his last message, he reported that he was 2,790 miles west of San Francisco.

Now Subaru was truly alone. "I began wondering what I had done in my life to deserve such bad luck," he says. "Everything seemed to be going wrong."

One windless day, with his boat at a near standstill, Subaru spotted a large ship on the horizon. As the freighter got closer and closer, Subaru saw it was heading toward his sailboat on a collision course. He frantically waved his arms. Finally someone aboard the ship saw the young sailor in his boat and changed course just in time to avoid disaster.

By the end of August, many people in Japan were convinced Subaru had been lost at sea. They had followed the radio reports of his voyage until

Subaru Takahashi poses with the Japanese flag shortly after becoming the youngest person to sail solo across the Pacific Ocean. Below, Subaru conducts the final check of his yacht *Advantage* before leaving Tokyo.

the reports stopped abruptly in mid-ocean. But his parents never gave up hope. In anticipation of his arrival, they traveled to San Francisco in September.

They were rewarded on September 13 when Subaru sailed under the Golden Gate Bridge and into San Francisco Bay. "Two days before my arrival, I was so excited I couldn't stop smiling and I couldn't sleep," he recalls. He was soon greeted by his parents and a group of reporters whose news reports made him an instant hero as the youngest person to sail solo across the Pacific Ocean.

As he stepped off the boat, he said, "This is the beginning for me, not the end." He was referring to another goal: sailing solo around the world — just as soon as he can get prepared.

Check Your Progress

In this theme you have read about several people with courage, from a thirteen-year-old girl to a Japanese diplomat. Now you will read and compare two new selections, practice your test-taking skills, and review what you've learned throughout the theme.

Look back at pages 23–24. Think about what courage means to Avi and to you. Which characters do you believe have shown the greatest courage so far?

Now read the two selections that follow. Compare the kinds of courage each selection tells about. Think about how difficult, or easy, it seems for these characters to be courageous. How do their courageous actions compare with others in the theme?

Read and Compare

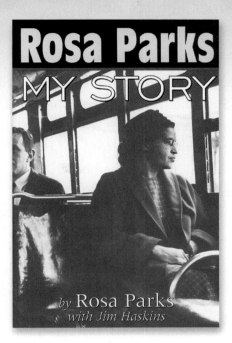

In the first selection, learn about Rosa Parks, whose act of defiance sparked the national civil rights movement.

Try these strategies:
Monitor and Clarify
Evaluate

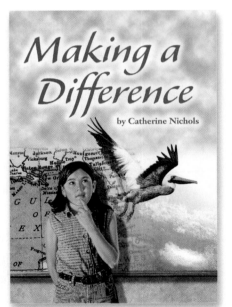

Then read a story about a girl who finds the courage to make a speech in front of her class.

Try these strategies:
Predict and Infer
Summarize

Strategies in Action *Remember to use all your reading strategies while you read.*

Rosa Parks

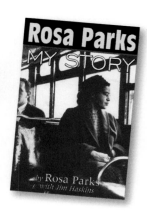

MY STORY

by Rosa Parks, with Jim Haskins

In 1955 Rosa Parks worked in a department store. She was also the secretary for Edgar Nixon, president of the Montgomery National Association for the Advancement of Colored People (NAACP). She, like many other people, took the bus to work. At that time, the buses of Montgomery, Alabama, were segregated, which meant that whites sat in the front part of the bus and African Americans sat in the back. Rosa Parks thought that this law was wrong. What she did on December 1, 1955, sparked the national civil rights movement in the United States.

THIS PART OF THE BUS FOR THE COLORED RACE

▲ The "colored" section at the back of the bus (Courtesy of NAACP Public Relations)

Back in the spring of 1955 a teenage girl named Claudette Colvin and an elderly woman refused to give up their seats in the middle section of a bus to white people. When the driver went to get the police, the elderly woman got off the bus, but Claudette refused to leave, saying she had already paid her dime and had no reason to move. When the police came, they dragged her from the bus and arrested her. Now, her name was familiar to me, and it turned out that Claudette Colvin was the great-granddaughter of Mr. Gus Vaughn, the black man with all the children back in Pine Level who refused to work for the white man. His great-granddaughter must have inherited his sense of pride. I took a particular interest in the girl and her case.

After Claudette's arrest, a group of activists took a petition to the bus company officials and city officials. The petition asked for more courteous treatment and for no visible signs of segregation. They didn't ask for the end of segregation, just for an understanding that whites would start sitting at the front of the bus and blacks would start sitting at the back, and wherever they met would be the dividing line. I think that petition also asked that black bus drivers be hired. The city officials and the bus company took months to answer that petition, and when they did, every request in it was turned down.

I did not go down with the others to present that petition to the bus company and the city officials, because I didn't feel anything could be accomplished. I had decided that I would not go anywhere with a piece of paper in my hand asking white folks for any favors. I had made that decision myself, as an individual.

Another bus incident involving a woman occurred that summer. I didn't know much about the girl. Her name was Louise Smith, and she was about eighteen years old. They say she paid her fine and didn't protest. Hers certainly wasn't a good case for Mr. Nixon to appeal to a higher court.

I knew they needed a plaintiff who was beyond reproach, because I was in on the discussions about the possible court cases. But that is not why I refused to give up my bus seat to a white man on Thursday, December 1, 1955. I did not intend to get arrested. If I had been paying attention, I wouldn't even have gotten on that bus.

I was very busy at that particular time. I was getting an NAACP workshop together for the 3rd and 4th of December, and I was trying to get the consent of Mr. H. Council Trenholm at Alabama State to have the Saturday meeting at the college. He did give permission, but I had a hard time getting to him to get permission to use the building. I was also getting the notices in the mail for the election of officers of the Senior Branch of the NAACP, which would be next week.

When I got off from work that evening of December 1, I went to Court Square as usual to catch the Cleveland Avenue bus home. I didn't look to see who was driving when I got on, and by the time I recognized him, I had already paid my fare. It was the same driver who had put me off the bus back in 1943, twelve years earlier. He was still tall and heavy, with red, rough-looking skin. And he was still mean-looking. I didn't know if he had been on that route before — they switched the drivers around sometimes. I do know that most of the time if I saw him on a bus, I wouldn't get on it.

I saw a vacant seat in the middle section of the bus and took it. I didn't even question why there was a vacant seat even though there were quite a few people standing in the back. If I had thought about it at all, I would probably have figured maybe someone saw me get on and did not take the seat but left it vacant for me. There was a man sitting next to the window and two women across the aisle.

The next stop was the Empire Theater, and some whites got on. They filled up the white seats, and one man was left standing. The driver looked back and noticed the man standing. Then he looked back at us. He said, "Let me have those front seats," because they were the front seats of the black section. Didn't anybody move. We just sat right where we were, the four of us. Then he spoke a second time: "Y'all better make it light on yourselves and let me have those seats."

The man in the window seat next to me stood up, and I moved to let him pass by me, and then I looked across the aisle and saw that the two women were also standing. I moved over to the window seat. I could not see how standing up was going to "make it light" for me. The more we gave in and complied, the worse they treated us.

People always say that I didn't give up my seat because I was tired, but that isn't true. I was not tired physically, or no more tired than I usually was at the end of a working day. I was not old, although some people have an image of me as being old then. I was forty-two. No, the only tired I was, was tired of giving in.

The driver of the bus saw me still sitting there, and he asked was I going to stand up. I said, "No." He said, "Well, I'm going to have you arrested." Then I said, "You may do that." These were the only words we said to each other. I didn't even know his name, which was James Blake, until we were in court together. He got out of the bus and stayed outside for a few minutes, waiting for the police.

▼ A "Day of Pilgrimage" protest begins with black Montgomery citizens walking to work, part of their boycott of buses in the wake of the Rosa Parks incident.

As I sat there, I tried not to think about what might happen. I knew that anything was possible. I could be manhandled or beaten. I could be arrested. People have asked me if it occurred to me then that I could be the test case the NAACP had been looking for. I did not think about that at all. In fact if I had let myself think too deeply about what might happen to me, I might have gotten off the bus. But I chose to remain.

◀ Rosa Parks is fingerprinted by D.H. Lackey of the Montgomery Police Department for participating in the bus boycott.

Rev. Martin Luther King, Jr., director of ▶ the segregated bus boycott, brimming with enthusiasm as he outlines boycott strategies to his organizers, including Rosa Parks

THE OUTCOME

After Rosa Parks was arrested for violating the segregation law, the African Americans of Montgomery organized a boycott of the city buses. Rosa Parks attended her trial and was given a suspended sentence. Martin Luther King, Jr., called for an end to the segregation of buses. By the time the United States Supreme Court ruled that segregation on Montgomery buses was unconstitutional, the boycott had lasted nearly a year.

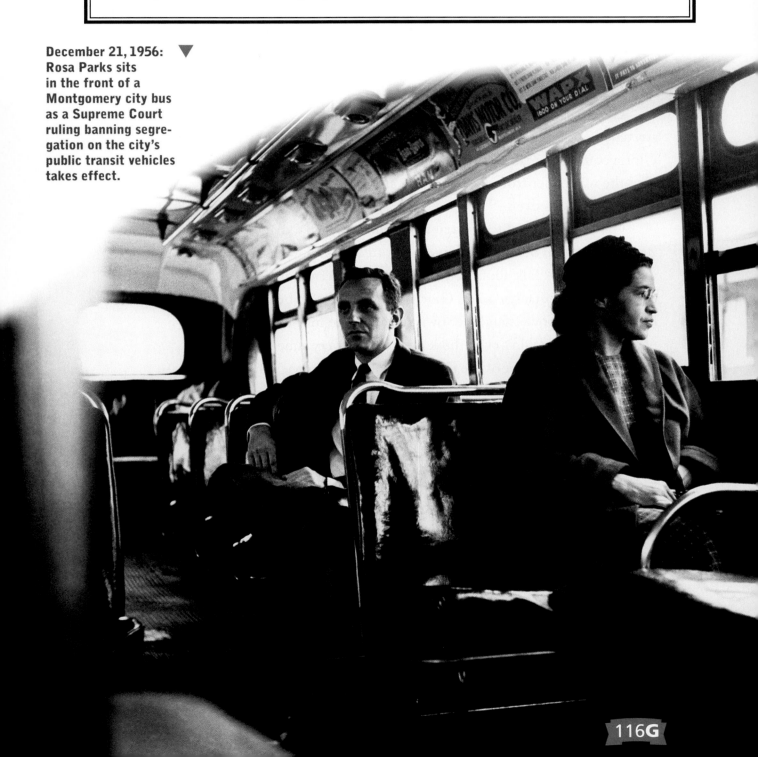

December 21, 1956: ▼
Rosa Parks sits in the front of a Montgomery city bus as a Supreme Court ruling banning segregation on the city's public transit vehicles takes effect.

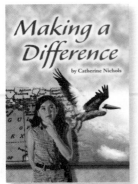

Making a Difference

by Catherine Nichols illustrated by Robert Rodriguez

Gloria ate the last bite of her *arepa*. Her older sister, Elena, lay stretched out beside her on the picnic blanket. Out on Tampa Bay, Gloria could just make out her father in his small boat. She crumpled the wax paper from her sandwich and shoved it into her knapsack. Lunch was over.

Gloria sighed and took a red notebook out of her knapsack. Inside, written in bold letters, was the word *Speech*. Her speech was due tomorrow. "Talk about something that concerns you," her teacher, Ms. Acosta, had said. Gloria had hoped she'd be inspired by being on Mangrove Island, her own special name for her favorite place. But she couldn't even think of a topic. Every time she tried, she saw herself in front of the classroom, and her stomach did a flip-flop. Nothing made her more nervous than the thought of getting up in front of people.

"I was the same way, *mi cielo*," Mami had told her. "The best way to get over it — do it! Get up and speak." Gloria wished she were more like Elena. Elena loved to talk. Giving a speech was nothing to her.

Gloria picked up her pen. She would just write something. Anything. Whatever came to mind. Before she could write a word, a frantic, fluttering noise came from the bushes. Gloria poked her sister. "Elena. Wake up."

Her sister rolled over lazily. "What is it?"

"I heard something," Gloria said. "In the bushes."

Elena lay back down. "You heard quiet, that's all." She closed her eyes.
A loud squawk was followed by more flapping noises. Elena sat up.

"Let's wait for Papi by the shore," Gloria said.

"No, come on," Elena said, scrambling to her feet. "Let's investigate."

Gloria followed her older sister, teeth chattering. She was scared — maybe even more scared than she was of giving a speech. But here she went, into the unknown in search of a strange sound. She dodged branches and bushes until they came to a clearing. There, by a mangrove, was a large brownish bird.

"*Mira!*" Gloria cried. "Look! The poor bird's wing is tangled in string."

The bird tried to get free, but the more it struggled, the more tangled it became.

"What do we do?" whispered Gloria.

"Watch me," Elena whispered back, stealthily approaching the bird. Just as she came within a foot or so, the bird lunged. "Ay!" Elena screamed and jumped back.

Gloria noticed that the other end of the string was several feet away, looped around the roots of another mangrove. "Wait," she said.

She crept forward and carefully unwound the plastic string from the roots. The bird stopped struggling, perhaps sensing that she was trying to help it. When the last of the string was off, the bird slipped free. Then it flapped its great wings and flew off.

Papi was waiting for them back at the blanket, a park ranger at his side. "*Niñas*, where have you been? I thought I told you to stay near the blanket."

"Oh, *Papi*, we saved a bird!" Elena cried.

"You girls did well," the ranger said when Elena finished telling what had happened. "In the future, though, you should find a ranger or some other adult to help. Even birds can be dangerous."

"What kind of bird was it?" Gloria asked.

"From what you described, it sounds like a brown pelican," he replied. "This is a nesting area of theirs, though they're not nesting now." He picked up the plastic string they had brought back. "And this is no ordinary string. This is fishing line. Trouble is, this stuff isn't biodegradable." He looked at the girls. "That's a fancy way of saying it doesn't break down. The lines collect and they can do a lot of harm. Hundreds of birds get tangled in them each year, and not all of them are as lucky as your bird. Most die."

"That's terrible!" Gloria cried.

During the car ride back to Ybor City, Gloria sat quietly in the back seat. She remembered how the bird had struggled to free itself. If she hadn't helped, it might have died. Tears pricked her eyes.

"Any volunteers to give the first speech?" Ms. Acosta asked the next day.

Gloria took a deep breath and raised her hand.

"Gloria Perez?" Ms. Acosta looked surprised but pleased. "Go right ahead."

Gloria walked to the front of the class. Her stomach made soft, rumbling noises. Facing the class, she noticed that her hands were trembling. Her throat and mouth felt dry. She remembered the pelican, its wing tangled in the fishing line, and took a deep breath. "I'd like to tell you about something I saw yesterday. . . ."

As she spoke, Gloria grew calmer. She told the class about the pelican and about how she and her sister had rescued it. She told them about the fishing line and how dangerous it was. She told them that the ranger said he could always use volunteers to help collect the fishing lines before they hurt wildlife. "I'm going this Saturday to help, and so is my family. I'd like to invite everyone in this class — and Ms. Acosta, too — to come with us. Together, we can make a difference."

Gloria made her way back to her seat. The entire classroom was quiet. The only sound Gloria heard was the *click clack* of her shoes. Back in her seat, she didn't look around. She guessed her speech hadn't gone over well. She guessed that no one cared about pelicans. Then she heard clapping. It grew louder and louder.

That Saturday, Class 5-1, armed with trash bags, piled out of two boats. Under the ranger's direction, they got to work clearing the island of fishing line and other trash. As she worked, Gloria thought about the birds that would now be able to live here safely and raise their families. With just one little speech, she *had* made a big difference.

Think and Compare

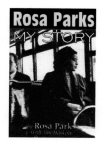

1. Compare Rosa Parks's story with Gloria's story. What do the two situations have in common? How are they different?

2. Why do you think the Montgomery buses were segregated in 1955? What do you think we have learned from the past?

3. Compare what Rosa Parks does with what Chiune Suguhara does in *Passage to Freedom*. How are their actions alike? How are they different?

4. How do Rosa Parks and Gloria show aspects of courage different from those shown by the characters in *Hatchet* or *Climb or Die*? Give examples.

5. Which selection in this theme best fits your own definition of courage? Explain your answer with examples from the selection.

Strategies in Action How did using the reading strategies help you read better during this theme?

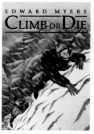

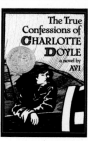

Write a Journal Entry

Choose a character from the theme. Think of how that character felt when he or she showed courage. Write one or two paragraphs about the experience in a journal entry.

Tips

- Use details from the selection to describe the character's experience.
- Describe events in the order in which they happened.
- Use action verbs.

Choosing the Best Answer

Many tests have multiple-choice items, or items with three to five answer choices. How do you choose the best answer? Look at this sample test item for *Rosa Parks: My Story.*

Read the question. In the answer row, fill in the circle that corresponds to the best answer.

1. What happens just before Rosa Parks refuses to give up her seat on the bus?

   A Rosa recognizes the bus driver.

   B Claudette Colvin is arrested by the police.

   C The driver gets out of the bus and waits for the police.

   D Rosa moves over to the window seat.

   ANSWER ROW 1   Ⓐ Ⓑ Ⓒ ●

 Understand the question.

Find the key words. Use them to understand what you need to do.

I think the most important words are *just before* and *refuses to give up her seat.* I need to find out what happens just before Rosa Parks refuses to give up her seat.

② Look back at the selection.

Think about where to find the answer. You may need to look in more than one place. Skim the selection, using the key words.

I'll look for the part where Rosa tells about getting on and riding the bus. That's where I'll find out what happens *just before* she refuses to leave her seat.

③ Narrow the choices. Then choose the best answer.

Find the choices that are clearly wrong. Have a good reason for choosing an answer. Guess only if you have to.

I know **B** doesn't happen on Rosa's bus. Choice **A** happens before Rosa sits down, and **C** happens after, not just before, Rosa refuses to move. I know from page 116D that Rosa moves to the window seat. The right answer is **D**.

POETRY

Poetry

What is Poetry? Who knows?

Not a rose, but the scent of the rose;

Not the sky, but the light in the sky;

Not the fly, but the gleam of the fly;

Not the sea, but the sound of the sea;

Not myself, but what makes me

See, hear, and feel something that prose

Cannot: and what it is, who knows?

Eleanor Farjeon

What Is Poetry?

Poems use words in ways that make you imagine and feel what's in and around you. The words of some poems **rhyme**. Other poems play with word sounds and **rhythm**.

Poems may remind you of experiences from your life. The poems that follow are about friends and family. Read on, and then write a poem of your own.

Contents

Friends

Good Hotdogs..121
by Sandra Cisneros

Losing Livie *from* **Out of the Dust**..............................123
by Karen Hesse

Poem..124
by Langston Hughes

The Pasture..125
by Robert Frost

Oranges..126
by Gary Soto

Family

Family Style..128
by Janet Wong

Sundays..129
by Paul Janeczko

My Own Man..130
by Nikki Grimes

From **The People, Yes** 131
by Carl Sandburg

Child Rest...132
by Phil George

Family Photo..133
by Ralph Fletcher

Friends

Here are five poems that express the ups and downs of friendship. While you read the poems, think about how you could compare and contrast two of them.

Good Hotdogs

Fifty cents apiece
To eat our lunch
We'd run
Straight from school
Instead of home
Two blocks
Then the store
That smelled like steam
You ordered
Because you had the money
Two hotdogs and two pops for here
Everything on the hotdogs
Except pickle lily

Dash those hotdogs
Into buns and splash on
All that good stuff
Yellow mustard and onions
And french fries piled on top all
Rolled up in a piece of wax
Paper for us to hold hot
In our hands
Quarters on the counter
Sit down
Good hotdogs
We'd eat
Fast till there was nothing left
But salt and poppy seeds even
Then little burnt tips
Of french fries
We'd eat
You humming
And me swinging my legs

— *Sandra Cisneros*

121

Losing Livie

Livie Killian moved away.
I didn't want her to go.
We'd been friends since first grade.

The farewell party was
Thursday night
at the Old Rock Schoolhouse.

Livie
had something to tease each of us
    about,
like Ray
sleeping through reading class,
and Hillary,
who on her speed-writing test put
an "even ton" of children
instead of an "even ten."

Livie said good-bye to each of us,
separately.
She gave me a picture she'd made
    of me sitting
in front of a piano,
wearing my straw hat,
an apple halfway to my mouth.

I handed Livie the memory book
    we'd all
filled with our different slants.
I couldn't get the muscles in my
    throat relaxed enough
to tell her how much I'd miss her.

Livie
helped clean up her own party,
wiping spilled lemonade,
gathering sandwich crusts,
sweeping cookie crumbs from the
    floor,
while the rest of us went home
to study for semester reviews.

Now Livie's gone west,
out of the dust,
on her way to California,
where the wind takes a rest
    sometimes.
And I'm wondering what kind of
    friend I am,
wanting my feet on that road to
    another place,
instead of Livie's.

from Out of the Dust
— *Karen Hesse*

Poem

I loved my friend.
He went away from me.
There's nothing more to say.
The poem ends,
Soft as it began —
I loved my friend.

— *Langston Hughes*

THE PASTURE

I'm going out to clean the pasture spring;
I'll only stop to rake the leaves away
(And wait to watch the water clear, I may)
I sha'n't be gone long. — You come too.

I'm going out to fetch the little calf
That's standing by the mother. It's so young
It totters when she licks it with her tongue.
I sha'n't be gone long. — You come too.

— *Robert Frost*

Oranges

The first time I walked
With a girl, I was twelve,
Cold, and weighted down
With two oranges in my jacket.
December. Frost cracking
Beneath my steps, my breath
Before me, then gone,
As I walked toward
Her house, the one whose

Porch light burned yellow
Night and day, in any weather.
A dog barked at me, until
She came out pulling
At her gloves, face bright
With rouge. I smiled,
Touched her shoulder, and led
Her down the street, across
A used car lot and a line

Of newly planted trees,
Until we were breathing
Before a drugstore. We
Entered, the tiny bell
Bringing a saleslady
Down a narrow aisle of goods.
I turned to the candies
Tiered like bleachers,
And asked what she wanted —
Light in her eyes, a smile
Starting at the corners
Of her mouth. I fingered
A nickel in my pocket,
And when she lifted a chocolate
That cost a dime,
I didn't say anything.
I took the nickel from
My pocket, then an orange,
And set them quietly on
The counter. When I looked up,
The lady's eyes met mine,
And held them, knowing
Very well what it was all
About.

Outside,
A few cars hissing past,
Fog hanging like old
Coats between the trees.
I took my girl's hand
In mine for two blocks,
Then released it to let
Her unwrap the chocolate.
I peeled my orange
That was so bright against
The gray of December
That, from some distance,
Someone might have thought
I was making a fire in my hands.

— *Gary Soto*

Family

Sometimes an image in a poem surprises you. As you read the next six poems about family, pick your favorite image.

Family Style

Like hungry sea gulls,
chopsticks fight, trying to snatch
the best piece of fish.

— *Janet Wong*

Sundays

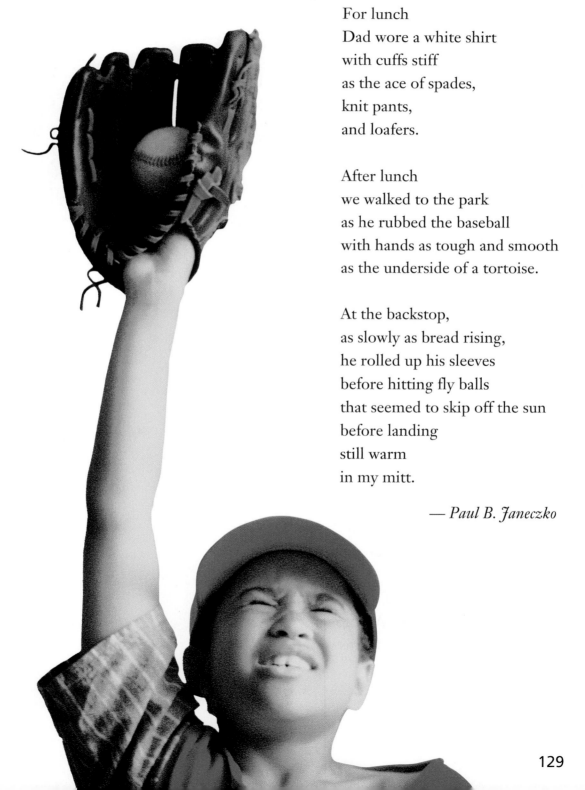

For lunch
Dad wore a white shirt
with cuffs stiff
as the ace of spades,
knit pants,
and loafers.

After lunch
we walked to the park
as he rubbed the baseball
with hands as tough and smooth
as the underside of a tortoise.

At the backstop,
as slowly as bread rising,
he rolled up his sleeves
before hitting fly balls
that seemed to skip off the sun
before landing
still warm
in my mitt.

— *Paul B. Janeczko*

My Own Man

When Mom works late I wait with busy
hands, pry soup cans open, spread spicy

mustard on rye with lettuce and tomatoes
sliced so thin the cheese peeks through.

It's my Cheddar Deluxe, which Mom loves
better than anything I cook. The boys next

door say, "How's that look? You fixin' supper
like some girl." I shrug off their teasing

and go on pleasing *me*. I read my books,
choose Jazz *and* Rap, and quiet over

chatter. Blue says, "What's the matter
with that?" And, if I take care of my mom

so what? She takes care of me. "Don't be
no Mama's boy," kids say. Well, tough.
                    I'm made this way.

— *Nikki Grimes*

130

From
The People, Yes

A father sees a son nearing manhood.
What shall he tell that son?
"Life is hard; be steel; be a rock."
And this might stand him for the storms
and serve him for humdrum and monotony
and guide him amid sudden betrayals
and tighten him for slack moments.
"Life is a soft loam; be gentle; go easy."
And this too might serve him.
Brutes have been gentled where lashes failed.
The growth of a frail flower in a path up
has sometimes shattered and split a rock.
A tough will counts. So does desire.
So does a rich soft wanting.
Without rich wanting nothing arrives.

— *Carl Sandburg*

Child Rest

Crispy, salty, fry bread, smoked, dried,
   deer meat
And ice water from the nearby spring —
Great grandmother's midday meal.
I nap.

In her lap she takes beeswax, needle,
   beads —
Her red and yellow flower needs an
   afternoon of sewing.
She half whistles, half hums an old song
   for me.
I sleep.

Faithful as a forest doe Kautsa watches
   over me.
Her red and yellow flower blossoms,
   beadwork complete.
Now, continuous humming, tapping of
   her moccasined foot stops . . .
I awake.

— *Phil George*

Family Photo

One last picture
before we head off
in different directions.

One last group shot of
all of us, smirking,
with rabbit ears.

Three generations,
kids on shoulders,
a baby cousin on my lap.

And in the middle
Grandma and Grandpa
who started all this.

We're ripples in a pond
spreading out
from a stone they threw.

— *Ralph Fletcher*

Think About the POETRY

1. Compare the poem on page 119 with the text that follows it. How do they define poetry? How would you define it?

2. How are the friendships in "Good Hotdogs" and "Losing Livie" alike? How do the moods in these two poems differ?

3. How do the poems in the "Friends" section describe the ups and downs of friendship? Give examples from your reading.

4. Which poem in the "Family" section appeals to you the most? How does the poet feel about this particular family?

5. Which poem best fits your own definition of poetry? Explain your answer with examples from the poem.

Internet

Post a Review

Choose a poem from either the "Friends" or "Family" section. Write a review of that poem. Post your review on Education Place. **www.eduplace.com/kids**

Write Your Own Poem

Choose someone you know well. It might be a friend or a family member. Is there a certain story or feeling you associate with that person? Write a poem about him or her.

2

What Really Happened?

"To be surprised,
to wonder, is to begin
to understand."

— *José Ortega y Gasset*

What Really Happened?

with Shelley Tanaka

Have you ever been left wondering about something you don't quite understand? Author Shelley Tanaka has. Find out why she investigates mysteries in science and history and read her descriptions of four fascinating mysteries.

Paleontologists find the bones of a ten-million-year-old rhinoceros (bottom right) and a long-necked dinosaur (upper right).

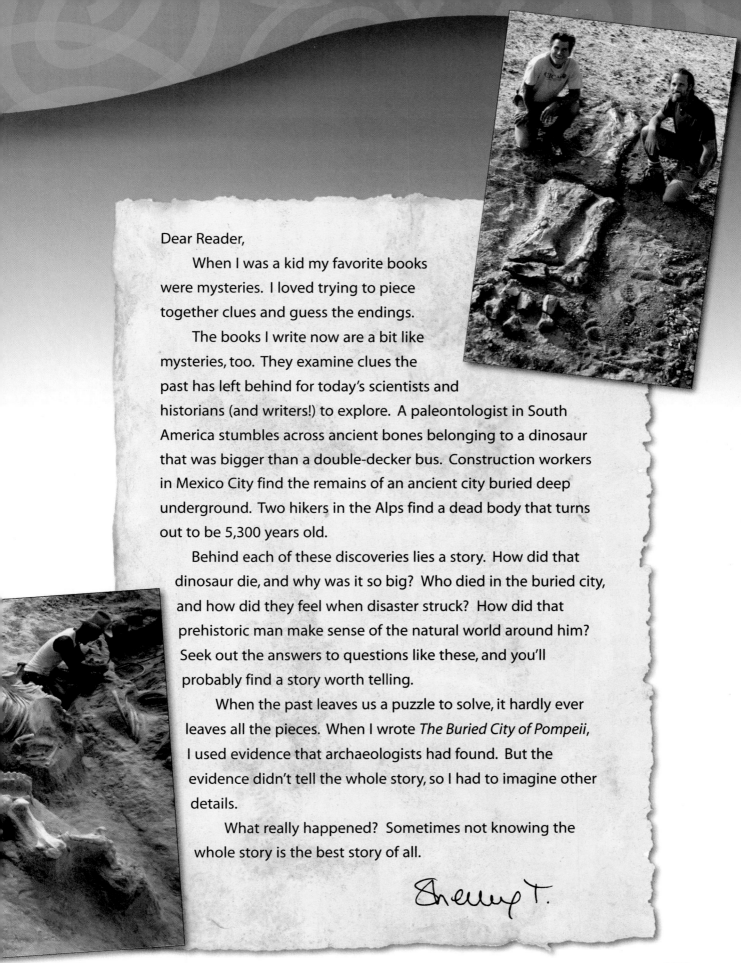

Dear Reader,

When I was a kid my favorite books were mysteries. I loved trying to piece together clues and guess the endings.

The books I write now are a bit like mysteries, too. They examine clues the past has left behind for today's scientists and historians (and writers!) to explore. A paleontologist in South America stumbles across ancient bones belonging to a dinosaur that was bigger than a double-decker bus. Construction workers in Mexico City find the remains of an ancient city buried deep underground. Two hikers in the Alps find a dead body that turns out to be 5,300 years old.

Behind each of these discoveries lies a story. How did that dinosaur die, and why was it so big? Who died in the buried city, and how did they feel when disaster struck? How did that prehistoric man make sense of the natural world around him? Seek out the answers to questions like these, and you'll probably find a story worth telling.

When the past leaves us a puzzle to solve, it hardly ever leaves all the pieces. When I wrote *The Buried City of Pompeii*, I used evidence that archaeologists had found. But the evidence didn't tell the whole story, so I had to imagine other details.

What really happened? Sometimes not knowing the whole story is the best story of all.

Shelley T.

Stonehenge

Four thousand years ago this giant stone circle was erected in southern England, but for a long time no one knew why it had been built. Was it an ancient temple or tomb? Recently scientists have realized that the stones were positioned according to the movements of the sun, moon, and planets — the beginning of an early calendar.

Piltdown Man

In 1912 a fossil collector reported finding pieces of an ancient-looking human skull and jawbone in a gravel pit in England. For years scientists thought the discovery provided a missing link in human evolution. Further study eventually proved that the skull was modern, and the jaw actually belonged to an orangutan.

Nazca Lines

Two thousand years ago the Nazca people of Peru created enormous drawings by carving wide lines in the desert. The drawings were up to eight miles long and could only be seen properly from high in the air. Were they made to please the gods above? Did they mark the way to sacred shrines? Or did they, like Stonehenge, have astronomical significance?

Nazca lines, Peru

The *Titanic*

The world's biggest ocean liner sank on her maiden voyage in 1912. For years no one could find the wreck, and many different stories were told about how she sank. In 1985 the *Titanic* was discovered at the bottom of the Atlantic Ocean. Experts were finally able to describe the ship's final moments.

Stonehenge, southern England

140

Puzzles to Solve...

Compare Shelley Tanaka's ideas about mysteries with your own. What makes an event or a discovery a real-life mystery? What mysteries have you read about or researched?

What unexplained discovery or event will you find in each selection below? As you read, think about what elements make each selection a mystery to be solved. How well does each proposed explanation succeed in solving each mystery? It's time to think about *what really happened.*

To learn about the authors in this theme, visit Education Place. www.eduplace.com/kids

Background and Vocabulary

First in Flight

Amelia Earhart: First Lady of Flight

JAN PARR

Read to find the meanings of these words.

e ● Glossary

accomplish

accounting

aviation

disappearance

inspiration

journal

runway

taxied

Amelia Earhart was the most famous female pilot of her time. She set many **aviation** records and was an **inspiration** to future pilots everywhere. *Amelia Earhart: First Lady of Flight* is an **accounting** of her last flight and the theories about her **disappearance**.

June 1928   As the first woman to cross the Atlantic Ocean as an airplane passenger, Amelia kept a **journal** of her historic flight.

May 1932 A cow pasture in Ireland served as Amelia's **runway** after she completed her solo flight across the Atlantic Ocean.

August 1932 There was very little Amelia couldn't **accomplish**. She set the women's nonstop cross-country speed record by flying from Los Angeles, California, to Newark, New Jersey.

January 1935 Amelia became the first person to fly solo across the Pacific Ocean from Honolulu, Hawaii, to Oakland, California. Thousands of people greeted Amelia after she landed and **taxied** her plane to a stop in Oakland.

About the Author
JAN PARR

As a girl, Jan Parr rode her bike to the bookmobile every week, checked out as many books as she could, and then rode home to read. Now, in addition to writing, she works as an online magazine editor. Her favorite story subjects are strong, independent people. When her editor suggested that she write about Amelia Earhart, she was thrilled, because Amelia was so far ahead of her time, and followed her heart.

To find out more about Jan Parr, visit Education Place.
www.eduplace.com/kids

144

BOOK REPORT BIOGRAPHIES

AMELIA EARHART

FIRST LADY OF FLIGHT

JAN PARR

In 1937, pilot Amelia Earhart planned to be the first to succeed in a dangerous flight. As you read, think of **questions** about the flight to discuss with your classmates.

Last Flight

In March 1937, Amelia Earhart attempted the first flight around the world at its widest point, the equator. With her husband George's financial and moral support, she was able to begin her historic flight. The plan was to fly an east-to-west course, starting from Oakland, California. The flight got off to a bad start when her plane, a Lockheed Electra, crash-landed on takeoff in Hawaii. Neither Amelia nor her navigator, Fred Noonan, was hurt. Two months later Amelia and Fred Noonan flew a west-to-east course, starting from Miami, Florida.

Amelia and Fred taxi for takeoff in their airplane, a Lockheed Electra, at Miami, Florida.

Amelia and Fred prepare for the flight.

Amelia says goodbye to her husband, George, before departing on her round-the-world flight.

On Her Way Around the World

Amelia and Fred Noonan left Miami on June 1, 1937. They left behind the telegraph key and the trailing communications antenna that had to be reeled in and out of the plane. Without them, they would be out of touch with homing signals for hours at a time. The telegraph would not have done them much good, anyway — neither Noonan nor Amelia had ever learned Morse code.

The first day, they flew to San Juan, Puerto Rico. The trip was underway. But Amelia was getting tired of these long-distance flights. In *Last Flight*, she wrote about hurrying to leave San Juan: "We're always pushing through, hurrying on our long way, trying to get to some other place instead of enjoying the place we'd already got to."

But she did push through — east toward Africa. As they approached the coast of West Africa in a thick haze, Fred Noonan, sitting at his chart table in the back of the plane, figured out where they were and sent a note to Amelia in the front. It told her when to turn south to head for Dakar, their planned stop in western Africa. To get the note to her, he attached it to a line on a fishing pole they had rigged up. (It was too noisy in the plane to talk.) She

read the note but believed Noonan had made an error. Her instinct told her to turn north, so she did, but they ended up in a town north of Dakar. Noonan had been right.

Then it was over to Karachi, India, south to Singapore, and across to Darwin, Australia. At each stop they rested, ate, and refueled and checked the plane. All along the way, Amelia was sending regular reports to George, who passed them along to newspaper reporters. All over the United States, anxious fans read her accounting of events in the newspaper.

They landed in Lae, New Guinea, on June 29. They had flown 22,000 miles (35,400 km) in one month, making thirty stops in nineteen countries on five continents. They were exhausted. In Lae, Amelia and Fred got some sleep while the plane was checked over and refueled. Bad weather kept them there for three days. From Lae she wrote in her journal, "I wish we could stay here peacefully for a time and see something of this strange land." But they had only 7,000 miles (11,300 km) to go.

Before they took off, Amelia packed up maps, clothing, and other things they would not need and sent them back home. She wanted the plane to be as light as possible. She also took survival equipment off the plane, so concerned was she about extra weight.

From Lae to Howland Island

The weather cleared, and they took off on July 2, heading for tiny Howland Island in the Pacific Ocean. The U.S. Department of the Interior had built a runway there for the Electra. From Howland, they were to fly to Hawaii, and from there to Oakland, California.

This was the most dangerous part of the trip. The airspace from Lae to Howland had never been mapped, and Howland would be hard to spot, even for the most experienced navigator. It was only two miles long and a half mile wide (3.2 by .8 km). Fred was expert at navigating by the stars, but this method would not work if the sky was cloudy. The U.S. Coast Guard provided a ship called the *Itasca*, stationed just off Howland Island, which would help guide the plane to the island. They would use black smoke signals and talk to the Electra on the radio.

The trip was expected to take about eighteen hours.

Radio operators were stationed on Howland Island and the *Itasca*. Amelia had said she would use frequency 3105 on the radio and report every half hour. The crew of the *Itasca* had a hard time hearing her. They asked her to switch to a stronger frequency but never received an answer. It seemed that she could not hear their requests.

They asked her several times to stay on the radio a few extra seconds so they could get a bearing on the plane. Each time, though, she signed off hurriedly.

At 4:53 A.M., a radioman on the *Itasca* thought he heard Amelia say "partly cloudy." There was a lot of static on the line. She said she would whistle into the microphone. She asked for a bearing on the plane, but she did not stay on the radio long enough to allow them to do this. She said she was 200 miles (320 km) out.

The crew of the *Itasca* grew alarmed. It was obvious there was a problem with the plane's radio or with the way Amelia was using it. They repeatedly tried to reach her, but she never answered. When they finally did hear from her, it did little to put them at ease. "We must be on you but cannot see you. Gas is running low," she said. "Been unable to reach you by radio. Flying at 1,000

In Indonesia, Amelia and Fred stopped to refuel their plane.

feet. Only half hour's gas left."

The *Itasca* began sending up thick black smoke signals. The sky was clear, and Amelia and Fred would surely have been able to see them if the plane was in the area.

At 8:47 A.M., Amelia's voice came in loud and clear, but hurried and panicked. "We are on line of position one five seven dash three three seven," Amelia said. "Will repeat this message on 6210 kilocycles. Wait, listening on 6210 kilocycles. We are running north and south."

The *Itasca* radioman responded immediately, asking her to stay on 3105 kilocycles. "Please stay on 3105 do not hear you on 6210," they said. But they did not hear from her again, on any frequency.

About an hour later, when the crew of the *Itasca* calculated that the Electra would have run out of fuel, a search party went out. Around Howland Island, and to the south and east, the weather was clear. To the north and west were heavy cloud banks. The Electra must have been in that area, they reasoned. This would explain why the plane could not see the smoke signals. It would also explain why Noonan had gotten so far off course, if he was not able to see the stars or the sun.

What followed was the largest sea search in the history of the U.S. Navy. As the days went on, a battleship, four destroyers, a minesweeper, a seaplane, and airplanes joined the search. They searched 25,000 square miles (65,000 sq km) of the Pacific. At first, the rescuers had high hopes of finding the fliers. Perhaps they were floating on a rubber raft or had been picked up by a Japanese fishing boat. Maybe the plane itself could float on its empty fuel tanks.

After many days of intense effort, however, the search teams found nothing.

What Happened to Amelia Earhart?

The search teams in the Pacific claimed that there was absolutely no trace of Amelia's plane. Or was there?

Did someone — the Japanese or the U.S. government — really know what happened to Amelia and Fred Noonan?

The disappearance of Amelia Earhart, Fred Noonan, and the Electra is one of the biggest mysteries of the twentieth century. The U.S. government's official position is that the plane ran out of gas shortly after the last time the *Itasca* heard from them, then it crashed at sea and sank. Many people do not believe this, however. For one thing, a plane that big would not have sunk right away. For another, the sunken plane would have left an oil or gas slick behind on the water. Nothing like this was ever found, despite the huge area of ocean they searched.

Many historians, aviation experts, reporters, and investigators have since tried to solve the puzzle. To date, no one knows for sure what happened. But here are some of the theories.

Did They Survive the Crash?

For several days after the *Itasca* heard its last message from Amelia, a number of ham radio operators say they heard messages that they are sure came from the Electra. A Pan Am operator on Wake Island in the Pacific filed an official report stating that he had heard this message the day after the search began:

SOS . . . SOS . . . SOS . . . SOS . . . Northwest unknown island 177 longitude . . . Quite down, but radio still working . . . Battery very weak . . . Don't know how long we can hold out . . . We are OK but a little wet . . . Calling [on] 3105 kilocycles . . . Give me a long call (fade out) KHAQQ [Amelia's call letters] . . . Plane on cay northwest Howland Island . . .

Amelia Earhart became an internationally certified pilot at the age of 25, as her license indicates.

Both OK. One wing broken. Bearing 337 . . . 58 minutes above equator L.A.T. Island 133 acres . . . Must be a new one.

Another operator, forty years after the incident, reported that he had heard Amelia say they had crashed and were floating in the sea. He was only fifteen at the time of the flight and did not think anyone would believe him. He said that as he listened, the woman's voice became frightened and that Japanese soldiers were beating Fred Noonan; she cried out, asking them not to hurt her. Then the transmission went dead.

Can we believe any of these reports? Were the transmissions fake? Perhaps there were other radio operators pretending to be Amelia as part of a cruel hoax? Or were the broadcasts real, and some people did not want the truth to come out?

Were They Spies?

One theory is that Amelia Earhart was spying for the U.S. government. Some people believe that her airplane was specially equipped with cameras to take pictures in the Pacific. At the time of the flight, the U.S. government believed the Japanese were getting ready to enter into warfare. (It was shortly before the start of World War II.) The government wanted to get evidence that the Japanese were building military bases in the Pacific, something they were not supposed to do.

Many things about Amelia's last flight do not add up. Why didn't she ever stay on the radio long enough to allow the *Itasca* to get her position? And why did she keep changing frequencies? There are three possible answers: one, she was an inexperienced radio operator; two, she did not want Japanese ships, which she knew were in the area, to know where she was; or three, she did not want the *Itasca* to know where she was because she was actually flying off course on purpose and spying for the U.S. government.

There are more questions. Why, for example, did she leave some of her radio equipment behind in Miami? Why did she switch course — from east-to-west to west-to-east — at the last minute? She ended up flying through many spring storms, though she said she had reversed the course to avoid them. Why did the government build a runway especially for Amelia at Howland Island? And why the huge and expensive search effort for two civilians? Other fliers had not received such attention.

In 1933, Amelia posed with President Franklin Delano Roosevelt (*far right*), his wife Eleanor Roosevelt (*far left*), and fellow fliers, James and Amy Mollison (*center*).

Amelia and crew inspect the damaged Lockheed Electra after a failed takeoff in Hawaii.

At least one investigator believes that after Amelia wrecked the Electra on takeoff in Honolulu, the U.S. government approached her about spying. When the plane was grounded after the crash, the team needed money for repairs in order to go on with the flight. According to this spy theory, instead of rebuilding the plane, they constructed a whole new Electra, a much faster and more powerful model, with cameras installed in the belly. It looked enough like the original to pass. The government could have had the ability to conduct such an operation — after all, Amelia and George were good friends with President Roosevelt himself. This theory would mean that all the calculations about the plane's location could be wrong because the new plane might have been able to go faster than people thought. This would explain why Amelia and Fred were not found in the search area — maybe they had flown out of it.

Whether the fliers were spying or not, the Japanese would have been suspicious of any plane flying over the territory. If a plane had gone down near them, they would have investigated the crash. It is quite possible that they would have taken Amelia and Fred prisoner. The Japanese did not let the U.S. search party into their waters, or onto the islands they controlled, to look for Amelia and Fred.

Was Amelia Still Alive?

In the early 1960s, U.S. Air Force Major Joe Gervais went to Saipan, an island some 2,660 miles (4,280 km) north of Howland. Saipan was an important military base for the Japanese during the war and had a military prison. Gervais had heard rumors that Fred and Amelia had been taken to Saipan, and he interviewed many people about the possibility. A short time later, Fred Goerner, a CBS reporter, also traveled to the island to interview residents who said they had seen the two.

More than one hundred of the island's residents who were living there in the time just before World War II said the same thing: they were sure the two were Amelia and Fred. When Goerner showed the islanders photographs of several women, all of them picked Amelia as the woman they had seen.

Some say that Amelia died of a disease called dysentery, and that Fred was shot by the Japanese when he made them mad. Others say they were both executed.

Many searches were made of the island, and in one search, some bones from two skeletons were found. When the bones were analyzed, however, it turned out they were not the remains of Fred and Amelia. Aside from the testimony of the residents of the island, no hard evidence could be found that Fred and Amelia were held on Saipan. A hot trail had gone cold.

Amelia's family did not give up the hope that Amelia was still alive. Some people suggested that Amelia had been brainwashed and was "Tokyo Rose," a woman who read propaganda reports over the radio meant to confuse American military personnel during World War II. George traveled to Japan to hear her; he denied the woman's voice was Amelia's. Fourteen months after Amelia disappeared, George had her declared legally dead, and he married another woman a short time later.

Amelia's mother and sister hoped that Amelia might return home after the war ended. They would be bitterly disappointed. Amy believed Amelia had left a large estate and fought with George over her will. She never wanted to admit that her daughter wasn't coming back and kept up hope until she died, at age ninety-five, in 1967. Muriel, who also had hopes of seeing her sister again, continued living in Massachusetts, lecturing and writing two books about Amelia; she was ninety-seven years old in 1997. Muriel believes that Amelia was "a tragedy of the sea."

Some evidence suggests that Amelia Earhart and Fred Noonan were held captive in this prison on the island of Saipan.

Several years ago, a writer digging through government documents on Amelia found a telegram. It was from China, addressed to George Palmer Putnam in California. The date of the telegram was August 28, 1945, after the liberation of a prison camp in China. It said, "Camp liberated; all well. Volumes to tell. Love to mother." Whether that telegram was really from Amelia or not, we do not know.

Another theory, which few people believe, is that Amelia survived the war, was released from prison camp afterward, and returned to the United States under a different name. Joe Gervais, who investigated a mystery woman named Irene Bolam, makes an interesting case. The woman lived in a house belonging to Amelia's good friend Jacqueline Cochran. The woman was also a pilot and a member of the Ninety-Nines and Zonta International, two flying groups to which Amelia belonged. When Gervais looked into their records, however, he found no Irene Bolam in their registers. She told him that she had been licensed under a different name. Still, she strongly denied that she was Amelia Earhart, and she sued author Joe Klaas to stop him from publishing a book that described Gervais's findings.

The Search Continues

We may never know for sure what became of Amelia and Fred and the Electra, but the search for the plane and clues continues. In 1997 a team of researchers searched an island called Nikumaroro, southeast of Howland. It was called Gardner Island in the 1940s. Many artifacts have been found there, including parts from a plane, but no one is sure they came from Amelia's Electra.

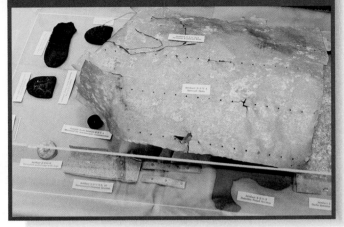

Researchers found these artifacts on the island of Nikumaroro. The large piece of aircraft skin in the center is made of the same material as the Electra. Also found was the sole of a woman's shoe (*top left*) that could have belonged to Amelia.

Though nothing has yet been confirmed, two compelling discoveries have been made at Nikumaroro: the remains of a shoe that was Amelia's size and a piece of metal that has been analyzed and found to be the same type of metal that Amelia's Electra was made of. The International Group for Historic Aircraft Recovery (TIGHAR), the team that searched the island, says that the U.S. government first searched Nikumaroro in the 1940s but did not go very far into it. TIGHAR reasons that Fred and Amelia may have taxied the plane into a cooler area under trees, where it would not have been seen by the search planes overhead.

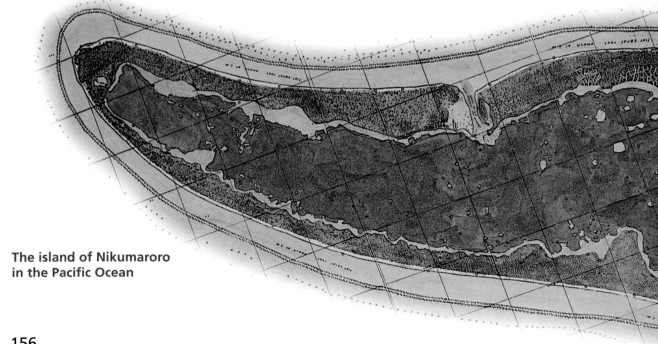

The island of Nikumaroro
in the Pacific Ocean

Fliers Elgen and Marie Long of California, along with a man named Roy Nesbit, believe the Electra probably ran out of gas and plunged into the ocean about 40 miles (64 km) northwest of Howland Island. Nesbit, relying on records from Lae, found that Amelia did not take off with a full tank of gas and only had enough to make it to Howland under perfect conditions. The Longs have established a fund to conduct the expensive search of the deep ocean bed. Only parts of the plane would still be intact today, but the mystery would be solved.

This is believed to be the last photograph taken of Amelia Earhart. She posed with a man named Jacobs (*center*) and Fred Noonan just before takeoff from Lae on July 2, 1937.

The controversy surrounding the plane's disappearance has captured the interest of countless people ever since that day in 1937. But did Amelia's last flight mean anything? Did it advance the cause of aviation or of women fliers, as she said she wanted it to? Yes. On a practical level, Amelia's flight led to new emergency procedures for fliers. For the future of aviation, people across the world could see that a plane was able to fly 22,000 miles (35,400 km) and more.

On another level, Amelia showed people that sometimes life is about taking risks, about proving things to yourself. She showed the world that women are risk-takers, too. Above all, she served as an inspiration to girls — and boys — everywhere. She lived her life exactly the way she wanted to, no matter what other people thought. In some ways, she always remained the girl in brown who walked alone. She spoke out about things that bothered her, and she fought for things she believed in. She was one of the true independent spirits of the twentieth century.

It is sad that Amelia did not live to see the day when people would fly places almost as easily as they board a bus, to see the day when millions of young girls would be able to gaze out of an airplane window and see the night sky Amelia loved so much and dream of the things they might accomplish.

Responding

Think About the Selection

1. On page 148 the author states that Amelia removed maps and clothing from the plane. Explain why this was important.

2. Which of the places Amelia Earhart stopped would you most like to visit? Why?

3. What decisions did Amelia and Fred make before and during their journey that lessened their chance of being rescued?

4. Why do you think Amelia kept signing off before the radio operators could get a bearing on her plane?

5. This selection lists several theories about why the Electra disappeared. Which theory do you agree with most? Give your reasons.

6. Why do you think the search for Amelia Earhart became "the largest sea search in the history of the U.S. Navy"?

7. **Connecting/Comparing** Why is *Amelia Earhart: First Lady of Flight* an appropriate choice for this theme?

Write a Sequel

What do you think happened to Amelia Earhart and Fred Noonan? Write a sequel — a follow-up to the story — about what might have happened to Amelia and Fred after they disappeared.

> **Tips**
> - Use details from the selection to describe Amelia, Fred, and the setting.
> - Make sure the sequence of events includes a problem, a climax, and a resolution.

Math

Calculate Averages

Look back at page 148 to see how many miles Amelia and Fred had flown in one month when they landed in New Guinea. If they had already made thirty stops, what was the average distance they flew between stops? between countries?

Bonus How many more miles did Amelia and Fred plan to fly on their journey? What fraction of their total flight would this last part represent?

Vocabulary and Speaking

Perform a Dialogue

With a partner, look for words in the selection that have to do with radio communication, including information about Amelia's call letters and the frequencies at which she attempted to communicate. Then use these words to create and perform a dialogue between Amelia Earhart and a radio operator on the *Itasca*.

Post a Review

Write a review of *Amelia Earhart: First Lady of Flight.* What did you like about her story? What didn't you like? Post your review on Education Place.

www.eduplace.com/kids

Skill: How to Outline an Article

❶ First, write the title of the article.

❷ On the next line, write the **main topic** of the first section. Label it Roman numeral *I*.

❸ List the important facts of the first section as **subtopics**, starting with the letter *A*.

❹ If you find a similar group of facts under a subtopic, group them together and write a **subheading** that describes them. There should be at least two details under a subheading.

❺ Repeat steps 2 and 3 for each paragraph of the article. Renumber when you start a new main topic.

BARNSTORMING BESSIE COLEMAN

by Sylvia Whitman

◀ *Bessie Coleman's first airplane, a Curtiss JN-4, or "Jenny."*

As Bessie Coleman's tiny plane swooped over Chicago in 1922, thousands of spectators oohed and aahed. Then they lined up for a ride. They had come to this air show because flying was still a novelty; the Wright brothers had made their first flight less than twenty years before. But many in the crowd also wanted to meet Coleman, the first African American woman to earn a pilot's license.

Probably no one that day appreciated Coleman's accomplishments more than her mother. An ex-slave, Susan Coleman had raised nine children alone in Texas after Bessie's father had left for Oklahoma. While most of the family picked cotton, Susan recognized Bessie's ability in math and assigned her the family bookkeeping chores.

When Bessie wanted to go to college, her mother let her keep the money she earned from doing other people's laundry. But Bessie could afford only one year's tuition. By 1917, she moved to Chicago and took a job as a manicurist in a barbershop. There she decided to become a pilot.

Because of her race, Coleman could find no one in America to teach her to fly. She learned French and, with the help of Robert Abbott, editor of the *Chicago Defender* newspaper, sailed to France to study parachuting and stunt flying. After earning her international pilot's license in 1921, she returned to the United States determined to open a school for African American aviators.

Like most pilots of the day, she was a "barnstormer," traveling around the country performing in air shows. (Organizers of these "flying circuses" often rented unused farmland for runways, and barns served as airplane hangars, thus the term "barnstormer.") Coleman cut a short, dashing figure in her leather helmet, goggles, longcoat, and leather boots. Admirers nicknamed her "Brave Bessie." After wowing mostly white crowds up north, Coleman inspired African American audiences in the South. On the side, she lectured at African American churches and community centers. To raise money for her school, she also flew advertising (pulled advertising banners with her plane).

As an African American woman and pilot, Bessie Coleman's flying so impressed spectators that she earned the nickname "Brave Bessie."

▼

Despite the glamour, piloting primitive cloth-and-steel aircraft was a dangerous business. In 1923, Coleman finally bought her own plane, a World War I Curtiss JN-4 (Jenny). As she cruised to an exhibition in California, the motor stalled, and the plane plunged to the ground. "Brave Bessie" broke three ribs and a leg. From her hospital bed, she sent a telegram to her fans: "Tell them all that as soon as I can walk I'm going to fly! And my faith in aviation and the [purpose] . . . it will serve in fulfilling the destiny of my people isn't shaken at all." Coleman knew that she was risking her life, but she said it was her "duty" to encourage African American aviators. She refused to perform where African American spectators were not welcome.

Bessie standing in front of a Model T car near her plane.

▼

Goggles protected
early pilots from
wind and the sun's
glare.

In 1926, Coleman entered an air show
in Jacksonville, Florida. Because no locals
would lend or rent a plane to an African
American, Coleman asked her mechanic,
William Wills, to bring her Jenny from
Texas. On the morning of April 30,
Wills piloted the Jenny over the field
while Coleman sat in the back scouting
sites for a parachute jump. She was
not wearing a seat belt because she
needed to lean over the edge of the
open cockpit to see. All of a sudden, the plane flipped,
hurling Coleman into a two-thousand-foot free fall that killed
her. Wills died minutes later when the plane crashed.

Coleman never realized her dream of establishing an
aviation school, but after her death Bessie Coleman Aero Clubs
began to spring up. Bessie Coleman continues to motivate
people because she proved that courage and determination
can give wings to a dream.

▲

Bessie Coleman's
aviation license. It
was the first ever
received by an
African American
woman.

A Story

A story is a narrative made up by the writer. Use this student's writing as a model when you write a story of your own.

The Girl Who Never Grew Up

A good story introduces the **characters** and the **setting** right away.

Dialogue makes the story real for the reader.

Details create mental pictures for the reader.

In a small town on Cape Cod lived a little girl named Madeline, who was eleven years old. Her mother's name was Jackie.

One day Madeline came home from school and told her mom about a new girl in school. "She has short red hair, Mom, . . . and lots of freckles too!"

"I had a friend when I was eleven, and she had short red hair too," said her mom. They both thought that was funny.

The next day when Madeline got home from school, she told her mom, "My new friend likes to play jump rope, but not just any jump rope. She only likes to play with a rope that is yellow, red, and black."

"So did my friend!" said her mom.

"What was your friend's name, Mom?" asked Madeline.

Jackie thought for a bit. "Laura," she said.

Madeline started to laugh. "Laura? That's my friend's name too!" How strange, she thought.

The next day Madeline invited Laura over to her house. When the two girls came into the kitchen, Jackie's eyes opened wide. "You look just like a friend I had named Laura when I was little!" The two girls laughed and disappeared upstairs to play.

About a week later, Madeline went to visit her grandmother. Her grandmother showed her a picture of her mom and her friend Laura when they were little. This Laura looked just like Madeline's friend Laura.

The next day at school Madeline showed Laura the picture. "This girl Laura looks just like you!"

"How strange — but it's not me!" said Laura.

"Okay," said Madeline. But she was starting to feel uneasy.

A good story often has **suspense**.

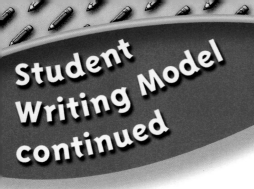

After school, Madeline decided to show her mother the picture that her grandmother had given her. Jackie took one look at the picture and ran out of the house. She headed straight for the house her friend Laura had lived in years ago. She nervously knocked on the door. No one answered. She knocked again; still no answer. She peeked in the front window.

She could not believe her eyes! Everything in the house looked exactly the way it did when she used to come to play with Laura twenty-five years ago. She saw the jump rope hanging on a chair just where Laura always hung it. She decided to try the front door again. It was unlocked. She slowly walked into the house.

She walked through all the rooms. No one was there. It was starting to make her very nervous. She quickly pushed open the front door and ran down the front steps. As she ran down the driveway, Jackie was surprised to see a car driving by that had a little girl with red hair in the back seat. She had her face pressed against the window, and she looked very sad.

As the car seemed to disappear around the corner, Jackie couldn't believe her eyes.

Madeline never saw her friend Laura again.

Meet the Author

Laura B.
Grade: six
State: Massachusetts
Hobbies: cheerleading, playing soccer
What she'd like to be when she grows up: an actress

Background and Vocabulary

THE GIRL WHO MARRIED THE MOON

TALES FROM NATIVE NORTH AMERICA
TOLD BY JOSEPH BRUCHAC AND GAYLE ROSS

The Girl Who Married the Moon

Read to find the meanings of these words.

e • Glossary

common room

hearth

mainland

phases

sod

sparkling

villages

Portrait of a People

People often use stories to try to answer the question *What Really Happened?* "The Girl Who Married the Moon" is one culture's way of explaining how the **phases** of the moon came to be. This story has been told for thousands of years by the Alutiiq (uh-LOO-tihk) — one of eight Native Alaskan peoples. Today about 4000 Alutiiq people live in fifteen rural **villages**, five towns, and all of Alaska's major cities.

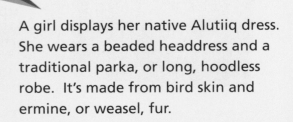

A girl displays her native Alutiiq dress. She wears a beaded headdress and a traditional parka, or long, hoodless robe. It's made from bird skin and ermine, or weasel, fur.

Map labels:

ALASKA

CANADA

Gulf of Alaska

Bristol Bay

Kodiak Island

PACIFIC OCEAN

N W E S

Kodiak Island, where about 2500 Alutiiq people live today, is thirty miles off the **mainland** of Alaska. Most natives no longer live in sod houses; their simple, modern homes sit on the shores of the Gulf of Alaska's **sparkling** blue waters.

Traditional Alutiiq housing was built out of **sod** — a mixture of soil, grass, and roots. Inside was a **common room** with a **hearth**, or fireplace, and rooms for sleeping, bathing, and food storage.

Meet the Author
JOSEPH BRUCHAC

Born: Saratoga Springs, New York

Careers: Legend collector, poet, editor, teacher, storyteller, publisher, and author of more than sixty books

Purposes for writing: "The first is to entertain. . . . The second is to teach."

Amazing fact: Once turned a gas station into a publishing company

Best-known books: Native American legends and folktales, especially legends of his ancestors, the Abenaki people, such as *Flying with the Eagle*, *Racing the Great Bear*, *Children of the Long House*, *The Great Ball Game*, *Dog People: Native Dog Stories*, and *The Story of the Milky Way*

Meet the Illustrator
LISA DESIMINI

Born: Brooklyn, New York

Sports she played while growing up: Running and softball

Favorite illustrators: Lane Smith, M.B. Goffstein, and Kate Spohn

Favorite hobbies: Yoga, cooking, and eating out

How she illustrated this story: By using a computer, she combined her painting, the photographs she took, and objects she found around the house — including a fur scarf, a suede glove, and her own hair.

To find out more about Joseph Bruchac and Lisa Desimini, visit Education Place. **www.eduplace.com/kids**

THE GIRL WHO MARRIED THE MOON

TALES FROM NATIVE NORTH AMERICA

TOLD BY JOSEPH BRUCHAC AND GAYLE ROSS

Strategy Focus

What happens when two cousins fall in love with the Moon, but he can marry only one of them? As you read, **summarize** in your own words what happens in the story.

Long ago, in the village of Chiniak, on the island of Kodiak, there were two cousins. Like the other girls of the village, they were skilled in many things. They knew how to weave beautiful hats and baskets from spruce roots. They were good at digging cranberry and other roots and finding the berries that were ready to be gathered in autumn. Like all the girls of their village, they had always been shown much love and understanding by their parents and the other elders. They had been given the freedom to do whatever they wished, but they had also been raised to be strong and brave. When they were very small, they had been placed many times in the cold salt water of the sea, yet they had never cried out.

Their lives were good in Chiniak. In the morning, they might watch the sunrise with their relatives, sitting on the sod roof of the big family house. During the day, when they were not out gathering food on the land or on the ocean in their two-person kayak, they might sit in the large common room by the hearth. Or they might take sweat baths in one of the small rooms attached to the common room, where steam would rise as they placed water on the heated stones. But whatever those cousins did, they always did it together.

Those two girls had reached the age when they could choose a husband. Both of them had just been given the chin tattoos that showed they were now women. Both of them were strong and good-looking, and they were so well liked that almost any young man would have agreed to marry them. Yet none of the young men

in the village of Chiniak or any of the other villages on the island or even the nearby mainland interested those cousins.

When the night had come and the work of the day was done, those two girls would always go down to the beach to play together in the sand and watch for the rising of the Moon above the water. As soon as he began to show his face, they would turn over their kayak and sit, leaning back against it, admiring the moon's beauty. They spent all their time at night staring at the sky. Whether it was winter or summer, they could always be found there at the beach.

One night, one of the girls said, "I have fallen in love with the Moon."

"I have fallen in love with the Moon, too," said the other girl. "If he ever comes down to the earth, I will marry him."

Their parents worried about them when they heard that the two girls wished to marry the Moon. But no one told them to stop going to the beach at night.

As they watched the Moon crossing the sky one night, it disappeared behind some heavy clouds.

"Why does the Moon have to hide his face so early in the night?" one cousin complained.

"Yes," said the other cousin, "I wish he would show himself again. I wish he would come here and choose one of us to marry him."

Suddenly they heard the sound of footsteps on the gravel of the beach and the voice of a young man.

"You have been saying that you love me," the voice said. "I have come to marry you."

The two girls leaped to their feet. A tall, handsome man wearing a beautiful mask on his face stood before them. That mask shone brightly, and they knew they were looking at the Moon.

"Yes," said the girls. "We will marry you."

"My work is hard," Moon said, "and I can take only one wife. I will take the one who is the most patient."

"We have always done everything together," said the girls. "You must take us both."

"Then you must close your eyes," Moon said. "Do not open them until I tell you."

The girls closed their eyes and waited. Moon reached down and held each of them by the long hair on her head, lifting them up into the air. The two cousins felt their feet leave the ground and they felt the wind whistling by them. They kept their eyes closed as they had been told, but when a long time had passed, one of the girls became impatient.

I must see where we are going, she thought. I will just open one eye a little.

But as soon as she opened her eye, she found herself falling down and landing back on the beach alone. Her long hair was gone from her head, and her cousin was gone from her forever.

The other girl, though, did not open her eyes. All through the night, she kept her eyes closed as Moon crossed the sky. When he told her to open her eyes at last, she found herself standing in Moon's house on the other side of the sky.

At first she was happy to be the wife of Moon.

"Go wherever you wish," her husband told her. "Only do not look behind the blanket and go into my storehouse."

Moon's wife agreed. She would do as her husband said. She settled down to her new life in the land on the other side of the sky, but it was not always easy. Sometimes her husband would spend a long time with her. Sometimes he would be gone all night and then sleep all day after he came home. She never knew when he was going to go or how long he would be gone. Soon she became bored.

"Why must you always leave me?" she said to her husband. "Why is it that you come and go in such a strange way?"

"It is the work I must do," said Moon. "That is why I cannot always be with you."

"Can I go with you when you do your work?"

"No," said Moon, "my work is too hard. You must stay home and be happy when I am with you."

Moon's wife listened, but she was not happy. That night when her husband left, she began to wander about the land on the other side of the sky. She walked farther and farther and came to a place where she saw many trails, and she began to follow one. At the end of that trail, she saw a person lying facedown.

"What are you doing?" she asked. But the person would not answer her or look her way.

She tried more trails and found the same thing at the end — a person lying facedown. And each time she asked what the person

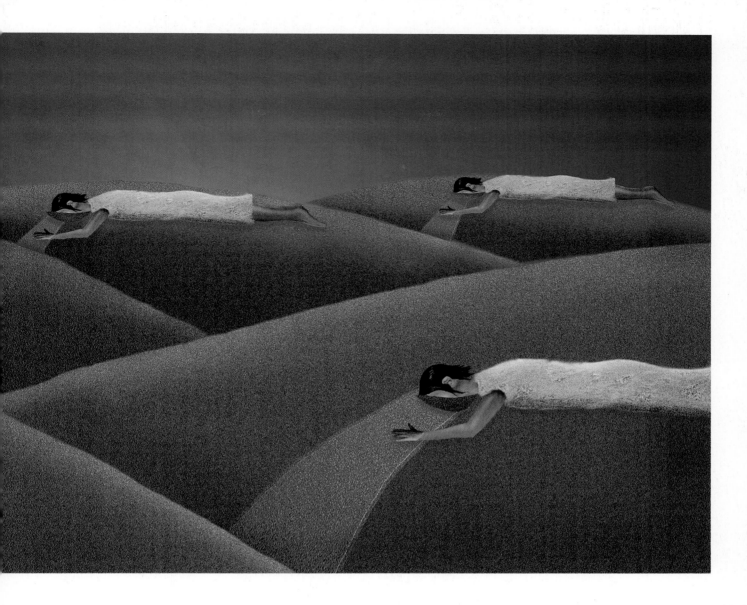

was doing, she received no answer. At last she could stand it
no longer. At the end of the next trail she took, when she found a
person lying down, she began to poke the person with her foot.

"Answer me," she said. "Answer me, answer me. What are
you doing?"

Finally that person turned and looked at her. She saw he had
only one bright eye, sparkling in the middle of his face. "I am
working," the person said. "Do not bother me."

When Moon's wife returned home, her husband had not
come back. She sat down to wait, but she was still bored. She
looked around and saw his storeroom, with a dark woven blanket
covering the door.

"It will not hurt to take one small look," she said. "Moon is my husband, and I should be able to go wherever I want in our house."

Then she went to the door and pulled aside the blanket. There in the storeroom were the pieces of light her husband wore when he crossed the sky. There was a half-moon, a quarter moon, and all the other phases. The only one missing was the full moon, which her husband had worn when he left that evening. The pieces of light were so beautiful that Moon's wife could not resist.

"I must try on one of them," she said, "to see how my husband feels when he is carrying them across the sky."

She reached down and picked up the one that was almost full and placed it on her face. As soon as she did so, it stuck there. She tried to remove it, but it would not budge. Although she wept and cried, the piece of moon would not come off. Then she heard her husband's steps coming across the sky.

She climbed into their bed and covered her head with a blanket.

"What is wrong?" Moon asked.

"I have a pain on my face," said his wife. "I do not feel well. Leave me alone."

But Moon became suspicious. He went to his storeroom and saw that one of the pieces of light was gone. He went back to his wife and pulled the covers from her head.

"Husband," Moon's wife said, "I became bored while you were gone. I tried on this piece of moon and now it is stuck."

Then Moon laughed. He laughed and laughed. And with careful hands, he pulled that piece of moon from her face.

"What else have you done today?" Moon said, still laughing.

His wife told him about following the many trails that led to people lying with their faces down and with a single bright eye in each of their heads.

"Those people are the stars," Moon said. "They should not be bothered while they are doing their work. It is clear to me that you need work to do also, my wife. Since you have shown that you are able to carry the moon you can help me. From now on, I will carry the pieces of moon each cycle until it is full, and then you can carry the pieces of moon until it is dark. That way, we will both have time to rest and neither of us will grow bored."

So it is to this day. The man of the moon carries the pieces of light from the time of the moon's first quarter until it is full, and the woman of the moon carries them from the time it is full until the moon grows dark. So they share the duty of carrying light across the night sky.

Think About the Selection

1. Why do you think the girls' parents are troubled when they hear that the girls want to marry the Moon?

2. How does the Moon's test of patience prepare his future wife for married life with him?

3. Do you think the Moon's wife is right or wrong to do what the Moon forbids? Explain.

4. In the end, how does the Moon show that he is devoted to his wife's happiness?

5. The two cousins are in love with something from nature. What in nature are you drawn to? Tell what you like about it.

6. Why do you think this story was created?

7. **Connecting/Comparing** Both Amelia Earhart and the Moon's wife take risks. Describe the risks that they take. Compare their reasons for taking these risks.

Write an Apology

Moon's wife has no idea that she is bothering the stars when she speaks to the people who are lying down. Write an apology she might post on the trails for the stars to read when they are not working.

Tips

- Give your apology a heading that tells whom the message is for.
- Make the tone of your message sincere by using polite language.

Social Studies

Find Cultural Clues

What information does the story provide about the Alutiiq culture on Kodiak Island? Make a list of occupations, food, and myths. Refer to "Portrait of a People" on pages 168–169 also.

Bonus Make a second list telling how each aspect of the culture relies on nature.

Listening and Speaking

Retell a Traditional Tale

"The Girl Who Married the Moon" is a story that explains how something in nature came to be. Read another similar tale, and retell it for a group. See if listeners can figure out what natural event is being explained. Then ask them to summarize the explanation.

Tips

- Speak slowly and clearly, and use expression to add excitement to your story.
- Repeat a section if your audience doesn't understand it.

 Internet

E-mail a Friend

The next time the moon is full, send an e-mail message to a friend. Describe the legend of the girl who married the Moon, and then tell who is "carrying the moon" on that night.

Images of the Moon

Poets view the moon in different ways. Myra Cohn Livingston calls it a man staring "down through a window" and "a pale lady"; Federico García Lorca calls it "a little mirror." These poems describe the moon as it moves through its phases — from full to a "slim curved crook." How would you describe the moon?

Skill: How to Read a Poem

Here are some tips:

❶ The end of a line doesn't always mark the end of a sentence. Read on until you come to the end of a thought.

❷ Poets often use figurative language to create vivid pictures. As you read, picture in your mind the comparisons the poet is making.

❸ The first time you read a poem, enjoy its rhythm and sound. Then reread it and think about what the poet is saying.

Moon

Why is
the moon always
changing? Sometimes a man
stares down through a window made of
white clouds.

Sometimes
a pale lady,
the dark earth's night mother,
a lace veil over her eyes, smiles
sadly.

How do
they turn themselves
sideways to watch the stars?
What is it they see when they look
away?

—— *Myra Cohn Livingston*

Summer Full Moon

The cloud tonight
is like a white
      Persian cat —

It lies among the stars
with eyes almost shut,
lapping the milk from
the moon's brimming dish.

—— James Kirkup

Brazilian Moon Tale

Did you hear the one
about the moon
being nibbled, gnawed,
eaten away,
by a rat, a jaguar,
a lion, until
in one great gulp
it was gone?

I didn't believe it
either,
until I looked up
and saw that moon,
the teethmarks
still on it,
growing smaller every night.

—— *Jane Yolen*

186

Half Moon

The moon goes over the water.
How tranquil the sky is!
She goes scything slowly
the old shimmer of the river;
meanwhile a young frog
takes her for a little mirror.

—— *Federico García Lorca*

Winter Moon

How thin and sharp is the moon tonight!
How thin and sharp and ghostly white
Is the slim curved crook of the moon tonight!

—— *Langston Hughes*

Background and Vocabulary

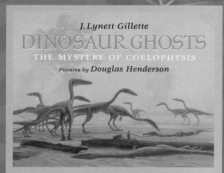

Dinosaur Ghosts

Read to find the meanings of these words.

e ○ Glossary

erosion

evidence

excavation

extinct

fossils

geologists

hypotheses

paleontologists

specimens

theory

Scientists at Work

188

Paleontologists are scientists who study prehistoric life. They often collect fossils of **extinct** animals, such as dinosaurs. Working in teams, they gather **specimens**, or individual parts, of dinosaurs. They hope the specimens will help them to prove or disprove a **theory**.

In *Dinosaur Ghosts*, scientists investigate an amazing discovery at Ghost Ranch in New Mexico. You will read about how they test various **hypotheses**, or scientific suggestions, based on **evidence** found there.

◀ A paleontologist's tools include hammers, brushes, and chisels.

▲ Here scientists work in a large **excavation**. They carefully note the arrangement of the bones before removing them for further study.

▲ Sometimes fossils are uncovered by **erosion** caused by wind or rain. Sometimes they are discovered by **geologists**, scientists who study the earth.

▶ A scientist examines **fossils** of turtle shells believed to be 65 million years old.

J. Lynett Gillette

DINOSAUR GHOSTS

THE MYSTERY OF COELOPHYSIS

Pictures by **Douglas Henderson**

Strategy Focus

Hundreds of dinosaurs once died in a small area in New Mexico. As you read about what might have happened, **monitor** your understanding. **Clarify** difficult parts by rereading or reading ahead.

There is a saying that the place called Ghost Ranch in New Mexico got its name because each night after dark, its fossils come out of the ground to play.

No one has really seen this happen, of course. But if there *were* such a thing as a dinosaur ghost, the red and green hills of this beautiful ranch would be filled with them. Hundreds of *Coelophysis* (SEEL-oh-FIE-sis) dinosaurs perished together here, in a tangle of necks, tails, arms, and legs. And for years scientists have been haunted by the question: Why did so many little dinosaurs die at Ghost Ranch?

To begin to answer that question, we must go back in time to the summer of 1947, when a scientist made a spectacular find.

A Big Find of Small Dinosaurs

Edwin Colbert listened carefully to his field assistant's excited report. Bones — lots of very small ones — lay on a hillside in a nearby canyon!

Ned Colbert was a paleontologist (a scientist who studies prehistoric life) from the American Museum of Natural History in New York City. His plan was to spend that summer of 1947 collecting fossils in Arizona. On his way to Arizona, Colbert had stopped to take a look around Ghost Ranch north of Albuquerque, New Mexico. He knew fossils had been collected there years earlier by several other paleontologists.

The red and green hills of Ghost Ranch

Edwin Colbert, left, with his American Museum of Natural History field crew at Ghost Ranch

Some of the earlier fossils had been found by a professor named Charles Camp. Most of the bones Camp discovered were from animals that had lived during the Triassic period of the earth's history, which lasted from 245 to 208 million years ago. Every fossil discovery was faithfully recorded in Camp's field diary. (In this same diary, Camp had mentioned his fantasy of the fossils coming out to dance at night.)

None of Camp's fossils had ever been found in the canyons of Ghost Ranch. But Ned Colbert had an open mind about the canyons. Whenever people asked him his secret for finding fossils, he answered, "Fossils are where you find them, and you find them in the darndest places." He decided to investigate his assistant's report.

Colbert and his two helpers followed a trail of bone uphill. When the trail ended, the men dug into the hill — and dinosaur skeletons began appearing. The team had found *Coelophysis,* a meat-eating dinosaur about the size of a dog.

Colbert wasn't the first to find this little dinosaur. Back in the 1880's, paleontologist Edward D. Cope hired a fossil collector to find bones for him in northern New Mexico. Traveling with a sure-footed burro, this fossil hunter discovered bits of backbones, a hipbone, a shoulder bone, and the end of a leg bone of a small reptile.

Cope said the fragile bones were those of a new small dinosaur. He named it *Coelophysis,* "hollow form," to suggest its hollow bones. The discovery didn't receive much publicity. Cope turned to other projects, and few people thought about this little dinosaur for nearly seventy years.

But in the summer of 1947 Colbert's team began finding dozens and dozens of *Coelophysis* skeletons, buried in 225 million-year-old rocks from near the end of the Triassic period. There were so many skeletons that Colbert had to send a telegram back to the American Museum to ask for more help with the excavation.

This was a great find. Most dinosaurs are known from just a few specimens. Up until that time, the most familiar small dinosaurs were two chicken-sized *Compsognathus* skeletons. In a few days *The New York Times* announced the discovery of *Coelophysis* on its front page. A photographer from *Life* magazine visited the site. *Coelophysis* became the best-known small dinosaur ever discovered.

But why were all those dinosaurs buried in one place? Colbert wasn't sure. With Ghost Ranch's permission, he cut blocks of rock with the bones still inside to take to New York for study.

Because the dinosaurs were packed so tightly together, the blocks were made extra large to avoid cutting through a skeleton. Each block weighed a ton or more. Blocks of bone were shared with other museums and universities around the United States for examination, and new paleontologists joined the study of *Coelophysis*.

The Colbert team digs to uncover more and more bones.

Bone Studies

Over the next fifty years a more complete picture of *Coelophysis* emerged. Paleontologists saw that the living animal had been a carnivore, or meat eater. Its teeth were sharp along the edges, much like a steak knife — perfect for slicing. Short front legs with sharp claws helped to hold the dinosaur's prey, but the long, flexible neck and strong jaws did most of the work.

They were lively, graceful animals, built for speed. The long, slender leg bones allowed *Coelophysis* to run upright, much like an African secretary bird does today. And much like a bird, *Coelophysis* had fragile, thin bones. If a technician working on *Coelophysis* sneezed, small bone fragments would fly into the air. Inside the whole length of each thin leg and arm bone was a very wide space called the marrow cavity, where red blood cells were made. Active animals need plenty of red blood cells to carry oxygen.

Scientists think *Coelophysis* may have lived in large family groups, possibly in herds. We know that the young stayed with the adults for several years because all ages except embryos in eggs and newborn hatchlings have been found at Ghost Ranch. They probably ate other reptiles — such as young phytosaurs, which resembled alligators — plus fish, crayfish, clams, and in some cases even their own kind. Two skeletons of *Coelophysis* have their last meal

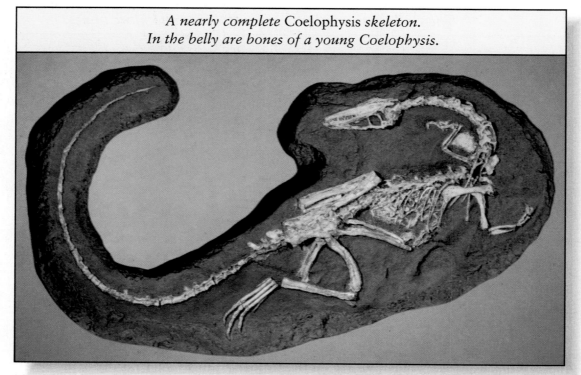

A nearly complete Coelophysis *skeleton.*
In the belly are bones of a young Coelophysis.

still in the belly: small bones of a young *Coelophysis*. Some reptiles today still have this habit of cannibalism.

Unlike many other Triassic reptiles, *Coelophysis* dinosaurs had no armor to shield them from predators. Instead, speed and agility gave an advantage to *Coelophysis* when facing a hungry armored phytosaur. Large eyes also may have helped *Coelophysis* find prey, even in the dim light of early morning and evening when more sluggish reptiles might be napping.

What Happened Here?

After studying the *Coelophysis* bones to learn what these dinosaurs were like when they were alive, the scientists turned their attention to the positions of the bones in the ground. The arrangement of the bones might give some clues to the mystery of what happened to all these dinosaurs. Why and how did they die?

Many nearly complete skeletons were found with almost all their bones still joined together. These skeletons lay flat on their sides with their heads, tails, hands, and feet all at about the same level. When these dinosaurs died, strong muscles in their necks tightened and pulled the neck and head back in a curve toward the tail.

In a different arrangement, some skeletons had missing bones and also were separated. Necks were no longer joined to bodies, tails were not attached to hips, ribs did not touch backbones. These bones had no unusual breaks or tooth marks, so we know the skeletons weren't scattered by predators.

All the skeletons — the nearly complete ones, stretched out on their sides, and the separated ones — lay close together. Some were even piled on top of one another. Other animals were discovered with the *Coelophysis* skeletons: a few fish, phytosaurs, small members of the crocodile family, and a very small lizard. The place where all these animals were buried is about thirty feet long and at least thirty feet wide. Around the bones are red rocks made of mud once carried by an ancient river.

Looking closely at the skeletons, paleontologists could see that none of the bones of any of the dinosaurs or the other animals seemed to be cracked from

drying a long time in the sun. After considering this fact and all the other clues from the bones, the scientists have suggested a number of possible scenes that might explain the *Coelophysis* burial ground at Ghost Ranch. We can test these scientific suggestions, or hypotheses, by comparing them with the evidence found in the bones and the rocks around them.

Stuck in the Mud?

A *Coelophysis* steps to the river's edge, coming to feed on several fish that are splashing in a pool of water. The dinosaur's feet sink deep in the dark, sticky earth. Other dinosaurs gather, also attracted by the splashing fish, but they too are caught in the treacherous ground. No matter how hard they struggle, they are all trapped, young and old alike.

The La Brea tar pits in California were once the site of scenes like this one. Thousands of animals were trapped there in sticky pools of black tar during the Ice Ages. Did a similar thing happen at Ghost Ranch?

Probably not. If the dinosaurs *had* been trapped in mud, as they struggled

their heavier legs would be buried more deeply than their arms and heads, and their bodies would be upright. (This is what scientists believe happened to a Triassic dinosaur from Europe called *Plateosaurus* that died after being trapped in mud.) Since so many *Coelophysis* were found lying on their sides, most likely they didn't die this way.

Volcanic Violence?

The little dinosaurs are surprised by an erupting volcano as they gather at a river's edge to eat. They cannot breathe in the hot, swiftly moving clouds of ash and sulfurous gases. In great panic they fall down as they scramble to escape. Soon they are buried by mud slides flowing down the river valley and by ash falling from the sky.

Many of the earth's great catastrophes have been caused by erupting volcanoes. When Mount St. Helens in Washington state blew its top in 1980, animals that couldn't run or burrow into the earth were killed by the heat, ash, and poisonous gases.

Does the scene at Ghost Ranch fit this picture? It doesn't seem likely to the geologists who have begun to study the rocks in which the *Coelophysis* skeletons are buried. If there were even traces of volcanic ash, under the microscope the rocks would have a few tiny smashed bubbles of the mineral silica. This silica would be present in the fiery blobs of ash shot into the sky. But no collapsed silica bubbles have been found yet in the rocks.

Asteroids from Outer Space?

The sun isn't as bright as usual, because high gray dust clouds shield the earth. The animals that the *Coelophysis* dinosaurs usually eat are becoming hard to find. The dinosaurs have become very thin; their scales are dull. Their tails — normally carried high — are drooping. Weak and exhausted, the dinosaurs fall, one by one, and do not get up.

Scientists Walter and Luis Alvarez of the University of California have suggested a reason why dinosaurs became extinct around 65 million years ago.

The Alvarezes said that maybe a huge asteroid falling out of orbit from outer space struck the earth. The collision would have sent great clouds of dust into the air that blocked sunlight and cooled the earth. A cooler earth couldn't support the same kinds of plants and animals. Many species that needed warm temperatures would die.

Not all paleontologists accept this reason for the extinction of dinosaurs, but it is an attractive one. A small amount of a rare element — iridium — has been found in many 65 million-year-old rocks. Asteroids often have more iridium than earth rocks, so an asteroid may indeed have brought this element to earth. Could an earlier asteroid, 225 million years ago, have caused climatic changes that killed *Coelophysis*?

The facts don't fit this picture at Ghost Ranch. The dinosaurs aren't scattered over a large area, as they would be if they collapsed, one by one, from hunger. And so far no one has found unusual amounts of iridium in the rocks. Asteroid extinctions don't seem to agree with what we have learned about *Coelophysis*.

Poisoned Water?

A group of *Coelophysis* gathers at a spring-fed pool of water along the river's edge. Balancing on their small front legs, they crouch down and drink, unaware that the water is poisoned. In a short time, one by one, they fall to the ground and die. Others come the next day, and the same thing happens again.

Do we find any poisons in the bones or the rocks around the dinosaur "graveyard" at Ghost Ranch? If the dinosaurs were killed this way, some poisons might remain, even after millions of years.

Geologists have tested the rocks and they did find a poison, arsenic, in both the rocks and the bones! But there are two problems with this theory.

First, we can't know exactly *when* the arsenic got into the bones and rocks. Just because arsenic is in the bones now doesn't mean that it was there when the dinosaurs died. The arsenic might have seeped in, carried by underground water, many years later.

201

202

And there's another idea to consider. Phytosaurs and fish were found with the dinosaurs. Could they have survived in a poisoned water hole? Poison that would kill dinosaurs would probably make the water unfit for other animals too — especially ones that had to live *in* the water. For this reason arsenic doesn't seem to fit what we know either.

A Fearsome Flood?

A group of *Coelophysis* dinosaurs sleep in their resting area away from the riverbank under tall evergreen trees. It has been raining for days. This night the rising water spills over the top of the river channel and rushes down a wide valley. *Coelophysis* groups from many areas wake and begin to run, but the water is too fast. They are caught up and drowned by the churning flood. A few dinosaurs who run up the valley, instead of down, are saved.

Soon the rain clouds pass, and the river returns to its old channel. Down the valley rest the bodies of hundreds of dinosaurs, with a few phytosaurs, fish, and other reptiles. They are wrapped together, necks over tails, one on top of the other.

The rains aren't finished yet. Another tropical storm begins, and the river floods again. New mud and water flow into the old riverbed and cover the dinosaurs before other predators arrive.

The tangled positions and good condition of the skeletons (no cracks from the sun, no tooth marks from predators) might well have been caused by a flood. After the dinosaurs drowned, they could have been thrown together by a rush of floodwater and mud and buried quickly.

But if this is true, how do we explain those dinosaur skeletons that were found on their sides with the necks curved toward the tails? This position happens only if a dead animal, such as a cow lying in a field, is undisturbed long enough for its muscles and ligaments to shrink. Why were these dinosaurs arranged differently than the rest? Even the suggestion of a flood doesn't fit all the clues.

Water Worries?

The sun has burned in a cloudless sky for days and days. Ponds, streams, and lakes are drying up. Plants are dying. Plant eaters are starving. Crayfish are burrowing deep into mud to wait for wetter days. Fish are trapped by the hundreds in ever smaller puddles. *Coelophysis* gather to scoop up the helpless fish, but even more than meat, the dinosaurs need water.

As more fish are trapped, more *Coelophysis* of all ages come to eat. But the feeding activity doesn't last. The dinosaurs are weak with hunger and thirst, and there isn't enough food or drink to satisfy everyone. Hundreds die as they crowd around the last of the puddles.

When paleontologists began looking at the rocks around the bones of these dinosaurs, they sometimes found mud cracks, suggesting that some of the animals died on sun-baked mud. The skeletons with the curved necks were arranged like any animal who dries out in the hot sun after death.

Most of the fish bones were underneath the dinosaurs, as if they had attracted the little hunters to the site. And the scientists found many places where crayfish had burrowed into the mud.

But the drought picture does not tell the whole story. We already know that the dinosaurs' bones were not cracked by drying a long time in the sun. What if they spent only a short time — just a few days — in the sun?

The real picture may be a combination of two suggestions — a drought *and* a flood.

Too Little Water — Then Too Much

Many of the little dinosaurs die at the end of a dry season when the earth is baked and the water holes are dry. One day the *Coelophysis* that are still alive discover a few sickly fish swimming slowly back and forth in a puddle at the bottom of the riverbed. Other fish bodies have already sunk into the mud. When a sudden rainstorm breaks the drought, a surge of water and thick mud flows swiftly over the riverbanks and down the valley. *Coelophysis* and other predators are trapped in the flood and drown.

When the waters dry up, they leave behind both the dinosaurs that had died a few days earlier in the drought and the newly drowned dinosaurs. Some are dropped in tangles; some lie alone, stretched out on the mud. The ones that lie in puddles begin to separate. Those outside the puddles begin to dry and shrink. Soon fresh rains bring more mud. The dinosaurs are buried completely in a few days, and they stay that way for millions of years. They are not uncovered until erosion in a canyon removes their blanket of rock in 1947.

This is our best idea for what happened to *Coelophysis* on those fateful days over two hundred million years ago. We can't say for sure that it is the right answer — but it's the explanation that fits most of the clues Ned Colbert and other scientists have discovered so far.

Could more information turn up that might point us toward a whole new scene? Of course, since the site is still being studied. Scientists are always ready to change their ideas to fit what they learn. New discoveries about the fossils and rocks at Ghost Ranch can still be made by anyone with the patience to study them — and the luck to find them "in the darndest places."

Meet the Author
J. LYNETT GILLETTE

Early interests: Stargazing and reading science fiction

How she got her start: Began to study fossils while working at a museum

Career: As curator for the new museum of paleontology at Ghost Ranch, Lynett Gillette runs the museum, leads school groups, *and* digs up fossils.

Advice: People should keep growing and learning all of their lives, and follow their interests wherever they lead.

Meet the Illustrator
DOUGLAS HENDERSON

First dinosaur book he remembers: So Long Ago, an old children's book with illustrations of Earth's early life

How he got his start: Starting as a landscape artist, Henderson would occasionally have a dinosaur "wander" into his artwork. Later he began drawing dinosaurs as illustrations for childrens' books.

Other books he has illustrated: How Dinosaurs Came to Be, Living with Dinosaurs, and *Dinosaur Tree,* which he also wrote.

To find out more about J. Lynett Gillette and Douglas Henderson, visit Education Place.

www.eduplace.com/kids

Think About the Selection

1. How did the *Coelophysis* studies at Ghost Ranch continue the work of other scientists? Explain.

2. What qualities do you think a good paleontologist needs to have? Why?

3. Why did scientists need to figure out what the dinosaurs were like before trying to figure out what caused them to die?

4. Why do scientists test theories by comparing them with evidence? Describe a time when you tested a theory with evidence.

5. Why does the author begin most sections about how *Coelophysis* died by asking a question?

6. The author says, "Scientists are always ready to change their ideas to fit what they learn." Give evidence to support this statement.

7. **Connecting/Comparing** How is solving the mystery of how *Coelophysis* died like solving the mystery of what happened to Amelia Earhart? How is it different?

Write a Travel Brochure

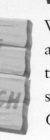

With a partner, write a travel brochure about Ghost Ranch. Tell visitors about the site and its history. Also explain some of the ideas about how *Coelophysis* died out.

Tips

- To make a brochure, fold a sheet of paper into three panels. Decide what to include on each panel. List the *most* important facts about Ghost Ranch.

- Add some interesting drawings.

Science

Make an Evidence Chart

With a partner, make a chart to show how evidence in fossils and rocks has led scientists to support or reject various theories about how this group of *Coelophysis* dinosaurs died. Label your columns *Theory, Supporting Evidence,* and *Opposing Evidence.* Then create a row for each theory. Fill in the information for each column.

Art

Create a Dinosaur

Review the illustrations of dinosaurs in *Dinosaur Ghosts* and the description on pages 194–195. Then, in small groups, create and display clay models of *Coelophysis.*

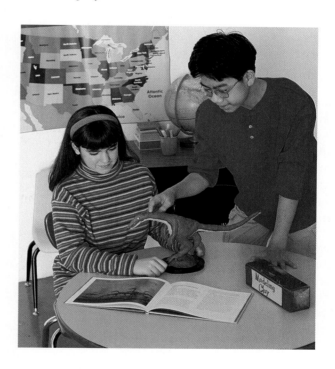

Complete a Web Crossword Puzzle

You've learned a lot of vocabulary related to dinosaurs and paleontology in this selection. Test your knowledge of these words by completing a crossword puzzle that can be printed from Education Place.

www.eduplace.com/kids

Skill: How to Categorize Information

As you read . . .

1 **Take notes**. When you come to an item or idea, identify what **category** or group of similar items or ideas it goes with. Write **headings** for each category.

2 Divide a big category into two or more **narrower categories**. List details or facts that belong to that category.

After you read . . .

Review your notes. **Remember** information by identifying the category to which it belongs.

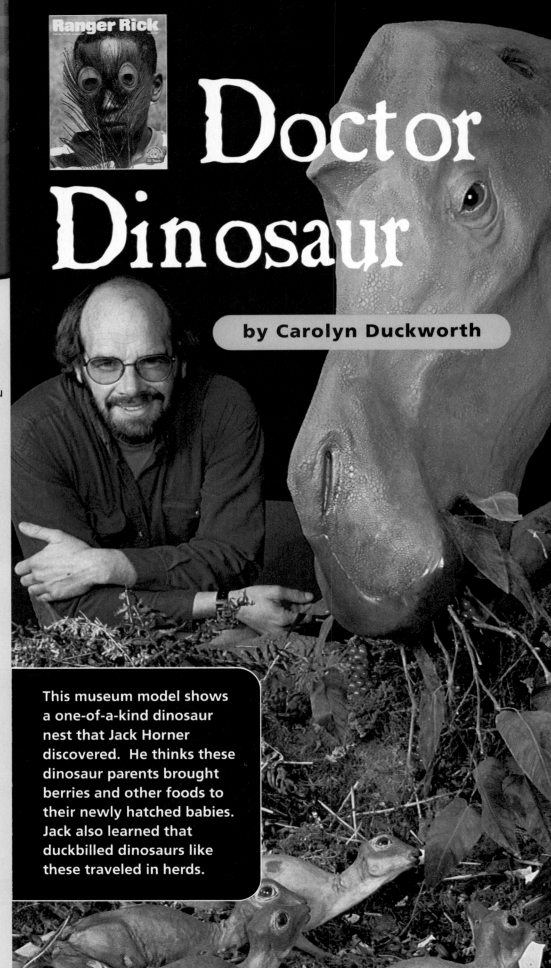

Doctor Dinosaur

by Carolyn Duckworth

This museum model shows a one-of-a-kind dinosaur nest that Jack Horner discovered. He thinks these dinosaur parents brought berries and other foods to their newly hatched babies. Jack also learned that duckbilled dinosaurs like these traveled in herds.

When Jack Horner was eight years old, he discovered his first dinosaur fossil near his home in Montana. From that point on, he never stopped looking. In the 1970s, he returned to Montana every summer to look for fossils with his friend Bob Makela.

Coffee-Can Question

In those days only one group of dino eggs and young had ever been found, and those were in Asia. No one could figure out where to find more. Jack thought there might be fossils of dino young in one part of Montana. In the summer of 1978, he and Bob went looking for the fossils, but didn't have much luck.

Then, at the end of the summer, the two diggers visited a store in a tiny Montana town. The storeowner showed them a coffee can full of fossil bones and asked what they were. The bones were from four different kinds of duckbilled dinosaurs. And since they were so tiny, Jack knew they had to be from *baby* dinos.

What a discovery! Jack and Bob were really excited. They got permission to dig in the spot where the storeowner had found the bones. Jack also got Princeton University to pay them for the work. Suddenly, he says, they weren't just two guys looking for fossils. They were a scientific expedition!

When Jack dug where the baby dino bones were found, he discovered a big, round piece of green stone. Jack and Bob dug all around it and lifted it out — like a giant scoop of green-stone ice cream.

The two diggers took this scoop back to their "lab" (Bob's backyard). They laid the scoop on some "lab equipment" (window screens). And they used a "lab tool" (garden hose) to wash away the dirt. Pretty soon they started to see a strange sight. The green stone held North America's first-known dinosaur nest!

Are Dinos Like Lizards?

For the next six years, Jack and Bob looked for more dino nests. It was hot, hard, tricky work. To find

When he's on a dinosaur dig in Montana, Jack stays in a tipi. Why? He digs far away from any town. And these tents can stand up to the toughest weather. Bad storms and fierce winds often howl across places where dinosaurs once roamed.

tiny pieces of eggshell, they couldn't just walk around. They had to crawl over rocks, which often cut their hands and knees. But all this work paid off. The diggers found eggs and nests from two different kinds of dinosaurs.

The nests really made Jack think. All the books he'd read said that dinosaurs probably were like lizards, which just lay their eggs and leave them. But in one kind of nest that Jack found, the eggshells were broken into tiny bits. Jack wondered why. Did the babies trample them?

Then Jack studied the bones of the baby dinosaurs. The joints looked weak, so he thought the babies couldn't have stood or walked easily. That and other evidence made Jack think that these dino babies had stayed in their nests for quite a while.

The babies also had worn-down teeth. Jack thought that showed the babies had been eating. But how did they get food if they were too weak to leave the nest? Jack thought the dino parents must have fed them. He named this kind of dinosaur *Maiasaura* (my-uh-SORE-uh), which means "good mother lizard."

Not-So-Good Mother?

Today, not everyone agrees with Jack's nesting ideas. Some scientists point out that ground-nesting birds such as chickens have weak leg joints, but those birds can run as soon as they hatch.

Other scientists point to another kind of baby dinosaur that was found still inside its egg. The dino's teeth were already ground down. The scientists wonder if *Maiasaura* babies also ground their teeth together before hatching. If so, their worn-down teeth wouldn't have to mean that the dinosaurs had been eating.

Jack still believes he's right. But he understands that people can look at the same fossils and come up with different ideas about the animals. That leads to more questions — which is what science is all about.

By discovering the nests of this dinosaur and others, Jack has shown people where to look for the fossils of dinosaur young. And every new discovery of dino young will help scientists find more clues and come up with new ideas. So even if Jack's ideas about *Maiasaura* turn out to be wrong, he still will have led the way to the truth.

Scientists think that eighty million years ago a *Maiasaura* baby pushed and poked its way out of an egg.

Check Your Progress

You have read about three mysterious events that many people have tried to explain. Now, continue developing your investigative powers as you read and compare two new selections and practice your test-taking skills.

Start by looking back at Shelley Tanaka's letter on pages 139–140. What does she mean when she writes, "Sometimes not knowing the whole story is the best story of all"? Which mysterious events from this theme do you think illustrate this idea best?

As you have discovered, knowing the whole story behind a mystery isn't always possible. As you read the next two selections, think about how we can sometimes use the facts we know to create a story that explains them. When you finish reading, you will compare the mystery of Mount Vesuvius with the others in the theme.

Read and Compare

POMPEII

by Shelley Tanaka

Find out about what might have happened to a man and his daughter during the eruption of Mount Vesuvius in A.D. 79.

Try these strategies:
Predict and Infer
Question

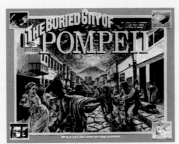

EPILOGUE

by Shelley Tanaka

Learn some of the facts that have been discovered about the actual eruption of Mount Vesuvius.

Try these strategies:
Monitor and Clarify
Summarize

Strategies in Action *Be sure to use all your reading strategies as you read these selections.*

POMPEII

August 24, A.D. 79 — 1 P.M.

by Shelley Tanaka   illustrated by Bleu Turrell

In a.d. 79, Mount Vesuvius erupted, burying the Roman city of Pompeii in layers of ash and pumice. More than 1,800 years later, archeologists uncovered the skeletons of a man and a little girl in one of the city's largest houses. The man, named Eros in this selection, may have been the steward, or head servant, of the household. The little girl, here named Silvia, may have been his daughter. This is the story of what might have happened to them on the day of the eruption.

Eros was jostled out of his doze as new bathers climbed into the hot pool. Outside, a noisy line was forming. He thought he could hear faint laughter coming from the women's baths on the other side of the wall.

He climbed out of the pool and walked over to the fountain of cold water that sat in an alcove at the end of the room. He splashed water on his face and leaned his hands on the edge of the basin. He looked down at the water through half-closed eyes. The light that streamed through the window above made the marble bottom gleam and sparkle.

He opened his eyes wider. The water in the basin had begun to tremble, as if it were beginning to boil. Then a boom, like a muffled clap of thunder, seemed to come from the floor beneath him. The water sloshed over the sides of the basin, splashing at his feet.

Eros turned around. All the men in the room had stopped talking. Some grabbed for the walls and each other as the floor continued to shudder.

Surely not another earthquake, he thought, his heart sinking. He remembered all the careful restoration work that had been done at the house. Everything was so close to being finished. It would be a terrible nuisance if more damage were done now.

He clutched the sides of the basin, waiting for the tremor to stop. But it didn't. Bottles of oil crashed to the floor in the next room. A man standing beside him was thrown off his feet. Then the window in the overhead dome began to grow dark, and soon the entire room was plunged into blackness.

Men screamed as they pushed toward the exits. A few slaves grabbed oil lamps and tried to light them with shaking hands. Finally they dropped the lamps in panic and ran.

Eros stumbled to the nearest door. Wet, naked men streamed into the street. The sky was very dark, and there was an odd yellowish cast to the air. People poured out of the surrounding buildings, their faces filled with confusion.

A pot of flowers fell from a second-story windowsill and smashed on the sidewalk below. Eros looked up. His gaze was drawn to the north, toward Vesuvius. And what he saw filled his throat with fear.

This was no earthquake.

The familiar outline of the mountain was transformed. An enormous black cloud billowed from the summit, which glowed a fiery red.

Tiny white pellets of pumice began to fall like a soft hailstorm. Eros felt as if he were being nipped by hordes of flying insects. Pieces the size of rice stuck to his hair and wet body. Bigger stones, like acorns, rolled underfoot.

People pulled their tunics over their heads and took shelter in doorways. The clatter of pumice on the cobblestones and tiled roofs grew louder, echoing through the narrow

streets. It drowned out the shouts of shop-
keepers who were trying to pull their wares
indoors. It muffled the sharp cries of children
calling for their parents.

Silvia. She was back at the house. He
must get to her.

He made his way down the road, but the
streets were clogged with carts and people.
Everyone seemed to be heading toward the
city gates. Toward the sea. Away from the
mountain.

Eros tried to push his way through the
crowds, but it was no use. The streets were
too narrow. He turned around and headed
back to the forum.

In the grand square, people fled from every
building. Shoppers and merchants swarmed
out of the market. Peddlers pulled their carts
behind them, their goods spilling out as they
ran. A bronze statue tumbled off its pedestal.
From inside the Temple of Jupiter came a long
scream. The cry was suddenly cut short by a
thundering crash within the building.

Eros pushed his way through the throng.
When he got to the bottom of the forum, he
stopped in dismay. Pompeii's main street, as
far as he could see, was filled with people, and
they all seemed to be coming his way. He
closed his eyes and began to shove past them.

The house was halfway across town. How
long would it take him to get there?

Donkeys, carts, dogs, and people were
everywhere. Benches in front of the
shops had been overturned.
Looters grabbed jugs and food.
A fighter from the
amphitheater, the net-
thrower, thundered
past. He still

wore his shoulder armor, and he waved his dagger wildly to clear a path in front of him.

The pumice fell steadily. Soon everything was covered with a ghostly cloak. Eros stumbled over one of the stepping stones in the middle of the road. His bare feet were bloody.

In front of him, a rich man in a sedan chair was cursing at the four slaves who were trying to carry his litter down the street. Their way was blocked by a cart that had been abandoned and overturned. The slaves were clumsily trying to make their way over it, while their master stayed in his chair and screamed at them.

"You fool!" someone yelled. "Why don't you just get out and walk? You're blocking the way for others!" As Eros watched, one of the slaves finally dropped his corner of the litter and fled. The rich man tumbled out onto the street and was trampled by the crowd.

By the time Eros reached his own block, he was limping. He hurried into the house. It was very quiet. In the garden, the workmen had disappeared.

He ran down the hallway, calling for Silvia. There was no answer. He headed for the stables.

She was on her knees, trying to free the dog from his rope. The animal was thrashing in panic. Eros could see that her face and arms were already scratched. He scooped her up and ran back into the house. He tried not to listen to the frenzied howls behind him, as the dog strained at its rope.

In the courtyard, a stew of fallen pumice floated in the fishpond. The pumice was coming down thickly now. It filled the courtyard like snow.

Eros stopped, panting. The house trembled and shook. It was crumbling before his eyes. His master would never have a chance to see the repairs now, to thank his loyal steward for all his effort.

Eros brushed a piece of pumice from Silvia's tear-stained cheek. Grains of it, like gravel, were tangled in her hair. She began to cough and pressed her face into her father's neck.

He ran down the narrow sloping corridor to his quarters. He put Silvia down on the bed. Then he went to the door and looked out. Across the street, a balcony crashed to the ground.

When Eros looked north now he could no longer see the mountain. It was as if a thick black blanket were gradually being lowered over the face of the city. The air was filled with a sharp, deadly smell.

Eros closed the door and went back inside. He looked down the hall past the slaves' quarters. From around the corner he could hear voices calling, the sound of running footsteps. He began to walk down the hall when rubble fell from the second story, blocking his way. The voices stopped.

Eros watched the dust settle around him. The passage to the rest of the house was blocked.

He tried to think clearly. Should they stay in the house and hope that the terrible storm would pass? Or should they take their chances at escape?

His ankle throbbed painfully. He would not get far carrying Silvia through the deadly downpour in the streets. Besides, how could he leave the house unattended? What about the treasure in the cellar? The master had entrusted it to his safekeeping . . .

He turned slowly back to his apartment. Silvia was sitting on a bucket beside the bed, her head buried in her arms. She was weeping softly.

Eros found his seal and the leather purse that contained his life's savings. He went into the bedroom and sat on the bed beside his daughter. He drew Silvia to him and held her tightly. Then he stared into his tiny courtyard and watched it slowly disappear beneath a sea of gray hail.

EPILOGUE

by Shelley Tanaka

Molten lava erupts from a modern-day active volcano (Kilauea, in Hawaii, USA, 1984)

Vesuvius erupted on August 24, A.D. 79. Pompeii had been experiencing earth tremors for a few days, and many people still remembered an earthquake that had damaged much of the city seventeen years before. But they did not realize that they were living in the lap of a deadly volcano.

At about 1 P.M., the mountain roared, and her summit cracked open. A huge column of pumice and ash shot up into the air like a rocket. When the column reached the height of twelve miles (twenty kilometers), it spread out like a fountain. Ash and pumice began to fall to the ground.

In horror, the people of Pompeii had to decide whether to flee or stay. Most chose to run, and soon the gates were clogged with humans and pack animals trying to push their way out of the city. Others hid in their homes, hoping that by some miracle, the rain of fire would soon stop.

But it didn't. With every passing hour, another 6 inches (15 centimeters) of pumice covered Pompeii. By late afternoon, the sky was almost black. Roofs caved in. Walls collapsed as earth tremors rocked the city.

At midnight, the column of ash and pumice finally collapsed back to earth. That's when superhot rock and gas spewed up out of the volcano and began to flow down the mountain, smothering and burning up the countryside.

The avalanche reached the walls of Pompeii at 5:30 the next morning. The people who remained in the city died from the extreme heat, or they were suffocated as they breathed in the hot ash. Within three hours, the city was completely buried.

After the eruption, many people returned to their homes, but Pompeii lay under a sea of pumice and ash. Some got shovels and tried to uncover the bodies of their loved ones. Some searched for their strongboxes and money. Others dug down to the majestic temples and public buildings, hoping to find valuable statues or building materials. Several of these diggers were buried when the ground caved in on top of them.

Eventually, though, the survivors drifted away. After many years, the slopes of Vesuvius were again covered with green forests and meadows.

But centuries later, people still remembered stories about an ancient buried city. And in 1748, they began to dig down to the city in earnest. At first the work was sloppy and disorganized. Treasure hunters ripped out priceless statues and artwork. Coins and vases were carted away.

Mount Vesuvius as it looks today

THE DAY VESUVIUS EXPLODED

On August 24, A.D. 79, a mushroom-shaped cloud of pumice and ash rose from the mouth of Vesuvius (below, top). Soon pumice began to fall steadily on Pompeii, followed later by a rain of fine ash. The town of Herculaneum, upwind from the volcano, received a lighter dusting of ash. Early the next morning, surges of hot ash and gas began to race down the mountain, followed by a flow of hot ash, rock, and pumice. Herculaneum was hit first; Pompeii was buried several hours later (below, bottom).

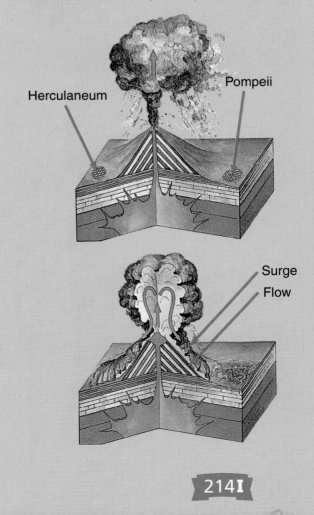

Herculaneum

Pompeii

Surge
Flow

For 1,500 years, Pompeii had been buried under a thick blanket of pumice and ash. This material had protected the city beautifully from the air and rain. But as soon as the buildings were uncovered, they began to crumble. The brilliant paintings on the walls began to fade.

In 1860, Giuseppe Fiorelli was put in charge of the excavation. Fiorelli was an archaeologist, and he knew that the town should be uncovered in an organized and scientific way. He made detailed maps and carefully recorded each new find. He began to restore the buildings and art, instead of hauling away the most valuable pieces and leaving the rest to rot.

Over the years, the excavations continued, making Pompeii one of the oldest and most studied archaeological sites in the world. Then, between 1927 and 1932, an archaeologist

An excavation in Pompeii during the late 1800s

named Amedeo Maiuri discovered one of the finest houses in the city, the House of the Menander. Here diggers found the remains of a grand residence that was undergoing major renovations. *Amphoras* full of plaster were found in the courtyard. Farm implements hung on the wall of the steward's apartment. In the cellar were two chests full of gold and silver coins, jewelry, and 118 beautiful silver dishes.

HOW DO WE KNOW ABOUT THE ERUPTION OF VESUVIUS?

Much of what we know about the eruption in A.D. 79 comes from two letters written by the Roman statesman and writer, Pliny. As a teenaged boy, Pliny watched the volcano from the home of his uncle, at Misenum, across the Bay of Naples. Years later, he described what he saw in letters that have become famous as the oldest eyewitness account of a major natural disaster. Pliny's uncle sailed across the bay to rescue survivors, but raining pumice prevented him from landing near Vesuvius. He died the next day on the beach at Stabiae (below), probably overcome by heat from the blast.

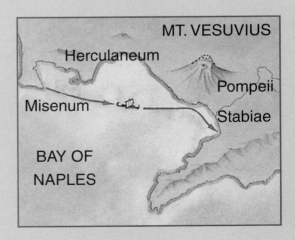

MT. VESUVIUS
Herculaneum
Misenum
Pompeii
Stabiae
BAY OF NAPLES

The diggers also found bodies. The skeleton of a dog lay in a corner of the stable yard. Several bodies were found in the hallway outside the slaves' quarters. And in the corner of a small room in the steward's apartment, a man lay on a narrow bed. He had a leather purse full of money and a seal that identified him as Eros, steward of one of the most important families in Pompeii. Nearby was the skeleton of a young girl. On the ground beside her were pieces of a tiny bronze ring engraved with a picture of a winged horse.

Did the skeletons in the hallway belong to servants or workmen who were in the house when the eruption occurred? Was the little girl the daughter of the steward? Had they stayed in the house to protect the treasure? Or had they for some reason been unable to run? No one knows for sure.

The skeletons cannot tell us their story. But Pompeii can still teach us a great deal about what life was like almost two thousand years ago. Every object, every building gives us a glimpse into this long-ago world.

The mummified corpse of a dog shows it twisting in an attempt to escape.

Plaster casts of two of the volcano's victims

Think and Compare

POMPEII

by Shelley Tanaka

EPILOGUE

by Shelley Tanaka

AMELIA EARHART

FIRST LADY OF FLIGHT

JAN PARR

THE GIRL WHO MARRIED THE MOON

TALES FROM NATIVE NORTH AMERICA

TOLD BY JOSEPH BRUCHAC AND GAYLE ROSS

J. Lynett Gillette

DINOSAUR GHOSTS

THE MYSTERY OF COELOPHYSIS

Pictures by Douglas Henderson

1. Compare the story of Eros with the description of the actual eruption in the Epilogue. What do the two stories have in common? How are they different?

2. How do we know the eruption that buried Pompeii really happened? Give examples from your reading.

3. How are the methods used by the scientists in *Dinosaur Ghosts* similar to those who excavated Pompeii? How are they different?

4. Compare what you learned about Amelia Earhart with what you learned in *The Buried City of Pompeii*. Which selection seems more mysterious? Use examples to tell why.

5. Which selection in this theme do you think best answers the question of *What Really Happened?* Explain your answer with examples from the selection.

Strategies in Action How have two or more of the reading strategies helped you read the selections in this theme?

Describing

Write a News Report

Write a TV news report describing the mysterious event in one of the selections. Be sure to include the known facts and details of the event.

Tips

- Use details from the story and illustrations.
- Use complete sentences.
- Include vivid adjectives and proper nouns in your description.

Taking Tests

 Filling in the Blank

Some test items ask you to complete a sentence. You will have several answers to choose from. How do you choose the best answer? Look at this sample test item for "Pompeii."

Read the sentence. Fill in the circle in the answer row for the answer that best completes the sentence.

1. Eros goes back to the house instead of escaping the city because _____.

   A the city is too noisy

   B he wants to get his daughter

   C he wants to guard the house against looters

   D the house provides protection from the ash and pumice

   ANSWER ROW 1   Ⓐ ● Ⓒ Ⓓ

 Understand the sentence.

Find the key words in the sentence. Use them to understand what you need to do.

> I think the key words are *back to the house* and *because.* I need to choose the reason why Eros goes back to the house.

② Look back at the selection.

Think about where to find the answer. You may need to look in more than one place. Skim the selection, using the key words.

I'll look back at the part where the eruption starts, because I know that's when Eros decides to go back to the house. I'll find the answer there.

③ Narrow the choices. Then choose the best answer.

Read the sentence, trying each answer choice in the blank. Find the choices that are clearly wrong. Have a good reason for choosing an answer. Guess only if you have to.

I know **A** isn't correct. It can't be **D**, because other buildings collapse during the eruption. Choice **C** might be correct, but on page 214D, it says that Eros must get to Silvia at the house. So **B** is the best answer.

Plays

Comedy and tragedy. Humor and drama. Every play brings the human experience to life through the **dialogue** and action of its **cast**. The **audience** feels what the characters feel. The reader does, too.

As you read these **scripts**, let the setting and **stage directions** guide you through two worlds. One play is realistic and serious, the other a funny fantasy. Each is about the experience of being human.

CONTENTS

The Diary of Anne Frank..............218
*by Frances Goodrich and
Albert Hackett*

A Better Mousetrap.....................226
by Colleen Neuman

The Diary of Anne Frank is a historical drama based on a real diary. It has a serious subject and a conventional structure.

During World War II (1939–1945), Jews throughout Europe fled their homes to escape the Nazi invasion. Many Jews were sent to concentration camps, while thousands went into hiding. In 1942, seven Jews entered the attic above an old warehouse in Amsterdam: Mr. and Mrs. Frank, their daughters Margot and Anne, Mr. and Mrs. Van Daan, and their son Peter. Miep Gies and her boss, Mr. Kraler, worked in the office below and brought the families food and news every day.

The Diary of Anne Frank

by Frances Goodrich and Albert Hackett

Characters:

Anne Frank	age 13
Peter Van Daan	age 16
Mr. Frank	Anne's father

Time: 1942

Setting: An attic above an old warehouse in Amsterdam. As the scene opens, Mr. Frank has just finished explaining the rules of the house and the two families are getting acquainted.

Anne: What's your cat's name?

Peter: Mouschi.

Anne: Mouschi! Mouschi! Mouschi! *(She picks up the cat, walking away with it. To Peter)* I love cats. I have one . . . a darling little cat. But they made me leave her behind. I left some food and a note for the neighbors to take care of her . . . I'm going to miss her terribly. What is yours? A him or a her?

Peter: He's a tom. He doesn't like strangers. *(He takes the cat from her, putting it back in its carrier.)*

Anne *(Unabashed)*: Then I'll have to stop being a stranger, won't I? Is he fixed?

Peter *(Startled)*: Huh?

Anne: Did you have him fixed?

Peter: No.

Anne: Oh, you ought to have him fixed — to keep him from — you know, fighting. Where did you go to school?

Peter: Jewish Secondary.

Anne: But that's where Margot and I go! I never saw you around.

Peter: I used to see you . . . sometimes . . .

Anne: You did?

Peter: . . . in the schoolyard. You were always in the middle of a bunch of kids. *(He takes a penknife from his pocket.)*

Anne: Why didn't you ever come over?

Peter: I'm sort of a lone wolf. *(He starts to rip off his Star of David.)*

Anne: What are you doing?

Peter: Taking it off.

Anne: But you can't do that. They'll arrest you if you go out without your star. *(He tosses his knife on the table.)*

Peter: Who's going out?

Anne: Why, of course! You're right! Of course we don't need them any more. *(She picks up his knife and starts to take her star off.)* I wonder what our friends will think when we don't show up today?

Peter: I didn't have any dates with anyone.

Anne: Oh, I did. I had a date with Jopie to go and play ping-pong at her house. Do you know Jopie de Waal?

Peter: No.

Anne: Jopie's my best friend. I wonder what she'll think when she telephones and there's no answer? . . . Probably she'll go over to the house . . . I wonder what she'll think . . . we left everything as if we'd suddenly been called away . . . breakfast dishes in the sink . . . beds not made . . . *(As she pulls* *off her star, the cloth underneath shows clearly the color and form of the star.)* Look! It's still there! *(Peter goes over to the stove with his star.)* What're you going to do with yours?

Peter: Burn it.

Anne *(She starts to throw hers in, and cannot.)*: It's funny, I can't throw mine away. I don't know why.

Peter: You can't throw . . . ? Something they branded you with . . . ? That they made you wear so they could spit on you?

Anne: I know. I know. But after all, it is the Star of David, isn't it? *(In the bedroom, right, Margot and Mrs. Frank are lying down. Mr. Frank starts quietly out.)*

Peter: Maybe it's different for a girl. *(Mr. Frank comes into the main room.)*

Mr. Frank: Forgive me, Peter. Now let me see. We must find a bed for your cat. *(He goes to a cupboard.)* I'm glad you brought your cat. Anne was feeling so badly about hers. *(Getting a used small washtub)* Here we are. Will it be comfortable in that?

Peter *(Gathering up his things)*: Thanks.

Mr. Frank *(Opening the door of the room on the left)*: And here is your room. But I warn you, Peter, you can't grow any more. Not an inch, or you'll have to sleep with your feet out of the skylight. Are you hungry?

Peter: No.

Mr. Frank: We have some bread and butter.

Peter: No, thank you.

Mr. Frank: You can have it for luncheon then. And tonight we will have a real supper . . . our first supper together.

Peter: Thanks. Thanks. *(He goes into his room. During the following scene he arranges his possessions in his new room.)*

Mr. Frank: That's a nice boy, Peter.

Anne: He's awfully shy, isn't he?

Mr. Frank: You'll like him, I know.

Anne: I certainly hope so, since he's the only boy I'm likely to see for months and months. *(Mr. Frank sits down, taking off his shoes.)*

Mr. Frank: Anneke, there's a box there. Will you open it? (*He indicates a carton on the couch. Anne brings it to the center table. In the street below there is the sound of children playing.*)

Anne (*As she opens the carton*): You know the way I'm going to think of it here? I'm going to think of it as a boarding house. A very peculiar summer boarding house, like the one that we — (*She breaks off as she pulls out some photographs.*) Father! My movie stars! I was wondering where they were! I was looking for them this morning . . . and Queen Wilhelmina! How wonderful!

Mr. Frank: There's something more. Go on. Look further. (*He goes over to the sink, pouring a glass of milk from a thermos bottle.*)

Anne (*Pulling out a pasteboard-bound book*): A diary! (*She throws her arms around her father.*) I've never had a diary. And I've always longed for one. (*She looks around the room.*) Pencil, pencil, pencil, pencil. (*She starts down the stairs.*) I'm going down to the office to get a pencil.

Mr. Frank: Anne! No! (*He goes after her, catching her by the arm and pulling her back.*)

Anne (*Startled*): But there's no one in the building now.

Mr. Frank: It doesn't matter. I don't want you ever to go beyond that door.

Anne (*Sobered*): Never . . . ? Not even at nighttime, when everyone is gone? Or on Sundays? Can't I go down to listen to the radio?

Mr. Frank: Never. I am sorry, Anneke. It isn't safe. No, you must never go beyond that door. (*For the first time Anne realizes what "going into hiding" means.*)

Anne: I see.

Mr. Frank: It'll be hard, I know. But always remember this, Anneke. There are no walls, there are no bolts, no locks that anyone can put on your mind. Miep will bring us books. We will read history, poetry, mythology. (*He gives her the glass of milk.*) Here's your milk. (*With his arm about her, they go over to the couch, sitting down side by side.*) As a matter of fact, between us, Anne, being here has certain advantages for you. For instance, you remember the battle you had with your mother the other day on the subject of overshoes? You said you'd rather die than wear overshoes? But in the end you had to wear them? Well now, you see, for as long as we are here you will never have

to wear overshoes! Isn't that good? And the coat that you inherited from Margot, you won't have to wear that any more. And the piano! You won't have to practice on the piano. I tell you, this is going to be a fine life for you! (*Anne's panic is gone. Peter appears in the doorway of his room, with a saucer in his hand. He is carrying his cat.*)

Peter: I . . . I . . . I thought I'd better get some water for Mouschi before . . .

Mr. Frank: Of course. (*As he starts toward the sink the carillon begins to chime the hour of eight. He tiptoes to the window at the back and looks down at the street below. He turns to Peter, indicating in pantomime that it is too late. Peter starts back for his room. He steps on a creaking board. The three of them are frozen for a minute in fear. As Peter starts away again, Anne tiptoes over to him and pours some of the milk from her glass into the saucer for the cat. Peter squats on the floor, putting the milk before the cat. Mr. Frank gives Anne his fountain pen, and then goes into the room at the right. For a second Anne watches the cat, then she goes over to the center table, and opens her diary.*)

In the room at the right, Mrs. Frank has sat up quickly at the sound of the carillon. Mr. Frank comes in and sits down beside her on the settee, his arm comfortingly around her.

Upstairs, in the attic room, Mr. and Mrs. Van Daan have hung their clothes in the closet and are now seated on the iron bed. Mrs. Van Daan leans back exhausted. Mr. Van Daan fans her with a newspaper.

Anne starts to write in her diary. The lights dim out, the curtain falls. In the darkness Anne's voice comes to us again, faintly at first, and then with growing strength.

Anne's voice: I expect I should be describing what it feels like to go into hiding. But I really don't know yet myself. I only know it's funny never to be able to go outdoors . . . never to breathe fresh air . . . never to run and shout and jump. It's the silence in the nights that frightens me most. Every time I hear a creak in the house, or a step on the street outside, I'm sure they're coming for us. The days aren't so bad. At least we know that Miep and Mr. Kraler are down there below us in the office. Our protectors, we call them. I asked Father what would happen to them if the Nazis found out they were hiding

us. Pim said that they would suffer the same fate that we would . . .
Imagine! They know this, and yet when they come up here, they're always
cheerful and gay as if there were nothing in the world to bother them . . .
Friday, the twenty-first of August, nineteen forty-two. Today I'm going to
tell you our general news. Mother is unbearable. She insists on treating me
like a baby, which I loathe. Otherwise things are going better. The weather
is . . . (*Anne's voice fades out as the scene ends.*)

Now that you've read a serious play, here's something much lighter.
A Better Mousetrap presents unusual characters in a ridiculous
situation. Get ready to laugh!

A Better Mousetrap
by Colleen Neuman

Wanted: state-of-the-art pest control for clever rodent...

Characters

Mouse	Four Corners	Catch One	Longer
Woman	Metal	Catch Two	Higher
Man	Bar	Wider	

Time: Now.

Setting: There are two chairs onstage: one far left, one up center.

At Rise: All performers sit in line on floor upstage, facing audience. Mouse crouches at end of line, far right; Woman sits at end of line, far left; Man sits in middle of line, center. All sit and hold same position until they get up to take part in the action. All but Woman and Man wear character name signs; signs are folded and taped up so that the audience can't read them.

226

Mouse: There was a mouse *(Untapes and turns down sign, showing Mouse to audience)* and a woman *(Woman stands, comes forward. Mouse goes right.)* who was afraid of the mouse.

Woman *(Seeing Mouse)*: Eek! Eek! A mouse! A mouse! Oh, help, help! *(Jumps up onto chair, left)* Ooh, ooh, ooh!!!

Man *(Standing and coming over to Woman)*: What's wrong, my dear?

Woman *(Hiding her face in her hands)*: A mouse! I saw a mouse!

Man *(Crossing center, looking carefully at Mouse)*: So it is. *(Politely; tips hat)* Morning, to you.

Mouse *(Tipping hat)*: Morning, sir.

Man You would seem to be a mouse.

Mouse: I am, indeed. And you are?

Man: I am Richard Esquith, Esquire, Sr., the Third. I own this house.

Mouse: And a charming abode it is.

Man: How kind of you to say.

Woman: Eek, eek!

Man: Oh, where are my manners? This is Dorothea Esquith, Esquire, Sr., the Third, my lovely wife.

Woman (*Crooking finger; through clenched teeth*): Richard, dear.

Man (*Going back to Woman*): Yes, dear?

Woman (*Icily, deliberately*): You-are-talking-to-the-mouse!

Man: Actually, it was more of an introduction than a talk . . .

Woman (*Shrieking*): Kill it!

Man: Oh, yes, of course, I was getting to that. Let's see — (*Checking pockets*) slingshot, hatchet, MTV, rap music — no, I don't seem to have anything lethal on me.

Woman (*Seething*): Set a mousetrap!

Man: A mousetrap! (*Hits forehead with hand*) Of course! A mousetrap! Obviously a mousetrap! (*Checking pockets*) I don't seem to have a mousetrap, so I'll have to build one.

Mouse (*Sighing heavily*): Here we go.

Man: A mousetrap is a rectangle, so I'll need four corners. (*Corners turn down their signs. Man notices them.*) Ah, there you are. Come right over here. Yes, that's right — (*Man puts them in sitting or lying positions where corners of mousetrap will be, then arranges their arms and legs at right angles to form corners.*) Here, and here, and here, and here. And a mousetrap has a metal bar. (*Metal and Bar turn down their signs.*) Yes, you two will do. Right over here. (*Man moves them to bend at waist, in center of trap, with outstretched arms touching. Then, as though with great effort, Man pushes them into an erect position.*) And I need a catch (*Catch One and Catch Two turn over their signs.*) to hold back the bar. Yes! You two! Over here! Quickly! (*They run over, reach up and hold arms of Metal Bar. Man lets go.*) Whew! And, of course, no mousetrap would be complete without a one-pound block of the finest cheddar . . . (*Takes cheese out of pocket*)

Mouse and Trap: Mm-m-m.

Man: . . . cheese. (*Sets cheese on floor in middle of trap*) Ah. There we are, my dear. All done. You may come down now.

Woman: Not until that disgusting rodent is dead.

Man: Well, I've built a very fine trap that will no doubt do the job sometime during the night.

Woman (*In relief*): I certainly hope so, dear. I'll look forward to it.

Man: Good night. See you in the morning.

Woman: Nighty-night. (*Man stands just right of Woman's chair. They both tilt heads to one side, rest cheeks on folded hands, close eyes, as if asleep.*)

Mouse: That was the first night.

Higher (*Raising alarm clock high above head, giving it a good shake*): R-r-r-ring!

Man: Good morning, Duck.

Woman: Morning, Cupcake.

Man (*Offering hand*): Let me help you down.

Woman: How splendid of you. (*Sees Mouse and screams*) Eek, eek!

Man: Is it the same disgusting rodent?

Woman (*Covering eyes, pointing at Mouse*): I can't bear to look!

Man (*Turning toward center*): The trap didn't work, I suppose?

Mouse and Trap (*Shaking heads, in unison*): Trap didn't work.

Mouse: It isn't that it's not a fine mousetrap. It's a very fine mousetrap. I just find it a bit small for me.

Man: Of course! *(Hits forehead with hand)* Why didn't I see that? It should be wider *(Wider turns over sign.)* and longer *(Longer turns over sign.)* and higher. *(Higher turns over sign.)* Yes, yes, all of you — over here and here and here. *(Wider lies along end of trap, Longer lies along the front, Higher stands on chair center.)* And the metal bar should have teeth! *(Metal Bar looks at audience, bares teeth.)* Ah, much better. *(Goes back to Woman)*

Woman: Well done, dear.

Man: Tonight will be the night, my sweet. Never fear.

Man and Woman: Nighty-night. *(They assume sleep positions again.)*

Mouse: That was the second night.

Higher *(Raising clock, shaking it)*: R-r-r-ring!

Man: Morning, Petunia.

Woman: Morning, Muffin. *(Notices Mouse and screams)* Eek, eek!

Man *(Turning to center stage)*: So, once again, the trap didn't work?

Mouse and Trap: Trap didn't work.

Mouse *(Matter-of-factly)*: It's the noise, you know.

Man: The noise? But there isn't any noise. It's as silent as a stone here.

Mouse: That's the problem. A mouse likes a noisy trap.

Man: Of course! *(Hits forehead with hand)* Noise! I should have thought of noise! *(To Trap)* Well, go ahead. Make some noise.

Corners: Wubba wubba.

Man *(To audience)*: Wubba wubba? *(To Metal Bar)* And you?

Metal Bar: Woosh woosh.

Man *(To Catches)*: And you?

Catches: Wibba wibba.

Man *(To Wider, Longer, Higher)*: And you?

Wider, Longer, Higher *(Together)*: Ugh!

Man *(Worried)*: Hm-m-m. Again. *(Points to each of them in turn)*

Corners: Wubba wubba.

Metal Bar: Woosh woosh.

Catches: Wibba wibba.

Wider, Longer, Higher: Ugh!

Man *(Pleased)*: Hm-m-m. Not bad. Again. *(He conducts. Performers in trap make their noises with even more rhythm this time, looking pleased with themselves.)*

Trap: Wubba wubba, woosh woosh, wibba wibba, ugh! Wubba wubba, woosh woosh, wibba wibba, ugh! Wubba wubba, woosh woosh, wibba wibba, ugh! *(Man stops conducting. Trap continues "noise" to end of play, though not so loudly that actors have to shout.)*

Man: Very good. Keep it up until tomorrow. *(To Woman)* Nighty-night, dear.

Woman: How will we sleep with all this noise?

Man: Probably not very well. Nighty-night. *(They assume sleep positions again.)*

Mouse: That was the third night.

Higher *(Raising clock, shaking it)*: R-r-r-ring!

Man: Morning, Dumpling.

Woman *(Annoyed)*: What?

Man *(Louder)*: I said: Morning, Dumpling.

Woman *(Screeching as she sees Mouse)*: Yikes!

Man *(Turning center)*: Don't tell me. Trap didn't work?

Mouse and Trap: Trap didn't work.

Mouse: You see, it doesn't move. And a trap that doesn't move is always such a disappointment.

Man: Well, you're in luck. Movement happens to be my specialty. Let me see. . . . *(Goes to each performer in trap and "starts" a movement — feet twitch back and forth, head nods, arm goes in circle, etc. — while ad libbing. Actions must be simple enough for actors to continue through end of play.)* This arm can do this. This leg can bend back. That's good. *(Etc. Stands next to Woman)* There we are! Isn't that just perfect? Who could resist a trap like that? Good night, Gumdrop.

Woman *(Wearily)*: Of course, right, whatever. *(They take sleep position.)*

Mouse: That was the fourth night.

Higher *(Raising clock, shaking it)*: R-r-r-ring!

Man: Good morning, my little Peppermint Drop.

Woman: Well, did it work? *(Man looks center; Mouse waves.)*

Man: Trap didn't work *(Trap stops noise briefly to speak next line with Mouse.)*

Mouse and Trap: Trap didn't work.

Mouse: May I make just one final suggestion?

Man: I would most appreciate it.

Woman: You're going to listen to that miserable rodent again? Every time you do, things just get worse.

Man: The way I see it is, who better to give advice on mousetraps, than a mouse? Besides, if I hadn't listened to him so far I wouldn't have made this lovely trap. *(To Mouse)* Now, you were saying?

Mouse: Though it is indeed a wonderful mousetrap, a marvelous mousetrap, it would be perfect if it were louder.

Man: Louder?

Mouse: Louder. And faster.

Man: Faster?

Mouse: Much faster. *(Trap looks worried.)*

Man: Louder . . . *(Turns "knob" — perhaps the ear or nose of a player — on Trap. Trap gets louder.)* . . . and faster. *(Pulls a lever — perhaps the arm or leg of*

another player — and Trap starts moving very fast. Actors' lines now have to be bellowed.) Nighty-night, Sweet Pea.

Woman: As if anybody could sleep standing on a chair in the middle of all this racket and commotion! *(They sleep. Woman tosses and turns.)*

Mouse: And this is the fifth night. *(Trap works frantically for a few more seconds, and then collapses into a big heap of bodies.)*

Trap: Boom!!! *(Actors lie very still after "explosion." They should not land on cheese.)*

Higher *(Raising arm out of pile, shaking clock)*: R-r-ring!

Man: Good morning, Lambiecakes.

Woman *(Testily)*: It is not a good morning, it wasn't a good night, and I'm not your lambiecakes! *(Thundering)* Did it work?

Man *(Looking over and gasping)*: It collapsed! No more trap?

Mouse and Trap: No more trap.

Man: Oh, my beautiful, clever, wonderful trap! Gone!

Woman: You fool! Five days and five nights I've stood on this chair. *(Gets down)* I'm hungry and tired and suffering from nervous exhaustion and all you care about is that ridiculous mousetrap! I can't take it anymore! I'm going to my sister's house to eat and sleep and take a bath — not necessarily in that order! *(Stomps off)*

Man: Oh. Well, if she's leaving, *(To Mouse)* I suppose you can stay.

Mouse: Why, thank you.

Man: And I guess I won't be needing a trap.

Mouse: How kind of you. It was a marvelous mousetrap, though, the best I've ever seen. *(Picks up cheese)* You wouldn't happen to have any crackers, would you? *(Comes center)*

Man *(Moving center)*: Why, yes, I believe I do. *(Takes crackers and plate from pocket, arranges crackers on plate)*

Mouse *(To audience, while taking slice of cheese from package)*: You see, while they did build a better mousetrap, what they didn't realize is they were dealing with . . . *(Turns down second sign)* a slightly better mouse *(Second sign reads Slightly Better Mouse)* . . . who wasn't hungry . . . *(Takes cracker, puts cheese on it)* until now. *(Takes bite. Quick curtain)*

The End

Characters: 14 or more male or female. You could, for example, have any number of actors play Wider, Longer, and Higher to expand size of mousetrap. The more performers added, the larger and more elaborate the mousetrap will be, and the bigger the explosion.

Playing Time: 10 minutes.

Costumes: Performers who are part of the mousetrap need only a sign, and may wear matching T-shirts and pants. Mouse wears gray baseball cap with gray felt or paper ears stapled to it, and also has a sign. Woman wears hat, long skirt, stole, jewelry. Man wears hat, suit coat, tie.

Properties: Cardboard signs worn in front of costumes should read: Mouse, Corner (four of them), Metal, Bar, Catch (two of them), Wider, Longer, Higher. Signs are folded in half and taped up to be concealed from audience, until tape is removed at appropriate moment, and sign unfolds. The words Slightly Better are written on separate piece of paper, folded and taped in space above Mouse sign; when indicated, the second sign is untaped to reveal new message reading: Slightly Better Mouse. Man has package of sliced cheese in one pocket, a small packet of crackers, and a small plate in another pocket. Higher holds an old-fashioned alarm clock.

Setting: There are two chairs on stage: one far left, one up center.

Lighting: No special effects.

Sound: Higher holds an alarm clock and "rings" it at various times during the play.

Think About the

PLAYS

1. How are the authors' attitudes towards the characters in the two plays similar? How are they different?

2. Compare Peter's attitude toward wearing the Star of David with Anne's. What do you think Peter means when he says "Maybe it's different for a girl"?

3. How do you know that the play about the mousetrap is a fantasy? Give examples from your reading.

4. Compare the relationship between Anne and Peter with the relationship between the Man and the Woman. What do the two couples have in common? How are they different?

5. Which play do you think your class would like to perform? Explain why.

Internet

Take an Online Poll

Have you ever performed in a play? Which do you like better, dramas or comedies? Visit Education Place to take an online poll. **www.eduplace.com/kids**

Creating

Write Your Own Scene

Write the script of a scene or a short play. It can be a comedy or a serious drama. Your play's story elements — a few characters and a simple plot and setting — can be traditional or offbeat, real or imaginary.

Tips

- Begin by thinking of a setting for your scene. Where and when will your scene take place?
- To help you create believable dialogue, try saying your characters' lines as you write them.
- Use stage directions to tell the actors how to move, speak, and use props.

237

3

Growing Up

We have tomorrow
Bright before us
Like a flame.

— *Langston Hughes
from "Youth"*

Growing Up

with E.L. Konigsburg

Hello!

Names say a lot about a person.

Before I got married and acquired my long, difficult last name, I had a short, difficult one: Lobl. That is what the *L* of E.L. Konigsburg stands for. The name is Hungarian, a language that is loaded with consonants. (My dad told me that the Hungarians dropped most of their vowels on Hawaii.) People usually add an *e* between the *b* and the *l* and call me *Low-BELL*. Wrong. Like most Hungarian words, the accent is on the first syllable: *LOW-bl*.

The *E* of *E.L.* stands for *Elaine*, my given name. When I was being named, *Elaine* was not particularly unusual. It fit right in with the names of other kids my age: Kenneth, Bert, Esther, Gwendolyn, Dolores.

When I was in the middle of fifth grade, my family moved, and I had to change schools, so I decided to change my name as well. I decided that I would be *Alayne*, pronounced *Ah–LANE*. My mother and my father would not cooperate. They told me that an important part of growing up is learning to accept who you are, so they insisted on calling me Elaine and spelling it exactly as it was spelled on my birth certificate.

In the sixth grade, my family moved again, but this time, I did not change my name or my school. Mr. Perkins, the principal, wanted me to continue at William McKinley Elementary School because I fit in there so well. So with my mother's consent, I was given an out-of-district permit, and I became the only girl who took a city bus to school and the only one who couldn't go home for lunch.

There I was — so much the same as everyone else that Mr. Perkins wanted to keep me, and there I was — so different from everyone else that I was the only person who ate lunch, all by herself, in back of her homeroom. There I was — like everyone else in the sixth grade but different. Just like my name. I was Elaine, the person who was not particularly unusual, but I was also Lobl, the person who was short, difficult, and missing a vowel.

It was there in the sixth grade at William McKinley Elementary School that I learned to accept being the same and being different at the same time. And it was there that I knew that I wanted to be loved for being both.

And now that I am grown up, that person, Elaine, and that person, Lobl, are still there, abbreviated as *E.L.*, but always right there, always right in front of Konigsburg. And now that I am grown up, I write stories about kids who are learning to accept themselves for being like everyone else at the same time they are learning to accept themselves for being different from everyone else. And the kids in the stories I write want to be loved for being both — at the same time. Just like me in the sixth grade. Just like Elaine Lobl Konigsburg now.

Sincerely,

E. L. Konigsburg

Growing Up Is...

Think about the events and feelings E.L. Konigsburg describes. Do you have times when you feel the same as everyone else, yet different in some way? What do you do when you feel that way?

As you read the selections below, ask what growing up means to each character. What do the characters learn about themselves? What would you do in the same situations? Find out what it's like to grow up in the country and in the city, in the past and in the present. Who knows? You may find many people who are different from, but just the same as, *you*.

To learn about the authors in this theme, visit Education Place. **www.eduplace.com/kids**

Background and Vocabulary

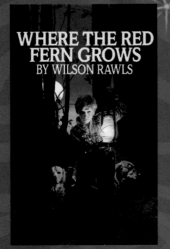

WHERE THE RED FERN GROWS
BY WILSON RAWLS

Where the Red Fern Grows

Read to find the meanings of these words.

e ● Glossary

cheap

determination

provisions

urgency

wares

The Great Depression

1929–1942

Where the Red Fern Grows tells about a boy growing up in an Ozark mountain valley during the Great Depression. Read on to find out more about this difficult time in our nation's history.

Job seekers have put signs on their car expressing their wish to work.

During the 1930s the United States was in the midst of the Great Depression, a time when businesses failed and many people were out of work. Prices were **cheap** because fewer goods were manufactured and people had no money to buy them. Many people with **determination** worked to save for **provisions** such as groceries, clothing, and other basic **wares**. With a sense of **urgency**, the federal government created new policies to relieve the hardships. It wasn't until after the United States entered World War II that the Depression finally ended.

Boy fishing, Oklahoma

Woman selling apples, New York City, 1929

General store, Moundville, Alabama

WHERE THE RED FERN GROWS
BY WILSON RAWLS

Strategy Focus

Billy Colman really wants a pair of dogs. Will his plan to get them succeed? As you read the selection, stop every few pages to **predict** what will happen next.

A valley in the Ozark mountains is a great place for dogs, and Billy Colman wanted dogs more than anything else in the world. Not just one dog, but two. One day he came across a magazine with an advertisement for hound pups — twenty-five dollars each. But it was the time of the Great Depression. Billy didn't have fifty dollars for two pups, and neither did his parents. So he decided to work hard and save the money. Using an old baking-powder can as his bank, he started with just twenty-three cents. One way or another, Billy would get his dogs.

All through that summer I worked like a beaver. In the small creek that wormed its way down through our fields, I caught crawfish with my bare hands. I trapped minnows with an old screen-wire trap I made myself, baited with yellow corn bread from my mother's kitchen. These were sold to the fishermen, along with fresh vegetables and roasting ears. I tore my way through the blackberry patches until my hands and feet were scratched raw and red from the thorns. I tramped the hills seeking out the huckleberry bushes. My grandfather paid me ten cents a bucket for my berries.

Once Grandpa asked me what I did with the money I earned. I told him I was saving it to buy some hunting dogs. I asked him if he would order them for me when I had saved enough. He said he would. I asked him not to say anything to my father. He promised me he wouldn't. I'm sure Grandpa paid little attention to my plans.

That winter I trapped harder than ever with the three little traps I owned. Grandpa sold my hides to fur buyers who came to his store all through the fur season. Prices were cheap: fifteen cents for a large opossum hide, twenty-five for a good skunk hide.

Little by little, the nickels and dimes added up. The old K. C. Baking Powder can grew heavy. I would heft its weight in the palm of my hand. With a straw, I'd measure from the lip of the can to the money. As the months went by, the straws grew shorter and shorter.

The next summer I followed the same routine.

"Would you like to buy some crawfish or minnows? Maybe you'd like some fresh vegetables or roasting ears."

The fishermen were wonderful, as true sportsmen are. They seemed to sense the urgency in my voice and always bought my wares. However, many was the time I'd find my vegetables left in the abandoned camp.

There never was a set price. Anything they offered was good enough for me.

A year passed. I was twelve. I was over the halfway mark. I had twenty-seven dollars and forty-six cents. My spirits soared. I worked harder.

Another year crawled slowly by, and then the great day came. The long hard grind was over. I had it — my fifty dollars! I cried as I counted it over and over.

As I set the can back in the shadowy eaves of the barn, it seemed to glow with a radiant whiteness I had never seen before. Perhaps it was all imagination. I don't know.

Lying back in the soft hay, I folded my hands behind my head, closed my eyes, and let my mind wander back over the two long years. I thought of the fishermen, the blackberry patches, and the huckleberry hills. I thought of the prayer I had said when I asked God to help me get two hound pups. I knew He had surely helped, for He had given me the heart, courage, and determination.

Early the next morning, with the can jammed deep in the pocket of my overalls, I flew to the store. As I trotted along, I whistled and sang. I felt as big as the tallest mountain in the Ozarks.

Arriving at my destination, I saw two wagons were tied up at the hitching rack. I knew some farmers had come to the store, so I waited until they left. As I walked in, I saw my grandfather behind the counter. Tugging and pulling, I worked the can out of my pocket and dumped it out in front of him and looked up.

Grandpa was dumbfounded. He tried to say something, but it wouldn't come out. He looked at me, and he looked at the pile of coins. Finally, in a voice much louder than he ordinarily used, he asked, "Where did you get all this?"

"I told you, Grandpa," I said, "I was saving my money so I could buy two hound pups, and I did. You said you would order them for me. I've got the money and now I want you to order them."

Grandpa stared at me over his glasses, and then back at the money.

"How long have you been saving this?" he asked.

"A long time, Grandpa," I said.

"How long?" he asked.

I told him, "Two years."

His mouth flew open and in a loud voice he said, "Two years!"

I nodded my head.

The way my grandfather stared at me made me uneasy. I was on needles and pins. Taking his eyes from me, he glanced back at the money. He saw the

faded yellow piece of paper sticking out from the coins. He worked it out, asking as he did, "What's this?"

I told him it was the ad, telling where to order my dogs.

He read it, turned it over, and glanced at the other side.

I saw the astonishment leave his eyes and the friendly-old-grandfather look come back. I felt much better.

Dropping the paper back on the money, he turned, picked up an old turkey-feather duster, and started dusting where there was no dust. He kept glancing at me out of the corner of his eye as he walked slowly down to the other end of the store, dusting here and there.

He put the duster down, came from behind the counter, and walked up to me. Laying a friendly old work-calloused hand on my head, he changed the conversation altogether, saying, "Son, you need a haircut."

I told him I didn't mind. I didn't like my hair short; flies and mosquitoes bothered me.

He glanced down at my bare feet and asked, "How come your feet are cut and scratched like that?"

I told him it was pretty tough picking blackberries barefoot.

He nodded his head.

It was too much for my grandfather. He turned and walked away. I saw the glasses come off, and the old red handkerchief come out. I heard the good excuse of blowing his nose. He stood for several seconds with his back toward me. When he turned around, I noticed his eyes were moist.

In a quavering voice, he said, "Well, son, it's your money. You worked for it, and you worked hard. You got it honestly, and you want some dogs. We're going to get those dogs."

He walked over and picked up the ad again, asking, "Is this two years old, too?"

I nodded.

"Well," he said, "the first thing we have to do is write this outfit. There may not even be a place like this in Kentucky any more. After all, a lot of things can happen in two years."

Seeing that I was worried, he said, "Now you go on home. I'll write to these kennels and I'll let you know when I get an answer. If we can't get the dogs there, we can get them someplace else. And I don't think, if I were you,

I'd let my Pa know anything about this right now. I happen to know he wants to buy that red mule from Old Man Potter."

I told him I wouldn't, and turned to leave the store.

As I reached the door, my grandfather said in a loud voice, "Say, it's been a long time since you've had any candy, hasn't it?"

I nodded my head.

He asked, "How long?"

I told him, "A long time."

"Well," he said, "we'll have to do something about that."

Walking over behind the counter, he reached out and got a sack. I noticed it wasn't one of the nickel sacks. It was one of the quarter kind.

My eyes never left my grandfather's hand. Time after time, it dipped in and out of the candy counter: peppermint sticks, jawbreakers, horehound, and gumdrops. The sack bulged. So did my eyes.

Handing the sack to me, he said, "Here. First big coon you catch with those dogs, you can pay me back."

I told him I would.

On my way home, with a jawbreaker in one side of my mouth and a piece of horehound in the other, I skipped and hopped, making half an effort to try to whistle and sing, and couldn't for the candy. I had the finest grandpa in the world and I was the happiest boy in the world.

I wanted to share my happiness with my sisters but decided not to say anything about ordering the pups.

Arriving home, I dumped the sack of candy out on the bed. Six little hands helped themselves. I was well repaid by the love and adoration I saw in the wide blue eyes of my three little sisters.

Day after day, I flew to the store, grandpa would shake his head. Then on a Monday, as I entered the store, I sensed a change in him. He was in high spirits, talking and laughing with half a dozen farmers. Every time I caught his eye, he would smile and wink at me. I thought the farmers would never leave, but finally the store was empty.

Grandpa told me the letter had come. The kennels were still there, and they had dogs for sale. He said he had made the mail buggy wait while he made out the order. And, another thing, the dog market had gone downhill. The price of dogs had dropped five dollars. He handed me a ten-dollar bill.

"Now, there's still one stump in the way," he said. "The mail buggy can't carry things like dogs, so they'll come as far as the depot at Tahlequah, but you'll get the notice here because I ordered them in your name."

I thanked my grandfather with all my heart and asked him how long I'd have to wait for the notice.

He said, "I don't know, but it shouldn't take more than a couple of weeks."

I asked how I was going to get my dogs out from Tahlequah.

"Well, there's always someone going in," he said, "and you could ride in with them."

That evening the silence of our supper was interrupted when I asked my father this question: "Papa, how far is it to Kentucky?"

I may as well have exploded a bomb. For an instant there was complete silence, and then my oldest sister giggled. The two little ones stared at me.

With a half-hearted laugh, my father said, "Well, now, I don't know, but it's a pretty good ways. What do you want to know for? Thinking of taking a trip to Kentucky?"

"No," I said. "I just wondered."

My youngest sister giggled and asked, "Can I go with you?"

I glared at her.

Mama broke into the conversation, "I declare, what kind of a question is that? How far is it to Kentucky? I don't know what's gotten into that mind of yours lately. You go around like you were lost, and you're losing weight. You're as skinny as a rail, and look at that hair. Just last Sunday they had a haircutting over at Tom Rolland's place, but you couldn't go. You had to go prowling around the river and the woods."

I told Mama that I'd get a haircut next time they had a cutting. And I just heard some fellows talking about Kentucky up at the store, and wondered how far away it was. Much to my relief, the conversation was ended.

The days dragged by. A week passed and still no word about my dogs. Terrible thoughts ran through my mind. Maybe my dogs were lost; the train had a wreck; someone stole my money; or perhaps the mailman lost my order. Then, at the end of the second week, the notice came.

My grandfather told me that he had talked to Jim Hodges that day. He was going into town in about a week and I could ride in with him to pick up my dogs. Again I thanked my grandfather.

I started for home. Walking along in deep thought, I decided it was time to tell my father the whole story. I fully intended to tell him that evening. I tried several times, but somehow I couldn't. I wasn't scared of him, for he never whipped me. He was always kind and gentle, but for some reason, I don't know why, I just couldn't tell him.

That night, snuggled deep in the soft folds of a feather bed, I lay thinking. I had waited so long for my dogs, and I so desperately wanted to see them and hold them. I didn't want to wait a whole week.

In a flash I made up my mind. Very quietly I got up and put on my clothes. I sneaked into the kitchen and got one of Mama's precious flour sacks. In it I put six eggs, some leftover corn bread, a little salt, and a few matches. Next I went to the smokehouse and cut off a piece of salt pork. I stopped at the barn and picked up a gunny sack. I put the flour sack inside the gunny sack. This I rolled up and crammed lengthwise in the bib of my overalls.

I was on my way. I was going after my dogs.

Tahlequah was a small country town with a population of about eight hundred. By the road it was thirty-two miles away, but as the crow flies, it was only twenty miles. I went as the crow flies, straight through the hills.

Although I had never been to town in my life, I knew what direction to take. Tahlequah and the railroad lay on the other side of the river from our

254

place. I had the Frisco Railroad on my right, and the Illinois River on my left. Not far from where the railroad crossed the river lay the town of Tahlequah. I knew if I bore to the right I would find the railroad, and if I bore to the left I had the river to guide me.

Some time that night, I crossed the river on a riffle somewhere in the Dripping Springs country. Coming out of the river bottoms, I scatted up a long hogback ridge, and broke out on top in the flats. In a mile-eating trot, I moved along. I had the wind of a deer, the muscles of a country boy, a heart full of dog love, and a strong determination. I wasn't scared of the darkness, or the mountains, for I was raised in those mountains.

On and on, mile after mile, I moved along. I saw faint gray streaks appear in the east. I knew daylight was close. My bare feet were getting sore from the flint rocks and saw briers. I stopped beside a mountain stream, soaked my feet in the cool water, rested for a spell, and then started on.

After leaving the mountain stream, my pace was much slower. The muscles of my legs were getting stiff. Feeling the pangs of hunger gnawing at my stomach, I decided I would stop and eat at the next stream I found. Then I remembered I had forgotten to include a can in which to boil my eggs.

I stopped and built a small fire. Cutting off a nice thick slab of salt pork, I roasted it, and with a piece of cold corn bread made a sandwich. Putting out my fire, I was on my way again. I ate as I trotted along. I felt much better.

I came into Tahlequah from the northeast. At the outskirts of town, I hid my flour sack and provisions, keeping the gunny sack. I walked into town.

I was scared of Tahlequah and the people. I had never seen such a big town and so many people. There was store after store, some of them two stories high. The wagon yard had wagons on top of wagons; teams, buggies, and horses.

Two young ladies about my age stopped, stared at me, and then giggled. My blood boiled, but I could understand. After all, I had three sisters. They couldn't help it because they were womenfolks. I went on.

I saw a big man coming up the street. The bright shiny star on his vest looked as big as a bucket. I saw the long, black gun at his side and I froze in my tracks. I'd heard of sheriffs and marshals, but had never seen one. Stories repeated about them in the mountains told how fast they were with a gun, and how many men they had killed.

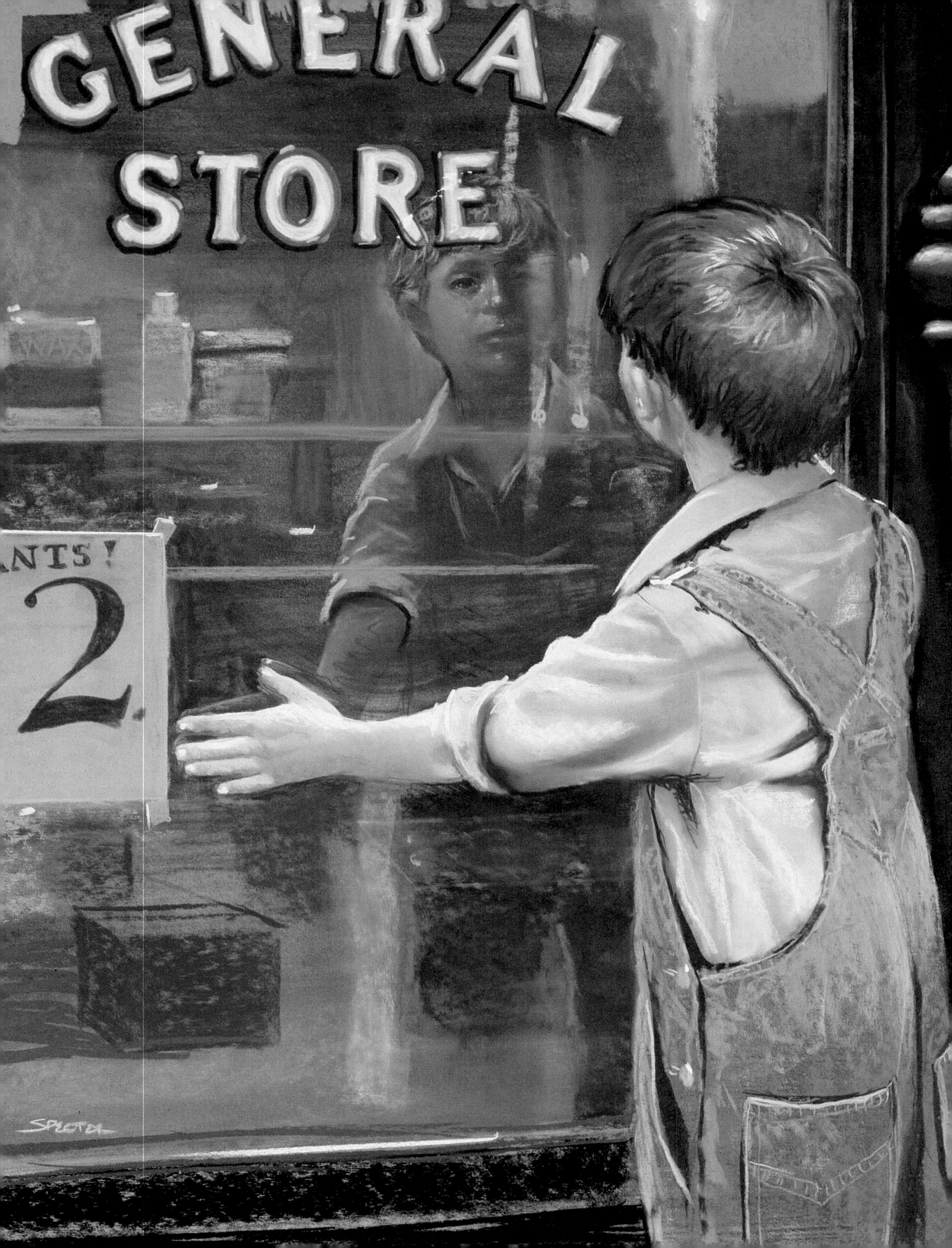
GENERAL
STORE
ANTS!
2.

The closer he came, the more frightened I got. I knew it was the end for me. It seemed like a miracle that he passed by, hardly glancing at me. Breathing a sigh, I walked on, seeing the wonders of the world.

Passing a large store window, I stopped and stared. There in the window was the most wonderful sight I had ever seen; everything under the sun; overalls, jackets, bolts of beautiful cloth, new harnesses, collars, bridles; and then my eyes did pop open.

I saw something else. The sun was just right, and the plate glass was a perfect mirror. I saw the full reflection of myself for the first time in my life.

I could see that I did look a little odd. My straw-colored hair was long and shaggy, and was bushed out like a corn tassle that had been hit by a wind. I tried to smooth it down with my hands. This helped some but not much. What it needed was a good combing and I had no comb.

My overalls were patched and faded but they were clean. My shirt had pulled out. I tucked it back in.

I took one look at my bare feet and winced. They were as brown as dead sycamore leaves. The spiderweb pattern of raw, red scratches looked odd in the saddle-brown skin. I thought, "Well, I won't have to pick any more blackberries and the scratches will soon go away."

I pumped up one of my arms and thought surely the muscle was going to pop right through my thin blue shirt. I stuck out my tongue. It was as red as pokeberry juice and anything that color was supposed to be healthy.

After making a few faces at myself, I put my thumbs in my ears and was making mule ears when two old women came by. They stopped and stared at me. I stared back. As they turned to go on their way, I heard one of them say something to the other. The words were hard to catch, but I did hear one word: "Wild." As I said before, they couldn't help it, they were womenfolks.

As I turned to leave, my eyes again fell on the overalls and the bolts of cloth. I thought of my mother, father, and sisters. Here was an opportunity to make amends for leaving home without telling anyone.

I entered the store. I bought a pair of overalls for Papa. After telling the storekeeper how big my mother and sisters were, I bought several yards of cloth. I also bought a large sack of candy.

Glancing down at my bare feet, the storekeeper said, "I have some good shoes."

I told him I didn't need any shoes.

He asked if that would be all.

I nodded.

He added up the bill. I handed him my ten dollars. He gave me my change.

After wrapping up the bundles, he helped me put them in my sack. Lifting it to my shoulder, I turned and left the store.

Out on the street, I picked out a friendly-looking old man and asked him where the depot was. He told me to go down to the last street and turn right, go as far as I could, and I couldn't miss it. I thanked him and started on my way.

Leaving the main part of town, I started up a long street through the residential section. I had never seen so many beautiful houses, and they were all different colors. The lawns were neat and clean and looked like green carpets. I saw a man pushing some kind of a mowing machine. I stopped to watch the whirling blades. He gawked at me. I hurried on.

I heard a lot of shouting and laughing ahead of me. Not wanting to miss anything, I walked a little faster. I saw what was making the noise. More kids than I had ever seen were playing around a big red brick building. I thought some rich man lived there and was giving a party for his children. Walking up to the edge of the playground, I stopped to watch.

The boys and girls were about my age, and were as thick as flies around a sorghum mill. They were milling, running, and jumping. Teeter-totters and swings were loaded down with them. Everyone was laughing and having a big time.

Over against the building, a large blue pipe ran up on an angle from the ground. A few feet from the top there was a bend in it. The pipe seemed to go into the building. Boys were crawling into its dark mouth. I counted nine of them. One boy stood about six feet from the opening with a stick in his hand.

Staring goggle-eyed, trying to figure out what they were doing, I got a surprise. Out of the hollow pipe spurted a boy. He sailed through the air and lit on his feet. The boy with the stick marked the ground where he landed. All nine of them came shooting out, one behind the other. As each boy landed, a new mark was scratched.

They ganged around looking at the lines. There was a lot of loud talking, pointing, and arguing. Then all lines were erased and a new scorekeeper was picked out. The others crawled back into the pipe.

I figured out how the game was played. After climbing to the top of the slide, the boys turned around and sat down. One at a time, they came flying down and out, feet first. The one that shot out the furthest was the winner. I thought how wonderful it would be if I could slide down just one time.

One boy, spying me standing on the corner, came over. Looking me up and down, he asked, "Do you go to school here?"

I said, "School?"

He said, "Sure. School. What did you think it was?"

"Oh. No, I don't go to school here."

"Do you go to Jefferson?"

"No. I don't go there either."

"Don't you go to school at all?"

"Sure I go to school."

"Where?"

"At home."

259

"You go to school at home?"

I nodded.

"What grade are you in?"

I said I wasn't in any grade.

Puzzled, he said, "You go to school at home, and don't know what grade you're in. Who teaches you?"

"My mother."

"What does she teach you?"

I said, "Reading, writing, and arithmetic, and I bet I'm just as good at it as you are."

He asked, "Don't you have any shoes?"

I said, "Sure, I have shoes."

"Why aren't you wearing them?"

"I don't wear shoes until it gets cold."

He laughed and asked where I lived.

I said, "Back in the hills."

He said, "Oh, you're a hillbilly."

He ran back to the mob. I saw him pointing at me and talking to several boys. They started my way, yelling, "Hillbilly, hillbilly."

Just before they reached me, a bell started ringing. Turning, they ran to the front of the building, lined up in two long lines, and, marching like little tin soldiers, disappeared inside the school.

The playground was silent. I was all alone, and felt lonely and sad.

I heard a noise on my right. I didn't have to turn around to recognize what it was. Someone was using a hoe. I'd know that sound if I heard it on a dark night. It was a little old white-headed woman working in a flower bed.

Looking again at the long, blue pipe, I thought, "There's no one around. Maybe I could have one slide anyway."

I eased over and looked up into the dark hollow. It looked scary, but I thought of all the other boys I had seen crawl into it. I could see the last mark on the ground, and thought, "I bet I can beat that."

Laying my sack down, I started climbing up. The farther I went, the darker and more scary it got. Just as I reached the top, my feet slipped. Down I sailed. All the way down I tried to grab on to something, but there was nothing to grab.

I'm sure some great champions had slid out of that pipe, and no doubt more than one world record had been broken, but if someone had been there when I came out, I know the record I set would stand today in all its glory.

I came out just like I went in, feet first and belly down. My legs were spread out like a bean-shooter stalk. Arms flailing the air, I zoomed out and up. I seemed to hang suspended in air at the peak of my climb. I could see the hard-packed ground far below.

As I started down, I shut my eyes tight and gritted my teeth. This didn't seem to help. With a splattering sound, I landed. I felt the air whoosh out between my teeth. I tried to scream, but had no wind left to make a sound.

After bouncing a couple of times, I finally settled down to earth. I lay spread-eagled for a few seconds, and then slowly got to my knees.

Hearing loud laughter, I looked around. It was the little old lady with the hoe in her hand. She hollered and asked how I liked it. Without answering, I grabbed up my gunny sack and left. Far up the street, I looked back. The little old lady was sitting down, rocking with laughter.

I couldn't understand these town people. If they weren't staring at a fellow, they were laughing at him.

On arriving at the depot, my nerve failed me. I was afraid to go in. I didn't know what I was scared of, but I was scared.

Before going around to the front, I peeked in a window. The stationmaster was in his office looking at some papers. He was wearing a funny little cap that had no top in it. He looked friendly enough but I still couldn't muster up enough courage to go in.

I cocked my ear to see if I could hear puppies crying, but could hear nothing. A bird started chirping. It was a yellow canary in a cage. The stationmaster walked over and gave it some water. I thought, "Anyone that is kind to birds surely wouldn't be mean to a boy."

With my courage built up I walked around to the front and eased myself past the office. He glanced at me and turned back to the papers. I walked clear around the depot and again walked slowly past the office. Glancing from the corner of my eye, I saw the stationmaster looking at me and smiling. He opened the door and came out on the platform. I stopped and leaned against the building.

Yawning and stretching his arms, he said, "It sure is hot today. It doesn't look like it's ever going to rain."

I looked up at the sky and said, "Yes, sir. It is hot and we sure could do with a good rain. We need one bad up where I come from."

He asked me where I lived.

I told him, "Up the river a ways."

"You know," he said, "I have some puppies in there for a boy that lives up on the river. His name is Billy Colman. I know his dad, but never have seen the boy. I figured he would be in after them today."

On hearing this remark, my heart jumped clear up in my throat. I thought surely it was going to hop right out on the depot platform. I looked up and tried to tell him who I was, but something went wrong. When the words finally came out they sounded like the squeaky old pulley on our well when Mama drew up a bucket of water.

I could see a twinkle in the stationmaster's eyes. He came over and laid his hand on my shoulder. In a friendly voice he said, "So you're Billy Colman. How is your dad?"

I told him Papa was fine and handed him the slip my grandpa had given me.

"They sure are fine-looking pups," he said. "You'll have to go around to the freight door."

I'm sure my feet never touched the ground as I flew around the building. He unlocked the door, and I stepped in, looking for my dogs. I couldn't see anything but boxes, barrels, old trunks, and some rolls of barbed wire.

The kindly stationmaster walked over to one of the boxes.

"Do you want box and all?" he asked.

I told him I didn't want the box. All I wanted was the dogs.

"How are you going to carry them?" he asked. "I think they're a little too young to follow."

I held out my gunny sack.

He looked at me and looked at the sack. Chuckling, he said, "Well, I guess dogs can be carried that way same as anything else, but we'll have to cut a couple of holes to stick their heads through so that they won't smother."

Getting a claw hammer, he started tearing off the top of the box. As nails gave way and boards splintered, I heard several puppy whimpers. I didn't walk over. I just stood and waited.

After what seemed like hours, the box was open. He reached in, lifted the pups out, and set them down on the floor.

"Well, there they are," he said. "What do you think of them?"

I didn't answer. I couldn't. All I could do was stare at them.

They seemed to be blinded by the light and kept blinking their eyes. One sat down on his little rear and started crying. The other one was waddling around and whimpering.

I wanted so much to step over and pick them up. Several times I tried to move my feet, but they seemed to be nailed to the floor. I knew the pups were mine, all mine, yet I couldn't move. My heart started acting like a grasshopper. I tried to swallow and couldn't. My Adam's apple wouldn't work.

One pup started my way. I held my breath. On he came until I felt a scratchy little foot on mine. The other pup followed. A warm puppy tongue caressed my sore foot.

I heard the stationmaster say, "They already know you."

MEET THE AUTHOR: WILSON RAWLS

Where he grew up: On the same farm he describes in his stories. At fifteen, his family moved to Tahlequah, Oklahoma — the town where Billy Colman got his dogs.

Who taught him to read: His grandmother

Favorite book as a boy: *The Call of the Wild*, by Jack London

Hard at work: Before writing full-time, Wilson worked on highways, dams, and shipyards.

Advice: "Do not wait to start writing. You are never too young to start."

WILSON RAWLS

MEET THE ILLUSTRATOR: JOEL SPECTOR

Home town: Havana, Cuba

Age when he came to U.S.: Twelve

Favorite hobby: Running after his children (all four of them)

Favorite way to make pictures: With pastel crayons

Why he became an illustrator: It's a great steady job for an artist.

Advice: Follow your dreams and learn your craft very well.

JOEL SPECTOR

To learn more about Wilson Rawls and Joel Spector, visit Education Place. **www.eduplace.com/kids**

Responding

Think About the Selection

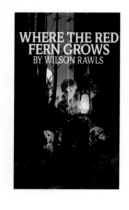

1. What things that Billy did to earn money did you find most interesting or surprising? Explain.

2. Give examples of ways Grandpa helped Billy to get his puppies. What conclusions can you draw about Grandpa?

3. What would have been different about Billy's journey if he had waited a week for a ride into town?

4. Think about the people in Tahlequah. Why do you think they acted the way they did toward Billy?

5. What clues led Billy to believe that the stationmaster was not a mean person?

6. Billy worked a long time to buy something, yet when he got it he couldn't move toward it. Has something like this ever happened to you? Give examples from your own life.

7. **Connecting/Comparing** What do Billy's experiences in this story show about the challenges of growing up?

Informing

Write a Paragraph of Advice

Billy worked hard and saved his money for something he wanted badly. Write a paragraph of advice, telling other young people how to earn and save money for something they want to buy or to do.

Tips

- Start by listing some ways to earn money and tips for saving money.
- Write a topic sentence for your paragraph. Then use your list items as supporting details.

Make a Compare/ Contrast Chart

Make a compare/contrast chart that lists the similarities and differences between Tahlequah and the country where Billy lived. Describe the differences in dress, speech, education, law enforcement, the way people spent money, and anything else you can think of.

	Countryside	Tahlequah
Land	Hills, River, Woods	Big Town
Education	Home	School
People		

Compare an Illustration and a Photograph

On page 256 the illustration shows Billy looking into a store window. Reread the passage in the selection that describes this scene. Compare this illustration with the photograph of the country store in "The Great Depression (1929–1942)" on page 245. Do you think the illustration does a good job of showing what Billy saw? Explain.

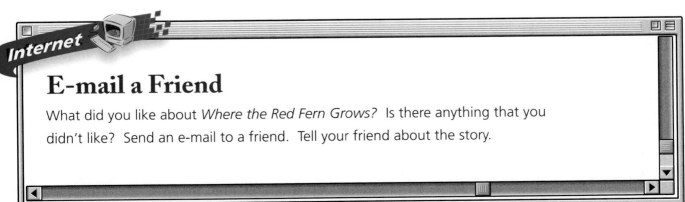

Internet

E-mail a Friend

What did you like about *Where the Red Fern Grows*? Is there anything that you didn't like? Send an e-mail to a friend. Tell your friend about the story.

This is a story about a girl and a dog. It's also about growing up, and learning, and helping someone you've never met.

Puppy Love

Skill: How to Skim and Scan

Skim to Identify Main Points

❶ **Preview** the title, the headings, and the introduction. Read the first and last paragraphs.

❷ Read the first sentence in each remaining paragraph. **Note key words** within paragraphs.

Scan to Find Information Quickly

Look quickly over the article with a particular topic or key word in mind.

A golden retriever puppy named Fanny romped into Leanne Roberts's life in the fall. That's when Leanne, nine, and her family became part of a puppy-raising program sponsored by the Guide Dog Foundation for the Blind, a group that trains dogs to help blind people.

Since guide dogs don't start official training until they're about fourteen months old, the foundation needs volunteer families to care for their puppies until it's time for training.

So when Leanne and her family welcomed three-month-old Fanny into their home, they also knew they'd say goodbye to her in about a year. Each day, as Fanny grew bigger and more mature, she was one day closer to going back to the foundation. After training, she would be matched with a blind owner.

Growing Up

Winter   Five months later, Fanny is much bigger. "Fanny is also calmer, and doesn't chew anymore," Leanne explains. "She's almost done teething, that's why." That's a big relief, as anyone who's raised a puppy knows. Along with all the fun of having a new puppy come the not-so-fun things like chewed-up telephone cords and lessons in housebreaking. Raising a puppy takes patience and hard work!

Now that Fanny's older, Leanne and her family work more on obedience commands. A trainer from the Guide Dog Foundation visits the family once every four weeks to help. And Fanny goes out more these days. Since guide dogs go practically everywhere with their blind owners, Leanne and her family must get Fanny used to places like grocery stores and restaurants — even the mall. Fanny always wears her yellow jacket, so business owners know she's part of the guide-dog program.

"People love to pet her and ask what kind of dog she is," says Leanne. "My friends think I'm very lucky to have a dog that I can take lots of different places. And I think so, too."

Fanny learns to wait patiently underneath the table while Leanne and her friends enjoy a meal.

Erin Cleary, a puppy trainer, takes Leanne and Fanny out for a leash lesson.

269

Saying Goodbye

Fall   Fanny's been with Leanne for just about a year. Together they've learned a lot and shared a lot — including a couple of under-the-table peanut butter and jelly sandwiches that got them both into trouble! Fanny has continued her work with a trainer, and she's done well. She's also passed important health tests needed to qualify as a guide dog. Now it's time for Fanny to go back to the Guide Dog Foundation for training.

On a bright September day, Leanne and her mom pack Fanny's things and take her to the Guide Dog Foundation. People there thank the Roberts family for helping to raise Fanny, and welcome Fanny into their training program.

This is a sad time, but it's a hopeful time, too. "I know Fanny will be happy helping someone," says Leanne. Someday Leanne and her family hope to meet Fanny's new owner. Someday they hope to see the results of their work, patience, and love. What a happy day that will be!

Leanne and Fanny are met by ▲ a representative at the Guide Dog Foundation.

◄

Erin shows Leanne a hand command that tells Fanny to sit.

A New Life

Fanny's ready to start her new life as a guide-dog-in-training. She now lives in a kennel at the foundation, along with nearly 100 other dogs who are in training. Here Fanny will be taught to perform all sorts of tasks, such as learning to stop at crosswalks. If she performs well during this first training, she'll be matched with a blind owner. Then the two of them will work together at the foundation until they graduate.

There is a possibility that Fanny won't do well enough to be matched with a blind person. If this happens, Leanne's family will have a chance to take Fanny back. If the Roberts family should decide not to keep Fanny, she'd be placed with someone who is on a waiting list for dogs that don't make it through the program.

Becoming a Puppy Raiser

Many groups are looking for volunteer puppy raisers all over the United States. Families have to meet requirements to qualify for the programs. Here are some of the requirements of the Guide Dog Foundation for the Blind:

- Family must be willing to devote time each day to the care and training of the puppy.

- Family must pay for the cost of feeding the puppy a special diet for the year. It costs about $30 a month.

- Family must be willing to take the puppy out in public to get it used to new people and places.

A Description

A description is a picture in words that helps the reader share the writer's experience. Use this student's writing as a model when you write a description of your own.

The **title** of a description should grab the reader's attention.

Good writers use **literal language** in their descriptions.

Similes and **metaphors** add spice to your writing.

Hockey: The Facts of Ice!

The sky is dim as dawn breaks on an icy cold winter day. The kitchen windows are frosted with moisture and I'm shaking. As I start to dress, the windows begin to drip as the heat in the house warms both me and the room.

My nylon suit is clammy and smooth at the same time. I hate the feeling of it on my skin. Hockey socks are next. They are warm and make my legs feel cozy. This huge chest protector, like a suit of armor, is heavy like the weight of bricks holding me down. As I put on each piece of equipment I feel more and more immobilized. I hate all this stuff. I can hardly move. Now I'm sweating and it's time to leave for the arena.

Like every arena, it is freezing, and you can see your breath and almost catch it in midair and break it up into ice cubes. Stepping onto the pristine ice, you can feel the quickness of your skates. The blades are so sharp they cut the ice as you glide on the untouched surface. It feels so beautiful when no one has been on it but you, and for a few minutes you can hear the hissing your skates make as if they're speaking to you and it's the only sound in the world. You glide like the wind and the cold air hits your face and you feel as if you are moving at 100 mph, your speed made more intense because of the stillness around you.

My hockey stick feels secure in my hand like an old friend I am at ease with. The shaft is worn and pieces of wood are fraying off like splinters, but it's comfortable. It's the security blanket I need because my coach is heading toward me. Reality hits; he's yelling orders out already. No matter how hard I try he's never happy. "You're dragging your heels," he hollers. "You're doggin' it," he barks again. He's only happy after I've done something 97 times over and over again and the sweat is pouring down my face.

My helmet is so hot, like an oven at 450. Now it's time for the sprints; stop and start, stop and start, crossovers and edge control, again and again. When will it stop?

I'm so glad it's over. The ice looks choppy like the sea during a bad storm. Chips and cracks are everywhere. There's not one bit of untouched surface. I've left my mark; my blades have scratched the once smooth surface with my signature in loops. The piles of snow left by my unending stops are evidence of my hour's work. It's over, let the Zamboni come on the ice, and in ten minutes you will never have known I was there.

Meet the Author

Billy D.
Grade: six
State: New Jersey
Hobbies: playing hockey and baseball
What he'd like to be when he grows up: a hockey player, a baseball player, or a sports announcer

Background and Vocabulary

Last Summer with Maizon

Read to find the meanings of these words.

e Glossary

daydreaming

express

previous

relieve

stoop

Life in the City

What is life like in a city neighborhood? In *Last Summer with Maizon,* a girl recalls good times with a friend who has moved away from their Brooklyn neighborhood.

▲

In the summer people in the city can spend time together on a **stoop**, or small porch, of their apartment building. Here neighbors may **express** their friendship by talking, joking, and telling stories.

Because summer days in the city can be very hot, playing in a fountain is a cool way to **relieve** the heat.

▼

▲ In the New York City subway, these friends are **daydreaming** about the things they might do at day camp.

Read on to discover how two best friends value their **previous** summer months together in the neighborhood.

MEET THE AUTHOR

Jacqueline Woodson

By fifth grade she was editor of her school's magazine. By seventh grade she was encouraged by her teacher to follow a career in writing. "I can't write about nice, easy topics," says Woodson, "because that won't change the world. And I do want to change the world — one reader at a time." Through her stories, Woodson shares with her readers "the idea of feeling like you're okay with who you are." Among her other books, Woodson has also written *Maizon at Blue Hill*, a sequel to *Last Summer with Maizon*.

MEET THE ILLUSTRATOR

Eric Velasquez

Eric Velasquez's parents used to buy art supplies and leave them around the house for him to use. By the time Velasquez was old enough for college, art school was the natural choice for the young man who loved to draw and paint. Today when he reads a story, Velasquez imagines the characters and begins sketching immediately. For *Last Summer with Maizon*, he went to Harlem and photographed people and subways to use in his illustrations.

To learn more about Jacqueline Woodson and Eric Velasquez, visit Education Place. **www.eduplace.com/kids**

Last Summer with Maizon

JACQUELINE WOODSON

Strategy Focus

Life won't be the same for Margaret now that her best friend Maizon is going away. As you read, **evaluate** how well the author shows that Margaret misses Maizon.

277

Margaret Tory and her best friend Maizon do everything together. They even live on the same block in Brooklyn, New York. But the summer they turn eleven, things change. Margaret's father passes away and Maizon is offered a scholarship to a boarding school in Connecticut. Now Margaret has to cope with her friend going away.

"Sure wish you weren't going away," Margaret said, choking back tears for what seemed like the millionth time. They were sitting on the M train, crossing the Williamsburg Bridge, and Margaret shivered as the train passed over the water. The L train would have made the trip easier but the L didn't go over the bridge and Maizon had wanted to ride over it once more before she left.

Maizon sat nervously drumming her fingers against the windowpane. "Me too," she said absently.

Margaret looked over at Mama and Grandma. Grandma stared out of her window. She looked old and out of place on the train.

"Maizon?" Margaret said, turning back toward her.

"Hmm?" Maizon frowned. She seemed to be concentrating on something in the water. It rippled and danced below them.

"Even though I wrote you those two letters, you only have to write me one back if you don't have a lot of time or something." Margaret looked down at her fingers. She had begun biting the cuticles, and now the skin surrounding her nails was red and ragged.

"I'll write you back," Maizon promised.

"Maizon . . ."

"What, Margaret!"

Margaret jumped and looked at Maizon. There was an uneasiness in her eyes she had never seen before.

"Forget it," she said.

Ms. Tory leaned over. "We'll be getting off in a few stops."

They rode the rest of the way in silence. At Delancey Street they changed for another train and a half hour later they were at Penn Station.

"I guess now we'll have to call each other to plan the same outfits," Maizon said as they waited for her train. Her voice sounded forced and fake, Margaret thought, like a grown-up trying to make a kid smile.

"I guess," Margaret said. The conductor called Maizon's train.

"I guess I gotta go," Maizon said softly, and Margaret felt a lump rise in her throat.

"I'll write you back, Margaret. Promise. Thanks for letting me keep the double-dutch trophy even if it is only second place." They hugged for a long time. Maizon sniffed loudly. "I'm scared, Margaret," she whispered.

Margaret didn't know what to say. "Don't be."

"Bye, Ms. Tory."

Margaret's mother bent down and hugged Maizon. "Be good," she said as Maizon and her grandmother made their way toward the train.

"Mama," Margaret said as they watched Maizon and her grandmother disappear into the tunnel.

"What, dear?"

"What's the difference between a best friend and an old friend?"

"I guess . . ." Her mother thought for a moment. "I guess an old friend is a friend you once had and a best friend is a friend you'll always have."

"Then maybe me and Maizon aren't best friends anymore."

"Don't be silly, Margaret. What else would you two be? Some people can barely tell you apart. I feel like I've lost a daughter."

"Maybe . . . I don't know . . . Maybe we're old friends now. Maybe this was our last summer as best friends. I feel like something's going to change now and I'm not going to be able to change it back."

Ms. Tory's heels made a clicking sound through the terminal. She stopped to buy tokens and turned to Margaret.

"Like when Daddy died?" she asked, looking worried.

Margaret swallowed. "No. I just feel empty instead of sad, Mama," she said.

Her mother squeezed her hand as they waited for the train. When it came, they took seats by the window.

Ms. Tory held on to Margaret's hand. "Sometimes it just takes a while for the pain of loss to set in."

"I feel like sometimes Maizon kept me from doing things, but now she's not here. Now I don't have any" — Margaret thought for a moment, but couldn't find the right words — "now I don't have any excuse not to do things."

When the train emerged from its tunnel, the late afternoon sun had turned a bright orange. Margaret watched it for a moment. She looked at her hands again and discovered a cuticle she had missed.

Margaret pressed her pencil to her lips and stared out the classroom window. The school yard was desolate and gray. But everything seemed that way since Maizon left. Especially since a whole week had passed now without even a letter from her. Margaret sighed and chewed her eraser.

"Margaret, are you working on this assignment?"

Margaret jumped and turned toward Ms. Peazle. Maizon had been right — Ms. Peazle was the crabbiest teacher in the school. Margaret wondered why she had been picked to teach the smartest class. If students were so smart, she thought, the least the school could do was reward them with a nice teacher.

"I'm trying to think about what to write, Ms. Peazle."

"Well, you won't find an essay on your summer vacation outside that window, I'm sure. Or is that where you spent it?"

The class snickered and Margaret looked down, embarrassed. "No, ma'am."

"I'm glad to hear that," Ms. Peazle continued, looking at Margaret over granny glasses. "And I'm sure in the next ten minutes you'll be able to read your essay to the class and prove to us all that you weren't just daydreaming. Am I right?"

"I hope so, ma'am," Margaret mumbled. She looked around the room. It seemed everyone in 6-1 knew each other from the previous year. On the first day, a lot of kids asked her about Maizon, but after that no one said much to her. Things had changed since Maizon left. Without her, a lot of the fun had gone out of sitting on the stoop with Ms. Dell, Hattie, and Li'l Jay. Maybe she could write about that. No, Margaret thought, looking down at the blank piece of paper in front of her. It was too much to tell. She'd never get finished and Ms. Peazle would scold her — making her feel too dumb to be in 6-1. Margaret chewed her eraser and stared out the window again. There had to be something she could write about quickly.

"Margaret Tory!" Ms. Peazle warned. "Am I going to have to change your seat?"

"Ma'am? I was just . . ."

"I think I'm going to have to move you away from that window unless you can prove to me that you can sit there without being distracted."

"I can, Ms. Peazle. It helps me write."

"Then I take it you should be ready to read your essay in" — Ms. Peazle looked at her watch — "the next seven minutes."

Margaret started writing frantically. When Ms. Peazle called her to the front of the room, her sheet of notebook paper shook in her hand. She pulled nervously at the hem of the maroon dress she and Maizon had picked out for school and tried not to look out at the twenty-six pairs of eyes she knew were on her.

"Last summer was the worst summer of my life. First my father died and then my best friend went away to a private boarding school. I didn't go anywhere except Manhattan. But that wasn't any fun because I was taking Maizon to the train. I hope next summer is a lot better."

She finished reading and walked silently back to her desk and tried to concentrate on not looking out the window. Instead, she rested her eyes on the half-written page. Margaret knew she could write better than that, but Ms. Peazle had rushed her. Anyway, she thought, that *is* what happened last summer.

"I'd like to see you after class, Margaret."

"Yes, ma'am," Margaret said softly. *This is the end,* she thought. One week in the smartest class and it's over. Maizon was smart enough to go to a better *school* and I can't even keep up in this class. Margaret sighed and tried not to stare out the window for the rest of the day.

When the three o'clock bell rang, she waited uneasily in her seat while Ms. Peazle led the rest of the class out to the school yard. Margaret heard the excited screams and laughter as everyone poured outside.

The empty classroom was quiet. She looked around at the desks. Many had words carved into them. They reminded her of the names she and Maizon had carved into the tar last summer. They were faded and illegible now.

Ms. Peazle came in and sat at the desk next to Margaret's. "Margaret," she said slowly, pausing for a moment to remove her glasses and rub her eyes tiredly. "I'm sorry to hear about your father . . ."

"That's okay." Margaret fidgeted.

"No, Margaret, it's not okay," Ms. Peazle continued, "not if it's going to affect your schoolwork."

"I can do better, Ms. Peazle, I really can!" Margaret looked up pleadingly. She was surprised at herself for wanting so badly to stay in Ms. Peazle's class.

"I know you can, Margaret. That's why I'm going to ask you to do this. For homework tonight . . ."

Margaret started to say that none of the other students had been assigned homework. She decided not to, though.

"I want you to write about your summer," Ms. Peazle continued. "I want it to express all of your feelings about your friend Maizon going away. Or it could be about your father's death and how you felt then. It doesn't matter what you write, a poem, an essay, a short story. Just so long as it expresses how you felt this summer. Is that understood?"

"Yes, ma'am." Margaret looked up at Ms. Peazle. "It's understood."

Ms. Peazle smiled. Without her glasses, Margaret thought, she wasn't that mean-looking.

"Good, then I'll see you bright and early tomorrow with something wonderful to read to the class."

Margaret slid out of the chair and walked toward the door.

"That's a very pretty dress, Margaret," Ms. Peazle said.

Margaret turned and started to tell her that Maizon was wearing the same one in Connecticut, but changed her mind. What did Ms. Peazle know about best friends who were almost cousins, anyway?

"Thanks, ma'am," she said instead, and ducked out of the classroom. All of a sudden, she had a wonderful idea!

The next morning Ms. Peazle tapped her ruler against the desk to quiet the class. "Margaret," she asked when the room was silent. "Do you have something you want to share with us today?"

Margaret nodded and Ms. Peazle beckoned her to the front of the room.

"This," Margaret said, handing Ms. Peazle the sheet of looseleaf paper. It had taken her most of the evening to finish the assignment.

Ms. Peazle looked it over and handed it back to her.

"We're ready to listen," she said, smiling.

Margaret looked out over the class and felt her stomach slide up to her throat. She swallowed and counted to ten. Though the day was cool, she found herself sweating. Margaret couldn't remember when she had been this afraid.

"My pen doesn't write anymore," she began reading.

"I can't hear," someone called out.

"My pen doesn't write anymore," Margaret repeated. In the back of the room, someone exaggerated a sigh. The class chuckled. Margaret ignored them and continued to read.

"It stumbles and trembles in my hand.
If my dad were here — he would understand.
Best of all — It'd be last summer again.

But they've turned off the fire hydrants
Locked green leaves away.
Sprinkled ashes on you
and sent you on your way.

I wouldn't mind the early autumn
if you came home today
I'd tell you how much I miss you
and know I'd be okay.

Mama isn't laughing now
She works hard and she cries
she wonders when true laughter
will relieve her of her sighs
And even when she's smiling
Her eyes don't smile along
her face is growing older

She doesn't seem as strong.
I worry cause I love her
Ms. Dell says, 'where there is love,
there is a way.'

It's funny how we never know
exactly how our life will go
It's funny how a dream can fade
With the break of day.

I'm not sure where you are now
though I see you in my dreams
Ms. Dell says the things we see
are not always as they seem.

So often I'm uncertain
if you have found a new home
and when I am uncertain
I usually write a poem.

Time can't erase the memory
and time can't bring you home
Last summer was a part of me
and now a part is gone."

The class stared at her blankly, silent. Margaret lowered her head and made her way back to her seat.

"Could you leave that assignment on my desk, Margaret?" Ms. Peazle asked. There was a small smile playing at the corners of her mouth.

"Yes, ma'am," Margaret said. Why didn't anyone say anything?

"Now, if everyone will open their history books to page two seventy-five, we'll continue with our lesson on the Civil War."

Margaret wondered what she had expected the class to do. Applaud? She missed Maizon more than she had in a long time. *She would know what I'm feeling,* Margaret thought. And if she didn't, she'd make believe she did.

Margaret snuck a look out the window. The day looked cold and still. *She'd tell me it's only a feeling poets get and that Nikki Giovanni feels this way all of the time.* When she turned back, there was a small piece of paper on her desk.

"I liked your poem, Margaret," the note read. There was no name.

Margaret looked around but no one looked as though they had slipped a note on her desk. She smiled to herself and tucked the piece of paper into her notebook.

The final bell rang. As the class rushed out, Margaret was bumped against Ms. Peazle's desk.

"Did you get my note?" Ms. Peazle whispered. Margaret nodded and floated home.

Ms. Dell, Hattie, and Li'l Jay were sitting on the stoop when she got home.

"If it weren't so cold," she said, squeezing in beside Hattie's spreading hips, "it would be like old times."

"Except for Maizon," Hattie said, cutting her eyes toward her mother.

"Hush, Hattie," Ms. Dell said. She shivered and pulled Li'l Jay closer to her. For a moment, Margaret thought she looked old.

"It's just this cold spell we're having," Ms. Dell said. "Ages a person. Makes them look older than they are."

Margaret smiled. "Reading minds is worse than eavesdropping, Ms. Dell."

"Try being her daughter for nineteen years," Hattie said.

"Hattie," Margaret said, moving closer to her for warmth. "How come you never liked Maizon?"

"No one said I never liked her."

"No one had to," Ms. Dell butted in.

"She was just too much ahead of everyone. At least she thought she was."

"But she was, Hattie. She was the smartest person at P.S. 102. Imagine being the smartest person."

"But she didn't have any common sense, Margaret. And when God gives a person that much brain, he's bound to leave out something else."

"Like what?"

Ms. Dell leaned over Li'l Jay's head and whispered loudly, "Like the truth."

She and Hattie laughed but Margaret couldn't see the humor. It wasn't like either of them to say something wrong about a person.

"She told the truth . . ." Margaret said weakly.

Ms. Dell and Hattie exchanged looks.

"How was school?" Hattie asked too brightly.

"Boring," Margaret said. She would tuck what they said away until she could figure it out.

"That's the only word you know since Maizon left. Seems there's gotta be somethin' else going on that's not so boring all the time," Ms. Dell said.

"Well, it's sure not school. I read a poem to that stupid class and no one but Ms. Peazle liked it." She sighed and rested her chin on her hand.

"That's the chance you gotta take with poetry," Ms. Dell said. "Either everybody likes it or everybody hates it, but you hardly ever know 'cause nobody says a word. Too afraid to offend you or, worse yet, make you feel good."

Margaret looked from Ms. Dell to Hattie then back to Ms. Dell again.

"How come you know so much about poetry?"

"You're not the first li'l black girl who wanted to be a poet."

"And you can bet your dress you won't be the last," Hattie concluded.

"You wanted to be a poet, Hattie??!!"

"Still do. Still make up poems in my head. Never write them down, though. The paper just yellows and clutters useful places. So this is where I keep it all now," she said, pointing to her head.

"A poem can't exist inside your head. You forget it," Margaret said doubtfully.

"Poems don't exist, Miss Know-It-All. Poems live! In your head is where a poem is born, isn't it?"

Margaret nodded and Hattie continued. "Well, my poetry chooses to live there!"

"Then recite one for me, please." Margaret folded her arms across her chest the way she had seen Ms. Dell do so many times.

"Some poems aren't meant to be heard, smarty-pants."

"Aw, Hattie," Ms. Dell interrupted, "let Margaret be the judge of that."

"All right. All right." Hattie's voice dropped to a whisper. "Brooklyn-bound robin redbreast followed me from down home / Brooklyn-bound robin, you're a long way from your own / So fly among the pigeons and circle the sky with your song."

They were quiet. Ms. Dell rocked Li'l Jay to sleep in her arms. Hattie looked somberly over the block in silence and Margaret thought of how much Hattie's poem made her think of Maizon. What was she doing now that the sun was almost down? she wondered. Had she found a new best friend?

288

"Maybe," she said after a long time. "Maybe it wasn't that the class didn't like my poem. Maybe it was like your poem, Hattie. You just have to sit quietly and think about all the things it makes you think about after you hear it. You have to let . . . let it sink in!"

"You have to feel it, Margaret," Hattie said softly, draping her arm over Margaret's shoulder.

"Yeah. Just like I felt when I wrote my poem, or you felt when you found a place for that one in your head!"

"Margaret," Ms. Dell said, "you gettin' too smart for us ol' ladies."

Margaret leaned against Hattie and listened to the fading sounds of construction. Soon the building on Palmetto Street would be finished. She closed her eyes and visions of last summer came into her head. She saw herself running down Madison Street arm in arm with Maizon. They were laughing. Then the picture faded into a new one. She and Maizon were sitting by the tree watching Li'l Jay take his first steps. He stumbled and fell into Maizon's arms. Now it all seemed like such a long time ago.

When she opened her eyes again, the moon was inching out from behind a cloud. It was barely visible in the late afternoon. The sky had turned a wintry blue and the streetlights flickered on. Margaret yawned, her head heavy all of a sudden from the long day.

"Looks like your mother's workin' late again. Bless that woman's heart. Seems she's workin' nonstop since your daddy passed."

"She's taking drawing classes. She wants to be an architect. Maybe she'll make a lot of money."

"Architects don't make a lot of money," Hattie said. "And anyway, you shouldn't be worrying your head over money."

"She has a gift," Ms. Dell said. "All of you Torys have gifts. You with your writing, your mama with her drawings, and remember the things your daddy did with wood. Oh, that man was something else!"

"What's Li'l Jay's going to be?"

Ms. Dell stood up and pressed Li'l Jay's face to her cheek.

"Time's gonna tell us, Margaret. Now, come inside and do your home-work while I fix you something to eat. No use sitting out in the cold."

Margaret rose and followed them inside.

"You hear anything from Maizon yet?" Hattie asked.

Margaret shook her head. If only Maizon were running up the block!

"I wrote her two letters and she hasn't written me one. Maybe she knows we're not really best friends anymore." Margaret sighed. She had been right in thinking she and Maizon were only old friends now, not the friends they used to be. "Still, I wish I knew how she was doing," she said, turning away so Hattie wouldn't see the tears in her eyes.

"We all do, honey," Hattie said, taking Margaret's hand. "We all do."

Responding

Think About the Selection

1. Give examples of ways Margaret and Maizon plan to keep in touch. What does their planning tell you about their friendship?

2. Why did Margaret think that she and Maizon were "old friends" now?

3. Find examples in the selection of things that made Ms. Peazle think Margaret was daydreaming.

4. Do you think Ms. Peazle should have given Margaret a homework assignment? Why or why not?

5. Which word best describes Margaret's experience for you: *desolate, distracting, empty,* or some other word? Explain why.

6. Ms. Dell told Margaret that "all of you Torys have gifts." What interests of yours could be seen as gifts?

7. **Connecting/Comparing** Compare Margaret's reading of her poem and her class's reaction to it with Billy's experience with the towns-people of Tahlequah in *Where the Red Fern Grows*. How were their situations alike and how were they different?

Creating

Write a Screenplay for a Scene

Write the script for a movie based on this story. Choose a scene from the story and rewrite it as a film script.

Tips

- Remember to note each character's name before his or her lines.
- Write your stage directions in parentheses — instructions telling the actors how to move, say their lines, and use props.

Art

Make a Collage

When you read a poem, you may see a picture of something in your mind. Make a collage about Margaret's poem, "My pen doesn't write anymore." Cut out pictures from magazines and add words or phrases from the poem to the images you selected.

Listening and Speaking

Listen to Poetry

Take turns reading Margaret's poem aloud with a partner. Then discuss the following questions with your partner. What are some of the rhyming words in this poem? Does this poem have regular, repeated rhythm, or is its rhythm irregular like speech?

Tips

- **What is the subject of the poem?**
- **Is the language colorful? direct? emotional?**
- **Is the speaker's manner and tone light? serious? friendly? excited?**

Internet

Post a Review

Write a review of *Last Summer with Maizon*. Post your review at Education Place.

www.eduplace.com/kids

Poetry Link

Skill: How to Read an Interview

Before you read . . .

❶ **Read** the title and introduction.

❷ **Identify** questions and answers.

❸ **Skim** the questions first to get a sense of what topics the interview will cover.

While you read . . .

❶ **Ask** yourself, "What am I learning about the person being interviewed?"

❷ **Reread** any answers you don't understand.

Poetic Power

by Ariel Eason, Julia Peters-Axtell, and Rebecca Owen

Read this interview from *New Moon* magazine. Then read on to discover a poem by Nikki Giovanni.

Dear Readers: Nikki Giovanni is a famous poet who has also written three books for kids: *Grand Mothers, Shimmy Shimmy Shimmy Like My Sister Kate,* and *The Genie in the Jar.* She is a professor of English at Virginia Tech in Blacksburg, Virginia. *New Moon* editors Ariel, Julia, and Rebecca talked with Nikki about her books and her love for poetry.

NEW MOON: When did you decide to become a poet?
NIKKI GIOVANNI: I was really kind of old. I was in college. I thought, "Well, wouldn't it be nice to be a poet?"

NM: What does it mean to be a poet?
NG: I have to observe and look at people and other things and the world in which we live — the floor, and space, and under the sea — because poets are great for looking at everything.

NM: Is being a poet fun?
NG: Yes it is! I enjoy it, and I think that everybody should write some poetry some time because it really makes you feel good about yourself.

NM: Did you read a lot of poetry when you were growing up?

NG: I read a lot of everything — poetry, stories, novels, and a lot of history, which I really love. Some plays — not many plays because I lived in a small town, and we didn't have a theater group. I never got to see plays until I was in high school. The only way that I could see a play was to read it.

NM: What do you write about?

NG: I mostly write about people because they fascinate me. I think they are interesting. We're an interesting species because we're illogical.

NM: How do you get ideas to write poems?

NG: I do a lot of reading. The two most important words for young writers are: "Why not?" You need to ask yourself, "Could this happen? Why not?" And then you begin to develop a story or an idea around the why not. You have to be curious. I am always asking myself, "Why not?"

NM: What do you think is easier? Speaking or writing your feelings?

NG: It's about the same thing, isn't it? Isn't writing expressing feelings with words? I will tell you that you can write because if you can think it and you can say it, then you can write it.

Nikki Giovanni at the festival "New York celebrates 30 years of Nikki Giovanni," May 1999.

NM: **Is there a certain place where you like to write?**

NG: I like my own den. I'm comfortable there. I've been writing on this same table for 26 years, and I have a rocking chair I've been using for 26 years, too. I sit there, and I am very comfortable.

NM: **What's your most recent book?**

NG: My most recent book is *Shimmy Shimmy Shimmy Like My Sister Kate*. It's about the Harlem Renaissance, for the young reader. (During the 1920s and `30s, wonderful books, poems, music, and art came from African-American writers, musicians, and artists who lived in and described the Harlem district of New York City. It was a time when African-Americans renewed pride in their heritage.)

NM: **Why did you write about the Harlem Renaissance?**

NG: It's a most fascinating period, I think. The Harlem Renaissance is very important. I couldn't imagine that people would grow up not realizing how much it has impacted their lives. I don't know what kind of music that kids listen to now, but we listened to rock and roll and that came right out of rhythm and blues of the Harlem Renaissance period. A lot of exciting changes came from this period, and I want people to know them.

NM: **Which book or poem is your favorite?**

NG: That would be like asking me which is my favorite dog, and I have four. I like all of my poems.

Nikki Giovanni receives an honorary degree of Doctor of Humane Letters from Indiana University Northwest, Gary, Indiana, 1991.

A Poem

by Nikki Giovanni

for langston hughes

diamonds are mined . . . oil is discovered
gold is found . . . but thoughts are uncovered

wool is sheared . . . silk is spun
weaving is hard . . . but words are fun

highways span . . . bridges connect
country roads ramble . . . but i suspect

    if i took a rainbow ride
    i could be there by your side

metaphor has its point of view
allusion and illusion . . . too

meter . . . verse . . . classical . . . free
poems are what you do to me

let's look at this one more time
since i've put this rap to rhyme

    when i take my rainbow ride
    you'll be right there at my side

hey bop hey bop hey re re bop

Winold Reiss.
Langston Hughes. c. 1920.
The National Gallery.

Background and Vocabulary

The Challenge

Read to find
the meanings
of these words.

e • Glossary

attention
awkward
conversation
encourage
notice
managed

Attention, Please!

What do you do when you want someone to **notice** you? In "The Challenge" you will read about how one boy tries to get the **attention** of the new girl in his class.

Friends sometimes **encourage** each other to show off. It might feel **awkward** to do this stunt by yourself, but with his friend, this boy feels more at ease.

Have you ever had a difficult time starting a **conversation** with someone? By doing a trick with a basketball, one boy gets the other's attention.

Knowing the answer to the question, this girl **managed** to get her teacher's attention. In what other ways can students get attention in school?

299

Meet the Author
Gary Soto

Gary Soto grew up in a Mexican-American community in Fresno, California. His family picked grapes and oranges and worked in factories. "I don't think I had any literary aspirations when I was a kid," says Soto. "We didn't have books . . . so my wanting to write poetry was kind of a fluke." It wasn't until he picked up a book of poetry in college that he decided to try writing. Gary Soto's many books include *Baseball in April and Other Stories*, *Neighborhood Odes*, and *Off and Running*.

Meet the Illustrator
David Diaz

"One day I realized that everything around me in my room — the chair, the door, the window — all started out as drawings at some point," remembers David Diaz. Building a skyscraper or a bridge out of popsicle sticks soon became one of Diaz's favorite homework assignments. As an adult, Diaz still likes to have fun with art by trying different ways to make pictures. His advice to young artists: "Experiment. Find something you love. You may think you want to be an artist but you might end up being a photographer or a website designer."

To discover more about Gary Soto and David Diaz, visit Education Place. **www.eduplace.com/kids**

LOCAL NEWS

by Gary Soto

The Challenge

by Gary Soto
Selection illustrated by David Diaz

Strategy Focus

José's bragging gets the attention of Estela, the new girl, but not in the way he expects. As you read, think of **questions** about the story to discuss with your classmates.

FOR THREE WEEKS José tried to get the attention of Estela, the new girl at his middle school. She's cute, he said to himself when he first saw her in the cafeteria, unloading her lunch of two sandwiches, potato chips, a piece of cake wrapped in waxed paper, and boxed juice from a brown paper bag. "Man, can she grub!"

On the way home from school he walked through the alleys of his town, Fresno, kicking cans. He was lost in a dream, trying to figure out a way to make Estela notice him. He thought of tripping in front of her while she was leaving her math class, but he had already tried that with a girl in sixth grade. All he did was rip his pants and bruise his knee, which kept him from playing in the championship soccer game. And that girl had just stepped over him as he lay on the ground, the shame of rejection reddening his face.

He thought of going up to Estela and saying, in his best James Bond voice, "Camacho. José Camacho, at your service." He imagined she would say, "Right-o," and together they would go off and talk in code.

He even tried doing his homework. Estela was in his history class, and so he knew she was as bright as a flashlight shining in your face. While they were studying Egypt, José amazed the teacher, Mrs. Flores, when he scored twenty out of twenty on a quiz — and then eighteen out of twenty when she retested him the same day because she thought that he had cheated.

"Mrs. Flores, I studied hard — ¡de veras! You can call my mom," he argued, his feelings hurt. And he *had* studied, so much that his mother had asked, "¿Qué pasó? What's wrong?"

"I'm going to start studying," he'd answered.

His mother bought him a lamp because she didn't want him to strain his eyes. She even fixed him hot chocolate and watched her son learn about the Egyptian god Osiris, about papyrus and mummification. The mummies had scared her so much that she had heated up a second cup of chocolate to soothe herself.

But when the quizzes had been returned and José bragged, "Another A-plus," Estela didn't turn her head and ask, "Who's that brilliant boy?" She just stuffed her quiz into her backpack and left the classroom, leaving José behind to retake the test.

One weekend he had wiped out while riding his bike, popping up over curbs with his eyes closed. He somersaulted over his handlebars and saw a flash of shooting stars as he felt the slap of his skin against the asphalt. Blood rushed from his nostrils like twin rivers. He bicycled home, his blood-darkened shirt pressed to his nose. When he examined his face in the mirror, he saw that he had a scrape on his chin, and he liked that. He thought Estela might pity him. In history class she would cry, "Oh, what happened?" and then he would talk nonsense about a fight with three guys.

But Estela had been absent the Monday and Tuesday after his mishap. By the time she returned on Wednesday his chin had nearly healed.

José figured out another way to get to know her. He had noticed the grimy, sweat-blackened handle of a racket poking out of her backpack. He snapped his fingers and said to himself, "Racquetball. I'll challenge her to a game."

He approached her during lunch. She was reading from her science book and biting into her second sandwich, which was thick with slabs of meat, cheese, and a blood-red tomato. "Hi," José said, sitting across the table from her. "How do you like our school?"

Estela swallowed, cleared her throat, drank from her milk carton until it collapsed, and said, "It's OK. But the hot water doesn't work in the girls' showers."

"It doesn't work in ours either," he remarked. Trying to push the conversation along, he continued, "Where are you from?"

"San Diego," she said. She took another monstrous bite of her sandwich, which amazed José and made him think of his father, a carpenter, who could eat more than anyone José knew.

José, eager to connect, took a deep breath and said, "I see that you play racquetball. You wanna play a game?"

"Are you good?" Estela asked flatly. She picked up a slice of tomato that had slid out of her sandwich.

"Pretty good," he said without thinking as he slipped into a lie. "I won a couple of tournaments."

He watched as the tomato slice slithered down Estela's throat. She wiped her mouth and said, "Sure. How about after school on Friday."

"That's tomorrow," José said.

"That's right. Today's Thursday and tomorrow's Friday." She flattened the empty milk carton with her fist, slapped her science book closed, and hurled the carton and her balled-up lunch bag at the plastic-lined garbage can. "What's your name?"

"Camacho. José Camacho."

"I'm Estela. My friends call me Stinger."

"Stinger?"

"Yeah, Stinger. I'll meet you at the courts at 3:45." She got up and headed toward the library.

After school José pedaled his bike over to his uncle Freddie's house. His uncle was sixteen, only three years older than José. It made José feel awkward when someone, usually a girl, asked, "Who's that hunk?" and he would have to answer, "My uncle."

"Freddie," José yelled, skidding to a stop in the driveway.

Freddie was in the garage lifting weights. He was dressed in sweats and a sweatshirt, the hem of his T-shirt sticking out in a fringe. He bench-pressed 180 pounds, then put the weight down and said, "Hey, dude."

"Freddie, I need to borrow your racquetball racket," José said.

Freddie rubbed his sweaty face on the sleeve of his sweatshirt. "I didn't know you played."

"I don't. I got a game tomorrow."

"But you don't know how to play."

José had been worrying about this on his bike ride over. He had told Estela that he had won tournaments.

"I'll learn," José said.

"In one day? Get serious."

"It's against a girl."

"So. She'll probably whip you twenty-one to *nada*."

"No way."

But José's mind twisted with worry. What if she did, he asked himself. What if she whipped him through and through. He recalled her crushing the milk carton with one blow of her fist. He recalled the sandwiches she downed at lunch. Still, he had never encountered a girl who was better than he was at sports, except for Dolores Ramirez, who could hit homers with the best of them.

Uncle Freddie pulled his racket from the garage wall. Then he explained to José how to grip the racket. He told him that the game was like handball, that the play was off the front, the ceiling, and the side walls. "Whatever you do, don't look behind you. The ball comes back — fast. You can get your *ojos* knocked out."

"Yeah, I got it," José said vaguely, feeling the weight of the racket in his hand. He liked how it felt when he pounded the sweet spot of the strings against his palm.

Freddie resumed lifting weights, and José biked home, swinging the racket as he rode.

That night after dinner José went outside and asked his father, "Dad, has a girl ever beaten you at anything?"

His father was watering the grass, his shirt off. His pale belly hung over his belt, just slightly, like a deflated ball.

"Only talking," he said. "They can outtalk a man any day of the week."

"No, in sports."

His father thought for a while and then said, "No, I don't think so."

His father's tone of voice didn't encourage José. So he took the racket and a tennis ball and began to practice against the side of the garage. The ball raced away like a rat. He retrieved it and tried again. Every time, he hit it either too softly or too hard, and he couldn't get the rhythm of a rally going.

"It's hard," he said to himself. But then he remembered that he was playing with a tennis ball, not a racquetball. He assumed that he would play better with a real ball.

The next day school was as dull as usual. He took a test in history and returned to his regular score of twelve out of twenty. Mrs. Flores was satisfied.

"I'll see you later," Estela said, hoisting her backpack onto one shoulder, the history quiz crumpled in her fist.

"OK, Estela," he said.

"Stinger," she corrected.

"Yeah, Stinger. 3:45."

José was beginning to wonder whether he really liked her. Now she seemed abrupt, not cute. She was starting to look like Dolores "Hit 'n' Spit" Ramirez — tough.

After school José walked slowly to the outdoor three-walled courts. They were empty, except for a gang of sparrows pecking at an old hamburger wrapper.

José practiced hitting the tennis ball against the wall. It was too confusing. The ball would hit the front wall, then ricochet off the side wall. He spent most of his time running after the ball or cursing himself for bragging that he had won tournaments.

Estela arrived, greeting José with a jerk of her chin and a "Hey, dude." She was dressed in white sweats. A pair of protective goggles dangled around her neck like a necklace, and she wore sweatbands on both wrists. She opened a can of balls and rolled one out into her palm, squeezing it so tightly that her forearm rippled with muscle. When she smacked the ball against the wall so hard that the echo hurt his ears, José realized that he was in trouble. He felt limp as a dead fish.

Estela hit the ball repeatedly. When she noticed that José was just standing there, his racket in one hand and a dog-slobbered tennis ball in the other, she asked, "Aren't you going to practice?"

"I forgot my balls at home," he said.

"Help yourself." She pointed with the racket toward the can.

José took a ball, squeezed it, and bounced it once. He was determined to give Estela a show. He bounced it again, swung with all his might, and hit it out of the court.

"Oops," he said. "I'll go get it, Stinger."

He found the ball in the gutter, splotched with mud that he wiped off on his pants. When he returned to the court Estela had peeled off her sweats and was working a pair of knee pads up her legs. José noticed that her legs were bigger than his, and they quivered like the flanks of a thoroughbred horse.

"You ready?" she asked, adjusting her goggles over her eyes. "I have to leave at five."

"Almost," he said. He took off his shirt, then put it back on when he realized how skinny his chest was. "Yeah, I'm ready. You go first."

Estela, sizing him up, said, "No, you go first."

José decided to accept the offer. He figured he needed all the help he could get. He bounced the ball and served it into the ground twice.

"You're out," she said, scooping the ball up onto her racket and walking briskly to the service box. José wanted to ask why, but he kept quiet. After all, he thought, I am the winner of several tournaments.

"Zero-zero," Estela said, then served the ball, which ricocheted off the front and side walls. José swung wildly and missed by at least a foot. Then he ran after the ball, which had rolled out of the court onto the grass. He returned it to Estela and said, "Nice, Estela."

"Stinger."

"Yeah, Stinger."

Estela called out, "One-nothing." She wound up again and sizzled the ball right at José's feet. He swung and hit his kneecap with the racket. The pain jolted him like a shock of electricity as he went down, holding his knee and grimacing. Estela chased the ball for him.

"Can you play?" she asked.

He nodded as he rose to his feet.

"Two-nothing," she said, again bouncing the ball off the front wall, this time slower so that José swung before the ball reached his racket. He swung again, the racket spinning like a whirlwind. The ball sailed slowly past him, and he had to chase it down again.

"I guess that's three to nothing, right?" José said lamely.

"Right." Estela lobbed the ball. As it came down, José swung hard. His racket slipped from his fingers and flew out of the court.

"Oops," he said. The racket was caught on the top of the chain-link fence surrounding the courts. For a moment José thought of pulling the racket down and running home. But he had to stick it out. Anyway, he thought, my backpack is at the court.

"Four-nothing," Estela called when she saw José running back to the court, his chest heaving. She served again, and José, closing his eyes, connected. The ball hit the wall, and for three seconds they had a rally going. But then Estela moved in and killed the ball with a low corner shot.

"Five-nothing," she said. "It's getting cold. Let me get my sweats back on."

She slipped into her sweats and threw off her sweatbands. José thought about asking to borrow the sweatbands because he had worked up a lather of sweat. But his pride kept him quiet.

Estela served again and again until the score was seventeen to nothing and José was ragged from running. He wished the game would end. He wished he would score just one point. He took off his shirt and said, "Hey, you're pretty good."

Estela served again, gently this time, and José managed to return the ball to the front wall. Estela didn't go after it, even though she was just a couple of feet from the ball. "Nice corner shot," she lied. "Your serve."

José served the ball and, hunching over with his racket poised, took crab steps to the left, waiting for the ball to bounce off the front wall. Instead he heard a thunderous smack and felt himself leap like a trout. The ball had hit him in the back, and it stung viciously. He ran off the court and threw himself on the grass, grimacing from the pain. It took him two minutes to recover, time enough for Estela to take a healthy swig from the water bottle in her sport bag. Finally, through his teeth, he muttered, "Good shot, Stinger."

"Sorry," Estela said. "You moved into my lane. Serve again."

José served and then cowered out of the way, his racket held to his face for protection. She fired the ball back, clean and low, and once again she was standing at the service line calling, "Service."

Uncle Freddie was right. He had lost twenty-one to *nada*. After a bone-jarring handshake and a pat on his aching back from Estela, he hobbled to his uncle's house, feeling miserable. Only three weeks ago he'd been hoping that Estela — Stinger — might like him. Now he hoped she would stay away from him.

Uncle Freddie was in the garage lifting weights. Without greeting him, José hung the racket back on the wall. Uncle Freddie lowered the weights, sat up, and asked, "So how did it go?"

José didn't feel like lying. He lifted his T-shirt and showed his uncle the big red mark the ball had raised on his back. "She's bad."

"It could have been your face," Freddie said as he wiped away sweat and lay back down on his bench. "Too bad."

José sat on a pile of bundled newspapers, hands in his lap. When his uncle finished his "reps," José got up slowly and peeled the weights down to sixty pounds. It was his turn to lift. He needed strength to mend his broken heart and for the slight chance that Stinger might come back, looking for another victory.

Responding

Think About the Selection

1. Give examples of how José tried to get Estela's attention. What might have been a better way? Explain.

2. Why do you think José imagined introducing himself like James Bond? Why do you think Estela introduced herself with the nickname "Stinger"?

3. Why do you think José exaggerated his racquetball experience? What have you exaggerated about yourself in order to impress someone?

4. What clues show that Estela probably knew José had never played racquetball before?

5. Do you think Estela will ask José for another racquetball game? Find clues in the story to support your answer.

6. Is the setting important to "The Challenge"? Explain why or why not.

7. **Connecting/Comparing** Compare the way José felt playing racquetball to the way Margaret felt reading her poem in front of the class in *Last Summer with Maizon*.

Describing

Write a Sportscast Script

Write the script of a sportscaster's coverage of the game between José and Estela.

Bonus Include a brief interview with each player after the game.

Tips

- While writing your script, try to imagine that you're calling the plays over a microphone.
- Include details that will let your readers picture the players in action.

314

Identify a Healthful Diet

Make a list of everything Estela eats for lunch on the day José talks to her in the cafeteria. Compare her lunch to the diet suggested in the food pyramid in your science book. What foods would Estela need to eat for breakfast and dinner to have a healthful diet?

Bonus Record everything on your school menu for the past two days. How does the menu compare to the food pyramid? How does it compare to Estela's lunch?

Have a Discussion

In a small group, have a discussion on this topic: What did José learn from his experience? How do you know he learned anything?

Tips

- Keep to the discussion topic.
- Speak clearly and listen carefully. Ask questions if something is unclear.
- Be polite, and don't interrupt. Respect the opinions of others.
- Be sure to take an active part in the discussion.

Internet

Send an E-Postcard

If you want to tell a friend what you've been reading in this theme, send an e-postcard. You'll find one at Education Place.

www.eduplace.com/kids

How to be a GOOD SPORT

People who are good sports add to everyone's fun — including their own. "Last one up the stairs is a rotten egg," Brenden yelled from the third step to his brother. Up the steps the two boys raced. Conor was just about to take the lead when Brenden stuck his foot out and tripped him. Brenden raced ahead and declared himself the winner. Was Brenden the winner? Of course not. He cheated. He figured if he couldn't win, he wanted to be sure no one else did. He was a poor sport.

Brenden isn't the only one showing off his poor sportsmanship. Occasionally, professional athletes seem to get away with bad sportsmanship. That's probably because professional sports is a lot more than a game. It is a *business*. It's all about having winning teams that make money. As long as the players keep scoring those points and basically following the rules of the game, they stay in the spotlight.

Sportsmanship matters

Basketball, baseball, football, tennis — all sports — are games. They're meant to be played. And you know the most important thing about any game: It's supposed to be fun.

When people follow the rules and play fair, the game stays fun. Being around a poor sport is no fun for anyone.

Dr. Darrell Burnett studies kids and sports. He is a clinical and sport psychologist in Laguna Niguel, California. He says participating in sports can make a big difference in your life. Staying involved with sports can make you more likely to graduate from school and less likely to get into trouble, he says.

Playing sports does other good stuff, too, says Dr. Burnett. "It gives you an instant sense of belonging."

It's the uniform, the feeling of being part of the team, the working together toward a common goal. And, when you're involved in sports, "You can watch yourself grow, see that you're getting better at things," he adds. This makes you feel good about yourself.

Dr. Burnett discovered that the number-one reason kids quit sports is that it stops being fun. It is possible to work really hard at perfecting your skills and still have fun. But it stops being fun when coaches, parents, or teammates encourage "winning at all cost" or put down players who aren't so good.

Being a good sport is not only more fun for everyone, it's better for you, too. When good sports win, they know they've won fair and square and haven't hurt anyone along the way.

What makes a good sport?

We already know that a good sport plays by the rules. Sara, a sixth-grade tennis and basketball player, says it's also "very important to be a good loser. I really hate to lose, but when I do, I want to do it in style." She says she's seen people throw their rackets when they lose and really "rub it in" when they win. She described "losing with style" as shaking her opponent's hand and "being nice about it, even though you lost. That's what I want her to do when I win."

That's good sportsmanship. Here are some other ways to be a good sport:

★ Cheer on your teammates and help them learn better skills.

★ Don't participate in trash talking.

★ Play fair.

★ Don't resort to dirty tricks to win.

★ Practice good teamwork.

★ Don't look for arguments.

★ Win *and* lose with style.

★ Don't gloat after a win.

★ Congratulate the opposing team.

★ Remember that each player is a person with feelings.

Some teams end every game with high-fives or handshakes. Sadly, other teams don't do this anymore because of fights that have broken out. Dr. Burnett still thinks taking the time to thank the other team is important. "After all, if that other team wasn't there, you wouldn't be playing. If they didn't play their best, you wouldn't have had a challenge."

Are you a good sport? Take Action!

1 The umpire calls an out, and you know you were solidly on second base when Jason tagged you. You:

a. argue with the umpire.

b. make your point, but do it politely: "I'm sure I was safe."

c. do nothing.

2 Your team just skunked the Muskrats. You say:

a. "Too bad, ya losers!"

b. "I'm sure glad we won."

c. "Good game."

3 You know you're the best player on your basketball team, so you:

a. remind everyone else how much they need you.

b. pretty much hog the ball, but make sure a couple of other players get a chance now and then.

c. share the ball and encourage your teammates so the team as a whole can improve.

4 You're playing volleyball. One of your teammates shouts out, "Mine!" She then misses the ball, causing you to lose the game. You:

a. call her an idiot and accuse her of losing the game.

b. glare at her, but keep your thoughts to yourself.

c. tell her it could happen to anyone.

5 You're the player who missed the ball in the last question. You:

a. blame the "idiot on the other team who didn't hit the ball right."

b. are embarrassed so you don't say anything.

c. apologize to your team after the game.

6 You're at bat, and someone on the sidelines is taunting you, saying, "Hey, you! You couldn't hit the broad side of a barn." You respond by:

a. yelling something back.

b. getting distracted and swinging wildly.

c. staying cool and trying to focus.

HOW DID YOU DO, SPORT?

Mostly C's? Congratulations! You're the kind of good sport that makes a team work.

Mostly B's? You're not a bad sport, but your sportsmanship could use a little fine-tuning.

Mostly A's? You're out of the running for the sportsmanship award.

Background and Vocabulary

Turtle PATROL

The View from Saturday

E. L. KONIGSBURG

Read to find the meanings of these words.

e ● Glossary

commute

hover

permitted

resettling

volunteers

The characters in *The View from Saturday* spend a lot of time observing loggerhead turtles. Find out what makes these turtles' lives so interesting!

After hatching, baby loggerhead turtles will live in the Sargasso Sea, fifty miles off the eastern coast of Florida. The turtles spend time **resettling** into their new surroundings. Later the turtles will **commute** up and down the Atlantic Ocean for many years. Only the females will return to their native beaches to lay eggs.

To track the turtles' movements, researchers attach satellite transmitters on the backs of grown loggerhead turtles. The transmitters will track them for most of their lives.

Turtle patrols made up of **permitted volunteers** also study loggerhead turtle nests. Photographers may **hover** nearby but are careful to stay out of the way. No one else is allowed near the fragile nests.

Two turtles wearing satellite transmitters are released on a beach.

Researchers look into a loggerhead turtle nest.

Hatchlings are attracted by a researcher's flashlight. The turtles make their way to the water safely after the light is turned off.

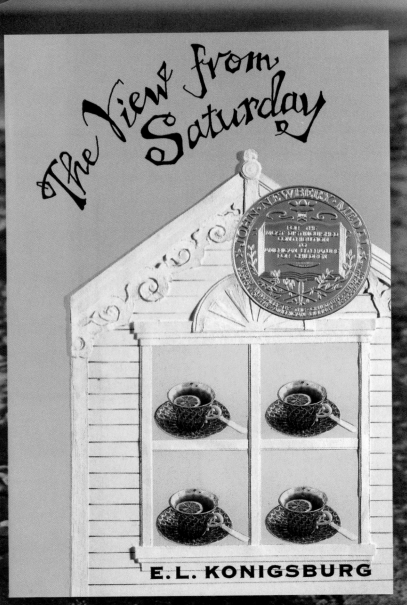

The View from Saturday

E. L. KONIGSBURG

Classmates Nadia, Ethan, and Noah share something in common: Nadia's Grandpa Izzy married Ethan's grandmother, Margaret. Noah was the best man at their wedding. Nadia and her father are staying in Florida after her parents' divorce, and she feels uncomfortable around Margaret.

Margaret was in charge of fifteen permitted volunteers. That meant that if she could not do the turtle patrol, one of them could. Permitted volunteers were licensed to move a nest or dig out a nest after the eggs had hatched, but they had to be supervised by her. All fifteen of Margaret's permitteds, plus friends and other interested parties showed up for the digging out. As soon as other beach walkers saw the hovering over the nest, they joined in. The audience was enthusiastic. They ooohed and aaahed, and at least once every three minutes, one way or another, someone said that nature was wonderful. Four people said, "Fascinating." Ethan did not oooh or aaah, and he did not say fascinating. He watched as patiently as a cameraman from *National Geographic*. My father hovered with the rest of them and said "fascinating" twice. Hovering had become his great recreational pastime.

Turtle patrols keep very close watch on all the nests on their stretches of beach, and they know when they are ripe for hatching, and sometimes they are lucky enough to be there when the turtle nests are emerging. That is what a hatching is called. When the turtles push their way out of the sand and start waddling toward the water's edge, they look like a bunch of wind-up toys escaped from a toy store. Watching a nest hatch is more interesting than digging one out after they've hatched, which is really only a matter of keeping inventory and making certain that everything that was or is living is cleared out. During old times, I had ooohed and aaahed at the digging out, but that evening it seemed as exciting as watching a red light change.

Like a proud parent, Margaret watched as Grandpa Izzy dug out the nest. Wearing a rubber glove on his hand, he reached down into the nest as far as his armpit. He removed:

96 empty egg shells
4 unhatched whole eggs
1 dead hatchling
3 turtles that were half-in/half-out of the shell but were dead. Those are called dead-pipped.
1 turtle that was half-in/half-out of the shell but was alive. Those are called live-pipped.
2 live ones

Margaret took notes, counted again, and said at last that it all added up.

Grandpa released the two live turtles onto the sand. Everyone lined up on either side of them as they made their way to the water's edge.

Turtles almost always hatch at night, and after they do, they head toward the light. Normally, the light they head for is the horizon on the ocean. However, if a hotel or high-rise along the ocean leaves its lights on, the turtles will head toward the brighter light of civilization and never make it to the ocean. They do not find food, and they die. Turtles are not trainable animals. Their brains are in the range of mini to micro.

When the two hatchlings reached the water, everyone along the parade route applauded, and my father said fascinating for the third time.

Back at the nest, Margaret examined the live-pipped. She announced, "I've decided to keep it." Judge, jury, and defending attorney.

Dad asked what would happen to it, and Margaret explained, "It'll take a few days to straighten itself out. We'll give it a safe, cool, dark place in the utility room and release it after sunset when it's ready."

Dad could have asked me. I did get an A on my report on Florida turtles.

When baby turtles come out of their shells, which are round — about the same size as a golf ball — they are squinched up into a round shape that fits inside the eggs. After they break through the shell, they spend three days down in the sand hole straightening themselves out. Sometimes they die before they make it out of the shell. Those are the dead-pipped. They are counted and discarded with the unhatched and the empties. A permitted person has to decide if the live-pipped are more alive than dead. If the decision is that they stand a good chance of surviving, they need care. They are lifted from the nest and

taken home and given shelter until they straighten themselves out, and then they are released onto the sand.

"We never carry them to the water," Margaret explained. "They must walk across their native sand. We think that something registers in their brains that kicks in twenty-five years later because they return to the beach where they were born to lay their eggs."

As Margaret was explaining this, I thought about my mother's returning to New York. Her birthday is September 12, and I wondered if her need to return to autumn in New York had anything to do with some switch that had been turned on when she emerged.

Back at the condo, Grandpa carried the bucket containing the live-pipped into the utility room, and we all sat down to have milk and cookies. Bubbe would have had homemade ruggelach. Margaret did not even know what ruggelach were until Grandpa Izzy took her to a kosher delicatessen and introduced her to them. She already knew about bagels because bagels have become popular even in places that never heard of them.

Margaret liked ruggelach, but I could tell she had no intention of learning how to make them. Grandpa Izzy, who had enjoyed ruggelach and bobka as much as anyone, had adjusted to store-bought cakes and cookies. I asked Ethan if he knew ruggelach. He did not.

Before the evening was over, Grandpa Izzy suggested that Dad bring me back early enough so that I could take the morning turtle walk with him and Margaret and Ethan.

Then Margaret said, "Allen, why don't you come, too? The exercise will be good for your foot." Dad had broken his foot on the day of their wedding, and it had not yet healed. Margaret believed that a bad mental attitude had slowed it down. Much to my surprise, Dad agreed. "What about Ginger?" I asked.

"No problem," Grandpa Izzy said. "Just keep her on a leash like old times."

I started to say that Ginger has grown to hate the leash, but once again a look on Dad's face told me something, and I said nothing. So it was from a look of Dad's and a sentence left unspoken that the sequel to the turtle habit got started.

Dad and I would leave his apartment early, meet Margaret, Grandpa, and

Ethan on the beach, and do our walk. Then Dad would return to Grandpa's and change into his business suit and leave for work. If time permitted, Dad would join us for breakfast. If not, the four of us would eat without him. We usually watched the rest of the *Today Show* before going for a swim.

Grandpa and Ethan got into an unofficial contest about how many laps they could do. I did not participate. I took a short swim, got out of the water, sat on the sidelines and read while Grandpa was teaching Ethan how to dive. He wanted to teach me, too, but I preferred not to.

One afternoon, we went to the movies. It was blazing hot and bright outside. We went into the movies where it was cool and dark, and then we came back out into the bright, hot sun. I felt as if I had sliced my afternoon into thirds, like a ribbon sandwich. Ethan, who never said much, had a lot to say about the camera angles and background music and described the star's performance as subtle. Never before in all my life had I heard a boy use the word subtle.

Dad had tickets for *The Phantom of the Opera*. This was the real Broadway show except that it was the road company. Not knowing that Ethan would be visiting, he had bought only four. As soon as he found out that Ethan would be in town, he started calling the ticket office to buy one more, but there were none to be had. He kindly volunteered to give up his ticket, but Grandpa Izzy and Margaret would not hear of it. Margaret said that she would stay home, and Grandpa Izzy said that he didn't want to go if she didn't.

I expected Ethan to do the polite thing and say that he would stay home. But he did not. Of course, Ethan usually said nothing. Even when it was appropriate to say something, Ethan could be counted on to say nothing. But on the subject of who should give up a ticket, Ethan was particularly silent, which was a subtle hint that he really wanted to go. At the very last minute, the problem was solved. One of Dad's clients mentioned that he had an extra ticket, and Dad bought it from him on the spot.

We met at the theater. Ethan had insisted upon taking the odd seat, saying that he would be fine. The odd seat was three rows in front of ours and closer to the center of the stage, but I do not think Ethan knew it at the time. I think he wanted to be alone, or, I should say, without us. At intermission, Ethan bought one of the ten-dollar souvenir programs, and after the show he thanked my father at least five times for getting him a ticket.

328

Dad was pleased with the way the evening had turned out. We went to a restaurant for ice-cream sundaes after the show. Ethan could hardly keep himself from thumbing through his ten-dollar program. His head must have stayed back at the theater long after we left, for when the waitress asked for his order, he said, "They must have more trapdoors on that stage than a magic act."

My father actually hummed as he looked over the menu, and then right after we placed our orders, he dropped his bombshell.

He asked Margaret if he could be listed on her permit. He would like to be able to substitute for her or Grandpa Izzy. His apartment house was not far from a beach, he explained, and he would transfer to someone's permit there after I went back north. Then he would like to train so that he could head up a turtle patrol. His goal was to get licensed.

"Like father, like son," he said, patting Grandpa Izzy on the back.

Margaret said, "We'll get the process started tomorrow." She must have been quite proud of her loggerheads. They got her my grandpa, and now they got her my dad.

I did not care. I had Ginger. I preferred animals with fur and some measure of intelligence. Ginger had grown sleek and muscular with our long turtle walks. She was more affectionate than ever. For example, when we got back to the apartment after *The Phantom of the Opera*, she greeted me as if I were the best friend she had ever had.

Inside me there was a lot of best friendship that no one but Ginger was using.

The day after Dad dropped his bombshell, he and Ethan, Margaret and Grandpa walked the beach together, a tight, three-generation foursome. They got ahead of Ginger and me, and I made no effort to catch up. Instead, I slowed down and walked at the water's edge so that I could kick at the waves as they rolled ashore. Ginger and I fell farther and farther behind the others. I saw Ethan stop to wait for Ginger and me to catch up. He did not call to us, and I pretended that I did not notice. Ethan waited until Ginger and I were midway between Grandpa, Dad, and Margaret — until we were half-pipped — and then I slowed down even more. Dad stopped, called to Ethan — not to me — to catch up. Ethan looked toward Ginger and me, then toward Grandpa and Margaret, waited another second or two, and then walked fast-forward until he caught up with Dad, Grandpa, and Margaret.

On Tuesday evening we watched a nest hatch. It was one of theirs. "Theirs" means that it was one that Margaret had moved. Like the one on the first night of our turtle walks, this one also contained a hundred and seven eggs, but this time all one hundred seven turtles emerged. "One hundred percent," Grandpa cried, and he hugged Margaret. Then he congratulated Ethan and Dad. Ginger and I stayed on the fringe because I had to hold Ginger on a short leash so that she would not start chasing the baby turtles. Grandpa did not hug or congratulate me.

We all returned to Grandpa's apartment, and Dad insisted on taking us all out to the ice-cream place to celebrate. Margaret ate a whole Peanut Buster Parfait without once mentioning cholesterol or calories.

I was sitting at poolside, reading. After doing our turtle walk, Margaret had gone to her volunteer duties at the garden club, and Grandpa Izzy had gone to his at the public library. Ethan and I were to let ourselves into their condo and start lunch. Ethan finished his laps and came out of the water. He sat at the deep end with his legs dangling into the water. I joined him at the pool's edge and put my feet into the water, too. I noticed that he had his key on an elastic cord around his ankle, and I also noticed that he had a key chain ornament that looked like a giant molar. As the daughter of a dental hygienist, I was interested in his key chain ornament and asked him where he got it.

"From your mother," he said.

I was not prepared for his answer. "My mother?" I asked in a voice that was too loud even for the out-of-doors.

"Well, yes. Your mother works for Dr. Gershom, doesn't she?"

"As a matter of fact, she does."

"She cleaned my teeth," he said.

There is not a worse feeling in this world than the feeling that someone knows something about you that he has known for almost a whole summer and has kept to himself. Even sharing what he knows about you with others is not as bad as knowing something and not telling you he knows. All you can think about is what he was really thinking the whole time he was speaking to you or walking the beach with you or swimming laps or playing fetch with your dog Ginger. I felt as if I had been spied on. I felt as if I had been stalked.

My heart was pumping gallons of blood up to my face. I could feel my neck throb. I controlled my voice so that it would not quiver. I said, "You should have told me that. You should have told me long before now. A person with good manners would have."

Ethan said, "I didn't think it was important."

I caught my breath and asked an intermediate question, "Does your mother also know Dr. Gershom?"

"He's our family dentist."

"And Margaret? Does she also know him?"

"I told you. He is our family dentist. Grandma Draper is part of our family. Before she moved to Florida, he was her dentist, too."

"Do not adopt that tone with me, Ethan Potter."

"What tone?"

"The tone of being patient and tolerant as if the questions I am asking are dumb questions. They are not dumb questions. I need to know what you know that I do not."

"I don't know what you don't know, so how can I know what I know and you don't?"

"Now, that is a dumb question. That is a really a very stupid question."

"I don't think so."

"Just tell me what you knew about my mother and me and my father before we met."

"Okay. I'll tell you what I knew about you if you'll tell me what you knew about me."

"All right. You go first."

"When your mother said that she was divorcing your father and wanted to move to New York where she grew up, my grandmother set things up with Dr. Gershom."

"Margaret set what things up?"

"The job interview."

"Mother's job interview with Dr. Gershom?"

"I thought that was what we were talking about — your mother's job with Dr. Gershom."

"We are talking about what you know that I do not."

"And I am trying to tell you. Your mother told Izzy and Grandma Draper that she wanted to move to New York State, so Grandma set up a job interview with Dr. Gershom."

I had stayed in Florida with Dad while Mother had gone north to find a job and a house. No one — not Dad, not Mother, not Grandpa Izzy — no one had told me that Margaret had set up Mother's job interview with Dr. Gershom. Margaret could have. The others should have. No one seemed to think that it would matter to me where I lived. No one seemed to think that it would matter to me whether I spent my life in New York or Florida or commuting between the two.

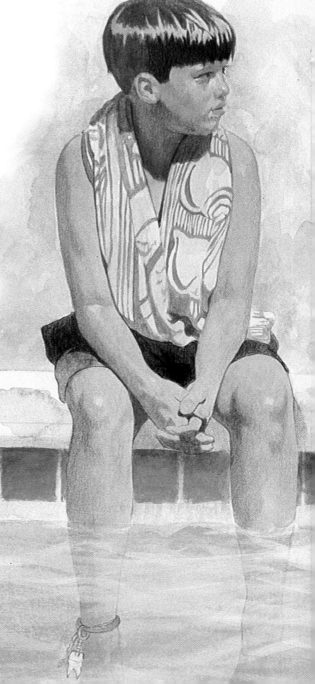

My throat was dry. I took a deep breath of the chlorine-saturated pool air and asked, "Is there anything else you know about me that I don't know?"

Ethan shrugged. "Only that Noah was best man at Grandma and Izzy's wedding."

"The whole world knows that. I am asking you one last time. What do you know about me that I do not know you know?"

"Not much. Only that Noah never said what nice guys your Dad and Izzy are."

"That is what you do not know. I was asking you what you do know." The pulse in my neck was about to break through the skin.

6 ft

"I do know that you're pretty mad right now, and I think now you ought to tell me what you knew about me."

"Nothing."

"My grandma told you nothing about me?"

"That is correct. She said nothing about you. She did not even tell me that you were coming even though she had several opportunities to do so."

Ethan then asked a strange question. "Did she tell you anything about Luke?"

"Luke what? Luke warm?"

"My brother Lucas, called Luke. Did she tell you anything about him?"

"She did not."

Ethan smiled, more to himself than to me. "Well," he said, "we Potters make an art of silence."

"Your grandmother is a Draper."

"See?" he said, grinning. "It comes to me from both sides of my family."

I did not speak to him for the rest of the day, and when he left the pool to return to the condo for lunch, I did not go with him. I thought that it would do him good to know how it felt to be the recipient rather than the giver of silence.

It was obvious that it was Margaret who had made possible my mother's leaving my father. Margaret Diamondstein, formerly Draper, helped my mother move to New York. She moved turtles from one nest to another. She moved Grandpa Izzy out of Century Village. And now, she was helping my father get permitted. By next turtle season, she will be helping him move to the beach. Margaret Diamondstein, formerly Draper, was an interfering person.

I did not need Margaret interfering with my life. I would have nothing more to do with her. That meant no more walking on the beach. That meant no more swimming and breakfast. That meant no more turtle walks.

Never again a turtle walk. Never.

I would stop and never tell her why.

Never.

I was still at the pool when Dad came to pick me up. I went back to the condo while they all went down to the beach to check on a nest. After I showered and dressed, I watched from the balcony, staying back by the wall where I could not be seen. Ginger whimpered to let me know that she wanted to be down there, but I thought that at the very least, my dog ought to stay by — and on — my side.

I wanted to leave my father's house. I wanted to go home, to autumn.

That evening as we were driving back, I asked my father if he knew that Margaret had set up Mother's job interview.

"I did."

"I think you could have told me."

"I didn't think it was important."

"Why does everyone think they know what is important to me? This was important. This *is* important. Do you think it is right that you should know and Ethan should know, and I should not?"

All he said was, "I didn't know that Ethan knew." I waited for Dad to say something more, to apologize, or simply tell me that I was right, but he did not. Like Ethan, my father has a strong taste for silence. Mother always said, "Your father is not a communicator." She made that statement more than once. Sometimes more than once a day. I was glad that I had made the decision not to go on any more turtle walks and not to communicate with anyone about my decision.

The following morning when Dad knocked on my door, I was still undressed. He called through the closed door, "Better hurry. We'll be late." I said nothing. He opened the door a crack and said, "Nadia? Nadia, are you all right?"

"I am not going," I said.

"What's the matter? Don't you feel well?"

"I feel fine. I have decided to stay here."

"Why?"

"It is not important."

Dad waited by the door, waited for me to explain, but I said nothing. I wanted silence to make him as miserable as it had made me. He hesitated, then came into my room, sat on the edge of the bed, and said nothing. He hovered. I struggled with silence until I could not stand it another second, so I said, "Did you know that I did a report on turtles last year?"

"Yes. I knew that."

"You never seemed very interested in turtles when I did my report."

"I guess I had other things on my mind."

The pulse in my ears was so strong, I hardly heard him. "I guess it took an invitation from Margaret to get you interested."

"Partly that and partly that I had the time."

"Your child custody time," I said. Dad let out a long sigh and looked so embarrassed that I almost did not say what I was about to say, but I did. "I have decided not to spend your child custody time on turtle walks with Margaret and her grandson. Not today. Not tomorrow. Not ever. If you want to take turtle walks, you go ahead and take turtle walks. You can get permitted without me. All you need are turtles and Margaret." I had not only broken my silence, I was almost screaming.

Dad looked at his watch. If there is one thing I really detest, it is having someone look at his watch as he is talking to me. It says to me that time spent elsewhere is more important than time spent talking to me. "I have an appointment at the office in an hour." He glanced at his watch again.

"I am sure it is an important appointment," I said.

"Yes, it is," he replied.

Dad was so preoccupied with time that he did not even notice the sarcasm in my voice.

"Let me call Margaret to let her know we won't be there."

"You can go," I said. "You go. I would not want you to miss a turtle walk for my sake. It might interfere with your getting permitted."

"There's no way I can make it up there and back in time for my appointment."

"Are you trying to tell me that I have kept you from your turtle walk?"

"Well, no. But, yes." He looked confused. "What I meant to say is that, yes, this conversation has kept me from going on a turtle walk, but no, that is not what I am trying to tell you. You know that if it had not been for your unwillingness to go, I would have."

He glanced at his watch again. "Let me call Margaret. Then we'll have time for breakfast, and we'll talk about it." He started out the door, turned back and said, "I won't tell her why you're not coming."

"Tell her. I do not care. She knows every other thing about me. Tell her," I said. "And do not count on me for breakfast. I do not want any." I turned my back to him and my face to the pillow.

The telephone rang in the middle of the morning. I let the recorder get it. It was Margaret, telling me that she would come pick me up if I would call. I did not. Instead, I took Ginger for a walk around the golf course. When we returned, I saw that there was a message on the machine. I played it. It was Grandpa Izzy asking me to please call. I erased the message. I sat out by the pool for a while and read, came back to the apartment for lunch, and that is when I ate the breakfast cereal that my dad had put out on the counter in the kitchen. He called while I was eating. I did not pick the phone up then either.

After lunch, I took Ginger for another walk, called the airline to see how much it would cost if I changed my ticket to go home early. Thirty-five dollars. I watched three talk shows on television. They were disgusting. The phone rang twice. It was my dad again, sounding worried that I was not answering. Then it was Margaret again, saying that she hoped we would come over since another nest was due to hatch.

I erased all the messages.

Not answering the phone but hearing what people on the other end were saying was a little bit like spying. I enjoyed it.

Dad walked into the apartment looking frazzled. He was looking very much like the unstrung self who had picked me up from the airport. "Where were you?" he demanded. "I have been calling every twenty minutes."

"I noticed," I said. When he asked me why I had not returned his calls, I said that I did not think they were important.

"I'm taking tomorrow off," he said.

"What are you going to do?" I asked. "Hover?"

"What do you mean?"

"Nothing." *Nothing* is a mean answer, but sometimes nothing works. Sometimes nothing else does.

"I thought we might go up to Disney World. You used to like Epcot."

"What will I do with Ginger?" I asked.

"Well, let me find out what accommodations they have for dogs . . ."

Just then the phone rang. Dad picked it up. I could tell by the way he was speaking that it was Grandpa Izzy asking if he would be coming over for the evening's turtle walk. When he hung up, Dad asked me if I would like to invite Ethan to come to Disney World with us. I could not believe he was asking me that question. I just stared at him.

"Well," he said, "he seemed to enjoy *The Phantom of the Opera* so much, I thought he might enjoy . . ." I continued to stare at my father and say nothing. He cleared his throat. "If you don't like the idea of asking Ethan, would you like to ask one of your friends from the old neighborhood?" He was practically pleading with me to ask someone. Without turtles my father did not know what to do with me.

Even though Disney World was only a two hours' drive from his apartment, Dad had decided that it might be more fun if we stayed overnight at one of Disney's theme hotels. He called and got us reservations, and we went to our rooms to pack our overnight bags.

That evening a northeaster hit the coast. The winds were thirty-five miles an hour with gales up to fifty. There was coastal flooding, which meant that the low lying highways and many side roads and ramps would be closed. That meant that the interstates that were normally bumper to bumper but moving would be bumber to bumper and not moving. Before we went to bed, Dad suggested that we avoid rush hour by starting out late in the morning instead of early.

The phone rang at midnight. Dad called in to me and said that I should pick up the phone. It was Grandpa Izzy.

"It's an emergency," he said, pleading. "Our hatchlings will be swept ashore by the winds. We have to harvest them early tomorrow before daylight. Before the birds get them. Margaret and I think you ought to drive up here now so that we can get an early start. Traffic will be impossible in the morning."

Grandpa was so sincere, so concerned about the turtles, so convinced that we would answer his 911 that it was obvious Dad had never told him that I had canceled all future turtle walks. I waited to see how Dad would turn him down. Dad did his best thing; he remained silent.

Grandpa said, "Nadia, are you there? Are you on the line, darling?"

"I am here, Grandpa . . ."

"You know what will happen if we don't gather them up. Can't you come?"

"Dad and I had plans . . ."

"What plans, darling? You don't want the baby turtles to be blown ashore and die, do you? These are babies, Nadia. They need help."

"Dad and I were going to Epcot . . ."

"Why do you want to go there to see Mr. Walter Disney's Version of the World when you can see Mother Nature's real thing?" I had to smile. Grandpa Izzy always called Disney World *Mr. Walter Disney's Version of the World*. Then he said, "Margaret and I need your help, Nadia. So do the turtles. Sometimes one species has to help another get settled." Grandpa was apologizing for not telling me about Margaret's meddling. I did not know what to say.

Dad finally spoke up. "Let Mother Nature worry about the turtles. They can take care of themselves."

But I knew that they could not. I said, "Let me talk to Dad, Grandpa. I will call you back."

After I hung up, I went into the living room. Dad was in his pajamas. Striped. I had never seen Dad sitting in the living room in striped pajamas. He said, "Don't worry about the turtles, Nadia."

I explained, "The turtles will be easy to spot — so out of place, washed up on shore. The birds will eat them."

"They couldn't possibly eat them all."

"Those that do not get eaten will be lost."

"But, surely, the tide will come back and carry the seaweed — and the turtles along with it — back out." He smiled again. "What comes ashore always washes back out. That's not a philosophical statement, Nadia. It's a fact."

"They will be lost at sea."

"Lost at sea? The sea is their home."

"They will be lost at sea," I repeated.

"Nadia," Dad said, "how can that happen?"

"You have to understand turtles to understand how that will happen."

"I don't think I do."

"I told Grandpa I would talk to you."

My father sat on the sofa, looking out of place in his striped pajamas. He nodded, a slow, thoughtful nod, and I knew that he would pay close attention, and I knew that I could explain it all.

"It all starts," I said, "the minute the new hatchlings scamper over the sand toward the light of the horizon. Once they reach the water, they begin a swimming frenzy. They do not eat. They just swim and swim until they reach the Sargasso Sea. That is when they stop, and that is when Mother Nature turns off the swimming-frenzy switch and turns on a graze-and-grow switch. For the next five to ten years, they will stay in the Sargasso Sea, feeding off the small sea animals that live in the floating mats of sargasso grass. Tonight when the wind blows that

seaweed ashore, there will be a lot of immature turtles in it — swept along with the sea grass they have called home."

I paused in my narrative. I focused hard on Dad, and he focused hard on me. "Are you with me?" I asked. My father nodded, so I continued. "Here is the tragic part. Even if the tide does wash them back into the water, they will not be able to get back home because once the swimming-frenzy switch is turned off, it is turned off forever. Turtles do not have an emergency power pack or a safety switch to turn it on. So, there they are, once again at the water's edge, but this time they are without a mechanism for swimming east. And that is why they will be lost at sea. They will want to graze. They will have an appetite, but they will not be where they can satisfy it, and they will not know how to get there because they cannot turn back their internal clock. They will not find home. They will not find food. They will starve and grow weak and be eaten."

My father did not once look at his watch or the clock on the table by the sofa. His listen-and-learn switch had been turned on, and his own internal clock was ticking. I studied my father, sitting on the pale gray living room sofa in his blue striped pajamas. The storm in our private lives had picked him up and put him out of place. Me, too. I, too, had been picked up from one place and set down in another. I, too, had been stranded. We both needed help resettling.

"When Grandpa says that we must harvest the turtles, he means that we must gather them up and save them in buckets. Then we take them to Marineland. When the seas calm down, they will be taken fifty miles offshore and placed in the Sargasso Sea."

Dad smiled. "They need a lift."

Ginger rubbed herself against my legs. I stroked her back. "Yes," I said, "they do."

Without another word, we returned to our rooms, Dad and I. We got dressed. When we ran out to the car, the rain was coming down in sheets, and the wind was blowing so hard that umbrellas were useless. I held the back door open for Ginger, and she hopped in. Dad and I got pretty wet just from that short run to the car, and Ginger sat on the back seat, panting and smelling like the great wet dog she was.

The rain battered the car, and the wipers danced back and forth, never really clearing the windshield. There were only a few cars on the road. We didn't pass any of them not only because it was dangerous to do so but also because we welcomed their red tail lights as a guide. Cars coming the other way made spray that splashed over the hood. Dad's hands were clenched on the steering wheel.

These northeasters dump rain in squalls that last for miles, and then they let up briefly. During one of the few lulls in the storm, Dad leaned back slightly and asked, "What do the turtles do after they've finished their five to ten years in the Sargasso Sea?"

"They go to the Azores and become bottom feeders for a few years."

"And then?"

"And then they grow up. When they are about twenty-five, they mate. The females come ashore and lay their eggs — on the same shore where they were born — and immediately return to the sea, not coming ashore again for

two or maybe three years when they are again ready to lay eggs. The males never return to shore."

Dad said, "You've left something out, Nadia. They are ten when they leave the Sargasso Sea, and they are twenty-five when they mate and lay eggs. What happens during the fifteen years between leaving the Azores and mating?"

Realization hit me. I laughed out loud. We were riding into a squall again, and Dad was concentrating so hard on driving that I was not sure he was even waiting for my answer. "What is it?" he asked.

"Another switch," I said.

He took his eyes off the road long enough to demand, "Tell me, what do they do?"

"In the years between leaving their second home and their return to their native beaches, they commute. Year after year, all up and down the Atlantic, turtles swim north in the summer and south in the winter. Did you already know that?"

"I didn't know for sure, but I had my suspicions."

I had to smile. "And did you have your suspicions about me?"

"For a while," he said. Then he took his eyes off the road long enough to return my smile. "But not now."

"Of course," I said, "I will be doing the same but opposite. I will commute north in the winter and south in the summer."

"Yep," he said. "And there will be times when you or I will need a lift between switches."

"Yes," I replied, "there will be times."

344

Meet the Author
E.L. Konigsburg

What E.L. stands for: Elaine Lobl

First job: Bookkeeper in a meat plant

Favorite food: Chocolate

Inspiration for her books: Kids she taught at school and her own children

On telling a good story: "[I try to] let the telling be like fudge-ripple ice cream. You keep licking the vanilla, but every now and then you come to something darker and deeper and with a stronger flavor."

A famous book she wrote: *From the Mixed-Up Files of Mrs. Basil E. Frankweiler*

Meet the Illustrator
Kevin Beilfuss

Born: March 10, 1963 in LaGrange, Illinois

Favorite children's books: *The Chronicles of Narnia* by C.S. Lewis

Favorite sports: Softball and skiing

How he creates his art: "It's like directing a play," says Beilfuss. He has models act out the scene and then uses oils or acrylics to recreate the mood.

Internet

For more interesting facts about E.L. Konigsburg and Kevin Beilfuss, visit Education Place.

www.eduplace.com/kids

Think About the Selection

1. Why is Nadia upset when her father wants to be licensed to head up a turtle patrol? Find a sentence in the story to back up your answer.

2. What do you learn about Nadia and Ethan from her thoughts and his behavior at *The Phantom of the Opera* and after the show?

3. If you were in Nadia's place, would you stay home the day before an exciting trip and not answer the phone? Why or why not?

4. Disprove this statement with information from the story: It is foolish for Nadia and her father to change their plans in order to help the turtles.

5. Why does Nadia's father compare the two of them to the turtles and say, "There will be times when you or I will need a lift between switches"?

6. Nadia is interested in helping baby turtles survive and may become a biologist. What special interests of yours might lead to a career?

7. **Connecting/Comparing** Compare Nadia's feelings about her parents' breakup with Margaret's feelings about losing her father in *Last Summer with Maizon*. How are their feelings alike and different?

Informing

Write a News Bulletin

A big storm has hit the Florida coast. Helpers are needed right away to save the hatchling turtles. Write a news bulletin about the situation. Explain why the turtles are in danger, what helpers will have to do, and where people who want to help should report.

Tips

- Remember that a news bulletin must answer these questions about the situation: *Who? What? When? Where? Why?* and *How?*

- Use language that will inspire people to help out.

Make a Circle Graph

Create a circle graph using details from the beginning of the selection. If there were a hundred eggs altogether, what percentage of them hatched live turtles? What percentage were unhatched? What percentage were dead-pipped? Live-pipped?

96 empty egg shells

4 unhatched whole eggs

1 dead hatchling

3 turtles that were half-in/half-out of the shell but were dead. Those are called dead-pipped.

1 turtle that was half-in/half-out of the shell but was alive. Those are called live-pipped.

2 live ones

Report on Turtle Migration

Go back into the selection to reread what Nadia tells her father about turtle migrations. Then combine your information with a partner's and together give an oral report about each area in the turtles' migration.

Bonus Draw a map of where loggerhead turtles go during their lifetime. Write and attach captions telling where the turtles migrate and other notable facts.

Complete a Crossword Puzzle

How much do you know about loggerhead turtles from reading *The View from Saturday?* Test what you know by completing a crossword puzzle that can be printed from Education Place. **www.eduplace.com/kids**

Home-Grown Butterflies

by Deborah Churchman

People in Barra del Colorado, a village in Costa Rica, had a big problem. For many years, the villagers had caught fish for a living. But then, because of pollution and overfishing, the fish began to disappear. Soon it became hard for the people to catch enough fish to feed to their families and sell for money. What could they do?

The village is on the edge of a beautiful rainforest. One thing the villagers could have done was chop down the trees. Then they could have sold the wood and farmed the land. They would have made money but destroyed the rainforest.

A scientist named Brent Davies had another idea about how the villagers could use the rainforest. And it would keep the forest alive. The villagers could raise and sell *butterflies*.

Many colorful butterflies flit around in the forest near Barra del Colorado. It would be easy to capture a few and use them to raise many more.

Brent knew that butterfly zoos around the world would pay for farm-raised butterflies. If the villagers could make money by selling them, they'd have a good reason to protect the insects' rainforest home. After all, without the forest, there would be no wild butterflies to capture. And without a steady supply of wild butterflies, the farm would fail.

Brent Davies and friends admire their new sign (above). In Spanish and English, it says that they're raising insects such as the butterflies on the opposite page.

Inside an enclosure (right), visitors can see plants grown for hungry caterpillars.

Brent wanted to show villagers how to raise butterflies to sell. And she knew just who could help: the school kids! If adults saw kids making money with butterflies, they might want to start their own farm — and protect the forest.

Schoolyard Farm

Butterflies drink nectar from certain flowers, and they lay their eggs on other plants. When the eggs hatch, caterpillars come out and eat those plants. They eat and grow, and grow and eat. When they've grown enough, the caterpillars turn into pupae (PEW-pee). And those are what butterfly zoos buy.

Brent knew that villagers could find some pupae in the rainforest to sell. But if the people could get butterflies to lay eggs in one place, they could *raise* caterpillars — and get many more pupae. They could even let some of the extra butterflies they raised go free in the rainforest. That would make sure the forest would always have plenty.

So, how to get started? To attract butterflies, Brent figured the villagers needed a garden full of nectar plants. They also needed an enclosure full of plants for caterpillars to eat. She talked to people at the school. Together they decided on a good spot in the schoolyard.

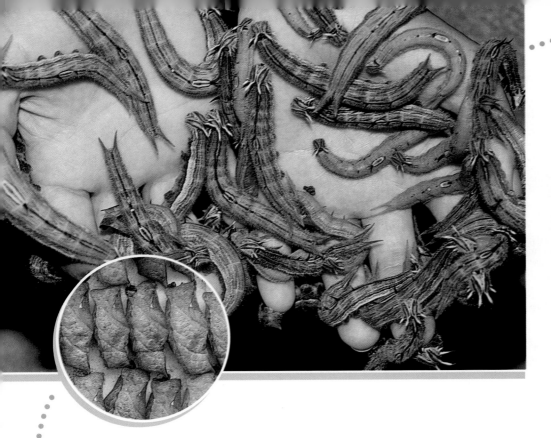

Two handfuls of hungry owl butterfly caterpillars (left) are being moved to a feeding box. These caterpillars will eat and grow. When they turn into pupae, they'll be packed into boxes (inset) and shipped out to butterfly zoos.

Clearing and Planting

First they had to clear a lot of trash out of the schoolyard. The kids pitched in and stuffed more than 100 sacks with trash. Soon people were stopping by to admire their work.

Then everyone helped dig up the soil so that plants could grow. That turned up lots of worms — which attracted lots of chickens. So the kids went on "chicken patrol," chasing the birds away. Their butterfly garden needed those worms!

Next, they planted flowers to attract the butterflies. Beside the flower garden, they built the enclosure for raising caterpillars. Then they put the right kinds of plants inside it.

Raising Butterflies

Butterflies from the forest flew to the garden to feed on the flowers. Brent taught the children how to capture the butterflies and take them into the enclosure. There, the butterflies laid tiny eggs on the special plants.

Brent also taught the children how to find caterpillars and eggs. (Some eggs are no bigger than the period at the end of this sentence.)

The kids learned to lift up leaves and look around the plants. They put the eggs and caterpillars they found into special feeding boxes. That way they could make sure the insects got plenty to eat.

In the boxes, the caterpillars fattened up on leaves. Then they turned into pupae. The kids picked the pupae just as if they were picking a crop. They let some of the pupae turn into butterflies, and they put those back in the rainforest. But they sold the other pupae.

Today, the farm sells about 250 pupae every month. The money that's earned goes to the school for materials and equipment. The first thing the kids bought was a ceiling fan so their schoolroom wouldn't be so hot!

The best news is that some adults in the village have started doing what the kids have done — making farms for butterflies. They've learned from the kids how to use the forest without harming it.

Meanwhile, Back Home

People at the San Diego Wild Animal Park helped start the butterfly farm in Costa Rica. Then they had another wild idea. Why not start this kind of farm at home in California?

They asked students at San Pasqual Union Elementary School if they wanted to get involved. People at the school agreed to do the same thing as the villagers in Costa Rica.

Kids and adults set up a butterfly garden and an enclosed area. Some of the money they earn pays for special things for their school, such as science equipment.

Students from California have started writing to the students in Costa Rica about their butterfly businesses. Both groups of kids feel great about what they're doing for nature!

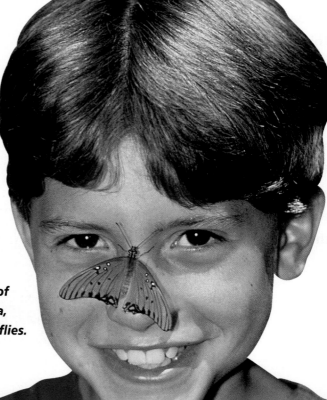

Kids such as Charlie Hanscom in the town of San Pasqual, California, are also raising butterflies.

351

Check Your Progress

You have read about the many aspects of growing up, including grief, humor, joy, and understanding. Keep in mind those feelings as you read and compare two new selections and polish your test-taking skills.

First, take another look at E.L. Konigsburg's letter on pages 240–242. She writes "about kids who are learning to accept themselves for being like everyone else at the same time they are learning to accept themselves for being different from everyone else." Think about how the characters you have read about so far have learned to accept themselves.

In the two selections that follow, you'll read about young people pursuing their dreams. Think about how pursuing a dream can be a way of accepting yourself. Then compare the people and their experiences with the other selections in this theme.

Read and Compare

Read about a Japanese boy who wants to become a cartoonist by studying with a master.

Try these strategies:
Predict and Infer
Evaluate

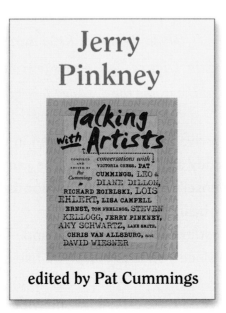

Enjoy an interview with an artist, beginning with the story of the artist's childhood.

Try these strategies:
Question
Monitor and Clarify

Strategies in Action *Call on all your reading strategies for help as you read.*

THE INK-KEEPER'S APPRENTICE

ALLEN SAY

THE INK-KEEPER'S APPRENTICE

WRITTEN AND ILLUSTRATED BY ALLEN SAY

Kiyoi is thirteen years old and living in Tokyo after World War Two. His dream is to be a cartoonist. One day he visits the studio of Noro Shinpei, a famous cartoonist, and asks to become his apprentice. Although Master Noro already has an apprentice, Tokida, he makes Kiyoi draw a horse as a test. Impressed by Kiyoi's dream, Master Noro agrees to become his sensei, or teacher. Kiyoi arrives at the studio the next day to begin his apprenticeship.

The next day I arrived at the studio at ten in the morning. Sensei and Tokida were already at work, sitting in the same places, wearing the same clothes. Sensei's small eyes were bloodshot and his face bristled with a heavy beard.

"You've come just in time to give us a hand. Tokida and I have been going nonstop since you left. Have you had breakfast?"

"Yes, sir."

"Pour yourself a cup of tea. A magazine reporter is coming over at two to pick up this installment. We'll relax after that. Here, I'll have another cup," he said and handed me his mug. Already I was beginning to feel useful, pouring tea for the master.

352B

"Ready to work, Kiyoi?" Tokida spoke to me for the first time.

"Yes, what can I do?"

"Don't worry, you'll have plenty to do. You don't know what you got yourself into," Tokida said. He spoke with a slight Osaka accent, which is softer and more melodious than the sharp, staccato speech of the Tokyo natives.

It was exciting, and a little eerie, to watch one of the best-known comic serials come to life in front of me. Tokida penciled in the frames on thick bristol boards with a ruler, and Sensei sketched in the rough figures with a soft-leaded pencil. He drew with tremendous speed and energy. Even when his pencil wasn't touching the paper his hand moved round and round as if drawing hundreds of small circles. I kept looking at his hand and noticed a pea-sized callus on the middle finger, and I wondered how many hundreds of hours I had to draw to work up a callus like Sensei's. I looked at Tokida's drawing hand and saw a budding pea. Then I saw that half of the little finger on Tokida's left hand had been lopped off.

Sensei didn't draw in any orderly way, but skipped from one frame to the next, as if he was working on his favorite scenes first. A steady stream of ideas seemed to rush through his head and flow out from the tip of his pencil. How did he know what size to make the balloons before putting in the words? I wondered, but was afraid to ask.

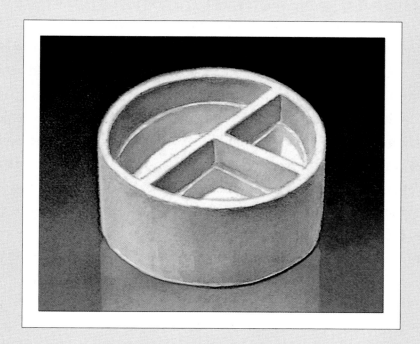

Sometimes the bristol boards became so heavily penciled it was hard to tell what was going on. Sensei would scribble a few words here and there inside the balloons and chuckle to himself. Then he would put a new nib in a pen holder and start to ink over the drawings. He used the pen as quickly and freely as he did a pencil, except with the pen he never went over the same line twice. He worked so fast I was afraid he might ruin a drawing, but he never did. The nib slid over the smooth paper effortlessly, and the gleaming streak of black ink flowed with ease and power. Suddenly a cartoon figure would emerge, almost leaping out of the page. It took my breath away.

"Do you know what a baseball player's uniform looks like?" asked Sensei.

Tokida and I looked at each other and nodded.

"Draw one for me."

It's another test, I thought. Tokida seemed as puzzled as I was, but we each drew a baseball uniform. Sensei glanced at our drawings.

"So you thought you knew what it looks like," he said. "You hardly know anything about it. You don't know where the seams come together, you're not sure about the length of the sleeves, and you don't know how many loops there are to hold up the pants. Soon I'm going to have you draw the backgrounds, and I want you to know what it is that you're drawing. For instance, when I ask you to draw a Shinto temple, I don't mean just any old temple, but a Shinto temple. Most of the time no one will know the difference, but I want you to know it. If you're not sure, look it up; don't rely on your memory."

Tokida and I said nothing. When Sensei asked us to draw the uniform I thought he was being silly. Baseball was the most popular sport in Japan, and of course everybody knew what the uniform looked like, or so I thought. Now I understood why so many books and magazines cluttered the studio. They were research materials. I wondered if I could draw anything from memory. The only consolation was that Tokida's drawing wasn't much better than mine.

"Kiyoi, watch Tokida and give him a hand," said Sensei.

Tokida moved over so I could sit next to him and watch what he was doing. With a brush he inked in the night skies, patterns on kimonos, hairdos — putting small touches here and there, giving life to the line drawings. When each frame was completed and the pencil lines erased, the finished drawings stood out against the sleek creamy paper. They were beautiful even before they were tinted with watercolor.

"Here, do this one," said Tokida casually, and gave me a board and a brush. "Fill in the large spots, like this man's coat. Always start from the top and work from left to right so you won't smudge the ink. And put a piece of paper under your hand so you won't grease up the board."

This was more frightening than drawing the horse yesterday. The master was actually going to let me work on his drawings. He and Tokida acted as though I'd been working with them for a long time. I felt like I was going into a duel with a real sword, without having gone through any training with a bamboo stick. Timidly, with a shaky hand, I started at a safe place — in the middle of a blank area — and worked outward. As I went near the edges, I unconsciously grasped the brush harder with each stroke, but the brush had a way of wandering off by itself, right over the outlines. I was making a mess.

"Don't worry about it; keep going," Tokida encouraged me.

"But I've ruined it," I said, nearly in tears.

"That's nothing," said Sensei. "You should have seen Tokida when he started; he has the shakiest hand I've ever seen. He'll show you what to do."

Tokida dipped a new brush into a jar of thick white paint and went over the mess I'd made.

"All you have to do is cover it up with white and the camera won't pick it up," he told me.

"What do you mean?"

"They photograph these drawings to make the printing plates."

What a relief! The drawing didn't have to be discarded. Now that I knew a dab of white paint would hide all my mistakes, I went to work with a renewed spirit. I ran the brush along the straight lines of the frame borders and found that I had more control when I painted with swift strokes.

"Very good, Kiyoi," said Sensei. "You used something sharp in the brush just now, like the edge of a knife. The brush is many things. Remember that edge."

He was right. There *was* something sharp in the brush, and I could cut a straight or curved line with a quick turn of my wrist. And the amount of ink on the brush had a lot to do with what you could do with it. I felt as if I was learning calligraphy all over again.

After I was through inking the piece, Tokida showed me how to accent rounded objects — wheels, balls, hairdos, and such — to give them a sense of volume. It was thrilling to see a flat line drawing suddenly become three-dimensional by putting in the highlights. At first I couldn't handle the brush well enough to use the white of the paper for the highlights, so I had to put them in with white paint, but after a while I got carried away and began to put in two or three highlights on a single object.

"The sun, the sun, Kiyoi," said Sensei. "One sun, one shadow, one highlight."

"Yes, sir."

At noon Sensei sent me to a restaurant to order our lunch.

"Noro Shinpei's place?" asked the woman who looked like the owner's wife.

"Yes, we'd like three bowls of noodles with shrimp, please."

"We haven't seen you before, have we?"

"No, I'm new."

"What happened to Tokida-san?"

"He's working with Sensei. I'm the new pupil."

"What, another one?" The woman looked me up and down. "But you seem so young. You must be awfully good to be his student."

Even the owner came out of the kitchen to inspect me. It was wonderful to have a famous master.

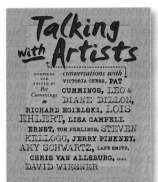

JERRY PINKNEY

from *Talking with Artists* by Pat Cummings
illustrations by Jerry Pinkney

Birthday:
December 22, 1939

MY STORY

I think I might have first gotten interested in art because of my two older brothers who drew. They liked to make pictures of airplanes, cars, things of that sort. I got started by mimicking them, trying to draw what they drew.

I remember an incident in the first grade when I was growing up in Philadelphia that sort of shaped the idea in my mind that I wanted to be an artist. For a Fire Prevention Week project I got to draw a red fire engine on a big sheet of brown paper. I got a lot of attention from that and I liked it. I was encouraged by my teacher and, as I kept drawing, I became the "class artist."

Probably part of the reason that I focused on my drawing so much was that I felt I wasn't very strong in other areas. I was able to escape some projects by drawing the assignments.

I was able to take private art classes when I was in junior high school. My father was a handyman who did painting, plumbing, electrical work, gardening — a bit of everything. He had several clients who knew of private art classes and I remember taking classes in different neighborhoods. Usually they were still-life painting classes.

When I was eleven or twelve years old I had a newspaper stand on the corner of a fairly large intersection in Philadelphia. I would take my drawing pad and sketch while I was there. An artist named John Liney, who was a cartoonist for the Henry comics, noticed me drawing. He took me to visit his studio, which was about a block away. From time to time I would go to see him and he would give me different materials to work with, different art supplies. So at that early age I had a sense that it was possible to make a living doing art. Knowing him and seeing how he worked helped me understand the possibilities of using one's talents.

Boy with a Wagon. Age 7.
Watercolor, 12" x 9".

One early influence was the work of Arthur Rackham, who was an illustrator of children's stories. I liked the quality of his drawing and how he used color.

I later went to Dobbins Vocational High School and took commercial art classes that introduced me to lettering and technical drawing, airbrush, and all kinds of media. In the twelfth grade, we even attended some figure-drawing evening classes.

There was a competition for scholarships to the Philadelphia Museum College of Art. Only four or five were available. I had to show a portfolio and write a paper stating why I wanted to attend. It felt great to win a scholarship, and I began studying advertising and design. But I soon realized that I enjoyed painting and printmaking classes even more, and drawing became very important to me.

I began doing greeting cards, advertising, and textbook illustration in Boston. The textbook work made me realize I liked illustration that was tied to a story.

> "Draw as much as possible if you want to one day be an illustrator. Especially, draw from life."
> — Jerry Pinkney

Book illustration seemed freer than some of the work I was doing. Working with a manuscript was very exciting. I also began to put some effort into looking at and researching African American artists. I admired Charles White, whose strong, graphic drawings gave such dignity to the black figure. I was also impressed by the photographs of James Van Der Zee. If you look at the work of these two men, I think you'll see their influence in my book *Home Place*.

I've won a lot of awards for my art and it feels wonderful to know that my work is appreciated. My work includes a mixture of things that I, myself, have appreciated. In some ways, it is a testimony to be able to state through my art, "Yes, these people have influenced me, and I'd like to say it now."

Black Cowboy, Wild Horses: A True Story by Julius Lester, 1998.
Published by Dial Books.

WHERE DO YOU GET YOUR IDEAS FROM?

Most of my work comes from the text, which I use as a sort of springboard. I try to find stories that allow me to make some kind of personal statement. For example, I'll find manuscripts that deal with the African Americans and our history in this country. So the ideas come from the story but also from my own personal commitment.

WHAT DO YOU ENJOY DRAWING THE MOST?

It varies. Perhaps I most enjoy drawing animals. Next to that would be using animals in an anthropomorphic way — giving them human characteristics, like dressing them in clothes or giving them human expressions. Combining them with people fascinates me and gives me so many areas to work on that I enjoy.

I try to keep a balance in my work. If I find that I'm working on projects that include an awful lot of animals and fewer people I want to balance it, so I go back and forth. When I get to a point where I've had it with drawing animals, I'll pick a project where there are more human figures involved. The variety can be quite, quite exciting.

Aesop's Fables by Aesop, 2000.
Published by Seastar Publishing Company.

I've always tried to focus on the things that give me the most enjoyment. Part of me always needs to try to do something that I've never done before or to bring a different point of view to my work. Often, this involves working on things that make me uncomfortable at the time. But the idea is to move through that uncomfortable stage and learn how to resolve the problem I'm having in my work and face it head on. Hopefully, that helps bring a freshness to the work.

For instance, for a while I showed most of the figures and animals in my paintings from a close-up point of view. There's not very much depth in those compositions, usually. Now I'm doing just the opposite of that and moving back and seeing characters in a much larger setting. That keeps me interested in what I'm doing. I like variety.

DO YOU EVER PUT PEOPLE YOU KNOW IN YOUR PICTURES?

Yes — especially my family. When my children were very young they were always turning up in my work. I think Brian has been a major character in a book and Myles and Scott and Troy have been on covers. Gloria, my wife, models for me all the time and also helps take photographs of the models.

Very often, when I get a manuscript I have to find models for the characters in the story. They're people that I don't know or don't know very well and, with the way I work, I like to introduce the models to the text and often have them act it out. Before it's all over, I end up knowing them very, very well because we've shared this kind of experience.

WHAT DO YOU USE TO MAKE YOUR PICTURES?

My work is done in pencil and watercolor on paper, usually. But I tend to use a lot of different media along with the watercolor: pastel, color pencils, and Cray-Pas. My worktable is just full of all these materials, and I use whatever I think will help me in getting the kind of effect that I want for the pictures.

HOW DID YOU GET TO DO YOUR FIRST BOOK?

My first book, *The Adventures of Spider* by Joyce Arkhurst, was published by Little, Brown in 1964. The book came as a result of my being in the Boston area where there are certainly a lot of book publishers. I had gotten some very nice recognition from art shows in which my work had appeared.

I think it also had a lot to do with the climate of the times. There were publishers who were interested in publishing African American writers. I think there was an awareness, if not pressure, that the African American artist could perhaps bring something unique to a text, something more personal. The publishers were actually looking for someone black to do this particular project, which was a collection of West African folktales. I showed them my portfolio, they liked my work, and that's how I got to do my first book.

The Adventures of Spider: West African Folktales by Joyce Cooper Arkhurst, 1964.
Published by Little, Brown.

Think and Compare

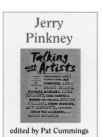

1. Compare the story of Kiyoi's wanting to be a cartoonist with Jerry Pinkney's story. How are the stories alike? In what ways are the stories unusual?

2. While growing up, Jerry Pinkney was encouraged by teachers and other people. Compare the support he received with another character's in the theme.

3. Compare Kiyoi's determination with that of Billy Colman's in *Where the Red Fern Grows*. How does their determination get them what they want?

4. What advice might Jerry Pinkney give Kiyoi about becoming an artist?

5. Which selection in this theme do you think best reflects your own experience of growing up? Give examples from the selection.

Strategies in Action Explain how you used one or more reading strategies while reading one of the selections.

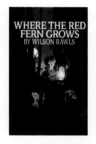

Write a Sequel

What do you think happened to your favorite character in this theme? Write a sequel — a follow-up to the story — about what might have happened to the character after he or she grows up.

Tips

- Use details from the story to describe the character and the setting.
- Make sure the plot includes a problem, a climax, and a resolution.

Writing a Personal Response

Some test items ask you to write a personal response to a topic, based on your ideas and experience. Here is a sample test topic about *The Ink-Keeper's Apprentice.*

> **Write your response to this question.**
>
> Compare Kiyoi's experience of learning to be a cartoonist with a learning experience of your own. Use examples from the selection and your own experience to support your answer.

1 Understand the question.

Find the key words. Use them to understand what you need to do. Decide what to write about.

2 Get ready to write.

Look back at the selection. List details that help answer the question. Think about yourself. List thoughts or experiences that help answer the question.

Here are some examples.

Selection Details	Personal Experiences
Kiyoi wants to be a cartoonist.	I want to play soccer well.
works with Tokida, learns to use brush, practices accents	practice with team, learn to pass, run plays
Sensei praises Kiyoi.	Coach asks me to lead a drill.

③ Write your answer.

Use details from both of your lists. Write a clear and complete answer.

Kiyoi's dream is to become a cartoonist. When he becomes Sensei's apprentice, Sensei asks Kiyoi to help Tokida with a drawing. Kiyoi is nervous, but he learns to use the brush well. He practices adding accents to Sensei's drawings, and Sensei praises him.

I want to play soccer well, so I practice with the team, and I learn how to pass the ball and run plays. When Coach asks me to help her show the team a passing drill, I feel proud, just like Kiyoi feels when Sensei praises him. The times when you're practicing and learning can be nervous times, but it's worth it.

354

4

Discovering Ancient Cultures

I should like to rise and go
Where the golden apples grow; . . .
And the rich goods from near and far
Hang for sale in the bazaar;
Where the Great Wall round China goes
And on one side the desert blows,
And with bell and voice and drum,
Cities on the other hum

— *Robert Louis Stevenson*
from "Travel"

Discovering Ancient Cultures

with Patricia C. and Fredrick L. McKissack

Dear Reader,

This theme is about discovery. Sometimes finding the past in the present is as interesting as the search. While researching *The Royal Kingdoms of Africa: Ghana, Mali, and Songhay* we traveled to Morocco, North Africa. We recorded our adventures in a journal. Here are a few of our journal entries.

JOURNAL

TANGIER

MARRAKECH

MOROCCO

TIMBUKTU

MALI

GHANA

MAP OF Africa

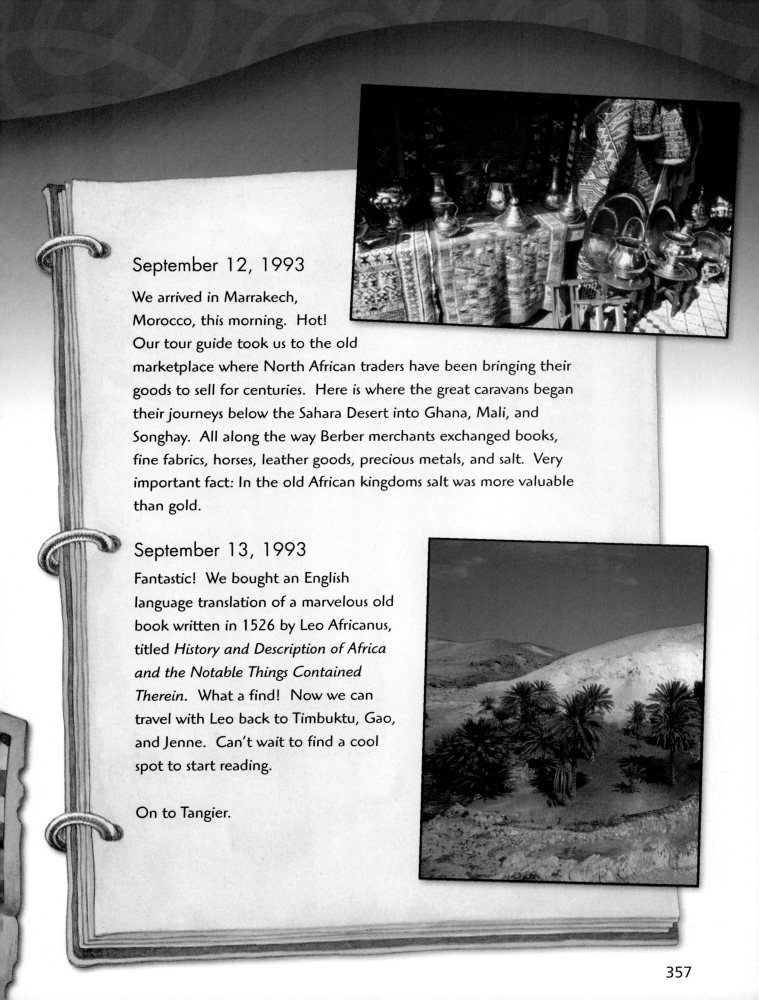

September 12, 1993

We arrived in Marrakech, Morocco, this morning. Hot! Our tour guide took us to the old marketplace where North African traders have been bringing their goods to sell for centuries. Here is where the great caravans began their journeys below the Sahara Desert into Ghana, Mali, and Songhay. All along the way Berber merchants exchanged books, fine fabrics, horses, leather goods, precious metals, and salt. Very important fact: In the old African kingdoms salt was more valuable than gold.

September 13, 1993

Fantastic! We bought an English language translation of a marvelous old book written in 1526 by Leo Africanus, titled *History and Description of Africa and the Notable Things Contained Therein.* What a find! Now we can travel with Leo back to Timbuktu, Gao, and Jenne. Can't wait to find a cool spot to start reading.

On to Tangier.

September 14, 1993

At the Tangier Museum of History and Culture, we studied old trade route maps and took pictures of the clothing and gear of a Berber trader. Then in the late afternoon, we went to a small town outside the city where we rode camels for the first time. It was so hot. The air was dry. A sea of sand stretched thousands of miles before us. Now we know how it felt being in a caravan, moving from oasis to oasis along the same routes we had seen in the maps earlier.

We have so much fun researching a book, it's hard to stop and begin writing. But our great discoveries make the writing a lot easier. We hope you'll have as much fun making discoveries while reading this theme.

Sincerely,

Patricia C. McKissack

Fredrick L. McKissack

Step Back in Time

Think about the details the McKissacks observe in their journal. Which details make you want to learn more? In this theme, you'll have your own chance to dig a little deeper. Each selection shown below tells about an ancient culture in a different way. As you read, think about how well each selection helps you understand the culture it describes.

Distant times and faraway lands await you! Set out to learn about the people of ancient Mexico, China, and Africa as you read *Discovering Ancient Cultures*.

To learn about the authors in this theme, visit Education Place. **www.eduplace.com/kids**

Background and Vocabulary

Lost Temple of the Aztecs

Read to find the meanings of these words.

e • Glossary

adorned

causeways

conquered

empire

excavation

intricate

mainland

metropolis

Excavating an AZTEC CITY

The Aztecs were a Native American people who founded the ancient city of Tenochtitlán *(tay-nohch-TEE-tlahn)* in Mexico in the mid-1300s. *Lost Temple of the Aztecs* tells about this hidden city, part of which was uncovered during an **excavation** in 1978 in what is now Mexico City.

Photo from 1978 excavation in Mexico City

A.D. 1325
City of Tenochtitlán founded by the Aztecs.

A.D. 1519
Cortés's expedition arrives in Mexico.

A.D. 1300   **1400**   **1500**   **160**

A.D. 1502–1520
Moctezuma II's rule.

The Aztecs worshipped many gods. This mask, made of gold and jade, represented the goddess of springs, rivers, lakes, and seas.

A turquoise and shell mosaic disc from the period A.D. 900–1521

During the rule of Moctezuma II (1502–1520), Tenochtitlán was the capital city of the Aztec **empire**. Tenochtitlán was a beautiful **metropolis** built on an island in Lake Texcoco. Long **causeways**, or raised roads over water, led from the **mainland** to the city, and the Great Temple rose from its center. The Aztecs began their empire with trading and later expanded when their warriors **conquered** neighboring groups.

Many artifacts were found when Tenochtitlán was discovered. These ranged from clay pots to jade and turquoise masks that were worn during festivals. The Aztec people also made **intricate** gold, silver, and platinum jewelry. Such jewels **adorned** only people of high status, like the ruler and his nobles.

An ornament worn as a mark of social status, made of gold and jade.

A.D. 1978
Workmen discover ancient moon goddess stone in Mexico City; excavation of Great Temple of the Aztecs begins.

| 1700 | 1800 | 1900 | 2000 |

LOST TEMPLE OF THE AZTECS

BY SHELLEY TANAKA
ILLUSTRATIONS BY GREG RUHL

I WAS THERE BOOK

What it was like when the Spaniards invaded Mexico

Strategy Focus

In 1519 the Spanish arrived in Tenochtitlán, capital of the Aztec empire. As you read, **evaluate** how the author portrays Moctezuma, the Aztec leader, and Cortés, the Spanish leader.

PROLOGUE
February 21, 1978

The zocalo was still dark. The trolley cars crossing the far corner of Mexico City's main square were not yet filled with people on their way to work. Between the cathedral and the presidential palace, workmen were digging ditches for electrical cables, anxious to beat the thick heat and pollution that would wrap around the city by midday.

Suddenly they struck something hard. It was a flat round stone covered with intricate, mysterious carvings.

A team of experts was called. They discovered that the giant disk, almost ten feet (three meters) in diameter, depicted Coyolxauhqui (coy-ohl-ZAH-kee), the ancient moon goddess. Further digging revealed that the stone lay at the foot of some buried steps. Beneath a block of stores and parking lots in the center of Mexico City, they had found the Great Temple of the Aztecs, the cornerstone of what was once the most powerful empire in North America.

Professor Eduardo Matos Moctezuma understood the excavation. He knew that he was witnessing the discovery of a lifetime. A graduate of the Mexican National School of Anthropology, he had long experience in excavating

Professor Eduardo Matos Moctezuma

363

The carvings on the great round stone show Coyolxauhqui, the Aztec moon goddess (*above*). An archaeologist carefully records discoveries at the excavation site in Mexico City (*left*).

Aztec sites. But his interest was more than professional. Through his mother's ancestors, his family tree led directly back to one of the most famous and tragic rulers in history. Long before the Europeans came to North America, a very different kind of metropolis stood on the spot where Mexico City is now. It was called Tenochtitlán (teh-NAWCH-tee-TLAHN), and it was the capital city of the Aztec empire.

Five hundred years ago, Tenochtitlán was a city of 250,000 people. It was built on an island in the middle of a sparkling blue lake. Canals crisscrossed the city between blocks of spotless white buildings and lush green gardens. Long causeways led to the mainland, where snowcapped mountains loomed in the distance.

The first Europeans who saw Tenochtitlán found the city so beautiful, they thought it must be enchanted.

The Great Temple stood at the heart of this remarkable city. Nine stories high, it faced a huge square surrounded by shrines and palaces. This was where the Aztecs worshipped their gods, where their conquered enemies brought gifts and tributes, and where the Aztec ruler Moctezuma received important guests.

One fateful day in 1519, an unusual group of visitors approached Tenochtitlán. The Aztecs had never seen such people. Their skin was oddly white, their faces were covered with hair, and they wore metal clothing from head to foot. They came with strange, wild-eyed beasts, and they carried heavy weapons that clanked and gleamed in the sun.

Were they friends, or enemies? Should they be destroyed or treated as guests?

Moctezuma decided to welcome the strangers. After all, what could his mighty nation of warriors have to fear here, within the walls of their great city?

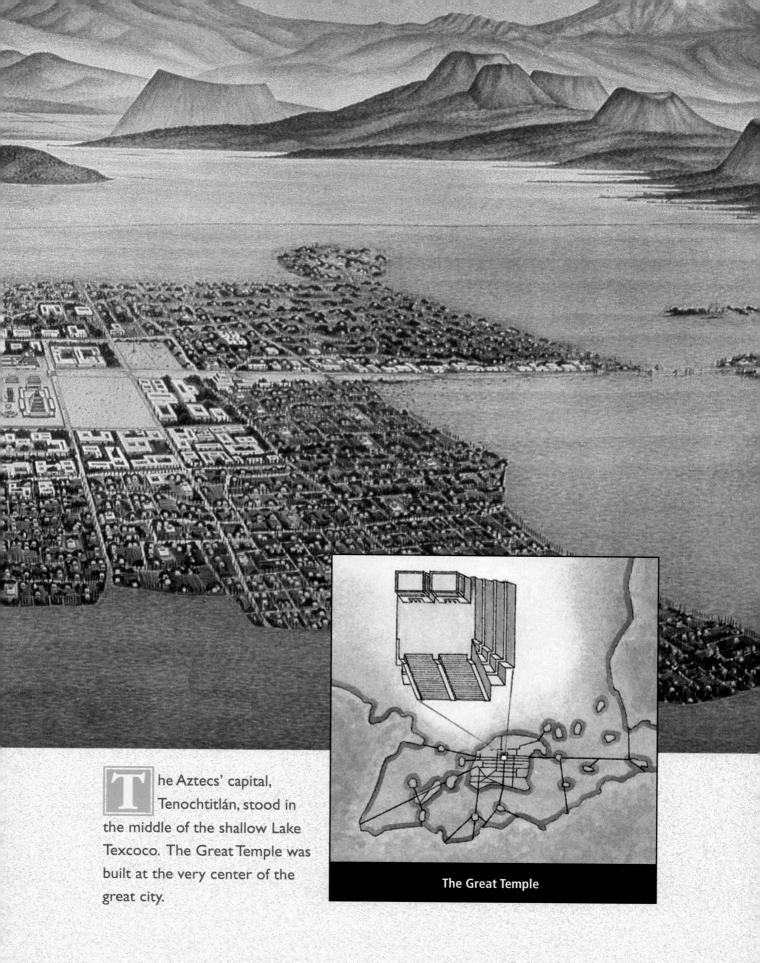

The Aztecs' capital, Tenochtitlán, stood in the middle of the shallow Lake Texcoco. The Great Temple was built at the very center of the great city.

The Great Temple

367

THE STRANGERS ARRIVE
April 1519

The ships came from the east. They just appeared on the horizon one day, as if they had dropped from the sky. They were bigger than any boats the people had ever seen, and they floated toward the shore like small mountains.

When Moctezuma's messengers saw the ships, they hurried back to Tenochtitlán.

"Strange people have come to the shores of the great sea," they told their ruler. "They have very light skin and long beards, and their hair only comes down to their ears. They sit on huge deer that carry them wherever they want to go."

Moctezuma listened to the news in silence. His mind raced.

Quetzalcoatl (keht´-zahl-COH-ah-tul) has appeared! he thought. He has come back to reclaim his throne!

It was happening, just as the ancient prophecy had foretold. Long ago, according to legend, Quetzalcoatl, the great god of learning and creation, had sailed east on a raft of serpents to a mysterious land across the ocean. But he had promised to come back, and this was the predicted year of his return.

Moctezuma knew there had already been signs that things were not well with the gods, that some momentous change was about to come to his people. Two years before, a great tongue of fire had streaked across the night sky, like a spear plunged into the very heart

An illustration from a Spanish book of the time shows Cortés's expedition coming ashore near what is today the city of Veracruz, Mexico.

of the heavens. At dawn, the sun destroyed the fire, but the next night it appeared again. And so it went on for the better part of a year, and each night the people watched with terror. Would the sun, the source of all life, continue to destroy the fire? Might the sun one day stop rising?

There were other signs of death and ruin. Temples burst into flames. The great lake that surrounded Tenochtitlán swirled and bubbled up as if it were boiling with rage. The nights echoed with the sound of a woman wailing.

Moctezuma was filled with fear and confusion at these unnatural happenings. The gods must be looking unfavorably on the richest and most powerful empire in the land.

And now, it seemed, one of the gods had returned. Quetzalcoatl had arrived.

WHO WERE THE AZTECS?

By the time Cortés arrived in 1519, the Aztecs ruled a great empire in what is now Mexico (*below and inset*). Originally from a land farther north called Aztlán, they arrived on the shores of Lake Texcoco in the fourteenth century. But the people living there wouldn't let them settle. So they created their city right in the lake, on rocky outcroppings and shallow marshes.

(According to legend, the Aztecs' priests had a vision of an eagle eating a snake atop a cactus (*below, right*) and, where they saw the eagle, they built their capital. Today the eagle on a cactus is part of the Mexican flag.) The Aztecs traded with people around the lake, and grew richer. Later, they expanded, creating an empire by defeating their neighbors in war.

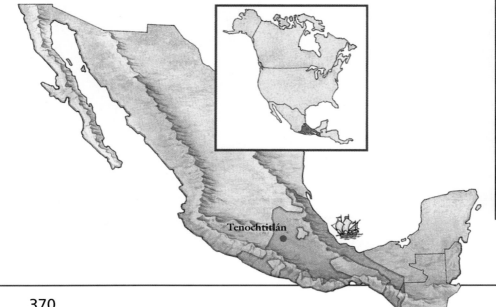

Tenochtitlán

THE AZTEC YEAR

The Aztec calendar was shown as
a round disk (*above*), since the
Aztecs saw time as being like a wheel,
endlessly turning. Each day had a name
(rain, crocodile, rabbit, and so forth) and
a number from 1 to 13. Every 13 days a
new month began, and there were 20
months in the Aztec year — which was
only 260 days long. The Aztecs also had
a 365-day calendar, which they used to
keep track of their many religious cere-
monies. Once every 52 years, the first
day of the 260-day calendar and the first
day of the 365-day calendar were the
same. This marked the start of a new
"century" or cycle, a very important
time in the Aztec world. By coincidence,
according to the Aztec calendar, the year
Cortés landed happened to be the year
given for the possible return of
Quetzalcoatl.

July 1519

Moctezuma gathered his chiefs around him. "Our lord, Quetzalcoatl, has arrived at last. Hurry to meet him. Tell him that his servant Moctezuma has sent you to welcome him back to his throne, and take him these gifts."

Moctezuma's messengers traveled to the coast. They placed their gifts in canoes and paddled out to where the huge ships floated offshore. The pale-skinned strangers let down a ladder, and the messengers climbed on board. They were taken to the leader, whom the strangers called Cortés. Surely he was Quetzalcoatl himself!

The messengers kissed the deck at Cortés's feet. "We bring these gifts from your servant Moctezuma," they told him. "He guards over your kingdom and keeps it safe for your return." Then they adorned Cortés with a serpent mask made of turquoise and a headdress of shimmering blue-green quetzal feathers.

Among the priceless treasures Moctezuma sent to Cortés was this pendant of a two-headed snake. This would be worn suspended on a chain that went around the neck. The snake was a symbol of the god Quetzalcoatl.

They draped gold and jade bands around his neck, arms, and legs. They placed a cape of ocelot skin and sandals of glistening black obsidian at his feet, along with the other gifts — serpent-head staffs and spears inlaid with green jade, masks, shields, and fans heavy with gold and turquoise.

Cortés looked at everything they had given him. "Are these your gifts of welcome?" he asked. "Is this all you have brought?"

"Yes, lord," the messengers replied. "This is everything."

Cortés ordered his men to fasten irons around the messengers' ankles and necks. Then he fired a huge gun. The messengers had never seen such a sight. They fainted from fear and fell to the deck.

The strangers revived them.

WHO WAS CORTÉS?

Hernan Cortés was a Spanish landowner who lived on the island of Cuba, which had been visited by Columbus in 1492 and then taken over by the Spanish. Like many men who had moved to the New World, Cortés dreamed of grasping a fortune for himself. With official backing from the governor of Cuba and using some of his own money, Cortés put together an expedition. The governor withdrew his official support, but Cortés left anyway, gambling on the success of his venture.

"I have heard about your people," Cortés said. "They say that one Aztec warrior can overpower twenty men. I want to see how strong you are." He gave them leather shields and iron swords. "Tomorrow, at dawn, you will fight, and then we will find out the truth."

"But this is not the wish of our lord and your servant, Moctezuma," the messengers answered. "He has only told us to greet you and bring you gifts."

"You will do as I say," said Cortés. "Tomorrow morning we shall eat. After that you will prepare for combat."

Then Cortés released them. Moctezuma's messengers got back in their boats and paddled away as quickly as they could. Some even paddled with their hands. When they reached land they scarcely stopped to catch their breath before hurrying back to Tenochtitlán to tell Moctezuma about the terrifying things that had happened.

WHO WAS MOCTEZUMA?

Moctezuma was the ninth Aztec emperor or *tlatoani*, an Aztec term that meant "speaker." He was the second ruler to bear the name Moctezuma. He had become emperor in 1502, picked, in the Aztec fashion, by the other nobles. Moctezuma was a little older than Cortés, thirty-eight to the Spaniard's thirty-three.

They described the strange sweet food they had eaten and the gun that had sounded to them like deafening thunder.

"A ball of stone comes out shooting sparks and raining fire. It makes smoke that smells of rotten mud. When the ball of stone hits a tree, the trunk splits into splinters, as if it has exploded from the inside.

"They cover their heads and bodies with metal. Their swords are metal, their bows are metal, their shields and spears are metal. Their deer carry them on their backs, making them as tall as the roof of a house."

When Moctezuma heard all this, he could not sleep or eat.

A few months later Moctezuma, against the advice of his chiefs, welcomed Cortés and his army as friends. The next year the Spaniards seized treasure and attacked the Aztecs during a festival. After retreating from the Aztecs, the Spaniards escaped. Moctezuma died during the fighting. Smallpox, a disease brought by the Europeans, killed thousands of Tenochtitlán's inhabitants. In May 1521 Cortés returned to attack Tenochtitlán and claimed victory after leaving the city in ruins.

MEET THE AUTHOR SHELLEY TANAKA

Shelley Tanaka grew up in Toronto, Canada, and attended university in Canada and Germany. She is the author of the "I Was There" series including *The Buried City of Pompeii*, *Discovering the Iceman*, *On Board the Titanic*, and *Secrets of the Mummies*. For more than twenty years she has been an editor of young adult and children's books. She currently lives in rural Ontario, Canada, with her family.

MEET THE ILLUSTRATOR GREG RUHL

Greg Ruhl is also a native Canadian. He graduated from the Ontario College of Art and has worked as a freelance illustrator in Canada for nearly twenty years. Ruhl worked previously with Shelley Tanaka on *The Buried City of Pompeii*.

To find out more about Shelley Tanaka and Greg Ruhl, visit Education Place.

www.eduplace.com/kids

Think About the Selection

1. Why did the men working on the electrical cables notify archaeological experts as soon as they discovered the carved stone?

2. Do you think Moctezuma's decision to treat the strangers as friends was a good one? Explain.

3. What does Cortés's treatment of the Aztec messengers reveal about him?

4. What do you think is the most exciting discovery that the archaeologists made while excavating the Great Temple? Explain.

5. The Aztec empire was one of the most advanced and powerful civilizations of its time. What details in the selection support this statement?

6. In your opinion, is it important to preserve artifacts from ancient cities such as Tenochtitlán? Why or why not?

7. **Connecting/Comparing** By reading *Lost Temple of the Aztecs*, what did you discover about the Aztec culture?

Expressing

Write a Letter

Write a letter to a friend describing the Aztec messengers who greeted Cortés. Also describe the gifts they brought with them.

Tips

- Look at the illustrations to help you describe the the messengers.
- Include vivid details in your description.
- Remember to include a date, a greeting, and a closing in your letter.

378

Math

Calculate Your Aztec Age

Reread the section on the Aztec year on page 371. Then, with a partner, calculate each other's ages in the Aztec 260-day calendar. Make a class chart listing all your classmates' ages in the 260-day Aztec calendar and in our 365-day calendar.

Bonus Calculate how many Aztec cycles, or "centuries," have passed since Cortés's arrival in Tenochtitlán.

	Age in 260-day calendar	Age in 365-day calendar
Bill		
Sara		
Tasha		
Jeremy		

Listening and Speaking

Role-Play a Scene

In a small group, role-play the scene in which the Aztec messengers board Cortés's ship, or the scene in which the messengers report their encounter with Cortés to Moctezuma.

Tips

- Use details from the selection to make the characters' dialogue seem real.
- Speak clearly and use gestures to enliven your performance.

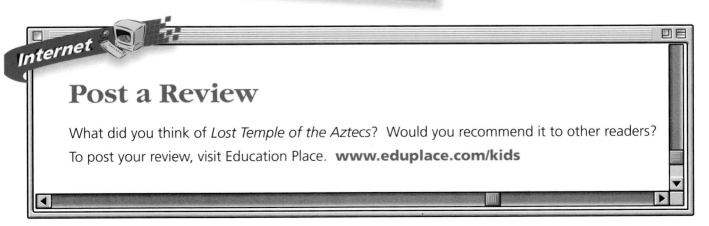

Internet

Post a Review

What did you think of *Lost Temple of the Aztecs*? Would you recommend it to other readers? To post your review, visit Education Place. **www.eduplace.com/kids**

Science Link

Skill: How to Adjust Your Rate of Reading

Before you read . . .

Identify the **purpose** of your reading. For example, are you studying for a test? Are you reading for pleasure? Your purpose will determine your reading rate.

As you read . . .

- Keep in mind the purpose of your reading.

- Stop occasionally to **monitor** your understanding. Ask yourself **questions** about your reading. If you don't understand the material, slow down. If the material is easy to understand, speed up your rate.

- Remember that it often helps to read nonfiction more slowly than fiction.

RAISING ROYAL TREASURES

Bit by bit, divers are recovering pieces of Cleopatra's lost palace.

It's a tale full of romance, sneaky tricks, tragedy and, most of all, girl power. On top of that, it's true. The real-life story of Cleopatra, a beautiful 17-year-old girl when she became the powerful ruler of ancient Egypt, has fascinated people for thousands of years. Dozens of plays, books and movies have told of her quest for power and love. Now new information about Cleopatra's life is coming to the surface. Parts of her ancient royal court have been found near Alexandria, Egypt — under water!

Finding a Lost Island

Ancient Egyptian writings and drawings show that Cleopatra owned a royal palace on an island named Antirhodos (An-teer-*uh*-dose). The island was near Alexandria, the capital city of Egypt during Cleopatra's reign in the first century B.C.

Although the city of Alexandria still exists today, floods and earthquakes buried Antirhodos under water more than 1,600 years ago. But it wasn't lost for good. In 1996 undersea explorer Franck Goddio found it beneath just 18 feet of water, off the shore of Alexandria. The ruins of what appears to be Cleopatra's palace lay buried in layers of mud, seaweed and garbage.

Goddio and his team of divers have spent two years uncovering statues, columns, pavement and pottery that may have belonged to the young queen. Their work is sponsored in part by the Discovery Channel, which broadcast a television special on the new findings.

Among the most sensational finds are two statues of sphinxes, imaginary creatures with the head of a human and the body of a lion. The faces of the sphinxes are in surprisingly good shape. So good, that experts have been able to identify one face as that of King Ptolemy (*Tall*-uh-mee) XII, Cleopatra's father.

How does it feel to come face to face underwater with an ancient sphinx? "It's fascinating!" Goddio told *Time for Kids*. "You see the sphinx, and it's looking at you. You know that it's the father of Cleopatra and that Cleopatra once saw it. It's like a dream."

A diver prepares an ancient stone for cleaning.

Even without a head, this statue is huge! It was probably made to honor an Egyptian king.

One Queen, Two Love Stories

Cleopatra and her brother Ptolemy XIII began to rule Egypt together in 51 B.C. But Ptolemy did not want to share the throne, and he forced Cleopatra out of the palace.

During this time, another great civilization was rising to power in Rome. Its main leader, Julius Caesar (*See-zer*), traveled to Egypt. In order to meet with him, Cleopatra is said to have sneaked into the palace rolled up in a carpet! Caesar soon fell in love with Cleopatra. He helped her push Ptolemy aside and take control of Egypt.

Romans were angered by Caesar's ties with Egypt's queen. Some feared that he had grown too powerful. Four years after meeting Cleopatra, Caesar was murdered by his enemies.

Three years passed before a new Roman leader, Mark Antony, met Cleopatra. Just like Caesar before him, Antony fell in love with her. He moved into Cleopatra's palace at Antirhodos.

Soon people back in Rome feared that Antony was more interested in Egypt than in his own empire. They turned against him and Egypt. In despair, Cleopatra and Antony took their own lives. Ancient Egypt's last queen died at the age of 39. Soon after her death, the Romans took control of Egypt.

Though her reign ended 2,000 years ago, Cleopatra continues to enchant people everywhere. For that reason, Goddio hopes to set up an underwater museum at the palace site. Visitors would be able to explore and experience Cleopatra's world up close. "To be there, underwater where she reigned and died," says Goddio, "is unbelievable."

DID YOU KNOW?

- Egypt began as two kingdoms, Upper and Lower Egypt. They were united in 3100 B.C.

- Egypt's kings were called pharaohs (*fair-ohs*).

- Ancient Egyptians loved games! Kids played leapfrog and tug-of-war. Grownups played a board game called senet. Players threw sticks to determine which way to move on the board.

- Egyptians invented a written alphabet called hieroglyphics. It used pictures to represent words.

- Egyptians worshipped hundreds of gods and goddesses. Ra (Rah), the sun god, was the most important, but there was even a cat goddess named Bastet!

Goddio's team lifting an ancient sphinx from the water near modern Alexandria.

A Research Report

A research report presents facts about a particular topic. Use this student's writing as a model when you write a research report of your own.

The Ancient Culture of the Inca

The ancient Inca culture of Peru formed a vast and powerful empire that extended from northern Ecuador to central Chile. The Inca Empire began in the 1100s and ended in the 1500s, when the Spanish army took control.

The Inca people were considered an empire, but in fact they were really a confederation of many nations located in South America. The Inca Empire was made up of what are today Peru, Ecuador, Bolivia, and parts of Argentina and Chile. These different nations were treated well as long as they followed the Inca leader and obeyed the laws.

> The first paragraph of a research report usually **introduces** the topic.

> **Topic sentences** present the **main idea** of a report.

The Inca people had a set social structure. The ruler, a descendant of the sun god, was considered divine. Then came the royal family, the immediate family of the ruler. Next came the heads of the various nations and their people, and the clans with their leaders. Finally, the common people were grouped by tens with their own leaders.

The Inca spoke a language called Quechua. All of the conquered people were required to learn and speak this language. Even today there are people in the Andes Mountains who speak Quechua.

A good report always has **supporting details**.

Inca culture formed a vast empire.

The Inca were good engineers. They were able to build huge forts, using perfectly cut stone that fit together so well that mortar was not needed. In fact, their forts are still standing today. They also built roads and tunnels through the mountains. They built bridges as well. The ability to perform all of these skills is amazing, since the Inca didn't have the tools and machinery that we have today. They were also able to make mountainous terrain into usable farmland on which they grew corn and potatoes and raised animals such as llama and alpaca.

The Inca raised animals, like this llama.

The Inca Empire finally came to an end in 1532, when the Spanish army, led by Francisco Pizarro, conquered the Inca leader and the royal family. After the capture of the royal family, it was easy for the Spanish army to gain control of the Empire.

A good report has a **strong conclusion**.

List of Sources

Beck, Barbara L., and Lorna Greenberg. *The Incas*. Rev. ed. Watts, 1983 For Young Readers.

The World Book Encyclopedia, World Book, Inc. Vol. 10, 1997.

Meet the Author

Stephanie S.
Grade: six
State: New York
Hobbies: movies, crafts, and reading
What she would like to be when she grows up: a teacher

Background and Vocabulary

The Great Wall

The story of thousands of miles of earth and stone that turned a nation into a fortress

By Elizabeth Mann

The Great Wall

Read to find the meanings of these words.

e • Glossary

craftsmen
domain
durable
dynasty
excluding
extravagance
laborers
massive
nomadic
steppe
terrain

TWO CULTURES, ONE WALL

For centuries the **terrain** of China protected its people from enemies on three sides. In the west lay mountains and a desert. To the south and the east lay the Pacific Ocean. Only in the north was there flat grassland called the **steppe**. This was where the Mongols, a **nomadic** tribe, could easily invade China's borders.

Because they lived in small groups and moved often, the Mongols had no need for **extravagance**. They herded sheep and horses. As skilled horsemen, they were fearsome warriors.

A Mongol leader sitting on a horse.

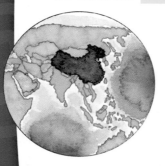

| 300 | B.C. | A.D. | 300 | 600 |

221 B.C.
Construction of the first long wall begins under Emperor Qin Shi Huangdi.

388

China's Great Wall

Most of the Chinese were farmers, while some were **laborers** and **craftsmen**. China was ruled by an emperor, and when power was passed along from generation to generation, the ruling family was called a **dynasty**.

The Chinese looked down upon the Mongols, yet they also feared them. When trade between the Mongols and the Chinese stopped, the Mongols would attack farms and cities. Many emperors tried various ways of **excluding** the Mongols from their **domain**. **Massive** walls were built over the centuries as a defense, but none of them proved to be as **durable** as the one you will read about in *The Great Wall*.

A Chinese farmer transports fruit trees with the aid of a yoke.

A.D. 1200
Mongols grow stronger under their leader Genghis Khan.

A.D. 1644
Manchus, another nomadic tribe, invade China; Great Wall abandoned.

| 900 | 1200 | 1500 | 1800 |

A.D. 1449
Building of the last Great Wall begins.

MEET THE AUTHOR

Elizabeth Mann

Elizabeth Mann was a public school teacher in New York City before she wrote her first nonfiction book. One day, while teaching her second grade students about the Brooklyn Bridge, she noticed how bored they all looked. The next day, she told them an extraordinary story about a family that spent fourteen years building the bridge. Suddenly, everyone was excited. That story became part of her first book, *The Brooklyn Bridge*. Mann has also written books about the Great Pyramid, the Panama Canal, and the Roman Colosseum.

MEET THE ILLUSTRATOR

Alan Witschonke

Alan Witschonke is an award-winning illustrator who has worked with Elizabeth Mann on *The Great Wall* and *The Brooklyn Bridge*. He lives in Belmont, Massachusetts, with his wife, Judith, who is also an illustrator, and their two sons.

Internet

To find out more about Elizabeth Mann and Alan Witschonke, visit Education Place. **www.eduplace.com/kids**

The Great Wall

The story of thousands of miles of earth and stone that turned a nation into a fortress

By Elizabeth Mann

Strategy Focus

The Chinese built a wall thousands of miles long to protect themselves from invaders. As you read, **summarize** how the wall was built.

For thousands of years, fierce Mongol warriors threatened China from the north. In 221 B.C., the Chinese began to build a thousand-mile-long wall to protect their farms and cities from the Mongols. Over the centuries, the wall crumbled. Other walls were built, but still the raids went on.

In A.D. 1449, the Mongol army grew much stronger. More and more Chinese soldiers were killed. After one devastating defeat, a young Chinese emperor, Zhu Qizhen, was kidnapped by a Mongol prince. When news of the kidnapping reached the Chinese government, the people were seized by fear. Too weak to fight back, they decided to build a stronger wall. The building of the Great Wall, the last long wall, went on for the next two centuries.

There was no masterplan or blueprint for a Great Wall. Each emperor built when and where he thought the Mongol threat was the greatest. Construction across northern China continued for the next two centuries. The routes through mountain passes that the Mongols used most often to reach China were blocked with walls. Those walls were then connected with other sections of wall.

In the western part of the country, walls were built of pounded earth, an ancient building technique. Peasants' homes, city walls, even Qin Shi Huangdi's first long wall had been made of pounded earth. In the dry, desert terrain of western China, earth was the only building material available in great quantity. It was simple to build with pounded earth. No skilled craftsmen were needed, just many, many laborers.

Toward the end of the Ming dynasty much building was done in the eastern mountains to protect the capital city, Peking. Builders began using bricks and blocks of stone instead of pounded earth. Walls built of stone and brick didn't erode in wind and rain. They didn't need constant repair as earth walls did.

Stone and brick walls were strong and durable, but they were more complicated to build. Progress was slow. Stone had to be dug from quarries, cut into blocks, and transported to the wall. Bricks were made from mud and then baked in kilns. Workers with special skills — stonemasons and brickmakers — were needed to handle the new materials.

Tens of thousands of workers were involved in building the Great Wall. The army provided many laborers. Soldiers became construction workers and generals became architects and engineers. Peasants were required to work on the wall. They worked for months at a time for little or no pay. Criminals served their sentences doing hard labor on the wall.

Even the most massive wall needed soldiers to patrol it. The Mongols were a determined enemy. If the wall was not guarded, they would find a way to get through. Many different kinds of fortifications were built along the wall for soldiers to live in. Some forts were large enough for one thousand soldiers. Watchtowers, built right into the wall, were sometimes so small they barely held twelve soldiers.

396

The wall and the soldiers who guarded it were part of an elaborate defense system across northern China. Nearly a million soldiers patrolled the Great Wall, but they were spread thinly across thousands of miles. The Mongol warriors were outnumbered, but they had an advantage. Thanks to their swift horses, they flowed like water across the steppe. They could assemble anywhere, at any time to launch an attack and then disappear just as quickly back into the steppe. To defend against their fast-moving enemy the Chinese used an ingenious system of communication to gather soldiers together for battle.

Stone platforms, called signal towers, were built on high ground near the wall. When Mongol horsemen were spotted, a smoky fire was built on top of the nearest signal tower. The smoke was visible for miles, and when guards at the next tower saw it they built their own fire, passing the signal along. Sometimes loud cannon shots accompanied the plumes of smoke. The number of smoke plumes and cannon shots was a code indicating how many enemy riders were approaching.

The wall was shaped to fit the landscape it passed through. In flat desert areas it ran in a straight line. In hilly areas it twisted and turned like a dragon. The Chinese took advantage of the terrain to make the wall even more insurmountable. They built along the crests of tall hills and mountain peaks. The wall plunged down into rivers and then continued on the far bank. At the eastern end it ran into the sea.

By 1644, the Great Wall ran from Jiayuguan in the west, past the Gobi Desert, across the Yellow River, past Peking, all the way to Shanhaiguan on the Bohai Sea in the east. A Mongol warrior could ride for miles in its shadow without coming to a gate. And work was still being done on it.

The wall demanded great sacrifices of the Chinese people. The workers who built it were separated from their families for long periods of time. Many didn't survive the grueling work and harsh conditions.

Life was no easier for the soldiers who guarded the wall. Winters in northern China were punishingly cold and the summers were dry and hot. They were paid very little, and had to grow their own food in order to survive. Farming was difficult in the dry climate, but they had no choice.

Even though soldiers were poorly paid, the wall was very expensive. Adding to it, repairing it, and patrolling it cost more every year. To pay for it, the Ming government taxed the people of China.

At the same time, the cost of supporting the Ming government was increasing. Tens of thousands of people were part of the court, and more were being added all the time. Officals and advisors, well-fed and dressed in silk, spent their days quarreling and endlessly vying for the emperor's favor. Paying for the extravagance inside the Forbidden City, or the palaces of the Ming emperors, placed another burden on Chinese taxpayers.

People grew angry at the extravagance and corruption in the Ming court, and at the taxes that were being imposed on them. Once again, peasants began to rebel against government officials. The Ming dynasty, which had been founded by a peasant, was now threatened by its own people. In 1644, an opportunity arose. A group of Chinese rebels stormed the Forbidden City and overthrew the last Ming emperor.

The world outside China was changing.

Once again lacking strong leadership, the Mongols were growing weaker and less united. Meanwhile, another nomadic tribe, the Manchus, had been gathering strength for years. They controlled a large area north and east of Peking and had conquered Mongol lands to the west. It was only a matter of time before they tried to expand their domain into China.

The Manchus waited. When rebels attacked the Forbidden City, they seized the opportunity. They quickly offered to come to the rescue of the Ming dynasty.

The Ming army gratefully threw open the gates and the Manchu forces marched through the Great Wall and on into Peking. The Manchus chased the rebels out of the Forbidden City, but they did not restore power to the Ming. Instead, they seized the throne and established their own dynasty, the Qing (ching).

Because the Ming dynasty had been disliked by many of its own people, it was easy for the Manchus to win Chinese support for the Qing dynasty. The combined Manchu and Chinese forces were far stronger than the Mongols. Subdued, the Mongols withdrew to distant parts of the steppe. Their fierce army, which had once so terrified the Chinese, was just a memory.

The Qing emperors ruled the land on both sides of the Great Wall. The Mongols were not a threat. The wall no longer marked a border, and it wasn't needed for defense. Construction stopped and the watchtowers were abandoned. Traders and travelers passed freely through gates that never closed.

Gossiping and scheming, as the two men at the lower left of this painting show, were as much a part of court life as beautiful silk robes and portrait painting.

In 1644 the Great Wall was longer, stronger, and better guarded than it had ever been before, but for the Manchus it was as though it didn't exist at all. They walked through it without a struggle and readily conquered China. The wall was meaningless.

But was it suddenly meaningless or had it been that way for a long time? Was it the wall or the Mongols' own lack of unity that prevented them from conquering China again during the Ming rule? Was excluding the Mongols the best, or the only, way of preventing their raids? Would negotiating peaceful trade with them have been effective? Or even possible? We will never know. We can only imagine the fear that the Ming emperors felt when facing the

Mongols, and how that fear influenced the choices they made in defending against them.

Looking at the Great Wall today we are amazed at its length, at how difficult it was to build, at the expense and effort that went into its construction. It was an extraordinary feat and the Great Wall has emerged as the most famous and enduring creation of the Ming dynasty. We are also aware that building it severely weakened the Ming government. Ironically, the greatest accomplishment of the Ming dynasty was an important cause of its downfall.

Think About the Selection

1. What unexpected circumstance led to the defeat of the Ming dynasty?

2. Do you think a nation would build a wall like the Great Wall of China today? Explain.

3. Describe what life was like for the Chinese people during the Ming dynasty. List specific examples from the selection.

4. What effects did the construction of the Great Wall have on the people of China?

5. Would you want to visit the Great Wall? Why or why not?

6. What lessons could a modern leader learn from the story of the Great Wall?

7. **Connecting/Comparing** Compare the conflict between the Mongols and the Chinese with the conflict between the Aztecs and the Spanish in *Lost Temple of the Aztecs*. How were their relationships alike, and how were they different?

Narrating

Write a Story

The selection provides many details about the lives of people who worked on the Great Wall. Write a short story about a typical day in the life of a soldier who guarded the wall.

Tips

- Use dialogue to show what your character thinks or feels.
- Use details from the selection to describe your character, the setting, and the day's events.

Science

Make a Poster

Review the different building methods and materials used by the builders of the Great Wall. Then make a poster showing the materials they used and advantages and disadvantages of each.

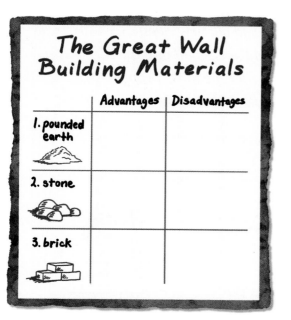

Viewing

Compare an Illustration and a Photograph

Look closely at the illustration of the Great Wall on page 396. Compare this to the photograph of the wall in "Two Cultures, One Wall" on page 389. What different things do you learn about the wall from each view? Discuss with a partner.

Internet

Go on a Web Field Trip

Visit Education Place to take an online field trip. **www.eduplace.com/kids**

Skill: How to Read a Timeline

Before you read...

- Notice how the time-line is organized. Timelines are read from left to right or from top to bottom.

- Determine the total number of years covered.

As you read...

- When you read about an event in the main text, locate the event on the timeline.

- As the years labeled **B.C.** get larger in number, they go back in time. To figure out how many years passed between B.C. events, subtract the smaller number from the larger number.

- To figure out how many years passed between a B.C. event and an **A.D.** event, add the B.C. number to the A.D. number.

BUILDING ANCIENT ROME

by Dr. Sarah McNeill

The Romans were skilled builders and engineers. They planned and laid out new cities, providing public lavatories and baths, good drains and a constant supply of water for the townspeople. Many of their constructions are still standing today.

Making Arches

To build an arch, a curved wooden support was put at the top of two stone columns.

Wedge-shaped stones were put around the support. When it was taken away, the arch stayed up on its own.

Working in Stone

Slaves cut out stone blocks from quarries by drilling holes and filling them with wooden wedges. Water swelled the wood and split the stone.

When Were They Built?

312 B.C.
First road and first aqueduct constructed in Rome

55 B.C.
First stone theater built in Rome

46 B.C.
Julius Caesar builds a new forum in Rome

20–16 B.C.
Pont du Gard aqueduct built in Gaul near Nîmes

13–11 B.C.
Theater of Marcellus built in Rome

A.D. 64
Fire destroys many of Rome's buildings

A.D. 79
Work on the Colosseum in Rome finishes

A.D. 98
Trajan's Column built in Rome

A.D. 100
Aqueduct at Segovia constructed in Spain

A.D. 118
Hadrian builds a great villa at Tivoli near Rome

A.D. 118–128
Pantheon built in Rome

A.D. 122–138
Hadrian's Wall built by Romans in Britain

A.D. 212–216
Baths of Caracalla built in Rome

100 B.C.

50 B.C.

B.C.

A.D.

A.D. 50

A.D. 100

A.D. 150

A.D. 200

A.D. 250

A stone theatre

Fire in Rome

Trajan's column

Biggest Buildings

The Colosseum, in Rome, was an enormous amphitheater built to stage gladiator fights. It seated crowds of up to 50,000 people and took ten years to build.

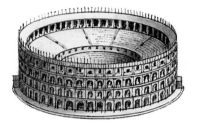

The Colosseum

The Pantheon was a temple with a large, circular hall. It was one of the most famous buildings of ancient times because of its vast domed roof, 141 feet in diameter. Built between A.D. 118 and 128, it has been used as a place of worship ever since.

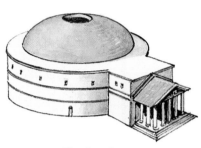

The Pantheon

The Baths of Caracalla in Rome were built on a grand scale. The main hall was enormous, over 100 x 25 yards in size. The baths could take up to 1,600 bathers every day. The buildings included shops, offices, libraries, gymnasiums and sports facilities.

Hadrian's Wall, a fortified wall 75 miles long, was built by Romans across ancient Britain to keep out warring tribes. The wall was of stone, up to 10 feet thick, with fortified positions along its length.

Hadrian's Wall

Central Heating

Wealthy Romans enjoyed central heating thanks to underfloor heating systems called hypocausts. Floors were supported on piles of bricks, with space underneath for air to circulate. A fire sent hot air into this space, warming the rooms above. Hypocausts were used in public baths as well as private houses.

Aqueducts and Bridges

The Romans were very skilled at building aqueducts and bridges. Aqueducts brought water to cities from springs and lakes in the hills. The Romans realized that they could use gravity to bring the water down to towns at lower levels. Eleven aqueducts brought water to Rome, from up to 30 miles away. Over 300 million gallons of water were brought to the city every day to supply fountains, baths and private houses.

 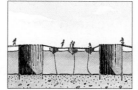  

1. To make a river crossing, first a temporary bridge was laid across a row of boats.

2. Then circles of wooden stakes were sunk into the river bed and the water pumped out of the space inside.

3. These spaces were filled with columns of stone blocks.

4. A wooden frame was lifted onto the columns by cranes to form the bridge.

Roads

Engineers built 50,000 miles of roads, to link all parts of the Empire to Rome. The roads enabled soldiers to move about the Empire, but they were also used by merchants. Roman roads took the shortest, straightest routes possible. Some roads involved tunneling through hills and cutting across valleys.

1. First, surveyors used a *groma* to make sure the land was level and marked out the road with stakes.

2. Then workmen dug a trench, up to 40 feet wide, and laid curbstones along the edges.

3. The trench was packed with sand, then stones, then rubble. These layers formed the foundation of the road.

4. The top layer of stone slabs, the road's surface, was curved to allow rain to drain off.

Background and Vocabulary

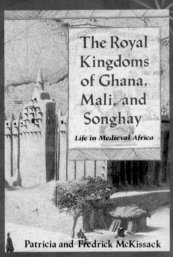

The Royal Kingdoms
of Ghana, Mali, and
Songhay
Life in Medieval Africa

Patricia and Fredrick McKissack

The Royal Kingdoms of Ghana, Mali, and Songhay

Read to find the meanings of these words.

e ● Glossary

caravans
flourishing
goods
primary
vicinity

The Rise of Ghana

FROM A.D. 500 TO 1700, civilization in western Africa was **flourishing**. In this selection from *The Royal Kingdoms of Ghana, Mali, and Songhay*, you'll discover the people and culture of ancient Ghana. The first great empire in Ghana was created by a group called the Soninke, a people who spoke the Mande language.

We know much about ancient Ghana from *griots* (GREE-ohs) — storytellers who pass along the Soninke people's oral history from generation to generation. Their musical and dramatic performances are the earliest accounts of Ghana's origin.

Aboure tribe elder telling tribal stories

A.D. 200	300	400	500

A.D. 200
Ghana first established by Soninke people of northwest Africa

The ancient kingdom of Ghana was located in present-day Mali and Mauritania in western Africa, in the **vicinity** of the Sahara desert. With its fertile land, Ghana quickly became a wealthy area with advanced methods of iron and gold work, carpentry, and pottery. The kingdom's **primary** source of wealth came from trading **goods** with surrounding areas. Trade wouldn't have been possible without the **caravans** that transported these goods.

A Samburu tribesman (above) leads a camel caravan through the wilderness.

A musical instrument from Ghana, made from a dried gourd and covered by seeds woven into a net

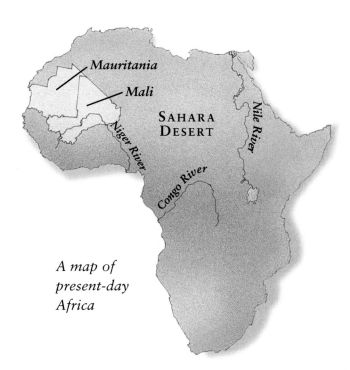

A map of present-day Africa

A.D. 990
Ghana, at height of its power, captures the Muslim city of Awdoghast.

A.D. 1050
Invasion of Ghana; wide disruption of trade

| 600 | 700 | 800 | 900 | 1000 |

A.D. 700–1000
Ghana is dominant power in Western Sudan

A.D. 1000
Al-Bakri writes history of Old Kingdom of Ghana.

Meet the Authors
Fredrick and Patricia McKissack

A life together: Fredrick and Patricia McKissack both grew up in Nashville, Tennessee, and attended the same university.

Beginnings: While working as a teacher, Patricia couldn't find good books about African Americans for her students. This led her to write her first biography.

Prolific writers: The McKissacks have published nearly a hundred books about the history of African Americans, including *Red-Tail Angels: The Story of the Tuskegee Airmen of World War II* and *African American Inventors*.

Their mission: "We try to enlighten, to change attitudes, to form new attitudes — to build bridges with books."

Meet the Illustrator Rob Wood

Southern roots: Like the McKissacks, Rob Wood grew up in Tennessee.

Artist's intuition: Wood says he "always wanted to become an illustrator." In the fourth grade, his teacher was an artist and encouraged him to follow his dream.

Hobbies: Sailing in the Chesapeake Bay, snorkeling, diving, and watching the stars and planets through his telescope

To find out more about Fredrick and Patricia McKissack and Rob Wood, visit Education Place. **www.eduplace.com/kids**

The Royal
Kingdoms
of Ghana,
Mali, and
Songhay

Life in Medieval Africa

Patricia and Fredrick McKissack

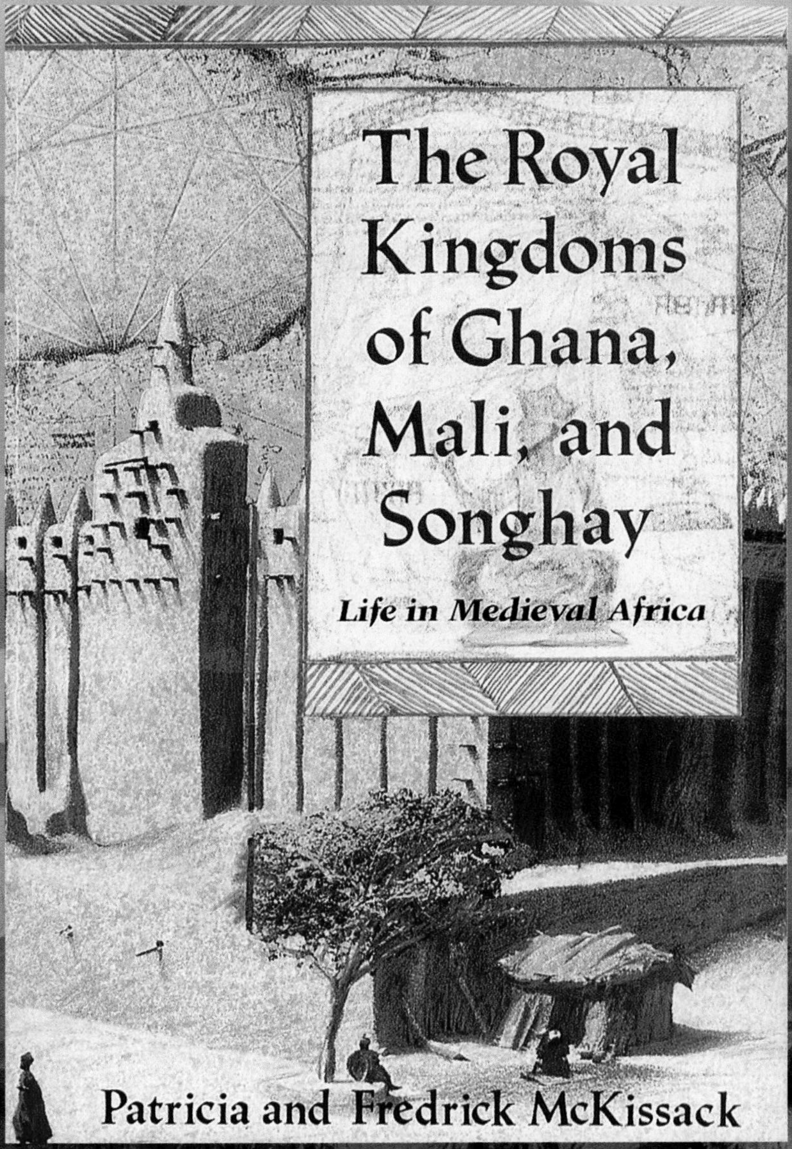

Strategy Focus

The people of ancient Ghana traded with peoples in faraway lands. As you read, **monitor** how well you understand the information. **Clarify** parts you don't understand by rereading or reading ahead.

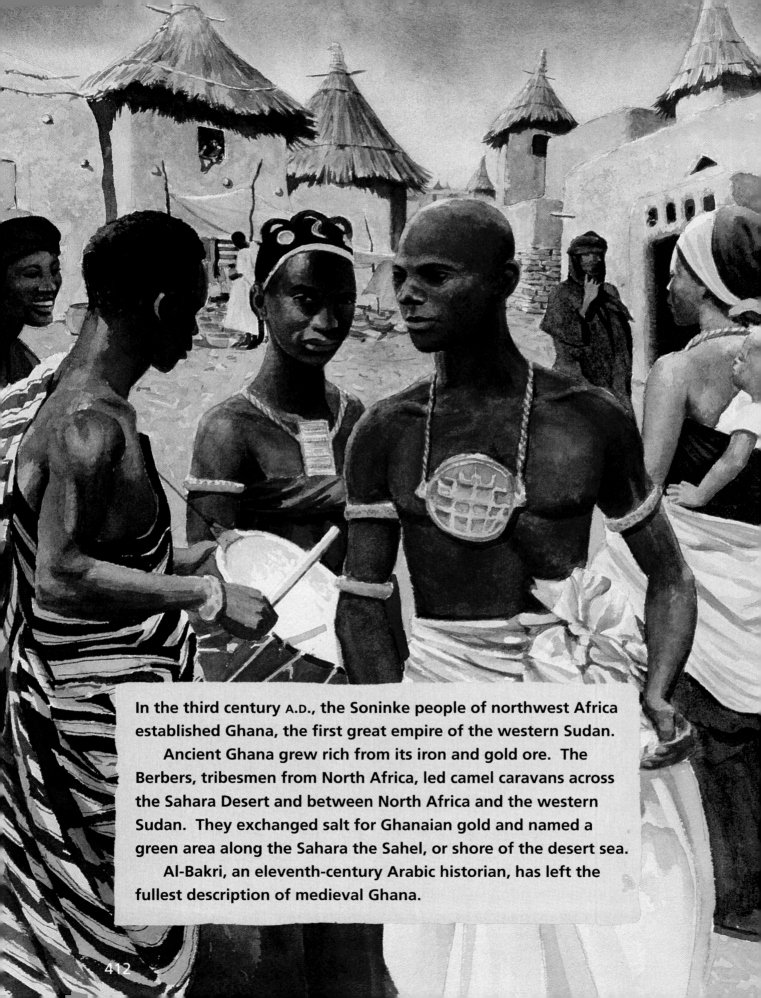

In the third century A.D., the Soninke people of northwest Africa established Ghana, the first great empire of the western Sudan.

Ancient Ghana grew rich from its iron and gold ore. The Berbers, tribesmen from North Africa, led camel caravans across the Sahara Desert and between North Africa and the western Sudan. They exchanged salt for Ghanaian gold and named a green area along the Sahara the Sahel, or shore of the desert sea.

Al-Bakri, an eleventh-century Arabic historian, has left the fullest description of medieval Ghana.

412

Gold for Salt

Ghana (GAH-nuh) had more than enough gold. Ordinary people adorned themselves with golden jewelry and wore cloth spun with strands of golden thread. Al-Bakri claimed that the king's hitching post was a gold nugget weighing close to forty pounds!

Everybody knew the location of the salt mines, but the exact location of the gold mines was a well-guarded secret. People assumed that the mines were located in the vicinity of Wangara.

An Arabic commentator, named al-Idrisi, described the city of Wangara as he saw it in the twelfth century:

> *In Wangara there are flourishing towns and famous fortresses. Its inhabitants are rich. They possess gold in abundance, and receive productions which are brought to them from the most distant countries of the world.*

Al-Idrisi also noted that Wangara was an island that was often flooded. When the water receded, gold could be found lying on top of the ground. Some scholars think that Bambuk, located on the headwaters of the Senegal River, and Bure (byur), at the headwaters of the Niger (NY-juhr) in modern-day Guinea, were the sites of Wangaran gold mines. Modern archeologists have found mine shafts, some as deep as fifty feet, at Bambuk and Bure. But not all archeologists are convinced that these are the remains of the mines that supplied old Ghana, and they are continuing to search the floodplain of the middle Niger for other possible sites.

By limiting outside contacts, the Wangaran miners protected the secret of their mines. According to a widespread tale, they even traded their gold dust for salt and other goods through a special, silent form of trade called dumb bartering.

Dumb Bartering

Al-Musadi, a tenth-century writer from Baghdad, reported that dumb bartering took place in this way: Their donkeys ladened with grains, leather, cloth, and salt, traders arrived at Wangara, where men lived in holes (no doubt, mines). There the traders spread out their goods along a stream or near a thicket. Then they announced their presence by beating on a special drum called a *deba*. The merchants went away.

The shy Wangaran miners crept from their hiding places and laid out a measure of gold dust. They, too, departed. Some time later the traders returned, and, if the amount of gold dust was acceptable, they took it and left. If not, they went away again and the Wangarans came back and made a counteroffer. Each group went back and forth until an agreement was satisfactory to both sides. Through years of experience, both sides had a general idea of what exchange would be acceptable, so the system generally moved quickly and smoothly. The silent miners inspired a lot of curiosity by trading in this manner. But, even if they were captured, as sometimes they were, the Wangaran miners chose death over betraying the location of the mines.

The Wangaran miners were secretive, but no less eager to trade. Trade was the lifeblood of Ghana. The king employed a standing, well-disciplined army whose primary responsibility was to defend his empire. The soldiers' peacetime duty was to protect the steady flow of caravans that came into the kingdom and the Berber traders who were Ghana's allies in the sub-Saharan trade system.

The Trade Caravans

Gold and salt weren't the only items traded in Ghana. Local donkey caravans arrived daily from all points in the empire, bringing slaves, honey, jewelry, tools, metal and leather goods, rare birds, livestock, horses, special cloth called *chigguyiya*, and, of course, news. Caravans also left Koumbi Saleh (KOOM-bee SAL-ay) and other large trading cities in the kingdom going to points north.

The arrival of a trans-Saharan camel caravan was a special event. Traders brought rare and wonderful treasures like jewels, silk, and furs from everywhere in the Islamic world, including Egypt, Arabia, Palestine, and even from as far away as central Asia.

During the period of old Ghana, caravans departed from Koumbi Saleh and usually took the western route through Awdoghast. Caravans from North Africa came through Sijilmasa in Morocco and down to the market towns of Awdoghast and Walata. From there the caravans split up and took short routes along the Senegal and Niger rivers.

The makeup of a long-distance caravan was as complex as it was colorful. Everything centered around the camels, which made trans-Saharan travel possible.

The camel was to the Berbers what the bison was to the Native American. The animal provided transportation, milk, wool, hides, and meat. These oddly shaped creatures adapted to desert travel so well because they have a double row of eyelashes, hairy ear openings, and the ability to close their nostrils to protect themselves from the sun and sand. Camels can endure the dry heat better than any other beast of burden. They can drink up to twenty-five gallons of water at a time, then go several days without food.

That's where praise for the camel ends. They are famous for being ill-tempered and make traveling in a caravan very difficult. They bite, spit, kick, run away, or refuse to move. Famously stubborn, camels cannot be handled by just anybody, so caravan leaders usually hired a full-time cameleer and crew to manage them.

Generally, several merchants pooled their resources to form a caravan. There was safety in numbers, too. On the day of departure, as many as a hundred camels were loaded with merchandise and supplies. An official made a strict accounting of all the goods for tax purposes. Then each merchant and his entourage assembled and were assigned their positions. Finally, when all the merchants, slaves, bodyguards, scholars, ambassadors, poets, and musicians had mounted their camels, the overland journey began.

There were four major trade routes that the caravans coming from the east could have traveled. Following an experienced guide, the caravan made its way through the ever-changing Saharan sands, clocking about three miles an hour, stopping only to observe the required prayer periods.

Mile after mile, day after day, the caravan pushed west and then south. Occasionally they must have been greeted by a lizard, a scorpion, or a snake, but no other life could endure the desert. The caravan moved from one oasis to another before the sun rose too high and temperatures soared to 130°F. During the hot part of the day the travelers rested at Berber-run caravanserai, much like our modern-day roadside rest stops.

Sometimes the caravan moved a few more miles at night by using the stars as their guide. More often, everyone slept, while guards stood watch for thieves, which were a real threat. But once a caravan reached the borders of Ghana, they were safe, for the king's soldiers guarded the area. Royal patrols maintained order and guaranteed safe passage to all visitors.

A typical caravan from Arabia to the Sahel took about forty days to complete. Coming out of the desert at a major city in Ghana must have been a wonderful sight to desert travelers who had endured such a long, hot journey.

Daily Life

Whether or not it was the capital of Ghana, Koumbi Saleh was certainly an important city, and there is growing evidence that there were other large trading centers on the Niger and Senegal rivers. By about A.D. 800, Jenne (JEHN-nay) alone had about 20,000 inhabitants, archeologists assure us. Most Soninke towns, though, had about 500 to 1,500 residents. These smaller towns were surrounded by walls with moats or pits in front of them.

City dwellers wore expensive clothing, owned objects of art, swords, copper utensils, foreign products, and ate exotic foods, especially citrus fruit, but a majority of the people didn't live that way.

Eighty percent of the population lived outside the towns, in small farming compounds, where a man and his sons' and daughters' families worked cooperatively. Several compounds of the same clan made up a village, but according to custom the land couldn't be bought or sold. Village leaders, appointed by the local king, allocated land to each family according to need. One family might be given the right to farm a piece of land, while another family might be given the right to harvest the fruit from the trees grown on the same land. If there was a dispute, each party could take their grievance to the local king, and even to the great king in the capital.

Anthropologists who have studied Soninke village life have discovered that eighth-century Mande people had advanced farming skills. They probably used dikes and earthen dams for irrigation, and their use of land was so well managed, farmers even grew enough to support the larger cities.

Ghana's major crops included millet, sorghum, cotton, ground nuts, rice, cow peas, okra, pumpkins, watermelons, kola nuts, sesame seeds, and shea nuts — butternuts — from which they made a spread.

Even in the villages, trade was an important aspect of daily life. A village that grew millet and cotton might trade with another that grew butternuts and watermelons. This local trading system helped unite the various groups who lived within the empire.

Men and women shared the workload, each taking responsibility for various chores. The men hunted and did most of the farming. The women were responsible for harvesting and processing the food for storage and sale. Women made pots and baskets and tended chickens. During the harvest season, men built houses, made tools, or spent a month on border duty in the military.

Because each man was expected to serve in the military for at least one month every year and to bring his own weapons, time was set aside for him to make bows and arrows and spears. At other times the men shared in making axes, hoes, and scythes. Women and men made baskets, pots, and utensils. Grinding stones for making meal from millet and sorghum were made by both men and women pooling their talents and resources.

Village houses were made of sun-dried mud or acacia wood and stone. Because of the hot climate, they were used mostly for sleeping and storage while a great many activities took place outside. Since the people were, in fact, a large family, the women cooked, ate, worked, and entertained together, and the men hunted and worked the fields together.

Inside furnishings were few and personal belongings were fewer still. The average household contained one sleeping mat or cot per person, rugs, and a stool. There might be a wooden or woven storage chest. The climate also made a lot of clothing unnecessary. Farmers wore woven cotton breeches, tunics, and sandals. Women wrapped their heads and draped themselves in cloth. Their diet was simple but adequate. Visitors were always welcome to share a meal, which most of the time consisted of rice stuffed in green peppers, milk, fruits, and wild game.

Although a farmer's possessions may seem meager by today's standards, he was not poor. Successful farmers had a good standard of living and they also had a respected place in society.

The Soninke people loved stories and poetry, and they still do today. An often-repeated theme in Mande proverbs is family. This one dates back to the old kingdom: *Kings may come and go, but the family endures.*

Among the Mande, family relationships were not defined as they are today. A child's oldest paternal uncle was her big father. Her youngest paternal uncle was her little father. A child's maternal aunt was his big mother and so on. Cousins were brothers and sisters. Therefore, there were no orphans or homeless people within their society. An elder surrounded and cared for by a big family was considered rich beyond measure. That's why the birth of a child was celebrated with feasting, dancing, and singing.

"Song of the Turtle" is a poem that dates back to the Ghanaian period:

> *We lived in freedom*
> *Before man appeared:*
> *Our world was undisturbed,*
> *One day followed the other joyfully.*
> *Dissent was never heard.*
> *Then man broke into our forest,*
> *With cunning and belligerence.*
> *He pursued us*
> *With greed and envy:*
> *Our freedom vanished.*

423

Responding

Think About the Selection

The Royal Kingdoms of Ghana, Mali, and Songhay
Life in Medieval Africa
Patricia and Fredrick McKissack

1. Why do you think the workers at the Wangaran gold mine refused to reveal the mine's location even when threatened with death?

2. What details support the main idea that trade was the "lifeblood of Ghana"?

3. Do you think that the ancient practice of bartering would be a successful way of doing business in today's world? Why or why not?

4. In what ways did the people of ancient Ghana make good use of the resources they had? Give specific examples.

5. Would you have liked to be part of a trans-Saharan camel caravan? If not, why not? If so, describe the role you would have wanted on the trip.

6. Based on information in the selection, describe the daily life in a Soninke village.

7. **Connecting/Comparing** Compare the life of a soldier guarding the Great Wall of China to the life of a farmer in Ghana. Which life would you prefer? Why?

Persuading

Write an Advertisement

Make a poster advertising the arrival of a camel caravan in the ancient city of Koumbi Saleh. Try to persuade people to come to greet the caravan and view the goods.

Tips

- Think of a head-line that will grab readers' interest.
- Use imperative sentences to urge people to attend.
- Include vivid details.

Social Studies

Compare Lifestyles

Make a chart that compares how village and city dwellers lived in ancient Ghana. Include the following categories in the chart: food and clothing; possessions; occupations; and family life.

	Village Life	City Life
food & clothing		
possessions		
occupations		
family life		

Listening and Speaking

Conduct a Trade

With a partner, act out a trade between a member of a trans-Saharan caravan and a city merchant. In the conversation, each person should describe what he or she has to trade and use bargaining skills to try to get the best deal possible.

Bonus Imagine that the traders speak different languages. Act out another version of the trade. Use movements and props instead of words.

Internet

Send an E-Postcard

Tell a friend about one or more of the ancient cultures you've read about in this theme. To send your friend an e-postcard, visit Education Place. **www.eduplace.com/kids**

Social Studies Link

Skill: How to Read a Diagram

Interpreting a Diagram

- Identify whether the diagram shows a **cross-section**, a **cut-away view**, or a view from above.

- Read **labels** to identify different items or parts of the diagram. Ask yourself: Are the labels clear? What do they add to my understanding?

- Compare the diagram to the text. Ask yourself: What does the diagram add to the text? How is the diagram useful? Should more information be included?

Daily Life in Ancient Greece

by Robert Nicholson

A GREEK HOME

Most Greeks were farmers or craftsmen living in simple houses. Businesses were family run with a few slaves to help out.

Greek houses were arranged around a court-yard with an altar in the middle. Ordinary Greek houses were made from mud bricks dried in the sun. It was easy to dig through the walls, so burglars were known as wall diggers.

The living rooms were on the ground floor, with bedrooms above. Often men and women had separate living areas and spent most of their time apart. Food was cooked over open fires in the kitchen. The smoke escaped through a hole in the roof.

Parts of this house have been cut away so you can see inside.

Inside a typical Greek house, walls were plain with just a few hangings. Chests were used for storage.

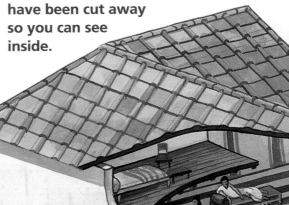

426

CLOTHES

Men's tunics were made from wool or linen. A plain square of material called a **chiton** was fastened over one or both shoulders and belted around the waist. Women wore a long tunic called a **peplos** or a long chiton. Wealthier people had tunics made from decorated material, while slaves had plain tunics. In classical times, it was fashionable for men to have short hair and a beard. Cloaks and shawls would be worn outside in colder weather and for traveling. Many people went barefoot most of the time. Shoes were leather sandals or boots.

Although Greek cities always had public baths, there was no soap, so the Greeks rubbed their bodies with olive oil to get clean. Then they would scrape the oil and dirt off with a tool called a **strigil**.

A gold necklace like the one worn by the woman in the vase painting below.

A seated woman is adorned with jewelry for her wedding. She wears a chiton sewn up both sides to cover her arms.

At the front of most houses stood a statue of the god Hermes — a **herm** — thought to act as a guard for the house.

Theme Wrap-Up

Check Your Progress

Your discovery of ancient cultures has taken you from Tenochtitlán to the western Sudan. Take the time to review how much you've discovered — and discover some more. Now you can revisit the theme by reading and comparing two new selections and practicing your test-taking skills.

Think about what it means to discover an ancient culture by revisiting the McKissacks' letter on pages 356–358. What do you think it would be like to visit an ancient culture?

As you read the two selections that follow, think about what each reveals about ancient Egypt. Compare how well they help you understand that culture. Then think about how these selections compare with the other selections in *Discovering Ancient Cultures*.

Read and Compare

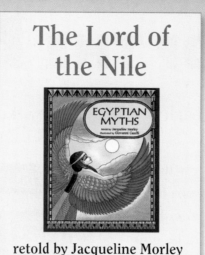

Discover a myth about how an Egyptian pharaoh brings back the yearly flooding of the Nile River after a long drought.

Try these strategies:
Predict and Infer
Evaluate

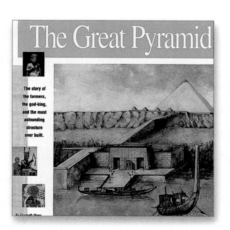

Learn about the Great Pyramid of Giza and the pharaoh who ordered its construction.

Try these strategies:
Monitor and Clarify
Summarize

Strategies in Action *Remember to use all your reading strategies while you read.*

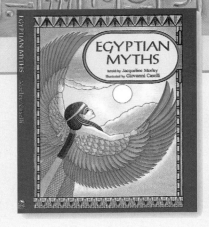

THE LORD OF THE NILE

retold by Jacqueline Morley

illustrated by Michael Jaroszko

Long ago, when the world was new, the gods lived on earth and were pharaohs in Egypt. By their wise example the gods showed Earth's people how their land should be governed and made them content. The last god to rule on Earth was Horus, the son of Isis. When he saw that his people lived peaceably together and had learned to bless the gods, he withdrew to the heavens and let mortals rule in Egypt. The people of Egypt still believed their pharaohs to be gods and thought that each one, when he died, would join his father Ra, and travel with him in the Boat of the Sun. Before departing, each pharaoh built an "everlasting home" — a tomb in which his body would be preserved forever. The Ancient Egyptians believed that without a perfectly preserved body to live in, the soul would die.

Now, about four thousand six hundred years ago, Zoser, a good and just king, ruled Egypt as pharaoh. He was anxious that his life in the next world should be blessed, but when he looked at the massive brick tombs of former pharaohs he doubted whether even they would last forever. So he asked his vizier, the great architect Imhotep the Wise, to build him a truly god–like tomb that would outlast time itself. Imhotep created a tomb of stone, which was made of many slabs of stone set one upon another, making a stairway to the sky. This was the first pyramid, known as the Step Pyramid, and it still stands today.

In the eighteenth year of Zoser's reign, disaster struck Egypt. The Nile, which flooded the land every year, was low and sluggish. Farmers waited anxiously for the river to coat their fields with the rich mud in which the crops grew tall, and to fill the canals that watered them, for rain is hardly known in Egypt. But the flood failed, and when Set sent the burning winds from the desert all growing things shriveled and died.

428**B**

Then Zoser fed his people from the granaries that held the surplus harvests of past years. But for seven years the Nile failed to flood, and then when the granaries were opened they yielded only gusts of empty air. People grew desperate; the strong stole from the weak; the old and the sick were left to starve. Angry crowds beat upon the doors of Zoser's palace demanding that he should use his god–like powers to make the river flood.

Zoser was at his wits' end. He had no idea how to make the Nile rise. Then an idea came to him.

"Call Imhotep," he commanded. "There is no man living wiser than he."

Imhotep listened thoughtfully to the pharaoh's agitated questioning, "Where is the birthplace of the Nile? What god or goddess rules there? I must be told, that I may beg this being to send my country life."

"Great Pharaoh," Imhotep replied, "I do not know, but at the Temple of Thoth at Hermopolis there are sacred books in which these secrets may lie hidden. I will go to Hermopolis, and if Thoth guides me I may learn the truth."

Before many days had passed Imhotep returned with an answer, "You must seek the mystery of the Nile in the beginning of all things. In the far south is an island called Abu, which means the City of the Beginning. This was the first dry land to rise from the waters of Nu. Here Ra stood when he spoke the names of all things. Here lies a cave where the river rests each year and is reborn. Then, with new strength it rushes forth through two caverns to nourish the land of Egypt. The lord of this cave is Khnemu the Nile god. Only he can make the river flood again."

Zoser sailed on the royal barge for many days towards the midday sun. At last he came to Abu, the birthplace of the Nile, and entered the Temple of Khnemu, which was a humble wooden building with a door made of reeds and a roof of the branches of trees. Zoser bowed before the shrine and piled offerings on the altar of the Lord of the Nile — bread–cakes, geese, legs of oxen, and all the things that please the gods.

Suddenly, in the darkness of the shrine, a majestic figure with the head of a ram with widespread horns appeared before him. This Being addressed him sternly, "I am Khnemu the Maker who knitted your body together and gave you a heart. I am Nu of the great waters, who was in being at the beginning of time. I am the Lord of the Nile. When I draw back the bolts of the cavern doors and strike the earth with my sandals, the flood pours out upon the land and the people of Egypt are fed and rejoice."

428E

Then Zoser asked fearfully, "Lord of the Nile, how has your servant offended you that for seven years you have not sent the flood?"

"Why does Pharaoh build for himself an everlasting home of stone, so splendid that the like of it has never been on Earth before, and yet neglect the gods?" Khnemu replied. "My temple stands on banks of granite, which is called the stone of Abu. And here are gold, silver, copper, lapis lazuli, crystal, and alabaster. Should these things lie untouched in the ground, while the Temple of Khnemu is a mere hut of reeds? Restore to the gods the honor that is their due and the Nile will rise again."

"It shall be done," said Zoser.

So Imhotep made a temple for Khnemu that outshone all others in the land. Its shrines were filled with statues of gold and silver and its walls were of malachite and lapis lazuli. And the pharaoh decreed that the harvests of the land for many leagues to the north and south of it should belong to the Temple Khnemu forever, so that his altars should never be bare. Then once more the Nile watered the land and the fields were yellow with ripe grain. But, from that time on, no pharaoh forgot that the wealth of Egypt, the comfort of its people and the glory of its kings, were the gift of the Lord of the Nile.

The Great Pyramid

by Elizabeth Mann, illustrated by Laura Lo Turco

Ancient Egyptians believed their pharaoh was the sky god Horus on Earth, who could watch over his people in the afterlife. They built tombs of stone that they believed would provide a passage to the heavens for the pharaoh and his *ka*, or spirit. About 4,500 years ago, the pharaoh Khufu declared himself both Horus and the sun god Re on Earth. To prepare for the afterlife, Khufu had to build the greatest pyramid of all.

Egypt prospered under Khufu and life was luxurious. He led extravagant sailing excursions, hunting expeditions, and fishing trips. Officials, nobles, and priests joined him at his palace for banquets. The guests wore fine linen, scented wigs, and dramatic eye makeup. Their gold jewelry was heavy with precious stones. While musicians and dancers performed tirelessly, servants carried trays heavy with meat and bread and fruit.

The pleasures and duties of a pharaoh's earthly life would only last a few years. His *ka* was expected to exist for eternity, so a pharaoh's most important responsibility was to prepare for the afterlife. For Khufu it was especially important. He had declared himself to be the greatest pharaoh ever. Now he had to build the greatest tomb ever.

He chose the location carefully. It had to be on high ground, above the flood waters. Like all Egyptian graves, it had to be in the Western Desert, close to where the Land of the Dead was believed to be. To set himself apart, Khufu wanted a site where no pharaoh had been buried before.

The Giza Plateau was all of these things, and more.

The plateau is solid limestone, firm enough to support the tremendous weight of a 50-story, 13-acre pyramid. There is so much limestone that quarries on the plateau could provide most of the stone blocks needed to build the pyramid. It was a practical location, and, with cliffs soaring 100 feet up from the valley, a very impressive one.

Khufu alerted his governors that he would need laborers. Every summer thousands and thousands of farmers would come to work for him while the Nile flooded their fields.

Once the workers arrived at Giza, bread had to be provided for them. They needed shelter and clothing. They needed tools, sharpened and in good repair. And they needed to be organized so that they did not get in each other's way on the construction site. It was a phenomenal undertaking. Work gangs were assembled, each with an overseer. The workers chose names for their gangs like "Enduring Gang" and "Beloved of Khufu." They painted them proudly in red on the stone blocks.

Stone from quarries hundreds of miles away came by boat to a man-made harbor near the Giza Plateau. Using only primitive tools, Egyptian stonemasons shaped blocks so skillfully that a knife couldn't slide between them.

Quarries all over Egypt echoed with the sound of mallets as massive blocks were carved out of the surrounding stone. From Fayyum came dark, greenish-black basalt for the temple floors. From Aswan came granite, so heavy that a single block weighed 40 tons. And from Tura came the fine white limestone to cover the outside of the pyramid.

The Great Pyramid had a tremendous effect on Egyptians who lived 4,500 years ago. Egyptians were farmers. Their lives had always centered on their fields and livestock, their villages and local gods. But those who left their homes every year and gathered at the Giza Plateau became part of a bigger world, a bigger society. They were loyal, not just to their village, but to the great work they were doing. By contributing to the afterlife of their pharaoh, they were insuring prosperity for all of Egypt. When they returned to their villages, they brought with them the sense of belonging to a larger community.

For some, the change in their lives was even greater. Many skilled workers did not return to their fields. They stayed at Giza with their families and worked year round for the pharaoh. Freed from the hard labor of farming, they developed remarkable talents as artists, boat builders, goldsmiths, and stonemasons.

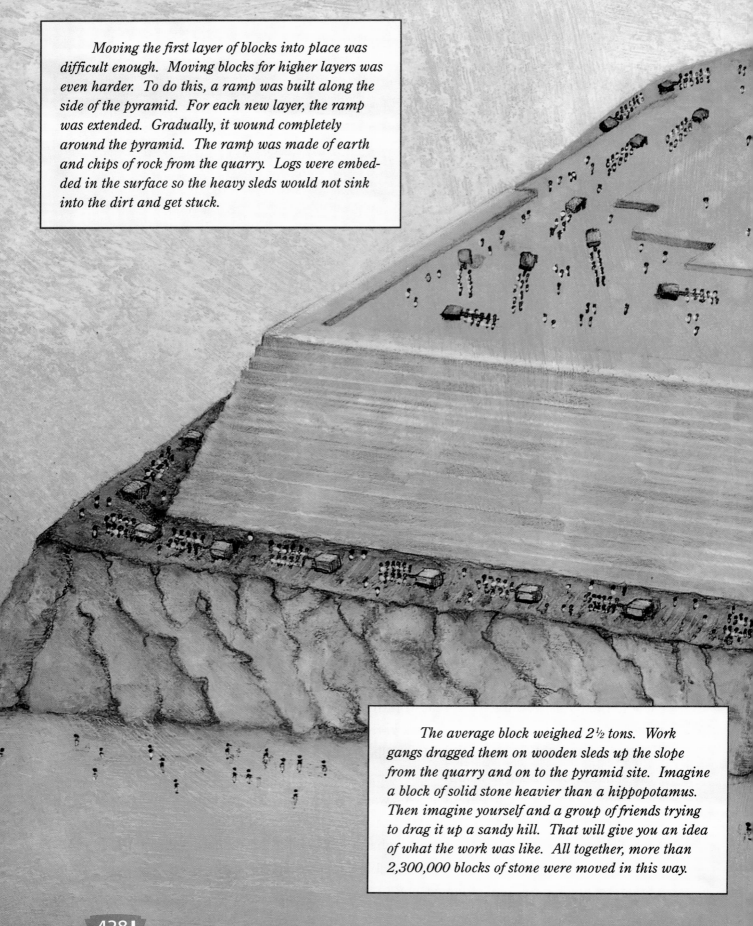

Moving the first layer of blocks into place was difficult enough. Moving blocks for higher layers was even harder. To do this, a ramp was built along the side of the pyramid. For each new layer, the ramp was extended. Gradually, it wound completely around the pyramid. The ramp was made of earth and chips of rock from the quarry. Logs were embedded in the surface so the heavy sleds would not sink into the dirt and get stuck.

The average block weighed 2½ tons. Work gangs dragged them on wooden sleds up the slope from the quarry and on to the pyramid site. Imagine a block of solid stone heavier than a hippopotamus. Then imagine yourself and a group of friends trying to drag it up a sandy hill. That will give you an idea of what the work was like. All together, more than 2,300,000 blocks of stone were moved in this way.

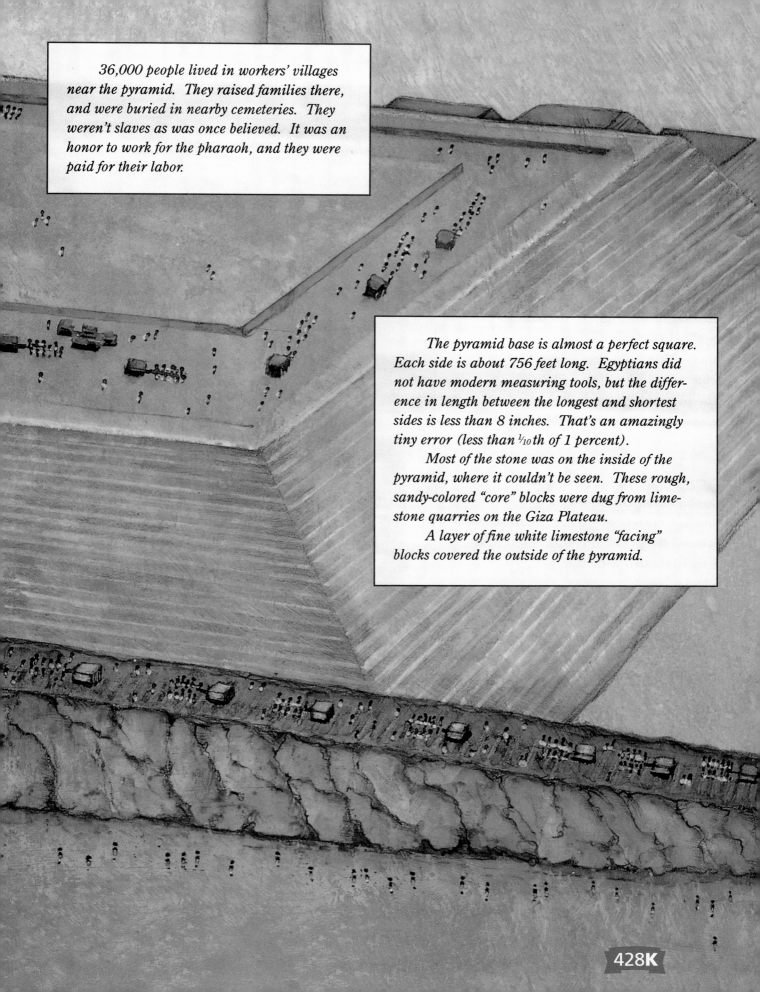

36,000 people lived in workers' villages near the pyramid. They raised families there, and were buried in nearby cemeteries. They weren't slaves as was once believed. It was an honor to work for the pharaoh, and they were paid for their labor.

The pyramid base is almost a perfect square. Each side is about 756 feet long. Egyptians did not have modern measuring tools, but the difference in length between the longest and shortest sides is less than 8 inches. That's an amazingly tiny error (less than 1/10th of 1 percent).

Most of the stone was on the inside of the pyramid, where it couldn't be seen. These rough, sandy-colored "core" blocks were dug from limestone quarries on the Giza Plateau.

A layer of fine white limestone "facing" blocks covered the outside of the pyramid.

The final block was the pyramid-shaped capstone. It was placed on the top and coated with gold. Then, from the top down, workers polished the white Tura limestone "facing" blocks until they gleamed.

Khufu had planned to be buried like earlier pharaohs, in a chamber beneath his pyramid. When he became Re on earth, he changed his mind. He built a second burial chamber, and then a third and final burial chamber, high in the middle of the pyramid. It was a way of showing that he was on the same level as the sun.

To prevent tomb robbers from getting in, the passageway to the burial chamber was blocked with huge slabs of granite and the pyramid entrance was concealed with "facing" blocks.

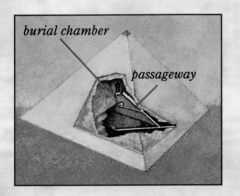

burial chamber

passageway

In the twenty-third year of his reign, the pharaoh Khufu died. Mourners stood along the Nile, striking sticks together and weeping as the funeral boat passed by. Priests waited at the valley temple to receive the body of their king. The painstaking job of mummification began. After 70 days, the body was ready for burial.

The coffin containing Khufu's mummy was lowered into the granite sarcophagus deep within the pyramid. The heavy lid was closed. Khufu's body was sealed inside the Great Pyramid. His *ka* was free.

Think and Compare

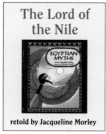

The Lord of the Nile

retold by Jacqueline Morley

The Great Pyramid

1. Compare the pharaoh Zoser with the pharaoh Khufu. How are the two rulers alike? How are they different?

2. How does the construction of The Great Pyramid affect the farmers of ancient Egypt? Describe their lives before and after construction begins.

3. Compare the construction of The Great Pyramid with that of The Great Wall. How are the reasons for their being built different?

4. Compare the two wrap-up selections. How are the myth and the nonfiction selection different? How are they alike in providing information?

5. Which ancient culture in this theme would you like to learn more about? Why?

The Great Wall

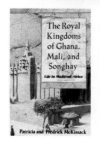

The Royal Kingdoms of Ghana, Mali, and Songhay

Patricia and Fredrick McKissack

Strategies in Action Explain which reading strategies you found most useful while reading this theme and why.

Write a Travel Brochure

Write a paragraph for a travel brochure about one of the ancient cultures in the theme. Tell readers about the culture and its history.

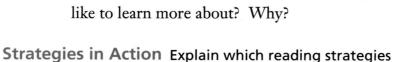

Tips

- **Explain how the people lived and how they were governed.**
- **Include a map with possible destinations.**

✓ Vocabulary Items

Some test items ask you to choose the word that has an opposite meaning, or an antonym. How do you choose the best answer? Below is a sample item for "The Lord of the Nile."

Read the question. Choose the best answer and fill in the circle in the answer row.

1. The author writes, "The Nile, which flooded the land every year, was low and sluggish." Which word means the opposite of *sluggish*?

    A slow

    B swift

    C slimy

    D bubbly

ANSWER ROW 1	Ⓐ ● Ⓒ Ⓓ

① Understand the question.

Find the word that the question asks about. Is it shown in context? Decide what you need to do.

> I need to find the opposite of the word *sluggish*. What can the sentence tell me about the word?

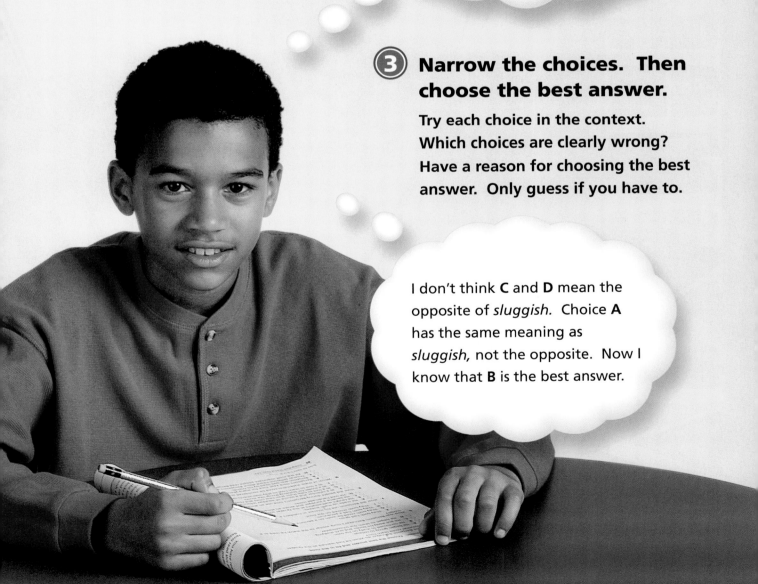

② Think about what the word means.

Think about the word's parts. Look for the base word and a prefix or suffix. How is the word used in the context?

The word *sluggish* has the word *slug* in it and the suffix *-ish*. I think *sluggish* can be used to describe the movement of a slug. The author must mean the Nile is slow right now.

③ Narrow the choices. Then choose the best answer.

Try each choice in the context. Which choices are clearly wrong? Have a reason for choosing the best answer. Only guess if you have to.

I don't think **C** and **D** mean the opposite of *sluggish*. Choice **A** has the same meaning as *sluggish*, not the opposite. Now I know that **B** is the best answer.

MYTHS

Myths

**Why do we have myths?
Simply to explain *why*.**

Myths are among our oldest
stories. People created **nature
myths** to explain the wonders of
nature. In **hero myths**, humans
defeated monsters to make the world
safer. **Creation myths** helped
explain how such things
as fire or music began.

Here are examples of these
three kinds of myths.

CONTENTS

Arachne the Spinner...............432
a myth from ancient Greece

Guitar Solo...................................437
a myth from ancient Mali

**How Music Was Fetched
Out of Heaven**..........................441
a myth from ancient Mexico

all retold by Geraldine McCaughrean

*Two heroes from Greek mythology, Achilles
and Ajax, are shown playing a game (left).*

As you read this nature myth from ancient Greece, think about why Athene was so angry. How could Arachne have changed the outcome of the contest?

Arachne the Spinner

Retold by Geraldine McCaughrean
Illustrated by Emma Chichester Clark

Once, when all cloths and clothes were woven by hand, there was a weaver called Arachne more skillful than all the rest. Her tapestries were so lovely that people paid a fortune to buy them. Tailors and weavers came from miles around just to watch Arachne at work on her loom. Her shuttle flew to and fro, and her fingers plucked the strands as if she were making music rather than cloth.

"The gods certainly gave you an amazing talent," said her friends.

"Gods? Bodkins! There's nothing the gods could teach me about weaving. I can weave better than any god or goddess."

432

Her friends turned rather pale. "Better not let the goddess Athene hear you say that."

"Don't care who hears it. I'm the best there is," said Arachne.

An old lady sitting behind her examined the yarns Arachne had spun that morning, feeling their delightful texture between finger and thumb. "So if there were a competition between you and the goddess Athene, you think you would win?" she said.

"She wouldn't stand a chance," said Arachne. "Not against me."

All of a sudden the old lady's gray hair began to float like smoke about her head and turn to golden light. A swish of wind blew her old coat into shreds and revealed a robe of dazzling white. She grew taller and taller until she stood head and shoulders above the crowd. There was no mistaking the beautiful gray-eyed goddess, Athene.

"Let it be so!" declared Athene. "A contest between you and me."

Arachne's friends fell on their faces in awe. But Arachne simply threaded another shuttle. And although her face was rather pale and her hands did tremble a little, she smiled and said, "A contest then. To see who is the best weaver in the world."

To and fro went the shuttles, faster than birds building a nest.

Athene wove a picture of Mount Olympus. All the gods were there: heroic, handsome, generous, clever, and kind. She wove all the creatures of creation onto her loom. And when she wove a kitten, the crowd sighed, "Aaaah!" When she wove a horse, they wanted to reach out and stroke it.

Alongside her sat Arachne, also weaving a picture of the gods.

But it was a comical picture. It showed all the silly things the gods had ever done: dressing up, squabbling, lazing about, and bragging. In fact she made them look just as foolish as ordinary folk.

But oh! when she pictured a butterfly sitting on a blade of grass, it looked as if it would fly away at any moment. When she wove a lion, the crowd shrieked and ran away in fright. Her sea shimmered and her corn waved, and her finished tapestry was more beautiful than nature itself.

Athene laid down her shuttle and came to look at Arachne's weaving. The crowd held its breath.

"You are the better weaver," said the goddess. "Your skill is matchless. Even I don't have your magic."

Arachne preened herself and grinned with smug satisfaction. "Didn't I tell you as much?"

"But your pride is even greater than your skill," said Athene. "And your irreverence is past all forgiving." She pointed at Arachne's tapestry. "Make fun of the gods, would you? Well, for that I'll make such an example of you that no one will ever make the same mistake again!"

She took the shuttle out of Arachne's hands and pushed it into her mouth. Then, just as Athene had changed from an old woman into her true shape, she transformed Arachne.

Arachne's arms stuck to her sides, and left only her long, clever fingers straining and scrabbling. Her body shrank down to a black blob no bigger than an ink blot: an end of thread still curled out of its mouth. Athene used the thread to hang Arachne up on a tree, and left her dangling there.

"Weave your tapestries forever!" said the goddess. "And however wonderful they are, people will only shudder at the sight of them and pull them to shreds."

It all came true. For Arachne had been turned into the first spider, doomed forever to spin webs in the corners of rooms, in bushes, in dark, unswept places. And though cobwebs are as lovely a piece of weaving as you'll ever see, just look how people hurry to sweep them away.

The Songhay people, who live by the upper Niger River in the African country of Mali, still tell this hero myth today. What makes this myth especially appealing?

Guitar Solo

by Geraldine McCaughrean
Illustrated by Bee Willey

In a place where six rivers join like the strings of a guitar, lived Zin the Nasty, Zin the Mean, Zin-Kibaru, the water spirit. Even above the noise of rushing water rose the sound of his magic guitar, and whenever he played it, the creatures of the river fell under his power. He summoned them to dance for him and to fetch him food and drink. In the daytime, the country-side rocked to the sound of Zin's partying.

But come nighttime, there was worse in store for Zin's neighbor, Faran. At night, Zin played his guitar in Faran's field, hidden by darkness and the tall plants. Faran was not rich. In

all the world he only had a field, a fishing rod, a canoe, and his mother. So when Zin began to play, Faran clapped his hands to his head and groaned, "Oh no! Not again!"

Out of the rivers came a million mesmerized fish, slithering up the bank, walking on their tails, glimmering silver. They trampled Faran's green shoots, gobbled his tall leaves, picked his ripe crop to carry home for Zin-Kibaru. Like a flock of crows they stripped his field, and no amount of shooing would drive them away. Not while Zin played his spiteful, magic guitar.

"We shall starve!" complained Faran to his mother.

"Well, boy," she said, "there's a saying I seem to recall: When the fish eat your food, it's time to eat the fish."

438

So Faran took his rod and his canoe and went fishing. All day he fished, but Zin's magic simply kept the fish away, and Faran caught nothing. All night he fished, too, and never a bite: the fish were too busy gathering the maize in his field.

"Nothing, nothing, nothing," said Faran in disgust, as he arrived home with his rod over his shoulder.

"Nothing?" said his mother seeing the bulging fishing basket.

"Well, nothing but two hippopotami," said Faran, "and we can't eat them, so I'd better let them go."

The hippopotami got out of Faran's basket and trotted away. And Faran went to where the rivers meet and grabbed Zin-Kibaru by the shirt. "I'll fight you for that guitar of yours!"

Now Zin was an ugly brute and got most of his fun from tormenting Faran and the fish. But he also loved to wrestle. "I'll fight you, boy," he said, "and if you win, you get my guitar. But if I win, I get your canoe. Agreed?"

"If I don't stop your magic, I shan't need no canoe," said Faran, "because I'll be starved right down to a skeleton, me and Mama both."

So, that was one night the magic guitar did not play in Faran's field — because Faran and Zin were wrestling.

All the animals watched. At first they cheered Zin: he had told them to. But soon they fell silent, a circle of glittering eyes.

All night Faran fought, because so much depended on it. "Can't lose my canoe!" he thought, each time he grew tired. "Must stop that music!" he thought, each time he hit the ground. "Must win, for Mama's sake!" he thought, each time Zin bit or kicked or scratched him.

And by morning it really seemed as if Faran might win.

"Come on, Faran!" whispered a monkey and a duck.

"COME ON, FARAN!" roared his mother.

Then Zin cheated.

He used a magic word.

"Zongballyhoshbuckericket!" he said, and Faran fell to the ground like spilled water. He could not move. Zin danced around him, hands clasped above his head — "I win! I win! I win!" — then laughed and laughed till he had to sit down.

"Oh, Mama!" sobbed Faran. "I'm sorry! I did my best, but I don't know no magic words to knock this bully down!"

"Oh yes, you do!" called his mama. "Don't you recall? You found them in your fishing basket one day!"

Then Faran remembered. The perfect magic words. And he used them. "Hippopotami? HELP!" Just like magic, the first hippopotamus Faran had caught came and sat down — just where Zin was sitting. I mean right on the spot where Zin was sitting. I mean right on top of Zin. And then his hippopotamus mate came and sat on his lap. And that, it was generally agreed, was when Faran won the fight. Zin was crushed.

So nowadays Faran floats half-asleep in his canoe, fishing or playing a small guitar. He has changed the strings, of course, so as to have no magic power over the creatures of the six rivers. But he does have plenty of friends to help him tend his maize and mend his roof and dance with his mother. And what more can a boy ask than that?

This is a very ancient creation myth of Quetzalcoatl (keht-zahl-COH-atl), the feathered serpent, the Lord of Spirit, in what is now Mexico. As you read, think about how Quetzalcoatl got his musicians and whether you approve or disapprove of what he did.

How Music Was Fetched Out of Heaven

by Geraldine McCaughrean
Illustrated by Bee Willey

Once the world suffered in Silence. Not that it was a quiet place, nor peaceful, for there was always the groan of the wind, the crash of the sea, the grumble of lava in the throats of volcanoes, and the grate of man's plowshare through the stony ground. Babies could be heard crying at night, and women in the daytime, because of the hardness of life and the great unfriendliness of Silence.

Tezcatlipoca, his body heavy as clay and his heart heavy as lead (for he was the Lord of Matter), spoke to Quetzalcoatl, feathery Lord of Spirit. He spoke from out of the four quarters of the Earth, from the north, south, easterly and westerly depths of the iron-hard ground. "The world needs music, Quetzalcoatl! In the thorny glades and on the bald seashore, in the square comfortless houses of the poor and in the dreams of the sleeping, there should be music, there ought to be song. Go to Heaven, Quetzalcoatl, and fetch it down!"

"How would I get there? Heaven is higher than wings will carry me."

"String a bridge out of cables of wind, and nail it with stars: a bridge to the Sun. At the feet of the Sun, sitting on the steps of his throne, you will find four musicians. Fetch them down here. For I am so sad in this Silence, and the People are sad, hearing the sound of Nothingness ringing in their ears."

"I will do as you say," said Quetzalcoatl, preening his green feathers in readiness for the journey. "But will they come, I ask myself. Will the musicians of the Sun want to come?"

He whistled up the winds like hounds. Like hounds they came bounding over the bending treetops, over the red places where dust rose up in twisting columns, and over the sea, whipping the waters into mountainous waves. Baying and howling, they carried Quetzalcoatl higher and higher — higher than all Creation — so high that he could glimpse the Sun ahead of him. Then the four mightiest winds braided themselves into a cable, and the cable swung out across the void of Heaven: a bridge planked with cloud and nailed with stars.

"Look out, here comes Quetzalcoatl," said the Sun, glowering, lowering, his red-rimmed eyes livid. Circling him in a cheerful dance, four musicians played and sang. One, dressed in white and shaking bells, was singing lullabies; one, dressed in red, was singing songs of war and passion as he beat on a drum; one, in sky-blue robes fleecy with cloud, sang the ballads of Heaven, the stories of the gods; one, in yellow, played on a golden flute.

This place was too hot for tears, too bright for shadows. In fact the shadows had all fled downward and clung fast to men. And yet all this sweet music had not served to make the Sun generous. "If you don't want to have to leave here and go down where it's dark, dank, dreary and dangerous, keep silent, my dears. Keep silent, keep secret and don't answer when Quetzalcoatl calls," he warned his musicians.

Across the bridge rang Quetzalcoatl's voice. "O singers! O marvelous makers of music. Come to me. The Lord of the World is calling!" The voice of Quetzalcoatl was masterful and inviting, but the Sun had made the musicians afraid. They kept silent, crouching low, pretending not to hear. Again and again Quetzalcoatl called them, but still they did not stir, and the Sun smiled smugly and thrummed his fingers on the sunny spokes of his chair back. He did not intend to give up his musicians, no matter who needed them.

So Quetzalcoatl withdrew to the rain-fringed horizon and, harnessing his four winds to the black thunder, had them drag the clouds closer, circling the Sun's citadel. When he triggered the lightning and loosed the thunderclaps, the noise was monumental. The Sun thought he was under siege.

Thunder clashed against the Sun with the noise of a great brass cymbal, and the musicians, their hands over their ears, ran this way and that looking for

help. "Come out to me, little makers of miracles," said Quetzalcoatl in a loud but gentle voice. *BANG* went the thunder, and all Heaven shook.

The crooner of lullabies fluttered down like a sheet blown from a bed. The singer of battle-songs spilled himself like blood along the floor of Heaven and covered his head with his arms. The singer of ballads, in his fright, quite forgot his histories of Heaven, and the flautist dropped his golden flute. Quetzalcoatl caught it.

As the musicians leapt from their fiery nest, he opened his arms and welcomed them into his embrace, stroking their heads in his lap. "Save us, Lord of Creation! The Sun is under siege!"

"Come, dear friends. Come where you are needed most."

The Sun shook and trembled with rage like a struck gong, but he knew he had been defeated, had lost his musicians to Quetzalcoatl.

At first the musicians were dismayed by the sadness and silence of the Earth. But no sooner did they begin to play than the babies in their cribs stopped squalling. Pregnant women laid a hand on their big stomachs and sighed with contentment. The man laboring in the field cupped a hand to his ear and shook himself, so that his shadow of sadness fell away in the noonday. Children started to hum. Young men and women got up to dance, and in dancing fell in love. Even the mourner at the graveside, hearing sweet flute music, stopped crying.

Quetzalcoatl himself swayed his snaky hips and lifted his hands in dance at the gate of Tezcatlipoca, and Tezcatlipoca came out of doors. Matter and Spirit whirled together in a dance so fast: had you been there, you would have thought you were seeing only one.

And suddenly every bird in the sky opened its beak and sang, and the stream moved by with a musical ripple. The sleeping child dreamed music and woke up singing. From that day onward, life was all music — rhythms and refrains, falling cadences and fluting calls. No one saw just where the Sun's musicians settled or made their homes, but their footprints were everywhere and their bright colors were found in corners that had previously been gray and cobwebbed with silence. The flowers turned up bright faces of red and yellow and white and blue, as if they could hear singing. Even the winds ceased to howl and roar and groan, and learned love songs.

Think About the MYTHS

1. Compare the three myths. What common elements do they share? How are the human characters in each myth portrayed differently?

2. In "Arachne the Spinner" and "Guitar Solo," humans compete against a god and a spirit. What is different about the way the competitions end?

3. Who is your favorite character in the myths? Why?

4. Do you think the way Quetzalcoatl brought the musicians down from the Sun was right? Why or why not?

5. How important is having larger-than-life characters in telling myths? Give examples from two of the myths.

Send an E-Postcard

If you want to tell a friend that you've been reading myths, send an e-postcard. You'll find one at Education Place. **www.eduplace.com/kids**

Write Your Own Myth

Myths use realism and fantasy to explain something. Think of a custom or a natural event that especially interests you. Then write one of the three kinds of myths—nature, hero, or creation—to explain it.

Remember that a myth often contains these three elements:

- **larger-than-life characters, such as gods, goddesses, and heroes**
- **long-ago, far-away settings**
- **amazing events**

447

5

Doers
and
Dreamers

"Shoot for the moon —
if you fail, you land
in the stars. That is not
bad company . . ."

— *Anonymous*

449

Doers and Dreamers

with Alma Flor Ada

Dear Reader,

It may seem that dreamers and doers have little in common beyond an initial *d*. After all, dreamers spend time thinking about what does not exist, while doers work to make things happen.

But doers are often dreamers working to make their dream, or someone else's dream, come true. Behind every notable invention, every great action, every unique creation, there has been a dream.

For centuries human beings dreamed of being able to fly. They made kites to give wings to their dreams. They went on risky ascents in hot-air balloons. The first "flying machines" were carrying not only their pilots, but also the dreams of people from all over the planet who wished to fly.

In the nineteenth century, French author Jules Verne wrote adventure novels that became popular all over the globe. He turned his own dreams into words. Millions of people have read his books *Twenty Thousand Leagues Under the Sea*, *Around the World in Eighty Days*, and *From the Earth to the Moon*. These novels have inspired movies and theme-park attractions. They have also inspired scientists to make these dreams a reality.

Imagine the audacity of those dreamers who dared to suggest that failing human organs could be replaced; that someone could see thanks to someone else's cornea; that someone could actually live with an artificial heart! Yet if it weren't for such audacious dreamers, many people today would not be able to see, and many lives would not be saved.

Of course, dreams alone cannot transform the world. The selections in this theme are about people who took action to bring their dreams to fruition. Such people as Jackie Joyner-Kersee and Chuck Close can inspire us to dream the highest dreams. If human beings are able to walk on the moon, we should also be able to eradicate hunger and disease, cruelty and violence, and protect the environment and every life form.

So here is a dream. Let us dream dreams of peace, kindness, and justice in a healthy and sound environment. And armed with our dreams, let us become doers, to bring about a world we can all be proud to have helped improve.

Your friend,

Alma Flor Ada

Follow Your Dreams...

To Alma Flor Ada, "doers are often dreamers working to make their dream, or someone else's dream, come true." Would you call yourself a doer or a dreamer? Do you think a person can be both?

Keep those thoughts in mind as you read the selections shown below. Ask yourself what makes the people you are going to read about doers as well as dreamers. What does it take to compete in the Olympics? Can helping with a family project make other people's dreams come true? How does a portrait painter overcome a physical disability to remain a successful artist? Find out about these people, and yourself, as you read *Doers and Dreamers*.

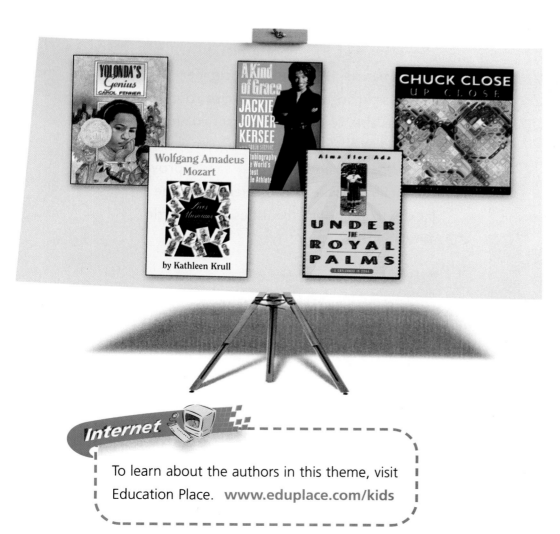

Internet

To learn about the authors in this theme, visit Education Place. **www.eduplace.com/kids**

Background and Vocabulary

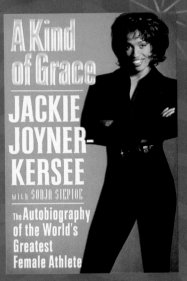

A Kind of Grace

Read to find the meanings of these words.

e ● Glossary

conditioning
discouraged
endurance
sessions
sprints
squad
unconventional

Making a Dream

Have you ever yearned to jump farther or run faster? Jackie Joyner-Kersee, winner of six Olympic medals, had that dream. Her autobiography, *A Kind of Grace*, shows how she made that dream come true. As a child, she sometimes felt **discouraged** by a poor athletic performance. By **conditioning** her muscles through regular exercise routines, she was able to improve her speed and **endurance**. By attending regular workout **sessions**, her entire **squad** saw improvement. As you'll discover in this selection, some of Jackie's conditioning routines were a little **unconventional**.

*Jackie often ran **sprints** at top speeds to improve her performance.*

Come True

Jackie Joyner-Kersee

Childhood in East St. Louis:
Jackie Joyner-Kersee spent many afternoons and weekends at the local community center doing homework, playing sports, and enjoying arts and crafts.

Early athletic success: In high school Joyner-Kersee set the Illinois girls' long-jump record and won four consecutive National Junior Championships in the pentathlon, a five-event competition.

School success: She graduated from high school tenth in her class with a basketball scholarship, another sport she excels in.

International triumphs: At both the 1988 and 1992 Olympics, Joyner-Kersee won the gold medal in the heptathlon, a seven-event competition.

To find out more about Jackie Joyner-Kersee, visit Education Place. **www.eduplace.com/kids**

A Kind of Grace

JACKIE JOYNER-KERSEE

with SONJA STEPTOE

The Autobiography of the World's Greatest Female Athlete

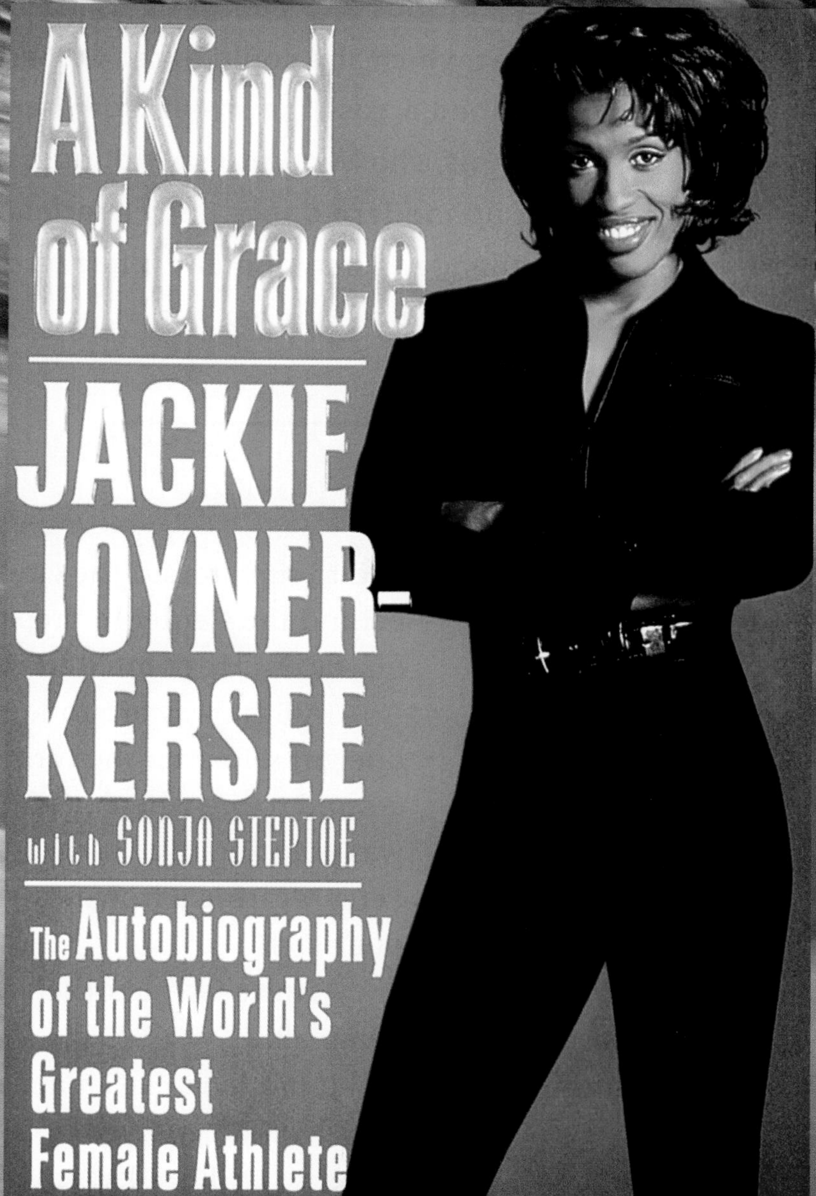

Strategy Focus

As you read Jackie Joyner-Kersee's story, **summarize** in your own words how her life as an athlete began.

Jackie Joyner was an ambitious and energetic child who longed to find something at which she could excel. When a new community center opened across the street from her house in East St. Louis, Illinois, she began to spend most of her free time there. She took up modern dance and cheerleading but wanted more of a challenge. Then one day a notice on the community center bulletin board caught her eye.

One day, in 1972, when I was ten, a sign-up sheet for girls' track appeared on the bulletin board at the Community Center. "If my legs are strong enough for dancing and jumping, maybe I can run fast, too," I thought to myself. I printed my name on the first line.

A bunch of girls, including Debra, Angie and me, showed up for the track team on a sunny afternoon in late May. We were dressed in T-shirts and shorts and we squinted and cupped our hands over our eyes to shield them from the sun as we looked up at our coach, Percy Harris. He explained that practice would be held every afternoon and that we had to run around the cinder track behind the Center to prepare for our races. He pointed to the area.

"All the way around there?" one girl said after she turned around to see where his finger was pointing. She turned back to Percy wearing a frown. "It's hot out here!"

"That's far!" another complained.

It did look like an awfully big circle, which grew wider as we got closer to it. But I kept my thoughts to myself. Momma and Daddy told us never to talk while adults were speaking. Besides, I wanted to see if I could make it all the way around. I was ready to run.

On June 16, 1978, Jackie does some stretching exercises before practicing long jumps.

When the Mary Brown Community Center first opened, Jackie was seven years old.

"If my legs are strong enough for dancing and jumping, maybe I can run fast, too," I thought.

459

That circular track, which still exists at the back of Lincoln Park and became a fixture of my teenage years, is unconventional. It measures about 550 yards around, roughly a third of a mile. A standard track is oval-shaped and measures 400 meters, a quarter-mile. Those of us who completed the lap were panting hard by the time we reached the end. We bent over and put our hands on our knees when we finished. The other girls had stopped running and were walking. Percy said we had to run around two more times without stopping to get in a mile workout. Some of the girls mumbled and rolled their eyes. I took off around the track.

Each day, fewer and fewer girls showed up until finally the track team consisted of the three Joyner girls, two of whom were there under protest. At that point, Percy gave up the idea of forming a team. But I wanted to continue running, so he introduced me to George Ward, who coached a half-dozen girls at Franklin Elementary and brought them to Lincoln Park in the summer to practice.

". . . If you win a ribbon, good. If not, that's okay, too," he said.

"I don't know if I'm good," I said shyly when Mr. Ward said I could join his team.

"Don't worry about that. We're just having fun. If you win a ribbon, good. If not, that's okay, too," he said. I breathed a sigh of relief.

The practice sessions with Mr. Ward's group were a lot of fun. Suddenly I had six new friends. I didn't know Gwen Brown or any of the others from Franklin Elementary because I attended John Robinson Elementary and the schools were in different parts of town. Most of the others had been training with Mr. Ward for over a year and, as I would soon discover, were already very strong, fast runners.

Jackie Joyner with her high school coach outside East St. Louis Lincoln High School in 1979.

The gold medal won by Jackie for the seven-event heptathalon at the 1992 Olympics in Barcelona, Spain.

The first race I ran for Mr. Ward was the 440-yard dash, now called the 400 meters. He lined us up opposite two bent steel poles. Then, stopwatch in hand, he walked around to the other side of the circle and stood on the board 440 yards away. From there, he yelled, "On your mark, get set, go!"

The rest of the girls charged ahead. I ran as hard as I could, but I couldn't catch them. I finished last. Once I caught my breath, I was disappointed.

After winning the silver medal in the 1984 Olympics, Jackie Joyner and two other East St. Louis athletes became local heroes. The poster Jackie's autographing reads: "Welcome home Al and Jackie 1984 Olympiad Heroes / East St. Louis is proud of you."

"Just keep coming to practice; you'll get better," he assured me.

I couldn't believe how fast the others were!

"What can I do to get faster?" I asked Mr. Ward.

"Just keep coming to practice; you'll get better," he assured me.

I finished last or nearly last in every race that summer. But Mr. Ward stuck with me. When school resumed, he picked me up every afternoon at home in the spring and drove me to track practice at his school. I looked forward to it all day. I was eleven. I would rush home after school, cram down a few oatmeal cookies or a bag of potato chips, quickly do my geography, math, spelling and science homework and then do my chores — or pay Debra to do them — so that I was ready when his car pulled up. I waved good-bye to Momma, who was getting home about the time I left, and hopped in Mr. Ward's car.

The practices were pressure-free, but there were rules. We weren't supposed to talk while running. But I chatted away with my new friends. Every time Mr. Ward caught me, he stopped us, pulled me out of the group and scolded me. As punishment, he made me run in the opposite direction from the others. I didn't mind. I was so happy to be out there with the others. With a smile on my face I ran clockwise while the others ran counter-clockwise.

One day I got sick while running. Mr. Ward asked me what I'd eaten. When I told him about the oatmeal cookies, he shook his head. Junk food was a no-no, he said. My punishment that time was three extra laps, all in the opposite direction. He said he wanted me to feel how eating junk food would affect my endurance. But it didn't bother me. I felt as if I could run forever. I just wasn't very fast yet.

After several more races and no ribbons, however, I became discouraged. "Am I ever going to win anything?" I asked.

He gave me a consoling pat on the back as we walked to his car. "You will if you keep working hard."

I wasn't crazy about running the 440-yard dash. But it was a challenge. I wanted to catch those other girls. My real love was jumping. But I was too shy to tell Mr. Ward. At the time I didn't know anything about the intricacies of the long jump. I just knew my legs were strong and I was a good jumper, based on my cheerleading and dancing performances.

For weeks, I watched Gwen Brown run down the long-jump track and leap into the air, like a plane taking off. I bit my lower lip as she practiced, yearning for just one chance to run down the dirt path and jump into the shallow sand. When I returned home that afternoon, I got a brainstorm. I found potato chip bags and convinced my sisters to go over to the sandbox in the park, fill the bags and help me bring the sand back to our house. Over the next several afternoons we secretly ferried sand from the park to the front yard, where I made a small sand pit. On the days when I didn't go to practice, I hopped onto our porch railing, which was about three feet high, crouched down with my back arched and leaped into the sand. The feeling was so satisfying and so much fun, I did it over and over again for about an hour.

One afternoon after all the other girls had left practice, while I waited for Mr. Ward to drive me home, I walked over to the runway. It was nothing more than a long strip of grass, marked off with a strip of tape at one end and a shallow hole with a thin layer of sand at the other end. The sun was ready to set, but the air remained hot and thick. I was tired after running sprints and conditioning drills in the oppressive heat. But standing there, looking down the long-jump lane for the first time, I was energized. I mimicked what I had seen Gwen doing. I charged down the lane as fast as I could, planted my right foot and jumped up as high as I could. I kicked my legs out in

Mr. Ward ran toward me. I was afraid he was going to be mad. But there was an excited look in his eyes.

front of me and pushed myself forward.

What a feeling! It was like flying. I stood up, content with myself and feeling daring. I smiled as I dusted the sand off my shorts and legs. Mr. Ward ran toward me. I was afraid he was going to be mad. But there was an excited look in his eyes.

"Do that again!" he shouted.

I trotted back to the starting line and repeated the process: charge, plant, push, kick, fly. His jaw dropped.

"I didn't know you could jump!" Mr. Ward said when I emerged from the sand.

"Oh, I love to jump," I said. "My legs are strong from cheerleading. I have wanted to try jumping for the longest."

DETROIT

Lev

ring

Jackie Joyner-Kersee gives the keynote speech at the NAACP's sports and business meeting, April, 1999.

Jackie enjoys meeting young people and talking to them about the importance of athletics.

"Starting tomorrow, come to the long-jump pit and I'll work with you and Gwen together," he said.

I was delighted. When he dropped me off, I skipped through the yard, bounded up the steps and ran inside to give everybody the news.

Mr. Ward was volunteering his time to the after-school track program. In coaching young girls, he and Nino Fennoy, a teacher at Lilly Freeman Elementary who had organized a girls' squad at that school, were exploring uncharted territory and exposing themselves to criticism. No one in town had ever tried cultivating athletic interest among girls. While boys had high school and junior high teams, Little League baseball and Pop Warner football, girls in our community had no organized sports activities whatsoever.

Congress had recently passed Title IX, the federal legislation requiring public schools to give girls and boys equal opportunities to participate in athletics. Mr. Ward and Mr. Fennoy used the new law to develop opportunities for girls in sports. The combined Franklin-Freeman Elementary School team competed against other schools during the academic year. In 1974, when I was twelve, the two men organized a track squad of male and female athletes from all the schools in town that competed in summer Amateur Athletic Union (AAU) track meets. The squad was called the East St. Louis Railers.

Although I didn't realize it at the time, my participation on the Railers squad set me on a course that would lead far beyond Piggott Avenue and the Arch, into a world full of life experiences both painful and joyous.

Jackie does stretching exercises while touring the Olympic stadium track in Barcelona, Spain, in July, 1992.

467

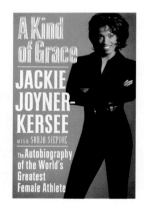

Think About the Selection

1. How did Jackie feel about coming to practice every day during her first summer on the team? What does this tell you about her?

2. Describe a dream or goal that you have. Explain what you think will be necessary to achieve it.

3. Why do you think Jackie waited so long before trying the long jump? Was there any benefit in waiting? Explain.

4. Was Mr. Ward an effective coach? Support your answer with examples from the selection.

5. Do you think girls today have an easier time pursuing athletic dreams than girls of Jackie's day did? Give examples.

6. On days when she didn't have practice, what did Jackie do to improve her jumping? What do you think of her way of practicing?

7. **Connecting/Comparing** The title of this theme is *Doers and Dreamers*. How is Jackie Joyner-Kersee both a doer and a dreamer?

Write an Introduction

Write an introduction for a speech by Jackie Joyner-Kersee at your school. The introduction should explain who she is and list her accomplishments.

Tips

- Give the speaker's name in the first sentence.
- Encourage the audience to give the speaker a warm welcome.

Math

Measure in Meters

The Lincoln Park track measured 550 yards; most tracks measure 400 meters. Convert the length of the Lincoln Park track to meters and compare it to the length of a standard running track.

BONUS Figure out the percentage difference between the length of a standard running track and the length of the Lincoln Park track.

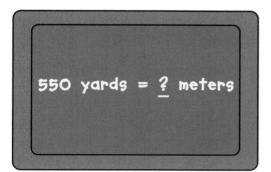

550 yards = ? meters

Listening and Speaking

Give a Speech

Write a speech that presents an argument for why girls should be given equal opportunities to participate in athletics. Use Jackie's story as an example. Then present the speech to a group.

Tips

- Use note cards instead of writing out your entire speech.
- Practice using your notes.
- Speak at an even pace. Make sure everyone in the audience can hear you.

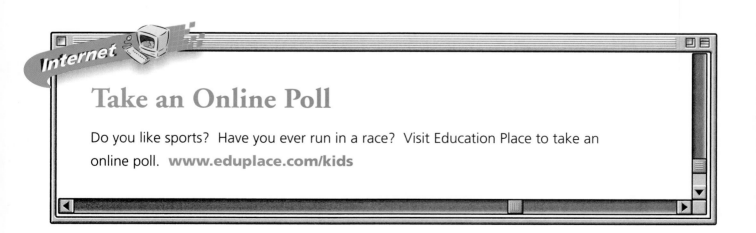

Take an Online Poll

Do you like sports? Have you ever run in a race? Visit Education Place to take an online poll. **www.eduplace.com/kids**

Music Link

Skill: How to Read a Magazine Article

Before you read . . .

❶ **Identify** the magazine that the article comes from. Ask: Who is the **audience** for this magazine? How can knowing the audience prepare me for reading the article?

❷ **Preview** the article. Notice headings, photos, and captions. If there is a **sidebar**, notice how it relates to the main article.

As you read . . .

❶ Keep in mind **the main idea** of each section. Think about how the details **support** the main ideas.

❷ Think about whether you agree with the main ideas. Think of **questions** to ask about the article.

A Real

by Gail Hennessey   from U.S.Kids Magazine

Practice plays a key role in many successful careers, from athletes like Jackie Joyner-Kersee, to the young musician described here.

Pretend you are shopping for music. Suddenly you see a familiar face on a CD cover. How familiar is it? If you are Sergio Salvatore, the face you see is your own. This twelve-year-old jazz pianist has already finished two CDs. He has performed in Japan, Italy, and Carnegie Hall in New York City.

How does a twelve-year-old get to record a CD? By working hard on his music for eight years. It also helps, as Sergio says, to be "in the right family at the right time." Sergio's father is a pianist, too. Sergio's mom used to perform as a singer. As he grew up, Sergio heard many different types of music in his house.

Jazzy Kid!

"I remember lying underneath the piano while Dad practiced," says Sergio. He started playing with the piano keys when he was two years old. Sergio was four when his father gave him his first lesson. "Some people think I just woke up and played like this," he says. "But what I'm doing takes a lot of work." Sergio practiced at least two hours every day for more than eight years. "It feels good that all that practicing has paid off," Sergio says.

Schoolwork Comes First

Sergio's career requires long hours, especially during recording sessions. "One night we worked from eight in the morning until two o'clock the next morning," Sergio recalls. Sergio took a short nap. Then he went to school. Even when he is performing in different cities around the country, Sergio is expected to complete any schoolwork he misses.

When he's not touring, Sergio is like a lot of kids at school. He plays the alto saxophone in his school's band. He likes tennis, swimming, and bike riding.

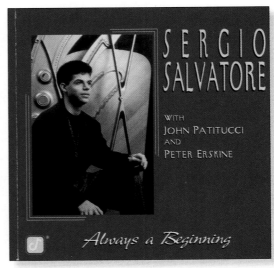

His friends weren't sure what to think when he told them that he had recorded a CD. "They didn't seem to believe I had a recording contract until they saw my album in the music stores," he says. "Some of them don't even know what jazz music is."

Jazz Is for Kids

That is something that Sergio would like to change. He thinks kids would like jazz as much as he does if they heard it more often. He hopes his albums will prove to kids that jazz can be fun. Songs like "Saturday Morning Cartoons" — a song he wrote about watching his favorite cartoons — are especially fun for kids to hear.

With two CDs behind him, Sergio thinks his career could go anywhere. He also has advice for kids who want to be their best in music or anything else they enjoy: "Find the best teacher you can and go for it!"

Then maybe someday you'll see a familiar face on a CD cover, too.

"I remember lying underneath the piano while my dad practiced," Sergio recalls. Today, Sergio is a professional pianist.

What Is Jazz?

What do classical and folk music, military marches, hymns, work songs, and African rhythms have in common? All these musical traditions contributed to the birth of jazz. Self-taught musicians in the American South created the new style of music about a hundred years ago.

Lively and rhythmic, jazz makes you want to snap your fingers or tap your feet. The all-important *beat* comes from a *rhythm section*, usually consisting of piano, bass, drums, and guitar. In addition to the basic rhythm section, many jazz bands add a trombone, a trumpet, a clarinet or saxophone, and sometimes a flute. Today's jazz bands often add computer-generated sounds. All of the instruments, including the drums, take turns playing solos.

Most of the musical notes in jazz are written down or memorized. But many notes are *improvised*. That means the musicians decide which notes to play on the spur of the moment, while they perform. When jazz musicians improvise, they often surprise their listeners. Each performance of a piece may sound very different!

Jazz musician Duke Ellington performing with his band in 1954.

Jazz band playing at a festival in Juan-les-Pins, France.

A Personal Essay

A personal essay explains the writer's opinion and gives reasons to support the opinion. Use this student's writing as a model when you write a personal essay of your own.

Student Council

A **beginning** that states a **personal opinion** captures the reader's attention.

     How important do you think it is to follow through with your goals? It's extremely important to me. I have run for student council for three years in a row. This is the story of my two unsuccessful runs for the student council of my elementary school, and how on my third attempt I finally won a seat on the student council of my middle school.

It's important to stay with the **focus** of an essay.

     When I entered fourth grade, I decided to run for student council the first time. My fourth grade teacher had the class choose a good representative, and my classmates selected me to be one of four finalists. I had to give a speech over the loudspeaker about why the school should vote for me. After all the votes were counted, I found out I had lost by a few votes.

Using **examples** shows the careful planning of the writer.

     When I entered fifth grade, I was selected to be a finalist. I gave my speech and again I lost by a few votes.

     Now I'm a sixth grader. I ran for homeroom representative a few weeks ago, and I had to give a speech to

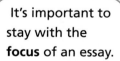

my classmates. After the speeches, my homeroom teacher handed out ballots to the class. My friend Kristen and I won. I finally won on my third attempt at running for student council representative.

With this goal accomplished, I thought it was time to reach a bit higher. The day after I won, we held our first student council meeting. I decided to run for vice-president.

This time the whole school was going to elect the officers. I made four campaign posters, one for each of the three floors of my school and one for the cafeteria. I prepared a speech, and I thought I did a really good job addressing the whole school inside the auditorium.

The next day we got the results. All the officers ended up being seventh graders, but I was second runner-up. I was disappointed, but I know that I will always have next year. I'll be a seventh grader then. Whatever happens in the future, I'm still a member of the student council. I'm happy that I didn't give up on my goals.

> Using **details** makes an essay come alive.

> A good **ending** ties the essay together.

Meet the Author

Olivia S.
Grade: six
State: Massachusetts
Hobbies: dancing, running, and talking online and on the phone
What she'd like to be when she grows up: a famous ballet, tap, or jazz dancer

Background and Vocabulary

Under the Royal Palms

Read to find the meanings of these words.

e • Glossary

accountant

certified

relegated

trinkets

Business Sense

What is it like to start a small business or open a store? In *Under the Royal Palms*, by Alma Flor Ada, you'll find out. You'll meet the author's mother, who opened a store in Cuba in the 1950s. As an **accountant**, Alma's mother was **certified** in the economics of running a business. Like all store owners, however, she had to decide what to sell. Should she offer cheap **trinkets** that would sell quickly? Would expensive merchandise be **relegated** to collect dust on the back shelves?

Every new business venture demands hard work and determination. In addition, this unusual business venture demanded a measure of love.

Alma's family around 1949–1950 (from left to right): Alma Flor Ada; her sister, Flora; her grandfather, Modesto Ada Barral; her father, Modesto Ada Rey; her mother, Alma Lafuente; her uncle, Mario Ada Rey.

Alma Flor Ada's family recorded each business purchase and sale in the narrow columns of a ledger book like this one.

To attract customers, some stores display merchandise outside the store.

Stores today keep track of their accounts through advanced computer technology.

Alma Flor Ada

Born: 1938 in Camaguey, Cuba

How she learned to read: Alma Flor Ada's grandmother would write the names of plants and flowers on the ground with a stick.

On deciding to write: "I made a firm commitment while in the fourth grade to devote my life to producing schoolbooks that would be fun — and since then I am having a lot of fun doing just that!"

Bilingual books: Many of Alma Flor Ada's books are published in both Spanish and English. Some of her other titles include *Where the Flame Trees Bloom* and *My Name Is María Isabel.*

Stephanie Garcia

Growing up: In suburban Los Angeles, Stephanie Garcia discovered her love for art at an early age. She often spent her time making vases out of soda bottles and painting macaroni gold.

How she makes her art today: Using antiques, sculpted objects, junk, and lots of paint

Advice to young artists: "Dream, make stuff, draw, draw, draw, work hard, go to a good art school, and never ever get discouraged."

To discover more about Alma Flor Ada and Stephanie Garcia, visit Education Place. **www.eduplace.com/kids**

Alma Flor Ada

UNDER
THE
ROYAL
PALMS

A CHILDHOOD IN CUBA

Strategy Focus

When Alma Flor Ada's family opened a small store in Cuba, they learned many things about running a business. As you read, pause from time to time to **predict** what decisions they need to make about their store.

Alma Flor Ada grew up in Cuba, in an old house called *La Quinta Simoni*. In her memoir *Under the Royal Palms* she describes her family's joys and tragedies, including the death of her daring Uncle Medardo. When her mother decides to open a store, Alma is not ready for the changes it will bring.

Until I was eight years old, my mother worked as an accountant for several small businesses. She would visit each store, collect the large ledgers and the voluminous envelopes filled with receipts, and bring them home. There she would spend many hours a day copying figures into the ledgers with her meticulous handwriting and adding the long columns of numbers. Then she would return the thick ledgers and envelopes and collect new ones from her next client.

My mother was very proud of her profession. She had completed her education going to school at night after I was born, and was very proud of being one of the first women who was certified as a public accountant in Cuba.

After my sister Flor was born, my mother decided that she was ready to have her own business. She rented a garage from a typewriter repair shop in Calle Avellaneda and opened a small store where she sold buttons and lace, scissors and thread, needles and yarn, as well as paper, pencils, pens, and erasers.

The customers tended to come in to the store at certain hours. Women came in the morning, on their way home from the market. Students came in

Mama

Flor

Alma

the afternoon, right after being let out from school. Young women came in the evening, on their way to night classes. No matter who they were, my mother always had a word of wisdom or encouragement for them, or a joke to make them laugh. Sometimes I suspect the customers came into the little store more for my mother's words than for the little trinkets they bought — especially the young women who came for a pad of paper or a pencil, but also asked my mother to go over their homework or explain a difficult math problem.

In the quiet hours of midday, my mother kept doing her accounting work, leaning on the countertop while she waited for a customer — a lady to browse among the lace, or a harried maid to select a zipper, or a young boy to buy a jar of glue to make a kite.

My baby sister, Flor, was kept in a large cardboard box which served as a makeshift playpen, and I did my homework sitting on the tile floor, grateful for its coolness in the hot afternoon.

One day my mother surprised everyone at home: my father, her younger sister Lolita, and Lolita's husband, Manolo, whom I called Tío Tony to distinguish him from my father's brother who was also named Manolo.

There had been a lot of talk of late about how difficult it was for the two young couples remaining to keep up the big *Quinta Simoni*. In a few years both my grandparents and my uncle Medardo had died. My two other aunts, Virginia and Mireya, had gone to work and live in Havana. And the big old house was expensive to run.

But my mother had an idea that was quite a surprise. She suggested they could all together purchase an old jewelry store that was for sale in the center of town.

It did not take long to convince the others. Here was an opportunity to have a business and to live on the premises. That would ease the economic situation. Also, I suspect that the large, rambling *Quinta Simoni* reminded them of how much they missed those who were no longer living with us.

So shortly afterward we moved to Calle República, to the house behind the Joyería El Sol, a few blocks away from the little store that had been my mother's first business venture.

483

For me, it was a most difficult time. I loved the old *Quinta Simoni,* where I had been born.

I loved its large rooms with high ceilings, the flat roof, where my father and I would lie gazing at the night sky while he told me stories about the constellations. I loved the pigeons and guinea pigs my aunt Lolita raised, and above all, my friends the flame trees, with their gnarled roots where I sat as if in the lap of my grandfather.

I realize that perhaps the house made the adults sad, after the deaths of my grandfather Medardo, my grandmother Lola, and my young uncle Medardo. But for me, they were still alive. I felt their presence in the hallways, on the porch and in the courtyard. All during the four years in which we lived in the city, I longed to return to live among the trees.

The only good times in the city, for me at least, were the feast of San Juan in June, which was celebrated almost like a Mardi Gras, and of course Las Navidades, or Christmastime.

As soon as they bought the Joyería El Sol, my family began to make improvements to the old jewelry store. My father, always ready to learn new things, learned how to fix watches. My mother, lover of innovations, had the storefront redone with large display cases. She also began to display a wider variety of merchandise.

The old jewelry and stopwatches were relegated to a few special counters. The other displays were filled with porcelain and crystal. During the first Christmas season, my mother brought in toys and the traditional figurines used to create Nativity scenes.

It was a Cuban tradition, common also in Spain and other Latin American countries, to set up a Nativity scene in the house during the month of December. It was a tradition shared by rich and poor alike, although the elaborateness of the scene varied greatly from home to home. More than a family's economic status, it was their willingness to make an effort, to set aside space, and to be creative that determined the size and originality of the scene.

The mountainous backdrop for the scene could be constructed with cardboard boxes covered with paper grocery sacks. The sand for the desert was brought in from a trip to the beach. The fields could be created by sprouting wheat in small cans or jars; a piece of broken mirror provided the surface for a lake. The figurines, though — the shepherds and their lambs, the three Wise Men, Mary, Joseph, and Jesus, the donkey and the cow — were usually store-bought.

My mother imported some figurines from Spain. They were made of clay and set in elaborately detailed and realistic settings carved out of cork. We cherished unpacking them, carefully lifting them from layers and layers of straw to discover the minute details of a kitchen with an old woman by the fire, a mother feeding her baby, a young girl spinning wool. Each one was a unique, handmade piece. But these figurines were very expensive, and very few people could afford them.

My mother then set out to find another source. In Havana she discovered an Italian artist who produced beautiful ceramic figurines. I still remember his name, Quirico Benigni, because he was the first Italian I had ever met. His figurines were carefully crafted, but they were made in series, not individually, so they were somewhat less expensive.

Even so, many people came into the store and handled the figurines, observed their beauty with a smile, but returned them to the shelves after seeing the price. And there were those who would not even enter the store, but simply looked longingly through the windows.

Then my father sprang into action. Though we were not Catholic, he understood the joy people found in re-creating the Nativity scenes. He considered it a creative project, in which every member of a family, young or old, could participate. And he decided we, too, would also have a family project, one that would make Nativity figurines accessible to all.

First he enlisted my aunt Lolita's artistic talent and had her model in clay each of the major figures of the Nativity scene: Mary, Joseph, the Baby, the three Wise Men, the donkey, and the cow. Then he constructed a series of hinged wooden boxes, each a little bigger than the figurines. He filled one side of each box with plaster of paris. Before the plaster hardened, he took one of the clay figurines, covered it with grease, and submerged one whole side of it into the plaster.

Once the plaster hardened, he removed the clay model, which had left an imprint in the plaster. He then repeated the same procedure with the other side of the box, and the other side of the model.

Through this simple process, he created a series of molds. Now we could grease the inside of each mold, close and lock the hinges, and pour in soft plaster of paris through a hole in the bottom of each box.

My father made several attempts until he determined how much time the plaster needed to harden in the molds. Then he was ready to operate. Several times a day, he would open his molds and take out the white figurines, which he set out to finish drying on the patio wall.

Every evening, after the little ones, my sister and cousin, had gone to sleep, the whole family would gather together to work on the figurines.

488

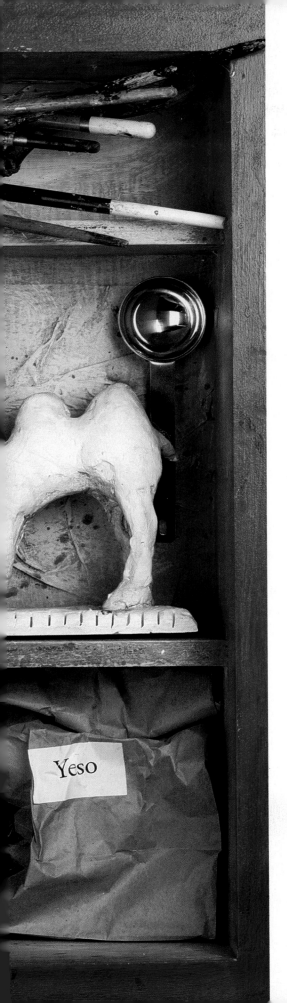

Yeso

It was my duty to clean with a knife the excess plaster that collected along the figurines' sides, where the two halves of the mold met. My mother then gave them a first coat of paint that colored Mary's mantle blue, the robes of the Wise Men red or green, the shepherds' cassocks brown.

Lastly, my aunt Lolita carefully painted their features with small brushes until the white plaster was all covered and the figurines became recognizable characters.

My uncle Manolo, Tío Tony, would prepare the plaster, clean the molds, and more than anything else, entertain us all with his unending stories.

The next day, some humble hands would happily exchange a few pennies for one of the figurines, which we had placed on a table by the door of the store, and take it home to add to their Nativity scene.

The pennies barely covered the cost of the materials, let alone the time spent by my parents or my aunt. In fact, the figurines were not very artistic, nor terribly graceful, I must confess. But we saw them go with the hope that they would bring others the same joy we had shared as we labored into the night together, believing that this was the essence of Christmas: a celebration in which all can take part, and find a way to express their love for one another.

Think About the Selection

1. Think of three character traits of Alma Flor Ada's mother. Support each trait with an example of something the author's mother says or does.

2. Prove or disprove this statement: Alma Flor Ada learned from her family how to be creative and innovative.

3. How did the author and the adults feel about leaving her family home? Why did they have different feelings?

4. What role did the author's father play in making the figurines? What do his actions tell you about his character?

5. In what way was the creation of the figurines important to Alma Flor Ada's family? to the community?

6. The family worked on a project in which every member had a role. Describe a project in which you participated. What was your role?

7. Connecting/Comparing Alma Flor Ada and Jackie Joyner-Kersee both wrote memoirs about important childhood events. What do you think each learned from these events?

Write a Description

Write a description of a shop you would like to open one day. Tell what items you would sell. Describe how you would display the goods to make your store inviting to shoppers.

> **Tips**
> - **Decide how to organize your description. You might organize it by the kinds of goods you will sell, or you might use spatial organization.**
> - **Include vivid adjectives to make your description appealing.**

Art

Make a Diagram

Alma Flor Ada writes that her family made improvements to the Joyería El Sol, the old jewelry store. Reread her description of the store on page 484. What do you think the store looked like after they made the improvements? Make a diagram showing a possible floor plan of the store and the location of merchandise. Then label the diagram using words from the selection, such as *storefront*, *display case*, and *crystal*.

Social Studies

Community Service

Alma Flor Ada's family worked hard to help their community through their store, the Joyería El Sol. Think about how stores in your neighborhood might help the community. With a partner, make a list of projects the stores might take on. Then create a poster that describes and illustrates one of these projects.

Bonus **Write a letter to a store in your neighborhood, proposing a community service project.**

Internet

Post a Review

Write a review of *Under the Royal Palms*. Post your review on the Education Place Web site. **www.eduplace.com/kids**

Social Studies Link

Skill: How to Skim and Scan

Skim to Identify Main Points

- Read the title and the headings. Read the first and last paragraph or section.

- Read the first sentence in each of the remaining paragraphs or sections. **Note key words.**

Scan to Find Information Quickly

Look quickly over the article with a particular topic or key word in mind. It may be helpful to run your index finger down the margin of the text as you look.

Help Wanted:
Groups Seek Kid Volunteers to Change the World. No Experience Necessary.

"You're too young to help — you're just a kid!" How many times have you heard this remark? Often, adults think kids aren't old enough to make a difference — especially when it comes to solving big problems like homelessness and the environment.

But millions of kids volunteer their time, energy and ideas to all kinds of causes — from saving rain forests to helping sick children.

The kid volunteers on these pages started their volunteer work in their own backyard. Now, they're making the world a better place for everyone. Meeting them might inspire you to make a world of a difference, too!

Make a Difference

Like these kids, you can make a huge impact on the world. You only have to give up a small amount of time to make a big difference. Thousands of organizations need volunteers. Here are just a few:

About F.A.C.E

Kids For a Clean Environment (Kids F.A.C.E.) is a popular organization for kids. Members recycle, pick up litter and plant trees. There are about 300,000 Kids F.A.C.E. members worldwide. One of those members is Jill Bader.

Jill has been involved in Kids F.A.C.E. for more than five years. "I started by doing neighborhood cleanups," she told CONTACT. Now she's leading the club's One in a Million project. "Our goal is for one million kids to plant one million trees by the year 2000."

Any kid in the U.S. can help out. Just plant a tree and tell Kids F.A.C.E. about it. The group will send you a certificate telling you the number of your tree. And soil from each state will be used to plant a tree in Washington, D.C.

This 13-year-old is serious about volunteering. Jill also works with handicapped kids, senior citizens and homeless people. She thinks it's important for kids to help others. "Once kids start volunteering, they'll see it's a great way to do exciting things and make life count."

Jill Bader "digs" volunteering for Kids F.A.C.E.

No Clowning Around

Ryan McDonald volunteers for the Ronald McDonald House in New Hyde Park, NY — but it's not because of his last name. The Ronald McDonald House is a place where families of hospitalized kids stay. "My brother was born with multiple birth defects," Ryan told CONTACT. "In the hospital, volunteers and nurses really

Ryan McDonald paves the way for other volunteers to help out.

supported us." Ryan saw volunteering for the House as a chance to be with other families like his own.

Ryan's been helping at Ronald McDonald House for two years. He's the youngest volunteer there, but that doesn't stop him. Last spring, the 14-year-old organized a huge fund-raiser. "I went to 45 schools on Long Island. I asked them to raise $100 through bake sales, car washes — whatever." The schools joined in and made a total of $5,000 for the House.

Ryan thinks kids can be awesome volunteers. "Kids can use computers and are good at learning languages," he says. "These things are great to know as a volunteer. The few hours kids can help will give them the best feeling — one they won't get anywhere else."

A Feather in Her KAP

"My mom taught me how much fun it is to volunteer," says Chelsea Horn. One of the organizations Chelsea volunteers for is Kids Against Pollution (KAP). This 12-year-old doesn't organize clean-ups. But as a KAP youth leader, she goes to meetings to learn about pollution. "I get to hang out with other kids and make a difference in the world," she told CONTACT.

A few months ago, Chelsea and other KAP members met with New York Congressman Sherwood Boehlert. They thanked him for writing a letter to President Clinton about clean air and environment.

"Clean air is important to me," Chelsea says. "If we didn't have it, we wouldn't live

Chelsea talks on the "horn" to get her message out.

very long." Chelsea thinks volunteers make a difference in the world. "There's always stuff to do. People who volunteer contribute a lot — and have lots of fun!"

T.E.A.M. Work

Why does 13-year-old David Garcia volunteer? "It's fun!" says the Fresno, CA, seventh-grader. So when the school principal challenged his class to clean up a neighborhood park, David was excited.

The clean-up was part of a contest for T.E.A.M. Sebastian (Teens for Environmental Awareness and Management). The five most active volunteers would win a trip to Costa Rica to learn about the rainforest.

At the park, David pulled weeds and picked up trash. At the end of the contest, he was chosen as one of the five winning kid environmentalists.

Winning the trip hasn't put an end to David's volunteering ways. He and his family also help their neighborhood cleanup group. "I want the environment and my community to look better for the future," David says.

David Garcia really "cleaned up" when he won a trip to Costa Rica!

Tips to Help You Help Others

1. What problems are important to you? Find out which organizations deal with them. Then decide how you can help.
2. Visit the organization or attend one of their functions. While you're there, chat it up with other volunteers.
3. How much time can you dedicate to your new cause?
4. Keep track of your volunteer hours. It could come in handy if you're earning a badge or school credit for volunteering.
5. Use the buddy system: If a friend or family member volunteers with you, you're less likely to call it quits.

Background and Vocabulary

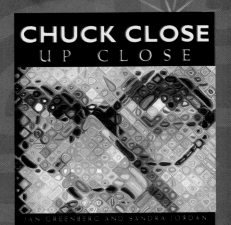

CHUCK CLOSE
UP CLOSE

JAN GREENBERG AND SANDRA JORDAN

Chuck Close,
Up Close

Read to find the meanings of these words.

e ▶ Glossary

abstract

canvas

exhibition

hyperrealistic

painstaking

palette

portrait

The Art of Portraits

With **painstaking** care, the artist applies paint to the **canvas**, one small dab of color at a time. A familiar shape begins to emerge from the many colors on the artist's **palette**. It is a person's face, a **portrait** of an individual, caught for one moment in time.

The human face has always fascinated artists, who recreate it in strikingly different ways. Some portraits show just a face, looking disembodied in space, while others show a complete figure. **Abstract** portraits barely resemble their real-life models. **Hyperrealistic** portraits look as if the subject is alive and might step right out of the canvas. You'll see some hyperrealistic portraits in the next selection, *Chuck Close, Up Close.*

An **exhibition** of portraits by different artists shows a wide variety of styles. What style of portrait do you like?

Hans Holbein, Edward V of England, *c. 1538. 22 3/4" x 17 3/8". Oil on wood panel.*

Gilbert Stuart, George Washington, *1796. 27" x 21 3/4". Oil on panel.*

Pablo Picasso, The Artist's Daughter with a Boat, *February 4, 1938. 28 3/4" x 23 5/8". Oil on canvas.*

Chuck Close, Lorna, *1995. 102" x 84". Oil on canvas.*

MEET THE AUTHORS

Jan Greenberg

Jan Greenberg lives in the city where she was born — St. Louis, Missouri. She began her first journal at ten, and she still keeps one. Greenberg says jotting down thoughts during the day helps her as a writer. She also has a passion for art: "Contact with other artists inspired me to write and develop my own creative skills."

Sandra Jordan

Sandra Jordan has worked with Jan Greenberg on other award-winning books about American artists, including *The American Eye: Eleven Artists of the Twentieth Century*, and *The Painter's Eye: Learning to Look at Contemporary American Art*. Their books were created to get young people more excited about art. Jordan lives in New York City.

To find out more about Jan Greenberg and Sandra Jordan, visit Education Place. **www.eduplace.com/kids**

498

CHUCK CLOSE
UP CLOSE

JAN GREENBERG AND SANDRA JORDAN

Chuck Close is an artist who has found an unusual way to paint portraits of people. As you read, think of **questions** about his art and career to discuss with your classmates.

Chuck Close has come a long way from his childhood, when he suffered from learning disorders in school. With strong self-discipline, Chuck overcame his problems and became an artist, eventually attending Yale University School of Art. The huge paintings in his first one-man show impressed art critics, and his career took off. Since then, Chuck Close has not stopped surprising his friends and fans with what he is able to accomplish.

"Putting Rocks in My Shoes"

It's summer. Chuck and his family have moved from New York City to a house/studio in Bridgehampton, New York. Even though he is surrounded by sea, sky, and rolling meadows, he is not tempted to paint a landscape. On the easel is a portrait of his friend, the artist Roy Lichtenstein.

Close says, "The greatest enemy for an artist is ease . . . repeating yourself once you get good at it." To keep his painting from becoming too "easy," he sets obstacles for himself. He calls it "putting rocks in my shoes."

"I think problem-solving is highly overrated. Problem creation is much more interesting. If you want to react personally you have to move away from other people's ideas. You have to back yourself into your own corner where no one else's solutions apply and ask yourself to behave as an individual."

The giant black-and-white paintings had been strikingly fresh in the late 1960s. Now he was ready to create another "problem" for himself — a new challenge. Around 1970 he invited some friends over to pose for a different set of "head shots," this time in color. He says there is a big advantage to using photographs. "If you paint from life, you have to do more than one sitting. The models gain weight, lose weight; their hair gets long; they cut it off. They're happy; they're sad. They're asleep or they're awake. But the camera provides the freshness and intimacy of one moment frozen in time."

To keep himself from making "the same old colors" on his palette, he found a way to mix the color directly on the canvas. Since color photo images are made up of three primary hues — red, blue, and yellow — he had the photographs separated into these three colors. Then he began to paint.

Chuck in his Bridgehampton, New York, studio painting Roy I, *1994.*
Finished painting is 102" x 84". Oil on canvas.

Five drawings from Linda/Eye *Series, 1977. Each 30" x 22 1/2". Watercolor on paper.*

I. Magenta

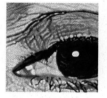

II. Cyan

III. Magenta

IV. Yellow

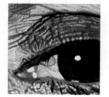

V. Magenta, Cyan, and Yellow

The task was slow and painstaking. It took fourteen months to complete one picture because each one was painted three times, one color on top of another.

Moving around such large canvases proved backbreaking. So he built a portable desk and chair on the prongs of a forklift. By pulling on a rope, he could raise or lower himself to reach the whole canvas, from the bottom to the top. On the forklift were his paints, a television, a telephone, a radio. While he painted all day, he listened to news and talk shows. As he put the last touches on a painting, he turned on an Aretha Franklin tape to celebrate.

In another series Close made paintings without using brushes. His tools were his fingerprints, sometimes just his thumb rubbed in stamp-pad ink. "I like using the body as a tool for painting. In a funny way you usually have to feel through a brush, through a pencil. But there's this object between the body and the surface of the canvas. By using my hands, I can feel just how much ink is on my finger, and then I can feel very clearly how much I'm depositing on the painting. This makes the ink easier to control." If you look at the background of this tender painting of his daughter Georgia (Figure 19), you can make out the artist's fingerprints in various colors.

The artist, seated on his forklift, painting Jud, *1987–1988.*

John, 1971–1972. 100" x 90". Acrylic on gessoed canvas. **a.** unpainted beard. **b.** beard with red layer. **c.** beard with red and blue layers. **d.** beard with red, blue, and yellow layers. **e.** finished painting.

a   b   c   d   e

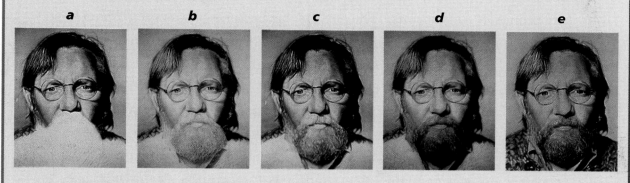

First the artist paints the red layer. Over the red he paints the same picture again, this time in blue. At last he paints the yellow layer. When these primary colors are mixed together in various degrees of intensity, they make up all the colors of the spectrum, from pinkish skin tones to midnight blue.

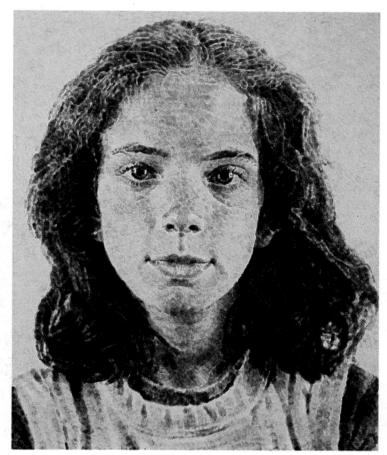

Figure 19. Georgia, *1984.*
48" x 38". Fingerpainting,
oil on canvas.

Even though he was now painting in color, Close hadn't given up black and white. Fanny was painted in his familiar hyperrealistic way with every fold and wrinkle of her face visible, but instead of the airbrush he built the image out of broken chunks of fingerprints. The surface has become soft, feathery, and mysterious. The fingerprints look rubbed, not crisp. From a distance you can't tell what method the artist used. Descriptive words that come to mind are wrinkled, gentle, warm, kind, weathered, and wise.

"I never intended to crank up the emotional content," Close says. "I found that if you present something straightforward, a person's face is a road map of his life."

Close's next great experiment involved thousands of vibrating dots of color. This time his aim was to "find a way that the colors would mix optically in your eye."

At three or four feet the individual dots of color that make up *Lucas II* are clear. They could be extra-large pixels on a color television or computer screen. If you prop up this open book and move away, your eyes will blend the dots. The confetti dots of crimson, green, azure, purple, and white merge into skin, hair, and eyes. With each step back the painting changes.

Now imagine walking into a gallery and being confronted by the actual painting of *Lucas II*. It is smaller than many of Close's heads — only three feet high — but its power dominates the room. His eyes drill into you. His hair crackles with electricity.

The starburst of color sucks you into a swirling vortex. Imagine a spaceship accelerating into hyperspace. On the other hand the painting also seems to radiate out, pulsing with an almost musical beat. Some descriptive words are speed, authority, explosion. If the head could talk, it would shout a command, not a polite request: "Do it now!" or "Follow me!"

Fanny, *1985. 102" x 84". Fingerpainting, oil on canvas.*

"Fanny, my wife's grandmother, was a person who had tremendous tragedy in her life. She was the only survivor from her whole large family in World War II. Given her experiences, it's amazing that she remained a very optimistic, lovely person. And both of those conditions are clearly present in her face."

Lucas II. *1987. 36" x 30". Oil on canvas.*

Figure 22. John, *1992 (finished painting, and in progress, right). 72" x 60". Oil on canvas.*

"The Event"

Chuck is busy painting today. He's preparing for an exhibition and feels pressured. At the far end of the studio a tilted canvas rises out of a trapdoor in the floor. The forklift has been retired. Now Chuck paints with a brush strapped to his arm. He works in this new way, dictated by what he matter-of-factly calls "the event," the event that changed his life.

"The event" happened in 1988, just before Christmas. Chuck was on the dais at the mayor's residence in New York City, facing a crowd of people. He was scheduled to give an art award but felt terrible, with a severe pain in his chest. He pleaded to be first on the program, quickly gave his speech, then staggered across the street to a hospital emergency room. Within a few hours he was paralyzed from the neck down.

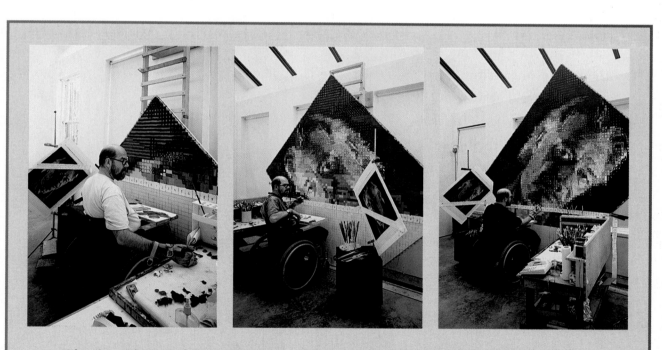

"I begin with one of the corners. After the squares are finished, I rotate the whole painting and go through it again. Finally the canvas is turned to its upright position. I go through the painting one more time, correcting, editing, changing, pulling one square out, putting one in. I'm always referring back to the photograph. It's like looking at a map so you don't get lost."

At first the doctors didn't know why. Eventually they diagnosed a rare spinal artery collapse. Sometimes injuries like this happen to football players during rough games or to people who have been in accidents. Nobody could figure out how it happened to Chuck. But art and medical experts agreed on one point: His career was finished.

Close knew better. He was alive, so he would continue to make art. But becoming a conceptual artist, counting on others to execute his ideas, didn't interest him. He yearned to get back to "the pure pleasure of pushing materials around, of getting into paint." The biggest question in his mind was how. "I was trapped in a body that didn't work, but somehow I was going to get the paint on canvas."

His wife, Leslie, understood and was determined to find a way. She encouraged him to move to Rusk Institute, a rehabilitation facility. "I was there for seven months. Besides my family and friends, the art world also really turned out for me. At the end of the day after physical therapy, I'd be lying there, and one visitor after another would appear at the foot of my bed. In the darkened room their faces loomed up. I realized just how important these disembodied images of heads were. It reconnected me. It was the first time I ever really accepted the fact that I was making portraits. Prior to that I'd always referred to my paintings as heads."

Richard, *1992. 72" x 60".*
Oil on canvas.

508

He spent painful months in rehabilitation. Though he'd never worked out in a gym before, he went every day. Eventually he gained partial use of his arms and legs, but he could walk only a few steps. He'd be dependent on a wheelchair for the rest of his life. And even worse for an artist, he still couldn't move his hands.

He labored with weights, strengthening the muscles in his arms. Finally, after many long weeks of struggle, he developed a way to work. Seated in his wheelchair, with a brush strapped to his hand, he could put paint on a canvas. His arms took the place of his fingers.

Lorna, *1995.*
102" x 84".
Oil on canvas.

"I used to like roughhousing on the grass with my kids, walking on the beach, or mowing the lawn. Since now there are so many activities I can't do, painting has assumed a larger share of my time. I'm really left with my relationship with my work, my family, my friends, and other artists."

Along with the complete change in his life, Close's portraits took on a new dimension. Before "the event" he was already painting in a looser, freer style, but now the shapes of each square were like fireworks — bursts of color. It was as if he were celebrating the sheer excitement of being able to paint again.

Step close to the canvas, and you see hundreds of little abstract paintings — multicolored ovals and gaudy squares, amoebas swimming before your eyes. Move back, and the portrait emerges. Perhaps first the mouth comes into focus, then the nose, the eyes, a full face beaming back at you.

A major leap! A triumph! A breakthrough, the critics would say. Close would simply say, "I was back to work."

509

Today Chuck Close is one of the most admired and successful artists in the world, with a hundred solo shows to his credit and a retrospective of his paintings at the Museum of Modern Art in New York City. How has he accomplished this? He says, "If you wait for inspiration, you'll never get anything done. When you look at my paintings, there is no way of knowing which days I was happy or which days I was sad, which days I was up or which days I was down. The important thing is getting into a rhythm and continuing it. It makes for a very positive experience. Every day when I roll out of the studio and look over my shoulder, I say, "That's what I did today."

Chuck Close's studio, with Self Portrait, *1997.*

(right, inset) April, *1990–1991. 100" x 84".*
Oil on canvas.

(main image) April, *(detail).*

Think About the Selection

1. Chuck Close says that "problem creation is much more interesting" than problem solving. What does he mean? Give examples.

2. Which word best describes Chuck Close for you: *creative, determined, hard-working,* or some other word? Explain your choice.

3. How important a role do you think technology has played in Chuck Close's success? Explain.

4. Chuck Close creates his portraits slowly. Do you work fast or slowly? Are you patient or impatient? Give examples from your experience.

5. How do the colors in the painting *Lucas II* look to your eyes? Do you like the effect of this kind of painting? Explain your answer.

6. What does Chuck Close mean by this statement?: "If you wait for inspiration, you'll never get anything done." Do you agree or disagree?

7. **Connecting/Comparing** Chuck Close and Jackie Joyner-Kersee both worked very hard to achieve success. Compare and contrast their goals and motivation.

Evaluating

Write an Art Review

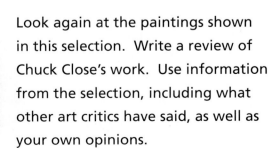

Look again at the paintings shown in this selection. Write a review of Chuck Close's work. Use information from the selection, including what other art critics have said, as well as your own opinions.

Tips

- If possible, start by reading a review of an art show.
- Begin your review with a short, general description of the artist's work.
- Then describe one or two paintings in detail.

Explore the Properties of Paint

Chuck Close often paints with oil paint, which is a mixture of powdered pigments and linseed oil. Why do artists use oil paint? Find out by mixing vegetable or linseed oil with different substances, such as flour, sand, cornstarch, and paint pigments. Then mix water with the same substances. Try spreading the different mixtures on paper and canvas. Time how long it takes for them to dry. Record your observations on a chart.

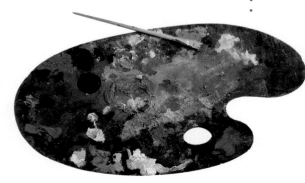

Comparing Portraits

Compare one of Chuck Close's paintings with the portraits shown in "The Art of Portraits" on page 497. List ways in which the paintings are similar. List ways in which they are different. Make a Venn diagram of your findings.

Tips

- Look for similar or repeated colors, shapes, or lines.
- Look at how light and shadows are used in both paintings.
- Look at the materials used by the artists.

Internet

Send an E-Mail Message

Send an e-mail to a friend or family member. Tell him or her what you learned about making dreams come true from the selections in this theme. Also tell which selection you think he or she might like to read, and why.

513

Art Link

Skill: How to Look at Fine Art

Identify the title, the time period, and the name of the artist. Note whether the painting is **representational** or **abstract**. Ask yourself these questions:

- What **shades** and **tones** of **color** are used in the painting? What feelings do the colors convey?

- What **shapes** appear in the painting? What do I think of these shapes?

- How has the artist used **horizontal** and **diagonal lines**? Are there many lines, or only a few? Why?

- What is the overall **composition** of the painting? How do the colors, shapes, and lines work together?

Different Strokes

by Samantha Bonar

Meet a girl whose passion for painting has made her a world-famous artist.

Thirteen-year-old Alexandra Nechita (neh–KEE–tuh) is at home, painting. Carefully she dips a brush into blueberry-colored paint. The glittery plastic bracelets click on her wrist as she swirls color onto the canvas, where a red and blue elephant is taking shape.

Like many girls, Alexandra wears braces, cracks her knuckles, and bites her nails. She loves eating Mexican food, playing basketball, and shopping with friends near her California home. But there's one big way in which Alexandra is different — she's a professional artist. Her paintings hang in homes, museums, and galleries around the world.

Even if she never sold another painting, though, Alexandra says she would still paint. "It's something I love," she says. "It's beyond my favorite thing to do!"

A trip to the zoo motivated Alexandra to paint the elephant she's working on above. "It's one of the most awful things, when you see all those animals caged," she says.

Daring to Be Different

Alexandra's passion for art began early. At age two, she spent so much time with her coloring books that her parents took them away from her, hoping she would spend more time playing with other kids. Instead, she made her own coloring books! By the time she was six, she was using acrylic and oil paints on canvas. "I loved working with bright colors," she says.

When Alexandra was eight, her paintings were shown at a library. There she sold her first painting — a picture of a plant with human heads. That might sound strange. But all of Alexandra's paintings have abstract qualities. Instead of copying the way

things look, Alexandra paints whatever she imagines — strange shapes, multi-colored animals, even faces with four eyes! "It's the way I express my thoughts," she says.

At first, some people thought her art was too different. Her parents took her out of an art class after a teacher told her to draw like everyone else. At school, her classmates said her paintings looked as if they were done by aliens from outer space!

"It was difficult," Alexandra recalls. Sometimes she came home from school crying. But one day she told herself, "If I continue to be afraid of everything they say, then that will

515

make me stop doing what I want to do, which is to paint."

A Painter's Process

Now, almost nothing stops Alexandra from painting. She paints for two or three hours after school and all day Saturday. Inside her studio, huge canvases lean against the walls among big buckets of paint. "I managed to convince my mom that an artist's studio is never fully organized!" she says.

Alexandra's canvases are like pages from a giant coloring book. She often begins by making a charcoal sketch on the canvas. Then, using acrylic paints, she starts filling in the shapes with color. She mixes her paints in plastic cups or muffin tins to get the right shades.

Alexandra trusts her feelings when she decides what colors to use. Some paintings, like one she did after the Oklahoma City bombing, use somber, dark colors. Other pic-

Alexandra gets inspired by many different subjects — from world events to her pet fish.

tures, like those of her little brother Maximillian, are bright and cheerful.

Because Alexandra likes to work on more than one painting at a time, it can take her weeks to complete a picture. "No painting is ever really finished," she says. "I always feel like I could add more." Once she is satisfied with a painting, she signs her name and gives her work a shiny coat of varnish.

Most of Alexandra's paintings are sold through an art agency. Alexandra refuses to part with some paintings, though — like those she did after a recent trip to Romania, where she was born. "I keep my most sentimental paintings," she says. "But every artist's work is special. You put all of your love, all of your thought, all of your creativity into it. You put your whole self into it."

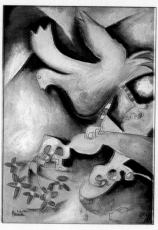

AG: *You chose this painting,* Sprinkle the Joy of Peace, *to show our readers. What does it mean to you?*

Alexandra: "The hands represent all the different nations and races. I showed hands and no human face because the hands have more control — they are symbolic. The dove represents peace, and the flowers represent joy. Every person wants to share and cultivate the joy of peace."

AG: *You're following your dream of being an artist. What advice would you give to a young artist about how to make their own dream come true?*

Alexandra: "The most important thing is to know that you love it and not to do it because you see somebody else doing it. Do it because it's from your heart. Do it because you have a true and sincere desire and it's something you have fun with. Because if you don't have fun with it, why do it?"

Check Your Progress

The doers and dreamers in this theme — an Olympic medalist, a family working together on a project, and a portrait painter — have made their dreams become a reality. Now you too can become a doer by reading and comparing two new selections and improving your test-taking skills.

Start by revisiting pages 450–452. In Alma Flor Ada's opinion, ". . . dreams alone cannot transform the world." How do the selections you've read so far support this opinion?

Next, as you read the two selections that follow, think about what makes someone a doer *and* a dreamer and how these individuals try to become both. How do these people and their dreams compare with each other and with the other doers and dreamers in this theme?

Read and Compare

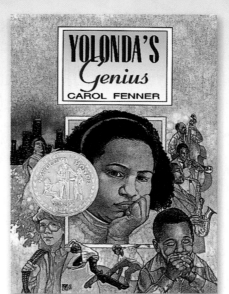

Read about a musically talented boy and his older sister, who tries to replace his broken harmonica with a new one.

Try these strategies:
Predict and Infer
Evaluate

Learn about the gifted composer Wolfgang Amadeus Mozart, including some events you may find surprising.

Try these strategies:
Question
Summarize

Strategies in Action *Look for ways to use all your reading strategies while you read.*

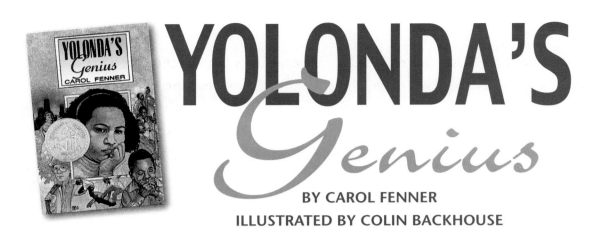

YOLONDA'S *Genius*

BY CAROL FENNER
ILLUSTRATED BY COLIN BACKHOUSE

Yolonda is a fierce protector of her younger brother, Andrew, and of his musical talent. When some older bullies destroy Andrew's harmonica, Yolonda looks for a way to replace it. She convinces the owner of a music store to listen to Andrew play. If the owner agrees that Andrew has talent, he will sell the harmonica to Yolonda at a lower price. Yolonda's plan puzzles Andrew, though; he's not sure what she wants him to do. Will Andrew overcome his confusion and earn his new harmonica?

Andrew wasn't sure where they were going. Yolonda had said something about a harmonica — not his dead one, the one that had the music in it, the one that sometimes spoke before he knew he had the thought. She wanted him to earn it. He was only a little worried. Yolonda never did anything to hurt him.

The bus ride was pretty long. Andrew was aware of Yolonda checking her watch and jiggling her leg impatiently. Every time the bus stopped to pick up a passenger, she let out an exasperated hiss. She was still perspiring, sweat running down her face.

Maybe she's still mad, thought Andrew. He'd never before seen the Yolonda he had just witnessed at Asphalt Hill — towering over those bad boys like Batman, bigger than Batman. He'd never seen her great power unleashed before, but he hadn't been surprised. He'd never doubted Yolonda could tackle anything. There wasn't anything she was afraid of. Some Yolonda sounds came into his head — great, powerful explosions. He'd need another instrument — drums maybe, a horn, both together. What instrument roared?

The bus stopped. Right in front of his favorite store. He checked the window with pleasure. There was a curled horn on a stand. Could the curled horn roar? He didn't think so.

Yolonda pushed open the wide glass doors. "Longhair might not be here, but I got a receipt somewhere." His sister fumbled in her jeans pocket.

Andrew stared at the wall lined with guitars, at the glass cases holding different kinds of pipes, bigger than his. There was a gigantic curved horn on a huge stand. Yolonda. Andrew was sure that horn could roar.

"Is this the genius?" A smiling man with gray hair that brushed his shoulders was leaning toward Andrew. Andrew scowled. There was that name again.

He could tell the man that his name was Andrew Blue, but his mouth was suddenly wishing for his old harmonica, the one he'd buried in the dark dirt of his mother's tulips, the dead harmonica. Where was it now?

Then he saw that the man was holding something out toward him.

"Where'd you get that?" asked Andrew, shocked and horrified.

There was his harmonica, only someone had fixed it up, polished it. The smiling man held it out toward him.

A sick feeling began to invade Andrew's stomach, and a faint hollow sound threatened his ears. Then it seemed as if all the instruments on the wall, on stands in the corners, inside the glass cases waited for him.

"All you gotta do to earn this baby is play something, Andrew." Yolonda eyed him. "Something great, that is. No chords. Play 'Round Midnight. Play Bart Simpson. Play the bacon."

Yolonda waited. The smiling man waited, holding out the harmonica. The other instruments waited. The hollow buzzing came into his ears.

"Andrew," said Yolonda in her impatient voice. "We got no time for games. The bus will leave. We aren't gonna wait another hour for the next one. I gotta dust before Momma gets home. You gotta play before we earn this harp. Come on, do your stuff."

The buzzing grew intense.

Yolonda grabbed the harmonica from the clerk, thrust it into Andrew's hands, and said, *"Play!"*

The harp in Andrew's hands felt stiff, wood and metal, no magic to it at all. No voice.

Yolonda's face grew more fierce. "Andrew! No more baby stuff. Come on!"

Andrew looked at the harmonica. He had no breath anymore, only a tiny little bit that sat in his throat, not enough to even whisper through the wooden holes. The air around him grew tight with everything waiting.

"They *really* robbed you, Andrew!" exploded Yolonda. She wheeled and headed for the door. "Give it back to the man. Get my eight bucks back. I'll try and hold the bus at the corner." She stomped toward the door.

Wait! cried Andrew's brain. Instinctively he lifted the harmonica to his mouth, felt with his lips and tongue the new wooden holes, felt with his hands the smoothness of metal, felt with his brain for the old voice living inside the wood and metal.

Wait! screamed the harmonica. *Wait! Help!* Yolonda froze, then turned slowly toward him.

Andrew wet the wood with his tongue, wept into the wooden holes; a crying spilled out of the Marine Band harmonica. Then jagged streaks of angry sound bled into the room.

"Whoooo!" cried the clerk. "Whoooo-eeee! Go for it, kid!"

Wait! yelled Andrew's harmonica. *Wait. Wait. Eee iiii eee iii oooh!*

"It's all yours, kid," said the clerk, clapping his hands. "You belong together." Then to Yolonda, "You owe me six bucks, sister."

Yolonda heaved a great sigh. "'Bout time," she grumbled.

Andrew looked at the harmonica while Yolonda counted out six dollars plus the sales tax from a great weight of quarters. His head felt like a balloon. It could float away maybe. He kept his eyes fastened to the Marine Band harmonica as if it were an anchor.

"Better take the case," said the man to Andrew. He held out a small black box. His smile was serious, and Andrew immediately trusted him. He could feel his head begin to come down to him again.

"What's it for?" Andrew asked.

"It'll protect your instrument — like a house around it — keep it from getting broken."

"Oh," said Andrew. His instrument. He took the case, opened it, and carefully placed the shiny Marine Band harmonica in its velvet bed. The lid snapped when he closed it. Safe.

On the bus as they headed home, Yolonda said, "Look, I don't have this all figured out yet, Andrew." She sighed.

Andrew waited.

"But you're *supposed* to have a harmonica. Maybe your genes did the deciding. Maybe the stars. Who knows?" She chewed her knuckles.

"Maybe just Daddy," offered Andrew, who could barely recall a large shape hovering over him. He'd been told where the Marine Band harmonica came from.

"Yeah, maybe just Daddy," said Yolonda. "Momma doesn't know you are supposed to have a harmonica. I thought she did, but she doesn't. She loves you, but she doesn't see that you're a genius. That takes a rare mind — to detect genius."

The bus rumbled on and Andrew waited for what Yolonda would say next. He knew Yolonda was very smart. Apparently a genius was a good thing to be.

"I don't have this figured out yet, Andrew," repeated Yolonda. "Maybe you shouldn't play the harmonica at home when Momma's there. No, that's not right. Play it whenever you have to."

What did she mean? Did genius have something to do with secrets? Would he have to be brave? He held the Marine Band harmonica in its case gently in both hands. His instrument. In his head he heard the sound bravery made, but he was afraid to play it.

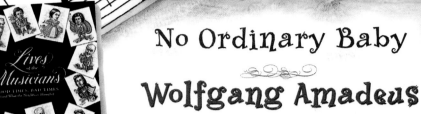

No Ordinary Baby

Wolfgang Amadeus MOZART

by Kathleen Krull & illustrated by Amanda Halsey and Trisha Tusa

Born in Salzburg, Austria, Mozart was a composer who in his short life (1756–1791) wrote many masterpieces, including symphonies, operas such as *The Magic Flute* and *Don Giovanni*, and piano music. He died in Vienna, Austria, at the age of thirty-five.

Until he was three, Wolfgang Amadeus Mozart was an ordinary baby. Then he began climbing up on the bench and imitating the clavier playing of his talented older sister Maria Anna. At age five, he made up his own compositions and studied violin. He insisted that all his activities be accompanied by music. His father noticed that it was difficult to teach him music — he seemed to know everything already. He would stay up late, practicing by candlelight.

The next year, six-year-old Mozart went on tour, traveling by stagecoach all around the bumpy roads of Europe. (From all of his travels, Mozart eventually learned to speak fifteen languages.) He played for royalty and for the well-known musicians of the day. At seven, he proposed marriage to Marie Antoinette (the future queen of France); at eight, he was composing symphonies; and at twelve, he composed his first opera. When composing, Mozart wore an apron to keep the ink off his clothes. He wore little velvet coats with lace ruffles and gold embroidery, and a little gold sword at his side.

He was known then as the most-kissed little boy in Europe. Today we think of him as the greatest musical prodigy who ever lived.

Mozart had a strange and exhausting childhood. He was so often ill that some people worried about how much longer he would live. He was sweet and affectionate, most anxious to please. His special talent meant he never had to go to school; his father gave him lessons. Mozart especially liked arithmetic and covered tablecloths and wallpaper with rows of figures.

Mozart loved animals. He sent the family dog, a terrier named Bimperl, greetings from cities all over Europe. In London, he broke off a concert to run after a cat that had wandered in. Later in life, he owned two other dogs (Goukerl and Katherl), a pet grasshopper, and various birds.

As a child Mozart was cute, with rosy cheeks and bright eyes. As an adult, though, his skin was yellowish, scarred from smallpox, and his blue eyes were bulgy. He was short and thin, and his head was too big for his body. Yet he was concerned about his appearance. He took care to have elegant clothes, and he had a barber work on his hair much more often than most people did.

Mozart fell madly in love with Aloysia Weber (cousin of composer Carl Maria von Weber), his landlady's daughter. But she rejected him, and he married Constanze Weber, her sister. Constanze was like Mozart in many ways: musical, not especially attractive (he called her "Little Mouse"), and playful. They had six children, but only two lived to adulthood.

Music was the one thing that made Mozart's face light up. He usually woke up at six, composed till nine, gave music lessons till one (though he didn't enjoy teaching), then had lunch at someone's house, where he had to entertain his hosts. Then, unless there was a concert to attend, he composed far into the night. He could get by on as little as four hours' sleep. Doctors told him he needed to get more regular recreation, which may be why he eventually bought a pool table.

He wrote music more quickly than almost any other composer in history, and he sometimes put things off till the very last minute. If he had to work through the night, Constanze would tell him tales about Cinderella or Aladdin to keep him awake.

His best ideas came when he was in a good mood, alone, and undisturbed. "What a delight this is I cannot tell!" he once wrote. "All this inventing, this producing, takes place in a pleasing, lively dream."

He could write down his ideas at meals (he liked liver dumplings and sauerkraut), while gossiping with friends, and even while playing pool. Once he held his wife's hand during childbirth and with his other hand wrote several pieces of music.

One day a visitor found Mozart and his wife dancing in their house, and Mozart explained that they had run out of firewood and were trying to stay warm. Mozart spent money faster than he could earn it, and he was always in debt. Part of the problem was that aristocrats paid him for music with things like watches — not the cash that he needed to live on. (A letter that he wrote asking for a loan sold, two centuries later, for one hundred times the amount he had pleaded for.)

There were plenty of people who didn't like Mozart. They thought he was rude, immature, and irresponsible. One person who knew Mozart well said that she never heard him say one serious thing. He could be impatient with people who were not as bright as he was.

Although his father was always bombarding him with advice on how to make money and meet the "right" people, Mozart had trouble finding and keeping jobs. Once he lost a court appointment by being obnoxious and got himself literally kicked out of court. "There is the door; I will have nothing more to do with such a villain," said the man who fired him.

Mozart was scared of ghosts and loud noises, and he was superstitious, which explains his reaction to the tall, mysterious stranger who came to his house one night. Dressed all in gray, the stranger commissioned him to write a requiem (or funeral) mass.

The stranger would never give his name, but kept nagging Mozart to finish. Fearful, and convinced somehow that he was writing his own burial music, Mozart worked feverishly. Eventually the stranger was revealed to be a messenger from an eccentric count who had a habit of having well-known composers write something he could pass off as his own in private performances.

But by that time Mozart had died of kidney failure and malnutrition.

Mozart had spent fourteen years of his short life on the road, and he had never been very healthy. He was only thirty-five when he died. Some people feel that fear of the stranger hastened his death. Plays, operas, and movies have been written about the theory that he was poisoned by rival composer Antonio Salieri, but this rumor has never been proved.

At the peak of his career, Mozart earned as much money in one concert as his father earned in a year. Yet, at the time of his death, he owned very little. He had six coats (five red, his favorite color, and one white for court); three silver spoons; and 346 books. His most expensive possessions were his walnut piano and his pool table.

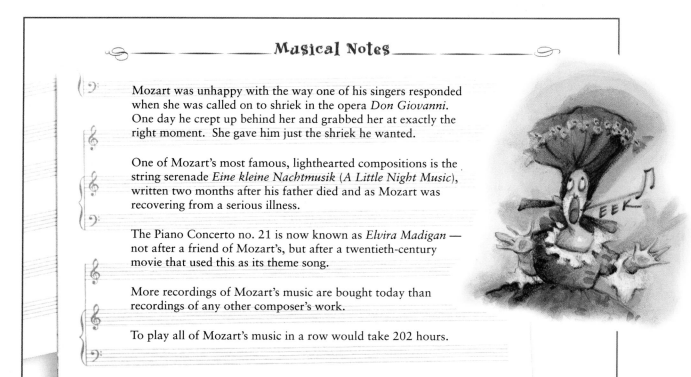

Musical Notes

Mozart was unhappy with the way one of his singers responded when she was called on to shriek in the opera *Don Giovanni*. One day he crept up behind her and grabbed her at exactly the right moment. She gave him just the shriek he wanted.

One of Mozart's most famous, lighthearted compositions is the string serenade *Eine kleine Nachtmusik (A Little Night Music)*, written two months after his father died and as Mozart was recovering from a serious illness.

The Piano Concerto no. 21 is now known as *Elvira Madigan* — not after a friend of Mozart's, but after a twentieth-century movie that used this as its theme song.

More recordings of Mozart's music are bought today than recordings of any other composer's work.

To play all of Mozart's music in a row would take 202 hours.

Think and Compare

Wolfgang Amadeus
Mozart

by Kathleen Krull

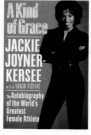

1. Compare the way Andrew's musical talent was described with the way Mozart's was described. What do the two musicians have in common? How are they different?

2. What would people today think of someone with Mozart's talent? Why do you think so?

3. Chuck Close creates his portraits at a different pace than the pace at which Mozart composed music. What do you think this tells you about each artist?

4. Which character in this theme seems most like Andrew? In what ways are the characters alike and different?

5. Which selection in the theme do you think is the most inspiring? Give examples from the selection.

Strategies in Action Tell about two or three places in *Yolonda's Genius* where you used reading strategies.

Write a Biography

Think of a character from the theme. Write the first few paragraphs of a biography of that person. Read your work to a small group.

> **Tips**
> - **Begin with simple details, such as the place and year the person was born.**
> - **Choose events and details that will make readers want to know more.**

Taking Tests

Writing an Answer to a Question

Many test items ask you to write an answer to a question about something you have read. Usually you can answer these questions with a few sentences. Here is a sample test question for *Yolonda's Genius*.

Write your answer to this question.

In *Yolonda's Genius*, why is Yolonda so determined to get another harmonica for Andrew?

---

1 Understand the question.

Find the key words in the question. Use them to understand what you need to do.

2 Get ready to write.

Skim the selection, using the key words. List the details that will help you answer the question.

Here is an example of a good list.

Selection Details

Yolonda wants to protect Andrew.
She feels that Andrew has musical talent.
She believes that Andrew needs to play music to be happy.

---

③ Write your answer.

Use details from your list. Write a clear and complete answer.

Now read a good answer to the test question.

Yolonda is angry that the bullies destroyed Andrew's harmonica. She is convinced that her brother has musical talent, and she believes that playing the harmonica makes Andrew happy. She wants to protect Andrew, and one of her ways to do that is to make sure he can play his music. So she tries to find a way to get him a new harmonica.

SPEECHES

Speeches

A **speech** calls for a speaker, an audience, and an important occasion. After an **opening** that grabs the audience's attention, a speech develops **main ideas**, then ends with a strong **conclusion**. As you read these speeches, think about how each one delivers its message.

CONTENTS

The Gettysburg Address.....................522
by Abraham Lincoln

A Story of Courage, Bravery, Strength, and Heroism........................525
by Shao Lee

On Accepting the Newbery Medal..................................529
by Jerry Spinelli

A Commencement Speech...............533
by Katherine Ortega

I Have a Dream...536
by Dr. Martin Luther King, Jr.

Gettysburg battlefield was dedicated as a military cemetery. President Abraham Lincoln spoke at the dedication. He worked out his brief speech with great care. Notice his choice of words in the first sentence, his repetition of the word *dedicate*, and the rhythm of his last sentence.

The Gettysburg Address

Abraham Lincoln

**President Lincoln and his son Tad (*above*).
A detail from the Lincoln Memorial in
Washington, D.C. (*right*).**

Fourscore and seven years ago our fathers brought forth on this
continent a new nation, conceived in liberty and dedicated to the
proposition that all men are created equal. Now we are engaged
in a great civil war, testing whether that nation, or any nation so
conceived and so dedicated, can long endure. We are met on a
great battlefield of that war. We have come to dedicate a portion
of that field as a final resting place for those who here gave their
lives that that nation might live. It is altogether fitting and proper
that we should do this. But, in a larger sense, we cannot dedicate
— we cannot consecrate — we cannot hallow — this ground.
The brave men, living and dead, who struggled here have conse-
crated it far above our poor power to add or to detract. The
world will little note nor long remember what we say here, but it
can never forget what they did here.

It is for us, the living, rather to be dedicated here to the unfinished work which they who fought here have thus far so nobly advanced. It is rather for us to be here dedicated to the great task remaining before us — that from these honored dead we take increased devotion to that cause for which they gave the last full measure of devotion; that we here highly resolve that these dead shall not have died in vain; that this nation, under God, shall have a new birth of freedom; and that government of the people, by the people, for the people, shall not perish from the earth.

President Abraham Lincoln visiting an army camp in 1862, during the Civil War.

States from Laos. She gave this speech at her 1995 graduation from the International School of Minnesota.

A Story of Courage, Bravery, Strength, and Heroism . . .

Shao Lee

How many ways are there to say good-bye? How many days will it take to say good-bye? I'd like to thank my father for tolerating, teaching, disciplining, and caring all these years. I'd like to thank my mother for her sweat, tears, toils, and morals. I'd like to thank my grandmother for her folklore, magic, and wisdom. David Willems, I'd like to thank you for your friendship and your faith in me.

I want to tell you a story of courage, of bravery, of strength, and of heroism. I've been in the United States for thirteen years. All this time I struggled with questions. How long does it take to be an American? An hour, a day, a year, a century?

Shao Lee remembers scenes like these from her childhood in rural Laos.

Does one have to be born in this country to be an American? I am a Hmong girl. I grew up in the mountains and jungles of Laos. Whenever I look back to my childhood, I always remember being so hungry and ill, without food, without clothing. There was an opportunity for a decent education, if and only if one's family was wealthy, and only males could attend. For those who did attend, some quit because their family needed them on the farm. Females weren't allowed to attend school; they were expected to care for their siblings, parents, cousins, and extended family. Otherwise they were married off, and they cared for their own children. The opportunities were very limited in Laos, especially for women.

My father, Youa Thao Lee, has influenced and inspired, motivated and supported me throughout my life. His experiences and stories gave me purpose, pride, and power. My father is an American and Hmong hero. His family were poor farmers, hunters, and gatherers. My father worked really hard as a young boy to get his education. He knew the secret. He knew knowledge was power. He knew education would advance him in society. He was one of the smallest boys from his village to go to school. He had to walk miles to his school. He had to stay at school on the weekdays, and then came home on the weekends. My father with his determination and effort was able to become a teacher. He could write, read, and was fluent in Thai, French, Laotian, and Hmong. He was a community leader.

Then the Vietnam War came. The Vietnam War was an unforgettable, tragic event for my father because many of his cousins, brothers, and uncles were murdered. My father fought in the "secret war." The Hmong people fought as spies for the United States. The Hmong people fought to keep their country from the communists, but they were outnumbered, abandoned by the United States, and defeated. After the American troops pulled out, the communists embarked upon a "killing fields" mentality and targeted the Hmong troops and their families. There was no peace, no human rights, no freedom, and no safety in Laos. It is easier to forget and harder to remember, but sometimes one doesn't want to remember, and the forgetting is bitter and painful. Even after the Vietnam War was declared over, people were still dying, still fighting. Yet those who died for the cause of saving their country, their homeland, their people, their children, died not in vain. Those who sacrificed their lives gave my family and me a safe journey to the United States.

Now here, I'm determined and devoted to serve my family and the Hmong community, owing my gratitude, my tribute to those who died and suffered, so they could give me a better future. What is a hero? Who is a hero? My father and those freedom fighters who fought should be honored as heroes. And I will not disappoint them. I will not disappoint my father. I will not abandon them. I will not abandon my heritage. I am determined to get the best education and learning I can. Using my best abilities and skills,

I will succeed, while also helping my Hmong people advance in what they never could have had in Laos. I will not let my Hmong people die in vain, because their dreams and beliefs live within me.

It is not what the world can do for you. It is not what your school can do for you. It is not what your parents can do for you. It is what you can do for yourself. Get your education. Get your opportunity. But keep your past, keep your history, keep your heritage. Know your language. Know your tongue. Know your voice. Make a great song. Make some noise. Do not define a century by one day. Do not define a civilization by one city. Do not define humanity by one man. Do not define a race by one color. What I wear, what I eat, what I own does not define me. My situation does not define me. I define who I am. I know who I am. I am Shao Lee. I am not afraid to say my name. I won't wait. I cannot wait for self-identity. I won't sleep. I have to awaken to my own voice. I'm too hungry to eat. My hunger is for knowledge. I'm too thirsty to drink. My thirst is for wisdom. My advice to my classmates: Seize the day, seize the moment. The moment is now, because now is the morning of our lives. Have no fear. We're young now. Now is the time to have faith in what we can do. Now is the time to have faith in yourself. Know yourself, know your name, say your name, see your worth, feel your value, touch your essence. In the mirror is your reflection, your face. The face of your father, the face of your mother, the face of your ancestors, the face of your progeny. Don't cover your face. Take your hands down from your face. No! Do not turn away! I am your mirror. Look at me! Have the courage to look at me! Don't hide your smile! For the last time look on every part. Then, know what you can truly become.

distinguished contribution to American literature for children. Jerry Spinelli was the winner of the 1991 Newbery Medal for his novel *Maniac Magee.* In this passage from his acceptance speech, Spinelli explains where he finds ideas for his stories.

On Accepting the Newbery Medal

Jerry Spinelli

Not long ago a kid in a group I was speaking to raised his hand and said, "Where do you get all that stuff?"

I looked out into a library full of cross-legged floor-sitters, their eyes wide, mouths agape, all wondering the same thing, their classmate having put his finger on their second most pressing question — the first being, of course, "How much money do you make?" I pointed to them all, and I smiled, and I said, "You. You're where I get all that stuff."

The expressions didn't change. They weren't buying it.

"Look," I said, "what do you think I do, make up all this stuff? I get it from you. I get it from the me that used to be you. From my own kids, your age-mates. For my first two books, I didn't even have to look outside my own house."

And I told them how I found *Space Station Seventh Grade* early one morning in my lunch bag, my fried chicken having been reduced to bones by one or more of the six sleeping angels upstairs. I told them that the warfare between Megamouth and El Grosso in *Who Put That Hair in My Toothbrush?* was nothing compared to the real battles between Molly and Jeffrey in my own house.

I pointed to them again. "You're the funny ones. You're the fascinating ones. You're the elusive and inspiring and promising and heroic and maddening ones. Don't you know that?"

I looked over the faces. No, for the most part, they did not know. And just as well. How regrettable if they did know, and thereby ceased to be themselves.

The obvious prompting of her teacher notwithstanding, how could anyone but an unselfconscious sixth-grader have written this:

Jerry Spinelli has enjoyed a successful writing career, publishing close to twenty books for young readers.

Spinelli often talks to students about his books, and welcomes their feedback.

Dear Mr. Spinelli,

I am very sorry that I was playing Tic-Tac-Toe while you were talking. I know that I had no right to do it. I should have listened to you. It was positively mean and rude of me and my friend to play Tic-Tac-Toe right under your nose. I regret it terribly and I seriously would understand if you hated me. I liked your talk and your books anyhow. If you do come back to Chatham, even after the rudeness of my friend and me, I hope that you get treated more kindly than this. Like I said before, I am really very, very sorry that I played Tic-Tac-Toe instead of listening to you. Please do not unlike the school because of our terrible rudeness. With all our heart we are sorry.

Most sincerely,
Katie Rose Loftus

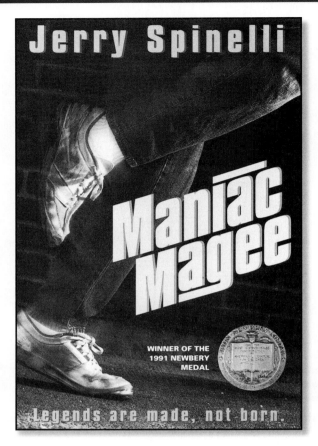

WINNER OF THE 1991 NEWBERY MEDAL

LEGENDS are made, not born.

The Newbery-Award-winning book *Maniac Magee* tells an unusual tale about a runaway orphan.

Where do I *get* this stuff?

I get it from Brooke Jacobs, who wrote, "When you came to our school, I thought I'd see a big, tall man in a suit looking rich. When I saw you, I got very relaxed."

I get it from the young lady who wrote, "I will not say I totally enjoyed your talk, because that would be untrue . . . Mr. Spinelli, you are a great writer. However, you, in my eyes, do need to work on your group speaking skills."

I get it from Niki Hollie, who wrote to me recently from Schuylkill Elementary, just a few blocks from my house: "I think no matter if people are black, white, or green, there is no difference in the way they get treated. It's the inside not the outside."

States from 1983 to 1989. Here is a selection from Ortega's comments to the 1985 graduating class of Kean State College, New Jersey.

A Commencement Speech

Katherine Ortega

I am sure there are some among you who think you are inheriting a highly uncertain world, a world burdened by armaments and a world ravaged by hunger, a world long on hypocrisy and short on opportunity. The world is an imperfect place. You do not need me to tell you that. But the world is also a perfectible place. If I did not believe that, I would not be here.

Now where, you are no doubt asking yourselves, did she ever come up with that idea? Well, let me tell you. When I was a girl, the youngest of nine children, I lived amidst the white sands and lunar landscape of New Mexico. When I was about your age, I hoped to become a school-teacher. But I was told not to bother. Why? Because in eastern New Mexico, the part of the state where the best paying jobs were to be found, employers simply did not believe in hiring Hispanics. But times have changed. They hire Hispanics now. More than a few Hispanics are themselves doing the hiring.

Katherine Ortega speaking at Kean State College in New Jersey and (*opposite page*) at the Republican National Convention in Dallas, Texas.

The United States Treasury Building

When I was a girl, my brothers wore tattered blue jeans long before they became fashionable attire. They sold perfume door-to-door to put bread on the Ortega family table. My father augmented his own income by nailing together custom-made coffins. The one thing he refused to bury was his unshakable conviction that each life is special, and that each one's calling was important not for the income it generated but the character it called forth. He dismissed both bloodlines and bank accounts as insignificant. He had contempt only for those who put on airs. "Get that chip off your shoulder," he used to say to us. "You are as good as anyone else." Then he said something to me, something in its own way as educational and as liberating as anything ever taught in a formal classroom. "If you are going to work for someone," he said, "give it the full eight hours plus. If you are going to do it at all, do it right."

These are the words that propelled me into the world of business and banking. Similar words, no doubt, have accompanied each of you on your way through Kean State. Do not ever forget them. Not for a moment. Because they are your ticket of admission to an America closer than ever before to the nation dreamed of by her founders. A country that is colorblind, a republic without walls.

535

Dr. Martin Luther King, Jr., gave an inspiring speech from the steps of the Lincoln Memorial. This last section of the speech is what listeners remember best.

from

I Have a Dream

Dr. Martin Luther King, Jr.

I say to you today, my friends, that in spite of the difficulties and frustrations of the moment I still have a dream. It is a dream deeply rooted in the American dream.

I have a dream that one day this nation will rise up and live out the true meaning of its creed: "We hold these truths to be self-evident; that all men are created equal."

I have a dream that one day on the red hills of Georgia the sons of former slaves and the sons of former slave owners will be able to sit down together at the table of brotherhood.

I have a dream that one day even the state of Mississippi, a desert state sweltering with the heat of injustice and oppression, will be transformed into an oasis of freedom and justice.

I have a dream that my four little children will one day live in a nation where they will not be judged by the color of their skin but by the content of their character.

I have a dream today.

I have a dream that one day the state of Alabama, whose governor's lips are presently dripping with the words of interposition and nullification, will be transformed into a situation where little black boys and black girls will be able to join hands with little white boys and white girls and walk together as sisters and brothers.

I have a dream today.

I have a dream that one day every valley shall be exalted, every hill and mountain shall be made low, the rough places will be made plains, and the crooked places will be made straight, and the glory of the Lord shall be revealed, and all flesh shall see it together.

This is our hope. This is the faith with which I return to the South. With this faith we will be able to hew out of the mountain of despair a stone of hope. With this faith we will be able to transform the jangling discords of our nation into a beautiful symphony of brotherhood. With this faith we will be able to work together, to pray together, to struggle together, to go to jail together, to stand up for freedom together, knowing that we will be free one day.

This will be the day when all of God's children will be able to sing with new meaning "My country 'tis of thee, sweet land of liberty, of thee I sing. Land where my fathers died, land of the pilgrim's pride, from every mountainside, let freedom ring."

And if America is to be a great nation this must become true. So let freedom ring from the prodigious hilltops of New Hampshire. Let freedom ring from the mighty mountains of New York. Let freedom ring from the heightening Alleghenies of Pennsylvania!

Let freedom ring from the snowcapped Rockies of Colorado!

Let freedom ring from the curvaceous peaks of California!

But not only that; let freedom ring from Stone Mountain of Georgia!

Let freedom ring from Lookout Mountain of Tennessee!

Let freedom ring from every hill and molehill of Mississippi. From every mountainside, let freedom ring.

When we let freedom ring, when we let it ring from every village and every hamlet, from every state and every city, we will be able to speed up that day when all of God's children, black men and white men, Jews and Gentiles, Protestants and Catholics, will be able to join hands and sing in the words of the old Negro spiritual, "Free at last! Free at last! Thank God Almighty, we are free at last!"

Martin Luther King, Jr. walks with his wife, Coretta Scott King, and other civil rights leaders during a march in Selma, Alabama in 1965.

Think About the
SPEECHES

1. How is giving a speech like performing in a play? How are the two different?

2. Did Abraham Lincoln and Martin Luther King, Jr., feel the same way about freedom and equality? Give examples from their speeches.

3. What elements do the graduation speeches by Shao Lee and Catherine Ortega have in common?

4. Choose two or three speeches. What do you learn about each person from the speech he or she gives?

5. Which speech do you think serves its purpose best? Why?

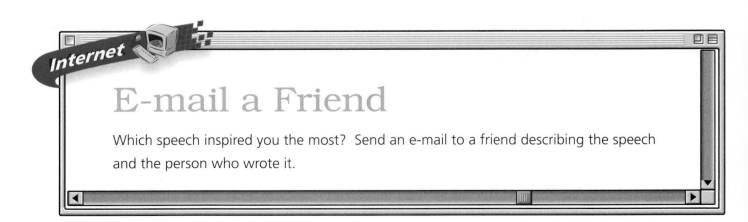

Internet

E-mail a Friend

Which speech inspired you the most? Send an e-mail to a friend describing the speech and the person who wrote it.

Expressing

Write Your Own Speech

Choose an occasion for a speech, such as a special ceremony or a school or community event. Then select a topic that interests you and might appeal to your audience. Write a speech that suits your purpose: to persuade, to inform, or to entertain. Then present the speech to your audience.

Tips

- Write key words on note cards to use as cues.
- Practice your speech in front of a mirror or with a friend.
- Speak slowly and clearly. Don't rush.

T h e m e **6**

New Frontiers:
Oceans
and Space

"Exploration is in our nature.
We began as wanderers, and
we are wanderers still."

— *Carl Sagan, from* Cosmos

New Frontiers: Oceans and Space

with Eugenie Clark

Dear Reader,

Since my first visit to the old New York Aquarium in Battery Park when I was nine years old, I have been fascinated with watching fishes. My mother let me have a fish tank of my own where I could watch these marvelous creatures swim, hide, eat, and produce babies. Nothing seemed to be more wonderful — until I discovered that I could go underwater myself, explore the shallow parts of the sea by snorkeling, then go deeper with SCUBA gear, and then finally really deep — 12,000 feet deep — in a submersible.

My first walk on the ocean floor was in a dense kelp forest off La Jolla, California. It was magical and weird, with giant kelp fronds flapping around me. My first SCUBA dive was in 1951 on

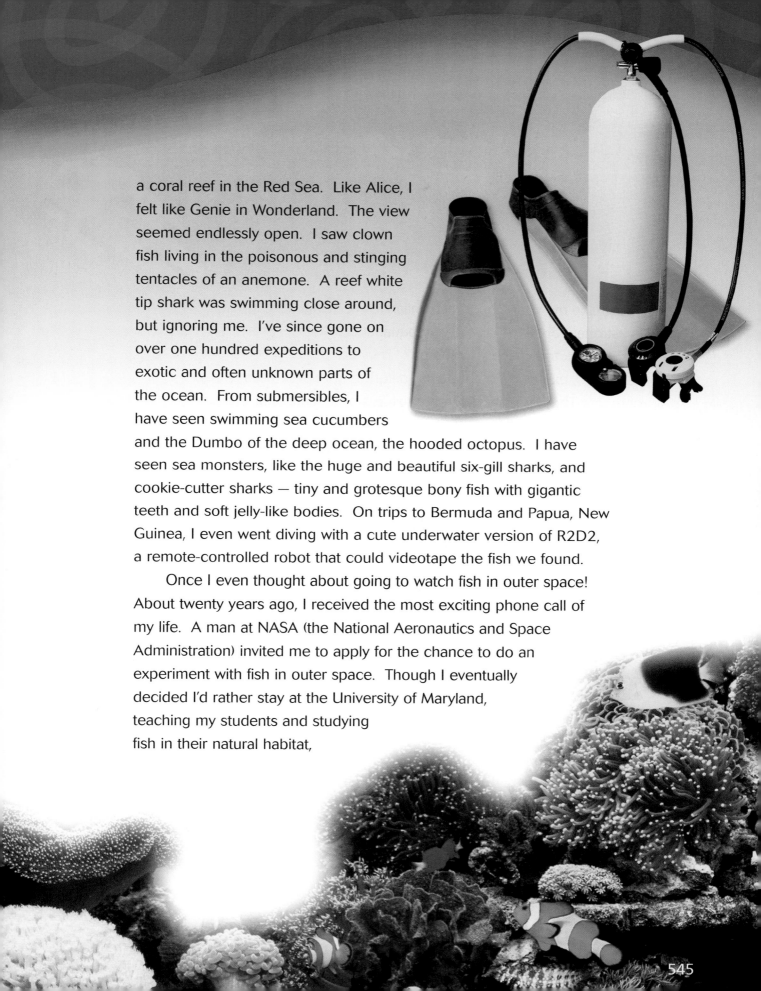

a coral reef in the Red Sea. Like Alice, I felt like Genie in Wonderland. The view seemed endlessly open. I saw clown fish living in the poisonous and stinging tentacles of an anemone. A reef white tip shark was swimming close around, but ignoring me. I've since gone on over one hundred expeditions to exotic and often unknown parts of the ocean. From submersibles, I have seen swimming sea cucumbers and the Dumbo of the deep ocean, the hooded octopus. I have seen sea monsters, like the huge and beautiful six-gill sharks, and cookie-cutter sharks — tiny and grotesque bony fish with gigantic teeth and soft jelly-like bodies. On trips to Bermuda and Papua, New Guinea, I even went diving with a cute underwater version of R2D2, a remote-controlled robot that could videotape the fish we found.

Once I even thought about going to watch fish in outer space! About twenty years ago, I received the most exciting phone call of my life. A man at NASA (the National Aeronautics and Space Administration) invited me to apply for the chance to do an experiment with fish in outer space. Though I eventually decided I'd rather stay at the University of Maryland, teaching my students and studying fish in their natural habitat,

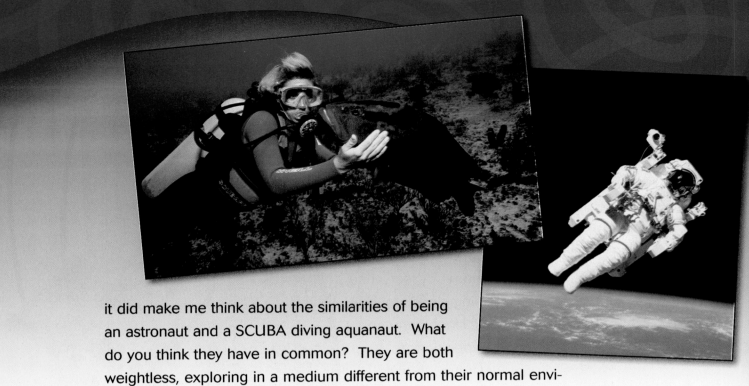

it did make me think about the similarities of being
an astronaut and a SCUBA diving aquanaut. What
do you think they have in common? They are both
weightless, exploring in a medium different from their normal environment. They breathe different mixtures of air and wear bulky
equipment and clothes, but they can fly and soar like birds in the air.
Their reward? Often they see and experience a spectacle or a fish
that no one else has ever seen before.

Many mysteries remain to be explored beneath the sea. And
outer space! WOW! First the moon and soon perhaps even Mars
will be explored by astronauts. In the next generation, you may be
part of this. Whether you go into outer space, dive into the depths
of the sea, or make exciting discoveries in a laboratory or a library,
these frontiers will certainly challenge your imagination and stimulate
wonderful ideas for the future. I hope this theme gives you some
ingredients for your dreams, and that some or all of them come true.

Sincerely,

Eugenie Clark

Explore New Frontiers

As a deep-sea scientist, Eugenie Clark has chosen a career of exploration and discovery. What do you think makes "watching fishes" so exciting for her? How do Dr. Clark's ideas about exploring compare with your own ideas?

Good exploration begins with good questions. Look at the selections shown below. What kinds of creatures live in the ocean depths? What can we learn by exploring outer space? Come along and wander the surface of Mars with Sojourner. Ask yourself what would it be like to discover a sea monster. Start asking questions, and look for the answers in these new frontiers.

beneath
BLUE WATERS
Meetings with Remarkable
Deep-Sea Creatures

Eugenie
Clark
Adventures of a Shark Scientist
by Ellen R. Butts & Joyce R. Schwartz

Standing Tall
**Franklin R.
Chang-Díaz**

ROGUE
THEODORE TAYLOR

Out There
by Theodore Taylor
illustrated by Rob Bolster

The Night of the
Pomegranate
Some of the Kinder Planets
by Tim Wynne-Jones

The Adventures of
Sojourner

Internet

To learn about the authors in this theme, visit
Education Place. **www.eduplace.com/kids**

Background and Vocabulary

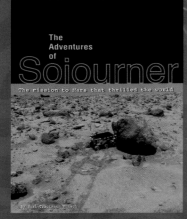

The Adventures of Sojourner

Read to find the meanings of these words.

e • Glossary

analysis
engineers
monitoring
navigation
rover
sensors

Adventure on Mars

Ever since space exploration began, scientists have dreamed of traveling to Mars, wondering what they might find there. Like Earth, Mars has seasons and an atmosphere. Water may once have flowed across its surface, making simple life possible. An **analysis** of rocks on Mars might unlock secrets about its history.

Now a way has been found to land an exploration vehicle on Mars. Using new technology, **engineers** have developed a small robot, called a **rover**. **Navigation** of the rover is by remote control, with scientists **monitoring** each inch of the rover's progress from 119 million miles away.

In 1997, the Pathfinder Mission sent a rover named *Sojourner* to Mars. Scientists wondered, Would the little remote control car really work? In *The Adventures of Sojourner,* you will discover their answer.

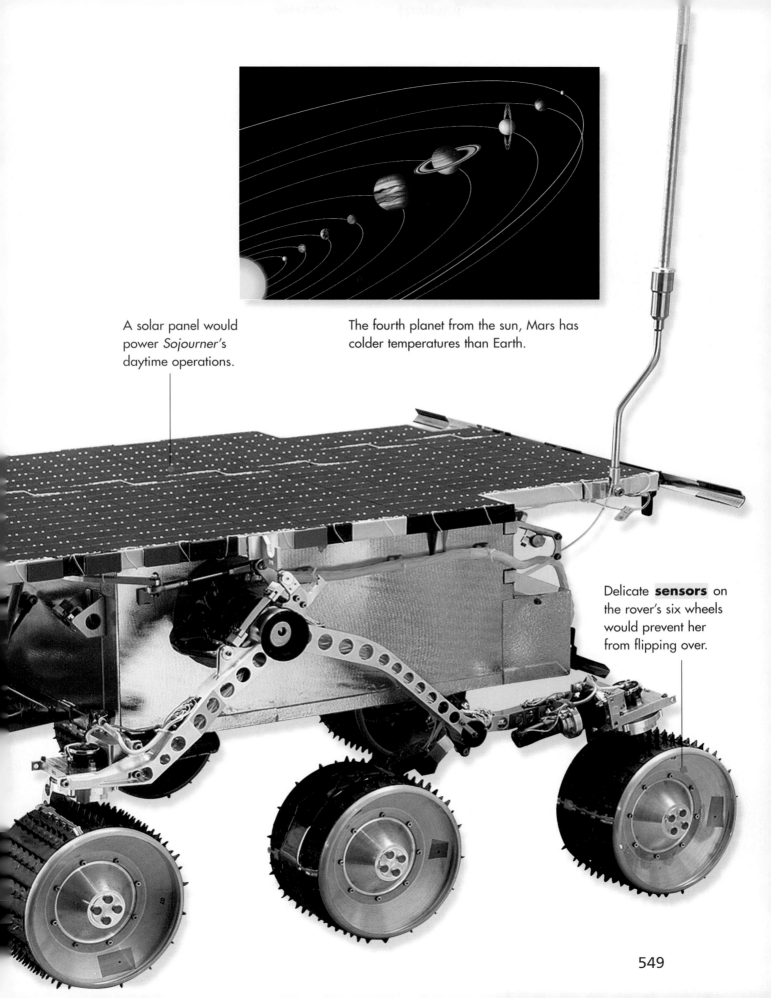

A solar panel would power *Sojourner*'s daytime operations.

The fourth planet from the sun, Mars has colder temperatures than Earth.

Delicate **sensors** on the rover's six wheels would prevent her from flipping over.

The
Adventures
of
Sojourner

The mission to Mars that thrilled the world

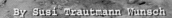

By Susi Trautmann Wunsch

Strategy Focus

As you read, **monitor** how well you understand the
purpose of the Pathfinder space mission. **Clarify** complex
parts by rereading the text and captions.

What: The Pathfinder Mission to Mars
Where: Eighty miles above the surface of Mars
When: July 4, 1997. Independence Day. Time until
            landing: 35 minutes

Never before had space scientists tried anything like this. They were about to land a remote control robot, called *Sojourner*, on Mars.

For three years, scientists had planned the Mission. Liftoff was in December, 1996. The journey to Mars had taken seven months.

Would the landing be successful? Would the rover operate on the surface of Mars as well as it had in the laboratory? Scientists would soon find out.

If you had been standing on Mars that day, here is what you would have seen: Glowing like a meteor, Pathfinder would have blazed across the predawn Martian sky. The Earth would have been visible as a blue morning star in the background.

In the Mission Operations room, a tense crowd clustered around Rob Manning, chief flight engineer, who was monitoring Pathfinder's entry, descent and landing. They waited.

A signal alerted Rob that Pathfinder's parachute had opened, slowing the descent to 150 miles per hour. What Rob could not hear was the fireworks on Mars that Independence Day. The explosion that opened Pathfinder's parachute was among 42 that were needed to trigger each step of the most complex landing system that the Jet Propulsion Laboratory had ever built.

Pathfinder's heat shield blew off. The lander detached from its backshell and whizzed down a 65-foot long tether like a fireman descending a firehouse pole.

Ten seconds before impact, the air bags inflated. Three small braking rockets fired, their thrust yanking the parachute and aeroshell up and away from the lander. Pathfinder hung motionless in midair for an instant before plunging the final 70 feet to the ground.

Entry, Descent and Landing/Friday, July 4, 1997
Landing at 10:07 a.m./Pacific Daylight Time

Pathfinder enters Mars atmosphere
Altitude: 80.8 miles
Time until landing: 5 minutes

Pathfinder separates from the cruise stage
Time until landing: 35 minutes

Parachute opens
Altitude: 5.8 miles
Time until landing: 134 seconds

Heat shield separates
Time until landing: 114 seconds

Lander separates, Pathfinder slides down tether
Time until landing: 94 seconds

Radar locates Martian surface
Altitude: 1 mile
Time until landing: 28.7 seconds

Members of the Pathfinder team eagerly await the first photographs of Martian terrain in more than 20 years.

Air bags inflate
Altitude: 1,164.7 feet
Time until landing: 10 seconds

The lander, bundled in its air bags, slammed into the red Martian dust at 30 miles per hour. It bounced 16 times — as high as 40 feet — like a giant beach ball. Then it rolled and rolled.

As it tumbled, a faint radio signal drifted in and out. The signal gained strength as Pathfinder came to a halt. The lander had survived its collision with Mars.

It was Sol 1. From then on, the mission would be counted in sols — Martian days — which last 24 hours and 37 minutes.

In the Mission Operations room at the Jet Propulsion Laboratory in Pasadena, hung with banners proclaiming "Mars or Bust," the Pathfinder team broke into applause. They yelled, cheered, shook hands and hugged each other. The project's leader, Donna Shirley, her dream realized, got tears in her eyes in the middle of an interview with a television reporter.

After their initial rush of excitement, flight controllers wondered what position Pathfinder had touched down in. If it had landed upside down, it would have to right itself by extending a petal and tipping itself over. But the lander signaled a thumbs-up to Earth. Not only had the spacecraft's unconventional belly-flop from the heavens succeeded, but Pathfinder had landed right side up.

The flight team was delighted, but geologist Dr. Matthew Golombek was worried about the smooth landing. What if it was too smooth? What if Pathfinder had come down on flat ground? What if there were no rocks? The painstaking selection of a landing site, although it had involved 60 scientists from the United States and Europe back in 1994, had been based on educated guesses about the geology of Ares Vallis, an ancient Martian flood plain. There were no guarantees. Matt waited uneasily for Pathfinder to send down the first photos. It didn't take long.

Rockets ignite
Altitude: 321.5 feet
Time until landing:
6 seconds

Tether cut
Altitude: 70.5 feet
Time until landing:
3.8 seconds

**Air bags deflate,
solar panels open**
Time after landing:
20 minutes

Air bags retract
Time after landing:
74 minutes

Air bags fully retracted
Time after landing:
87 minutes

Sojourner's radio could transmit only as far as a walkie-talkie, so she could not communicate directly with Earth. Instead, Sojourner talked to the lander and the lander talked to Earth. Transmissions were made 2 or 3 times each day during the approximately 12 hours the Earth appeared above the horizon on Mars.

Pathfinder pointed its antenna toward Earth, ready to transmit images and data. Now its camera could start taking pictures. The scientists and engineers could hardly wait. The first priority was to confirm that the air bags had retracted properly. The initial image, a black and white photo about the size of a bathroom tile, showed a section of the lander and a deflated air bag billowing like an untucked shirttail.

As Pathfinder beamed down 2 images per minute, more of the air bags came into view. The pictures revealed that one had bunched up over the petal that Sojourner would use to exit the lander. It was blocking Sojourner's path to the Martian surface. Fortunately, engineer David "Gremlin" Gruel had foreseen such a problem and had a solution. Controllers told Pathfinder to lift one of its petals about 45 degrees and reel in the offending air bag.

More photos streamed down. Finally, the view of Mars beyond the lander took shape, giving the scientists what they had come for. "Rocks!" cried Matthew Golombek.

After months of rehearsals in the test bed, the scientists had become accustomed to rocks hauled in from a local building supply company. Now they saw real Martian rocks. An incredible array of shapes, sizes and textures stretched out before them, dark gray in color with weathered surfaces or coatings of bright red dust.

"Looks a lot like Tucson," someone — not a geologist — commented, as he scanned the boulders and hills that jutted out in the distance.

Matt Golombek noted that the rocks leaned toward the northwest, the direction of the long ago flood. His eyes were drawn to a 10-inch tall rock. Unlike those around it, it was darker and studded with bumps that reminded Matt of barnacles. It was close to the exit ramp, within easy reach of the rover. Barnacle Bill, the science team decided, would be the first rock that Sojourner would investigate. Eventually, photos of the landing site would bloom with little yellow stickers bearing fanciful names — Yogi, Scooby Doo, Casper, Wedge, Shark, Half Dome.

On Sol 2, Sojourner was ready to leave the lander. Explosive bolts blew off the cables securing her to the lander petal and 3-foot long exit ramps extended onto the surface. The rover gathered herself up to her full 12-inch height and hoisted her antenna.

Sojourner's big moment was at hand. The little rover slowly drove backwards down the rear ramp and then rolled onto Martian soil, imprints from her wheel treads trailing behind. Shouts and cheers rang out in the Mission Operations room as the lander beamed to Earth the first pictures of the rover on Mars.

On Sol 3, Sojourner got to work. Rover driver Brian Cooper adjusted his goggles and gave her the command to swing her rear end to the left and then back toward Barnacle Bill. Although Sojourner only had to travel a short distance, she had to be in just the right position. Her main instrument, the APXS — a mini-radiation gun used to identify different kinds of rock — had to press its 2-inch nozzle securely against the rock in order to do a successful analysis of its chemical content. Bull's-eye! The APXS fitted perfectly against Barnacle Bill on the first try.

This is what Brian Cooper could see on his screen as he guided Sojourner toward Barnacle Bill.

The extraordinary pictures from the lander's camera helped Brian Cooper to guide Sojourner. From its perch 5 feet above the ground, the camera rotated 360 degrees, taking detailed shots of the entire landing site in black and white and color. Because Pathfinder's camera was stereoscopic, the pictures appeared 3-D. These images were used to construct a "virtual reality" map of the landing site. Looking at the map through his goggles, Brian could sense depth and pick out possible hazards. He could even "soar" like a bird above the landing site to check rock sizes, shapes and the distances between them.

Within minutes of receiving photographs, the science team posted them on the Internet via web sites that the Jet Propulsion Laboratory had launched. This was very unusual. Scientists typically wait to publish their data until after they have interpreted it themselves. In keeping with the spirit of the mission, though, everyone agreed to release the photos immediately.

On Sol 4, 46 million people logged onto the web sites, many wearing cardboard 3-D glasses to see the 3-D views. During the mission, they could browse through daily operations updates, check the latest Martian weather reports, view a photograph of sunrise on Mars or chat live with a Mars Pathfinder Team member. A "web cam" located in the Mission Operations room even allowed Internet users to eavesdrop on the team at work.

On Sol 6, Sojourner left Barnacle Bill and drove to a much bigger rock about 15 feet from the lander. It would be a more eventful run-in than anyone anticipated.

Geologists had named the rock Yogi because its shape reminded them of a certain cartoon bear. At 3 feet tall, Yogi towered over the rover. Unintimidated, Sojourner, her wheels encrusted with Martian soil, approached Yogi and set about her work. She tested the soil with her APXS, then focused her camera on Yogi's pitted surface.

The "virtual reality" map of the landing site was a big help when it came time for Sojourner to place her APXS against Yogi. The 3-D, bird's-eye view warned the rover team that Yogi's face, which had appeared flat, actually curved inward. Aiming for the middle could cause Sojourner to bump her head on the protruding

The little rover's collision with Yogi was the first interplanetary fender bender.

edge of the rock, possibly activating sensors that would instantly shut her down. The rover would have to be pointed slightly to the left.

An alternate rover driver had the tricky job that day of judging exactly how far to tell Sojourner to turn and back up in order for the APXS to make contact. His estimate was off by a little bit and the rover ran aground, her left rear wheel riding up on Yogi's cold shoulder. Sojourner halted immediately, as she had been programmed to do, and stayed there, hanging on the rock, patiently awaiting instructions.

Guiding a rover from a computer screen 119 million miles away is a complex task. Accidents were expected. During months of rehearsals in the test bed, Brian Cooper had practiced maneuvers to free Sojourner from just such a predicament. This was the real thing.

Under Brian's guidance, Sojourner slowly backed off Yogi. Her rear wheel dropped to the ground, but there was no damage to the sturdy little rover. Now Brian had to reposition the APXS so that it made contact with Yogi. He instructed Sojourner to

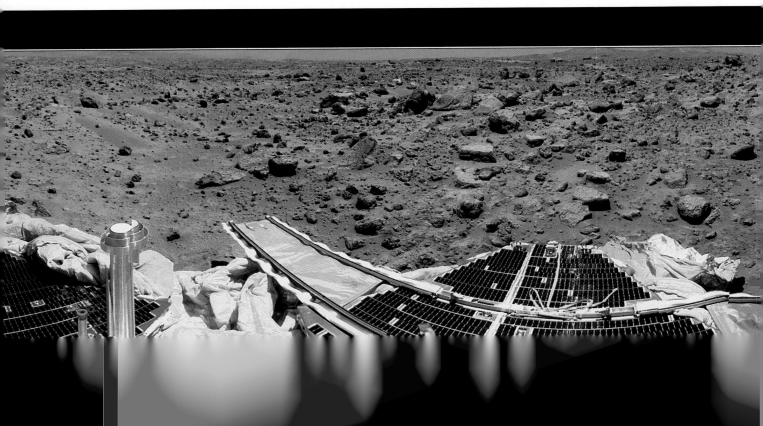

make one turn to the left, then another to the right. Slowly Sojourner extended her APXS and gently touched Yogi.

Until now, every move Sojourner made had been carefully plotted by its drivers. On Sol 12, Sojourner made her first try at independent navigation. Brian directed Sojourner to use her hazard avoidance systems to drive herself part way to the next target, a flat, white rock called Scooby Doo. She did it easily.

On Sol 20, Sojourner became even more independent when she made her way to a rock called Soufflé. This time, she not only had to use her hazard avoidance systems to find her way, she had to locate Soufflé by herself. Using her lasers, she made it to the center of the rock, right on target.

Sojourner settled into a routine. It always began with a song that her controllers on Earth played to start their work day. This was in keeping with the tradition of sending musical wake-up calls to astronauts. There was a different song each day. "Final

This panorama was made up of thousands of images taken by the lander camera over the course of the mission. The camera photographed a different section of the landing site at the same time each day to ensure that the lighting would be consistent throughout.

Frontier," the theme from the television program, "Mad About You," was the first.

Sojourner was awakened and her computer was turned on. She sent to Earth the APXS readings she had collected overnight. She updated her position. Then she was ready to rove.

By Sol 27 (July 31, 1997), the Pathfinder lander had met the goals set for its one-month mission. The mission team announced that the lander would shut down each night. Sojourner would continue to investigate as many additional rocks as possible with her APXS.

Her designers had hoped that Sojourner would survive for at least a week in the unforgiving cold of Mars. By Sol 27, she had lasted almost 3 weeks longer than that, earning the title "the little engine that could."

Sojourner began to travel greater distances. On Sol 30, she set out for the Rock Garden. Much of her remaining time was spent navigating this imposing cluster of boulders and smaller rocks. The Rock Garden had interested scientists from the start because its steep-faced rocks were relatively uncontaminated by dust. This would give the APXS the purest reading of their chemical content.

The next target was a Rock Garden specimen called Shark. Reaching it would be one of Sojourner's toughest assignments. While a counterclockwise path around the lander would have been the most direct, it was too rocky. Brian Cooper had decided that the little rover should follow a longer and only slightly less perilous clockwise trail. Threading through the maze of rocks that formed the gateway to Rock Garden proved so tricky that Brian and his team dubbed it the Bermuda Triangle. Several times the rover's hazard avoidance systems turned her off automatically to prevent spills. To make matters worse, her gyroscope had not been working properly. It now caused her to drift so badly that Brian finally turned it off.

Sojourner reached Shark on Sol 52. Six days later, the rover's backup batteries ran down. The rover team had to adjust

Pathfinder lander photographed by Sojourner.

Sojourner's schedule so that she did not start her work until the sun was up high enough to provide sufficient power to run her computer. From then on, the rover could only take APXS readings during the day. Still, she managed to complete readings of Half Dome and Chimp.

After finishing her exploration of the Rock Garden, Sojourner was to head back to Pathfinder. The team would never know whether she made it.

The lander sent its last complete transmission to Earth on Sol 83 (September 27, 1997). When the operations team tried to set up their usual communications link on the following day, there was no reply from Pathfinder. The team was able to lock onto a signal from Pathfinder's auxiliary transmitter on October 1, which indicated that the spacecraft was still functioning. There was one final blip on October 7, and then nothing more.

No one was sure exactly what had happened. As expected, the lander's battery had finally run down. With the battery dead,

Pathfinder could no longer run its heaters at night. Some people think that daily swings in the temperature of the lander may have put stress on the electronics and caused something to break.

After 5 days without word from Pathfinder, Sojourner's computer program would have told her to return to the lander. Still waking each morning, she would have circled Pathfinder at a distance of about 10 feet. She would have repeatedly asked the lander for commands from Earth, but there would have been no reply.

On November 4, 1997, the Mars Pathfinder team finally and reluctantly announced the end of the mission. They would still try once a month to pick up a signal from the lander, but they were not successful.

The team's sadness was tempered with joy at its achievements. It was less a "so long" than a "see you later," because, thanks to Pathfinder, more missions to Mars lay ahead.

Pathfinder had demonstrated that a lander could be parachuted safely onto Mars, that a microrover is an effective vehicle to explore another planet, and that space exploration can be done quickly and relatively cheaply. The mission had cost $266 million, exactly what had been budgeted.

Sojourner had only driven around an area the size of a big back yard, but she had gathered a wealth of valuable scientific data. The mission returned 2.3 billion bits of information, including more than 16,500 lander images and 550 from Sojourner, 15 thorough chemical analyses of rocks and soil from Sojourner's APXS, and millions of readings of Martian temperature, pressure and wind.

The mission confirmed that liquid water had once flowed through the Ares Vallis and that the planet had been shaped by a warmer atmosphere. Mars had once had conditions to support life.

Sojourner's APXS measurements of the Martian rocks revealed surprises. The geologists expected the mineral content to resemble that of meteorites from Mars. But some of Sojourner's targets, including Barnacle Bill and Shark, had more in common with Earth rocks. The scientists do not know why.

Meet the Author

SUSI TRAUTMANN WUNSCH

Susi Trautmann Wunsch has always been interested in science. As a young girl, she built a biology and chemistry lab in her basement and "conducted all kinds of smelly and smoky experiments." *The Adventures of Sojourner* is her first children's book, but she plans to write more. Currently she is working on a fictional story set in outer space. Wunsch lives with her husband, two sons, and a guinea pig in New York City.

For more interesting facts about Susi Trautmann Wunsch, visit Education Place.

www.eduplace.com/kids

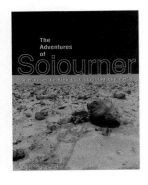

Think About the Selection

1. Find examples from the selection to prove or disprove this statement: People in the Mission Operations room were tense during Pathfinder's descent and landing.

2. The pictures transmitted from Pathfinder's camera were three-dimensional. What advantages did this give the scientists on Earth?

3. Scientists published the photos of Mars immediately, "in keeping with the spirit of the mission." What do you think this means?

4. In what ways did the Internet contribute to the Pathfinder mission to Mars?

5. How is anticipating problems important when planning a space mission? Give examples from the selection.

6. Of the different jobs described in the selection, which one would you want to have? Explain your choice.

7. **Connecting/Comparing** How have Sojourner's findings changed scientists' view of space as a "new frontier"?

Write a Description

Write a description of Sojourner and her job on Mars. Use details from the photographs and text to describe her appearance, her special features, and what she did on the Martian surface.

Tips

- Use vivid adjectives and verbs in your description.
- Begin a new paragraph for each new idea.
- Include a topic sentence in each paragraph.

Math

Calculate Time of Day

Pathfinder's entry and descent took 35 minutes, landing on Mars at 10:07 A.M. Use the information about the Pathfinder landing on pages 552–553 to calculate the time of day when each event leading up to the landing occurred. (Use Pacific Daylight Time and do not calculate fractions of seconds.) The first time should be for "Pathfinder separates from the cruise stage."

Bonus Extend the activity to include the times of the key events that occurred in the 87 minutes after Pathfinder touched down.

Listening and Speaking

Make an Announcement

Prepare and deliver an announcement that a member of the Mission Control team might give to the press. Include information about the successful landing of Pathfinder and about Sojourner's activities.

Tips

- Write notes about the key points you want to make.
- Speak slowly and clearly.
- Project your voice so that all the members of the audience can hear you.
- Be prepared to answer questions.

Internet

Take an Online Poll

What do you think scientists' goals should be for space exploration? How should they decide what to explore? State your opinion by taking an online poll at Education Place. **www.eduplace.com/kids**

Technology Link

Little Brother, Big Idea

by Ethan Herberman

How did a teenage boy come to design a new space exploration tool for NASA?

When Enrique Garcia was 10 years old, he was so shy he could barely speak to an unfamiliar adult. He lived in a Pasadena (Calif.) neighborhood so rough he wasn't allowed to play outside. And his mother, Eduarda, an immigrant from Mexico, thought he'd be doing well just to get a job after high school.

Last year, at age 16, Enrique spoke before a group of the country's top space officials, telling them about his ideas for equipment to be taken on a mission to Mars. And this year, the National Aeronautics and Space Administration (NASA) is spending about $200,000 to turn some of Enrique's concepts into working models.

Jet Propulsion Laboratory summer employee Enrique Garcia is pictured next to a prototype of the inflatable solar array that he helped to design in 1997 at the age of 16.

First Pizza, Then NASA

What happened to turn the shy 10-year-old into a pioneer in the field of space exploration? He met Art Chmielewski, an engineer at the Jet Propulsion Laboratory (JPL) in Pasadena. Chmielewski wanted to prevent kids from getting into trouble, so he joined Catholic Big Brothers. A "big brother" is a man who acts as a friend and guide to a fatherless boy. Chmielewski's "little brother" turned out to be Enrique.

Chmielewski took Enrique to baseball games and pizza parlors. He encouraged the boy to develop his talent for drawing and, above all, to communicate. Chmielewski also got Enrique a summer job at JPL, a NASA center where spacecraft, space tools, and unpiloted missions are designed.

A Simple Idea

"At first," said Enrique, "nobody noticed me." But Enrique noticed the people around him as they discussed their plans for an inflatable rover, or robot car, that would explore Mars. One lunchtime, Enrique drew some pictures showing how such a vehicle might look.

Said Chmielewski: "I walked by and saw [the drawings] and said, 'Oh, oh, how did you do that?'" The following week, Enrique found himself in front of JPL's managers, presenting his ideas.

Enrique's key innovation, said Chmielewski, was a new kind of solar array. Solar arrays are rows of solar cells, which generate an electrical current when struck by sunlight. Such a current can power a small motor on a rover.

Solar arrays have always had a major drawback, though. They have to be repositioned constantly to catch the sun's rays. Enrique's bright idea was this: Make the array inflatable, like the rest of the rover, and make it spherical — ball-shaped. That way, the array wouldn't have to be repositioned. It would catch sunlight from every angle.

JPL's engineers have made Enrique's array more umbrellalike than spherical, so it can be retracted into the rover during dust storms. Nevertheless, spherical arrays may be perfect for vehicles in outer space, Chmielewski said, where weather isn't a problem. "When I showed the concept to a NASA engineer," Chmielewski added, "he said, 'Gee, how come I didn't think of that?'"

Court in a Cup

Chmielewski calls devices such as Enrique's array *inflatables*, and said that eventually they'll have many uses, both in space and on other planets. Made of lightweight cellophanelike materials, they'll be launched at low cost, he said. They'll also be folded for launch using the techniques of origami — the Japanese art of paper folding. As new materials are perfected, Chmielewski said, squeezing an object the size of a tennis court into a container the size of a coffee cup will be possible.

This is Enrique's first computer model of a round solar array. The final design was umbrella-shaped.

Anyone familiar with balloons might be skeptical of Chmielewski's claims. One might ask, "Isn't space filled with speeding bits of dust that would make an inflatable object pop?"

Here's Chmielewski's answer: "Get rid of your intuition about balloons. To inflate anything on the ground, you have to overcome the pressure of the air around it. You have to fill the object with billions of gas molecules. But in

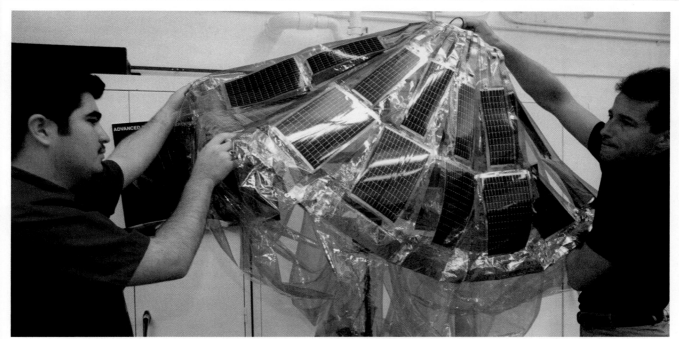

Enrique Garcia and Art Chmielewski unfurl the solar array designed by Enrique.

space, where there is no atmospheric pressure, you need about 10,000 times less gas to inflate an object by the same amount."

Because there are so few gas molecules bouncing around inside an inflatable, Chmielewski said, those molecules will "find" any hole in the structure only very gradually. So a damaged inflatable will take a long time to deflate. In fact, Chmielewski explained, a huge orbiting antenna or girder pumped up with nitrogen or helium might "have 200,000 holes in three years and still work fine."

Kids Can

Another myth that Chmielewski punctures is that "you need two PhDs to work with NASA. There's certainly room for teenagers and college students," he said. "That's why NASA hires them every summer."

As for Enrique, he is now attending community college, studying computer animation and awaiting a moment, perhaps as early as 2005, when he'll watch a vehicle he helped design set off to explore Mars.

A Persuasive Essay

The purpose of a persuasive essay is to convince the reader to think or act in a particular way. Use this student's writing as a model when you write a persuasive essay of your own.

Join STARS

> A persuasive essay usually states the goal in the introduction.

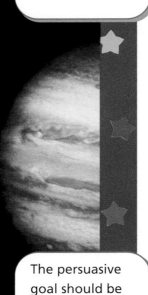

> The persuasive goal should be supported by **reasons**.

Are you interested in space? Do you want to be an astronaut when you grow up? Then become a member of STARS. It's the after-school organization for students who want to learn about space exploration. It can prepare you to be a professional astronaut. STARS is very educational and fascinating. If you are interested in astronomy, I suggest that you join STARS.

STARS has many activities related to space exploration. It is located in Room 221 in my school. There are 20 telescopes, and if you become a member you can use and enjoy them. Use the library at STARS to find out more about Saturn's 18 moons or Jupiter's 16 moons. There are many magazines and books about space. You can read them and find out about what is new in space. You can read about the new planet called HR 4796. Did you know that it is being compared to Earth? You can find out more about this and other things like it in the library at STARS.

Members of STARS can also use the planetarium. In this room you can see the sky the way it looks in real life. You can find the Big Dipper or see the distance between Earth and the other planets.

On Thursdays after school, members of STARS get to talk online with real astronauts. You can ask them questions about what they do. They will tell you how to become an astronaut too. They can tell you about Web pages you can go to and have fun. STARS has a lot to offer students who find astronomy exciting.

When you become a member, you will also have the chance to visit NASA. Each year, STARS has an essay contest. Five winners are selected, and they get to take a trip to NASA to see how things are really done.

STARS is a good organization for helping students learn more about space exploration. You will appreciate being a member of STARS. It will bring you closer to the stars.

It's important to state **facts** and to give **examples**.

A good **conclusion** brings the essay to a satisfactory close.

Meet the Author

Hashim L.

Grade: six
State: Massachusetts
Hobbies: playing all sports, and reading biographies, riddle books, and realistic fiction
What he wants to be when he grows up: a professional basketball player

Background and Vocabulary

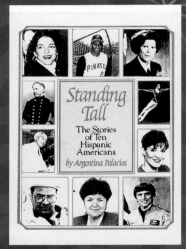

Franklin R. Chang-Díaz

Read to find the meanings of these words.

e • Glossary

aeronautics

applicants

astronaut

laboratory

physics

qualifications

rocketry

simulate

The Training of an Astronaut

Would you like to view Earth from outer space? experience weightlessness? conduct a scientific experiment in a tiny **laboratory** while orbiting the globe at 17,500 miles an hour?

As the next selection explains, Dr. Franklin Chang-Díaz dreamed of doing all these things. He discovered how tough it is to meet the **qualifications** to become an **astronaut**. Out of hundreds of **applicants**, only a handful are chosen. Applicants must have a degree in engineering, biology, **physics**, or math. They must pass a strict physical examination, be between 5 feet 4 inches and 6 feet 1 inch tall, and have at least 1000 hours of flying time in a jet aircraft.

If chosen, prospective astronauts undergo a year-long training period. They study modern **rocketry** and aircraft navigation, or **aeronautics**. In the laboratory, they practice working under conditions that **simulate** zero gravity, or weightlessness. Many of the chosen trainees fail to make it through the difficult program. Today, only about 140 astronauts are trained to travel in space.

Cosmonaut Boris V. Morukov, mission specialist representing the Russian Space Agency (RSA), descends from the top of the crew cabin of the Full Fuselage Trainer during an emergency egress training session. ▶

▲ *Two astronauts join SCUBA-equipped divers in the Neutral Buoyancy Laboratory (NBL) during an emergency egress training session.*

Astronaut Franklin R. Chang-Díaz, STS 61-C mission specialist, while checking cargo in Columbia's payload bay, turns to smile at a fellow crewman.
▼

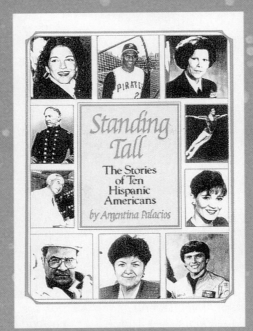

Standing Tall
The Stories of Ten Hispanic Americans
by Argentina Palacios

Franklin R. Chang-Díaz

Strategy Focus

As a child, Franklin Chang-Díaz fell in love with outer space. As you read, **evaluate** how well the author shows why Chang-Díaz wanted to become an astronaut.

he National Aeronautics and Space Administration called Dr. Franklin Ramón Chang-Díaz at the Charles Stark Draper Laboratory in Cambridge, Massachusetts, one day in May 1980. The call was unexpected and when he answered the phone, Dr. Chang-Díaz was not in his own office at the lab but in another office across the street. He was told that he had been selected to be an astronaut and if he wanted to work for the agency and fly in space he had to go to the Johnson Space Center in Houston, Texas, for training.

"When I went back to the lab, I was so excited . . . it was as if I already were in space . . . I had to cross a well-traveled street and started crossing without looking," Dr. Chang-Díaz recalls. "I was almost killed! What I had dreamed of all those years almost didn't happen."

That might have been the only time emotion overtook this man so completely — but it happened before he became an astronaut. Astronauts must always have their emotions under control, have "nerves of steel," as it is often said. Franklin Chang-Díaz has demonstrated time and again that he has what it takes to be an astronaut.

When Franklin Chang-Díaz was seven years old, and living in San Juan de los Morros, Venezuela, he was quite interested in observing the stars in the deep blue sky. That year, the then-Soviet Union, which included Russia, launched the first satellite into space, *Sputnik I*. Newspapers and radio stations throughout the world carried the news.

"The year 1957 was a key year, an important year for me — maybe for many people," says Chang-Díaz. "I was fascinated by the idea that a machine made by human beings was now a new

Franklin Chang-Díaz at age seven, at the time of the *Sputnik* launch.

A wood engraving in *From the Earth to the Moon* by Jules Verne, whose science fiction Chang-Díaz read as a boy.

Sputnik I, the first Russian satellite to enter space, displayed on a stand shortly before its launch on October 4, 1957.

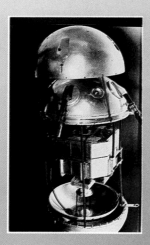

The Soviet cosmonaut Yugi Gagarin made headlines around the world as the first man in space in 1961. The country of Romania even featured him on a postage stamp.

'star' in the sky. I remember my mother telling me that if I looked hard after sunset I might get to see that little 'star.' I used to go to a park near our house, climb up a mango tree, and try to find it."

The seven-year-old never saw *Sputnik I* from his perch but the boy fell in love with outer space. That love was so great that it has remained with the man all his life.

Franklin Ramón Chang-Díaz was born in San José, Costa Rica, on April 5, 1950. His parents, Ramón A. Chang-Morales and María Eugenia Díaz de Chang, had six children, three girls and three boys; Franklin was the second child, the oldest of the boys. His paternal grandfather was born in China, the rest of his immediate ancestors, in Costa Rica.

His parents were poor and didn't have much schooling, but Ramón Chang-Morales was filled with the spirit of adventure. So he headed for Venezuela with his family when the oil boom in that South American country required extra workers. Mr. Chang-Morales easily found employment with the Ministry of Public Works as a fore-man on a construction crew.

"There were no astronauts then," says Chang-Díaz, "but I read a lot of science fiction, Jules Verne's stories, for example, and other stories about space conquests. I made up my mind then that I would become a 'space explorer,' my concept of what later became an 'astronaut.'

"All of this was before there were manned spacecrafts, before the Russians sent a little dog named Laika into space."

The so-called space race between the Soviet Union and the United States had started. The Soviet Union selected its first cosmonauts. The United States selected seven men to be its first astronauts.

Chang-Díaz continues his reminiscences during an interview. "Then came another important event — the first man went into space, [Soviet cosmonaut] Yuri Gagarin. I believe it was in 1961. We had returned to Costa Rica and I was going to school, with the idea [of flying in space] always in my mind. In those days I didn't know any English. I remember clipping every article [about space] I found in newspapers and magazines . . . gathering information."

By age ten or eleven, he was playing astronaut, lying on his back in a large cardboard box equipped with parts of old radios and TV sets, trying to simulate being in a space capsule. "My friends and I used to get inside this makeshift spaceship. We would go to a countdown, a liftoff, and we would go off and explore make-believe new planets," he says.

In his high school yearbook, there's a picture of Chang-Díaz and a friend in their multistage rocket, designed for the school science fair. While his friends also played space explorer and designed spacecrafts for the science fair, they followed different paths and careers when they grew up. Only Chang-Díaz became an astronaut.

When Chang-Díaz finished in La Salle, a parochial high school in San José, Costa Rica (1967), he tells us, "I started making plans to realize my dream. That's when I wrote to NASA, to the famous scientist Werner von Braun, the father of modern rocketry." He wrote asking how to become an astronaut.

"I received an answer from NASA," the astronaut says. "It was a form letter, nothing personalized, but at least I made contact." It has been reported that the answer said you should study science if you want to become an astronaut.

Now it was time to put the plan into action. "I decided to leave Costa Rica and go to the United States and find the way to embark on this adventure," says Chang-Díaz. "I didn't know, really, how I was going to do it, but I knew I wanted a career in science. That was very clear in my mind, that in order to be an astronaut I should first be a scientist."

Methodically, like the good scientist he would become, Franklin Chang-Díaz started working on his plan. "As soon as I graduated from high school, I took a job in a bank, the Banco Nacional de Costa Rica, in order to save money for my trip," he says. "I couldn't save too much because, to tell you the truth, salaries weren't very high."

Nine or ten months later, with his entire savings of $50 and a one-way ticket, young Chang-Díaz took a flight to the United States. Ramón Chang-Morales, the family adventurer, "a man so full of self-confidence that he could do anything," bought the ticket for his son.

Lino and Betty Zúñiga and their children, distant relatives of the Chang-Díaz family, were then living in Hartford, Connecticut. Franklin Chang-Díaz had contacted them from Costa Rica and they readily welcomed him into their home. "I owe them a lot; they were the ones who helped me with my first steps in this country," he says. "They were very hard-working people but with a very low income, and there were ten of them, now eleven."

When he first arrived, there were a few important things to do. "I thought that to find my way in this society I had to learn English," says Chang-Díaz. "Second, I had to prepare for winter, which was coming. I had never seen snow. I only had my clothes from Costa Rica, so I spent 35 of my 50 dollars on a coat." With the help of Mr. and Mrs. Zúñiga, Chang-Díaz enrolled as a senior-year student at Hartford High School. This, he thought, could lead him to learning English and to a scholarship.

In high school, Franklin Chang-Díaz knew and understood very little of his new language and was sent to a special class to learn English. "Only the teacher spoke English in that class, I talked to the other kids in Spanish all the time," he says. He began to fail so he begged the principal and the counselor to send him to the regular classes. The young student persuaded them, after much reluctance on their part, to let him try.

For a while, Franklin Chang-Díaz continued to get very poor grades because he didn't understand or converse easily in English. But after about three months, he was able to communicate in this new language and by the end of the school year, he was in the top portion of his class. The boy no longer felt as homesick and lonely as he had felt on his first Christmas away, when he wanted to return to Costa Rica.

NASA's space program was now in full swing. President John F. Kennedy had declared that the United States would put a man on the moon before the end of the 1960s. In fact, U.S. astronauts walked on the moon in 1969, the same year the young Costa Rican dreamer graduated from a U.S. high school. "I remember exactly where I was when those men landed on the moon. I remember getting chills and telling myself that one day I'd be doing something like that," says Chang-Díaz.

"I remember exactly where I was when those men landed on the moon. I remember getting chills and telling myself that one day I'd be doing something like that."

Edwin "Buzz" Aldrin poses next to the United States flag on the first mission to the moon, July 20, 1969.

Photos from Franklin Chang-Díaz's high school yearbook. Franklin stands at far left with the rocket he and classmate José Gamboa designed for the school science fair.

School officials were very impressed with the future astronaut's progress. They recommended him for a scholarship given by the State of Connecticut. "It wasn't necessarily the grades that interested them, it was my effort and change, from the very bottom to very high," he says. A scholarship was granted for Chang-Díaz to attend the University of Connecticut.

"When I went to register at the University of Connecticut," says the astronaut, "they told me they were very sorry but they couldn't accept me. I couldn't have the scholarship because an error had been made, they said. They thought I was from Puerto Rico instead of Costa Rica. A Puerto Rican is a U.S. citizen; a Costa Rican is not."

State scholarships are to be granted to U.S. citizens or permanent residents in the United States. Franklin Chang-Díaz hadn't known that requirement at the time. He was neither a citizen nor a permanent resident — he had only a temporary tourist visa.

The news was a shock because he had been accepted by several other universities but had already told them he was going to the University of Connecticut. Now he had no money, no job, no scholarship, no admission. Franklin Chang-Díaz didn't panic, however, and went to discuss the matter with school officials.

The school officials were moved by Chang-Díaz's plight and went to the state legislature to try to change the law. The legislature met in an extraordinary session, made an exception, and granted the Costa Rican a one-year scholarship, "to rectify the error." "That's one of the nicest things that ever happened to me in this country," says the astronaut today. "For me, that's the United States of America, where the concept of fairness is very important."

With that hurdle out of the way, Chang-Díaz changed his tourist visa to a foreign student visa, which made it possible for him to work legally in certain jobs related to his studies. He immediately found a position in a physics lab at the university, a post he kept during his four years at the school.

When classes were in session, Chang-Díaz worked part time. During summer vacations, and between sessions, he worked full time. Thus he was able to leave the Zúñigas and provide for himself. He decided to be on his own not because the Zúñigas didn't want him living with them, but because he felt that one more person to feed was an additional burden for the family.

In the 1970s, after the moon landings, interest in the space program decreased in the United States. NASA's budget was cut and aerospace engineers were laid off. But for Franklin Chang-Díaz, the dream was still very much alive. "I used to tell people I was studying to be an astronaut, and everybody told me I was a little crazy," he recalls with a chuckle.

"At first I thought of studying aerospace engineering," he says, "but then I thought I wanted to be more than a conventional aerospace engineer, I wanted to be a rocket inventor — something like my great idol, Dr. von Braun — and go to other planets. That's why I studied mechanical engineering."

> " I used to tell people I was studying to be an astronaut, and everybody told me I was a little crazy."

In four years time, Franklin Chang-Díaz received a bachelor of science degree with a double major in physics and mechanical engineering. In 1973, he went on to graduate school, at the Massachusetts Institute of Technology (MIT) in Cambridge, Massachusetts. Chang-Díaz became involved with a project he calls very "futuristic" in which people from many countries were involved. It was called *controlled thermonuclear fusion.* That's the same process used in the hydrogen bomb, he explains, but in a controlled manner, to produce electricity.

"This was almost like the science fiction I had read as a child, and it fascinated me," the scientist says. "I figured that in the future, spaceships would use that type of energy to move about in space. I could see a close connection between this [project] and the space program."

Chang-Díaz studied plasma physics, the area in which controlled thermonuclear fusion belongs, and graduated with a Ph.D. from MIT in 1977.

As luck would have it, in 1977 the Charles Stark Draper Laboratory, "around the corner from MIT," had a job opening for a mechanical engineer-scientist. That lab had designed all the navigational and control systems used in NASA's *Apollo* program, the spaceships that had gone to the moon. Draper needed someone to design control systems for atomic fusion reactors. The job had nothing to do with the space program but it was the same type of work, and Dr. Chang-Díaz, having the right qualifications, was hired.

As soon as his work started at Draper, Chang-Díaz learned that the space shuttle had been built and NASA was beginning to test it. "The idea of becoming an astronaut, which had sort of receded in my mind — because the space program was somewhat dormant — awakened," he says. "NASA began soliciting applicants in 1977, and my 'light bulb' was turned on!"

At this time, Chang-Díaz was going through the process of becoming a U.S. citizen. Most of the paperwork was done by then, but the whole process takes several years. No matter, Chang-Díaz prepared the paperwork to apply to become an astronaut.

The future astronaut was not accepted the first time. "I have never been told why, but I have the feeling it was because my [U.S.] citizenship had not been granted yet," he says. "I decided I would not give up after just one try — I had worked so hard towards my goal — so I said to myself, 'I'll stay

The Massachusetts Institute of Technology is a world-famous center for scientific research.

Official NASA portrait of Franklin Chang-Díaz in 1988

"NASA began soliciting applicants in 1977, and my 'light bulb' was turned on!"

here [at the lab] and get some more experience, and there will be another opportunity.'"

Teresa Gómez, chief assistant at NASA's Astronaut Selection Office, recently told an interviewer, "About 10 percent [of the applicants] are disqualified immediately because they don't meet the qualifications — they aren't U.S. citizens, or they don't have a degree in science or engineering."

In 1979, when NASA solicited applicants again, Chang-Díaz took out his papers from his file, updated his résumé, and applied again. By now he was a U.S. citizen.

Several months later, a letter and a phone call from NASA invited Chang-Díaz to go to the Johnson Space Center for preliminary interviews and tests. He had passed the preselection process and was to spend one week in Houston.

"I met lots of men and women who wanted to be astronauts, everyone an adventurer and visionary, everyone a highly qualified scientist," Chang-Díaz says. "For the first time I could see myself reflected in those people. But I was the only Latin, the only Spanish-speaking person born in another country."

Other astronauts have been born in different countries, but their parents were U.S. citizens. Two other Hispanics were in space before Chang-Díaz: Arnaldo Tamayo Méndez, from Cuba, in a Soviet mission; and Rodolfo Neri Vela, from Mexico, in the American mission just before Chang-Díaz's first mission. However, both these men were on a special one-time assignment. Franklin R. Chang-Díaz is the first Hispanic to be in the space program for the long run.

After the tests, Chang-Díaz went home. Many months passed without news from Houston. At last, in 1980, came that exciting, hoped-for call. From hundreds and hundreds of highly qualified applicants, only nineteen had been selected. Chang-Díaz called his parents in Costa Rica as soon as he got to his

" I met lots of men and women who wanted to be astronauts, everyone an adventurer and visionary, everyone a highly qualified scientist. For the first time I could see myself reflected in those people."

584

desk. "My father cried," he says, "the emotion was too much for him. I had worked so hard for this. He was so happy for me."

Dr. Franklin Chang-Díaz moved to Houston, Texas, in 1980, and became an astronaut in training. He still lives in Houston, with his second wife, the former Peggy Margaret Doncaster, and his three daughters, Jean, Sonia, and Lidia.

He was officially named an astronaut in August 1981. This is how NASA documents describe his activities:

While in training, he was also involved in flight software checkout at the Shuttle Avionics Integration Laboratory (SAIL), and participated in the early space station design studies. In late 1982, he was designated as support crew for the first Spacelab mission and, in November 1983, served as an orbit capsule communicator (CAP-COM) during that flight.

From October 1984 to August 1985, he was leader of the astronaut support team at the Kennedy Space Center. His duties included astronaut support during the processing of the various vehicles and payloads, as well as flight crew support during the final phases of the launch countdown.

STS 61-C, the official designation of Chang-Díaz's first mission, was scheduled for launching at the end of 1985 but, for a variety of reasons, it was postponed seven times.

The Shuttle *Columbia*'s flawless launch on January 12, 1986.

At long last, the big day for Chang-Díaz dawned at the launching site at Kennedy Space Center, Florida, on January 12, 1986. The flight marked the return to service of the Shuttle *Columbia,* which had been undergoing renovation since 1983.

As that spaceship finally took off, in one of the most flawless launches NASA has ever had, Franklin Chang-Díaz's lifelong quest was no longer a dream. "When I was strapped in that spaceship ready for liftoff, all I could think about was my childhood games in a cardboard box," the astronaut says. "It seemed incredible that this was for real." ■

MEET THE AUTHOR

Argentina Palacios

Personal journey: Born in Panama, Palacios moved to the United States in 1961. She now lives in New York City.

Important accomplishment: Translated almost 100 children's books by other authors from English into Spanish

Other jobs: Book editor, Spanish teacher, professional storyteller

Books of note: *A Christmas Surprise for Chabelita*, a story based on her childhood in Panama; *The Llama's Secret*, a retelling of a Peruvian legend

To find out more about Argentina Palacios, visit Education Place. **www.eduplace.com/kids**

Think About the Selection

1. Find examples in the selection to support this statement: "Franklin Chang-Díaz has demonstrated time and again that he has what it takes to be an astronaut."

2. Why was Franklin Chang-Díaz denied a scholarship to the University of Connecticut? Do you think this was fair? Explain.

3. Which word do you think best describes Franklin Chang-Díaz: *smart*, *lucky*, *hard-working*, or some other word? Explain your choice.

4. If a young person wrote to Franklin Chang-Díaz for advice on becoming an astronaut, what response do you think he would give?

5. Franklin Chang-Díaz remembers the first astronauts landing on the moon. Tell about an important or historic event that influenced you.

6. Chang-Díaz needed a background in science to be an astronaut. What preparation do you need to pursue a dream of yours?

7. **Connecting/Comparing** If Franklin Chang-Díaz had worked on the *Pathfinder* mission, what job do you think he would have preferred? Use evidence from the selection to support your answer.

Write a FAX Message

Write the FAX message that NASA might have sent to Franklin Chang-Díaz informing him of his acceptance into the astronaut training program. Then write the message he might have sent to his family telling them the good news.

 Tips

- Include facts from the selection.
- Use words of congratulation in the first FAX message, and words of excitement in the second.

588

Social Studies

Make a Timeline

This selection mentions many dates and events that were important in the life of Franklin Chang-Díaz. Some, such as *Sputnik I*, were historic events. Some, such as the phone call from NASA, were important to Chang-Díaz's career. Make a timeline that gives the year each event took place. Use the timeline on page 405 as a guide.

Vocabulary

Make a Guide for Foreign Students

When Franklin Chang-Díaz first came to the United States, he had to learn a lot about being a student here. What advice would have been helpful for him? With a partner, write a guide for foreign students. Include information about how to get a scholarship. Include the following words in your guide: *applicants*, *foreign student visa*, *scholarship*, *register*, *qualifications*, and *admission*.

Bonus Add information on how to become a citizen. Include these words: *process*, *converse*, *citizenship*, *preliminary*, and *tourist visa*.

Internet

Go on a Web Field Trip

How do astronauts train at the space center in Houston, Texas? What does the Kennedy Space Center in Florida look like? Visit Education Place and find out.

www.eduplace.com/kids

BUILD AND LAUNCH A PAPER ROCKET!

Model Rocketry

Flying paper airplanes is low-tech, low-cost, and LOTS of fun! Launching paper rockets is all that and a perfectly safe BLAST, too! You won't even need a launch pad for the rocket you're going to build. Just one mighty puff of your breath will send it off.

You know that an efficient rocket engine (in this case, your lungs) is only one part of a successful rocket — and a successful rocket launch. Your rocket must also be *stable* — smooth in performance and uniform in direction — during flight. Unstable rockets are dangerous because it's impossible to predict where they will go. A stable rocket requires some kind of control system — in this case, fins. Your paper rocket will enable you to experiment with the proper size and placement of fins to make your rocket soar!

You Need:

Ruler
Scissors
Cellophane tape
Scrap bond paper
Sharpened fat pencil
Milk shake straw
   (slightly thinner than the pencil)

Time to Build

1.

Cut a narrow strip of paper about 3 centimeters wide and 13 centimeters long and roll it tightly around the fat pencil. Tape this "cylinder" so it holds its shape and remove it from the pencil.

2.

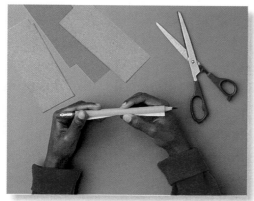

a. a. Draw points at one end of cylinder.

b. b. Cut points (do this by cutting out 3 tiny triangles).

c. c. Pinch points together to form a cone.

3.

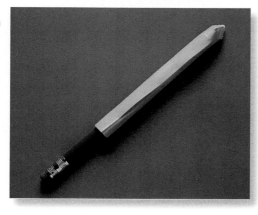

Slide the cone end onto the pencil tip. Squeeze and tape it together to seal the end and form a nose cone. (The pencil point provides support for taping.)

4.

Remove the cylinder from the pencil and gently blow into the open end to check for leaks. If air easily escapes, use more tape to seal the leaks.

5.

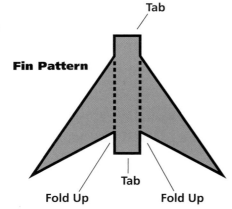

Tab

Fin Pattern

Fold Up   Tab   Fold Up

Trace and cut out 2 sets of fins using this pattern. Fold up each fin at the dotted lines. Tape the fins near the open end of the cylinder. The tabs make taping easy.

Launch Time

6.

Slip the straw into the rocket's opening. Point the rocket in a safe direction and blow sharply through the straw. The rocket will shoot away.

Caution: Be careful not to aim the rocket toward anyone because the rocket could poke an eye.

How High and Far Will It Fly?

- Try flying your paper rocket with the fins placed on the front end of the cylinder. Also, try attaching delta-shaped wings to achieve a gliding flight.

- Add some extra fins. Take some away. How many fins are required? Can you make them smaller and still stabilize the rocket?

- What will happen if the lower tips of the fins are bent pinwheel fashion?

- Test fly different paper rockets to see which ones travel higher or farther. Investigate the designs of the rockets that travel the farthest and the shortest distances. What makes one rocket perform better than another? (Don't forget to consider the weight of each rocket. Extra tape and larger fins make a difference!)

- Are fins necessary to stabilize a rocket in outer space?

Background and Vocabulary

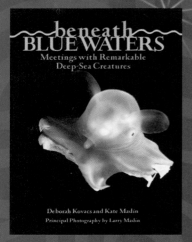

Beneath Blue Waters

Read to find the meanings of these words.

e ● Glossary

menagerie

oceanographers

submersible

unfathomable

Scuba divers can reach 164 ft. (50 m.) below sea level.

Sylvia Earle dove to 1,250 ft. (381 m.) in the "Jim" diving suit in 1979.

How Deep Is Deep?

The oceans of the earth are deeper than the highest mountains and cover most of its surface. Few people have ever traveled deeper than 450 feet (150 meters) below the ocean's surface. In a small diving vehicle called a **submersible**, **oceanographers** can now travel into the deepest zones. At **unfathomable** and uncharted depths, they are observing a strange **menagerie** of creatures. In the next selection, *Beneath Blue Waters*, you will observe this mysterious world with them.

In 1960, the bathyscaphe *Trieste* explored the Marianas Trench — at 35,800 ft. (11,275 m.), the deepest known place in the sea.

Diagram not to scale

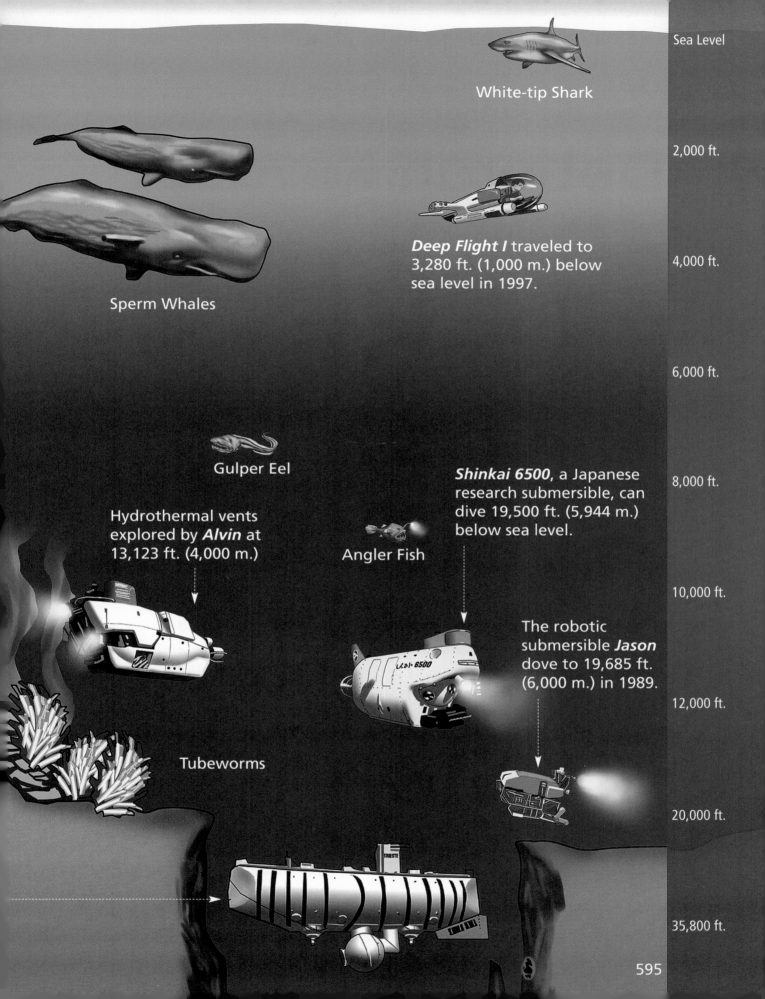

White-tip Shark

Sperm Whales

Deep Flight I traveled to 3,280 ft. (1,000 m.) below sea level in 1997.

Gulper Eel

Hydrothermal vents explored by *Alvin* at 13,123 ft. (4,000 m.)

Angler Fish

Shinkai 6500, a Japanese research submersible, can dive 19,500 ft. (5,944 m.) below sea level.

The robotic submersible *Jason* dove to 19,685 ft. (6,000 m.) in 1989.

Tubeworms

Sea Level

2,000 ft.

4,000 ft.

6,000 ft.

8,000 ft.

10,000 ft.

12,000 ft.

20,000 ft.

35,800 ft.

Meet the Authors

Deborah Kovacs

Deborah Kovacs's career has always focused on children. She began by developing toys and games for *Sesame Street*. She started writing nature stories for children after moving to a remote spot near the ocean. Her love of nature is seen in such books as *Dive to the Deep Ocean* and *Off to Sea: An Inside Look at a Research Cruise,* and in her computer-based interactive stories for the *Audubon Wildlife Adventure* series. She is also the editor of a magazine called *Ocean Explorer.*

Kate Madin

Dr. Katherine Madin works at the Woods Hole Oceanographic Institution, which owns the submersible *Alvin*. Her husband, Dr. Laurence Madin, shot most of the photographs for *Beneath Blue Waters*. The Madins live in Falmouth, Massachusetts.

To find out more about Deborah Kovacs and Kate Madin, visit Education Place. **www.eduplace.com/kids**

beneath BLUE WATERS
Meetings with Remarkable Deep-Sea Creatures

Deborah Kovacs and Kate Madin

Principal Photography by Larry Madin

Strategy Focus

Deep under the ocean's surface, scientists are discovering a new world. As you read, think of **questions** to discuss with your classmates about what scientists have found.

In the deepest part of the ocean, water is almost as cold as ice, and the pressure is a hundred times greater than we feel on land. This is where the strangest creatures live in utter darkness, and where humans are only just beginning to explore.

More than one mile below the surface, in the total darkness and near freezing temperature of the deep sea, pulses a jellyfish with a body that looks like an Easter bonnet. The creature, called *Benthocodon pedunculata*, spends most of its time looking for food, as do all creatures who live in this harsh place.

Joining the three or four people who have ever seen this animal in its natural environment is the three-person crew of the submersible *Alvin*. Crammed into *Alvin*'s tiny passenger sphere, which is less than 7 feet (2 meters) in diameter, are the pilot, a chemist, and a biologist — who is now busy videotaping the *Benthocodon*'s search for food. Despite the discomfort of their tight quarters, the scientists are thrilled at this chance to explore a region where only *Alvin* and four other existing subs can go. For most oceanographers, a day on *Alvin* is a once-in-a-lifetime experience.

During the three decades in which deep-sea submersibles and crewless robot vehicles have been around, these craft have explored undersea mountain ranges far larger than those on land. They have plunged into slashes in the earth's crust that are as deep as 35,000 feet (11,000 meters) — deeper than Mount Everest is tall! They have traveled to the sites of undersea earthquakes and volcanoes. And they've discovered life, amazing forms of life, in places nobody ever suspected.

Alvin, which has been in operation since 1964, has seen all this and more. The sub's long and proud history of deep-sea exploration is unmatched. *Alvin* has gone where no people have gone before, and has been used to locate

598

Alvin *being lowered from its mother ship,* Atlantis.

Benthocodon pedunculata (behn-thah-KOH-dahn pih-DUHNG-kyuh-LAH-tuh) .

lost hydrogen bombs, to find sunken ships, including the famous *Titanic* and *Bismarck*, and to discover new life. Once, during a launch from her previous mother ship, *Alvin* slid off the launch platform and took on water. As the pilot and passengers scrambled out to safety, the sub filled with water and sank to the seafloor. *Alvin* was finally recovered after ten months. It was fine, as was the bologna sandwich left in it by a crew member. Preserved by a combination of high pressure and cold temperature, the sandwich was still good enough to eat.

In the 1970s, *Alvin* was exploring a hydrothermal vent, a crack in the seafloor that sends up clouds of poisonous chemicals and water heated by the earth's core. Nobody imagined that anything could live in such a place, where the temperature is as hot as 650° Fahrenheit (around 350° Celsius) and the chemicals coming out of the vents are highly toxic to almost all known forms of life. Yet, incredibly, the area around the vent turned out to be an oasis of life, home to tubeworms as tall as a person, clams the size of dinner plates, and an entire menagerie of never-before-seen animals. Unlike most of the living things on our planet, these animals do not depend on the sun's energy for life, nor on the prey that supports the creatures of the sunless mesopelagic (mehz-uh-puh-LAH-jihk) zone. They get their life energy directly from the toxic stew of chemicals that shoots out of the earth's crust.

Alvin *begins its descent.*

The tiny styrofoam cup at right, which was tied to the outside of Alvin before a dive, is a favorite souvenir of those lucky enough to journey in the sub. The water pressure the sub endures is so great that it forces every molecule of air out, miniaturizing the cup.

If such an unimaginable community can exist and thrive, what other new life forms and environments can be found on the seafloor? Each submersible dive offers a tantalizing opportunity to glimpse the unknown. But these glimpses are all too brief — five hours is all the time the crew of Alvin has for their mission in the deep waters — and all too rare. It's incredibly hard to reach this world!

This day's dive has been in the works for four years and has required the efforts of many people. The success of the dive today depends not only on *Alvin*'s pilot and crew, but also on the many people aboard *Alvin*'s mother ship,

Atlantis II, which carried the submersible to this dive site. These include a crew of specially trained *Alvin* technicians, divers who help launch and retrieve the sub, the crew who operate the mother ship, and other scientists waiting for their chance to dive, as well as backup technical and scientific crew.

The scientists stay alert to all that is happening outside *Alvin*'s three tiny portholes. To see anything, the biologist has to push his face right up close to the Plexiglas window beside his seat. A tape recorder hangs by a chain nearby, ready to record any of his observations. He holds his own still camera and video camera on his lap. There's also a reading light, a flashlight, and a monitor displaying depth and time. The chemist has the same setup on the other side of the sub, just an arm's reach away.

Outside *Alvin*'s window, more than twelve lights are mounted. A 35-millimeter camera that takes in a panoramic view of the area around the sub is mounted on *Alvin*'s prow, along with a video camera specially adapted to record images in low light. A color video camera on Alvin's starboard side records close-up views. The two scientists can see images recorded by all three cameras on video monitors.

It's chilly inside *Alvin*, about 40° F (5° C), so everyone is dressed warmly. It's taken two hours for the sub to reach the seafloor, where the crew can begin the first of their experiments. The chemist has had sediment traps carried down by *Alvin*. She wants to collect the particles that have fallen to the seafloor, to analyze them for their chemical components and to measure the rate at which they fall. The sub pilot uses *Alvin*'s special features, and soon he has the traps skillfully positioned on the ocean floor. *Alvin*, whose location is being recorded by *Atlantis*, will return to this site on a later dive to retrieve the traps.

A ctenophore that has not been named yet.

Deep-sea cucumber or Enypniastes eximia
(eh-nip-nee-AHS-tees ex-IH-mee-uh).

Meanwhile, the biologist peers into the blackness, hoping to spot another creature. He looks down at the seafloor. It looks sandy, but not like a sandy beach; the grains are rough rather than fine. The floor isn't really made up of sand at all, but of the sediment and marine snow that has drifted down from the waters above. Nothing appears to be moving here, either.

Suddenly, something catches his eye. He picks up the camera in time to get a picture of a ctenophore (TEHN-uh-fawr) the size and shape of a football coming out of the blackness. As with many animals of the mesopelagic zone above, this one appears bright red in the sub's lights, though at this depth it would appear black to any predator using bioluminescence to illuminate the area. It drags its tentacles over the sediment in search of food. Finding a small crustacean, it entangles its prey with a sticky substance secreted by its tentacles and draws it up to its mouth. The biologist feels lucky to be able to videotape this event, as this animal probably gets a chance to eat only rarely. The deep sea is a cold, unchanging environment with sparse food supplies. Animals that live here can't waste any energy and must live at a very slow pace.

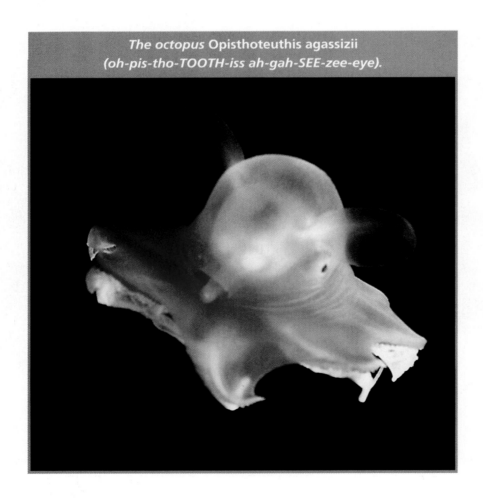

The octopus Opisthoteuthis agassizii
(oh-pis-tho-TOOTH-iss ah-gah-SEE-zee-eye).

No one knows how old these animals are, or why the jelly-like animals of the deep sea are so large in comparison to their shallow-water relatives. It's believed that they take a very long time to grow to this size. They do not actively hunt. They drift along and, if they are lucky, they will eventually drift by some food. They may use a sense similar to smell, or a vibration-detection sense, to home in on their meals. Their large size also probably improves their chances of bumping into some food.

Having successfully fed, the ctenophore drifts out of range of the sub's lights, and the biologist waits patiently for the next creature to come into view. But it is the chemist who spots a deep-sea cucumber flying over the seafloor, propelled by a waving collar of fluttering, fused tube feet. As it passes beneath, *Alvin* continues to hunt for creatures.

The pilot slowly cruises along the bottom with all the sub's lights on. Now it's his turn to spot something, an animal he nicknames "Dumbo." He quickly maneuvers the sub so the animal comes into the biologist's view. There's no denying that the little octopus does look for all the world like the cartoon elephant. The scientist films "Dumbo" as it flutters down to the seafloor, coming to rest in the sediment, its tentacles curved around it like spit curls.

It takes three pictures to show the size of Deepstaria enigmatica (deep-STAR-ee-uh en-ig-MAT-ik-uh). The large ripple in the middle and bottom pictures is made by contractions of the creature's muscle bands.

Periphylla jellyfish

Alvin continues to move slowly over the seafloor. Nothing much other than a few flakes of marine snow can be seen for a time. Then a creature that looks like a fried egg is suddenly illuminated by the sub's lights. It's a siphonophore (sy-FAHN-uh-fawr), but not one the biologist has ever seen before. He studies the animal closely. The "yolk" is probably a gas-filled float that the creature uses to raise or lower itself in the water. Its body is ringed by gelatinous bells, some of which it uses for swimming, some for feeding. Like all siphonophores, this one has nematocysts (NEHM-uh-tuh-sihsts), stinging cells, on the ends of its dangling tentacles. As the siphonophore shifts, giving the biologist a sidelong view, its body parts look like petals around a yellow-centered flower.

The biologist debates collecting the siphonophore, but decides against it. It's probably too fragile to survive the trip back to the surface. But he still has the video recording and pictures he's been taking all along, which he can later use to identify the siphonophore.

The pilot brings Alvin up slightly, so that it hovers at about 330 feet (100 meters) above the seafloor. The biologist, his face pressed against his porthole, is startled to see a very large jellyfish, *Deepstaria enigmatica*, rising up past the sub. It is so large that it takes several moments for its body to move past the small window. Though the biologist never gets a look at the whole animal, he can see it "flexing its muscles," as a wave of contracting muscle bands travels up through the animal's body.

The jellyfish looks and operates like a trash bag. It drifts, hunting for prey, its huge mouth open to surround anything it encounters. Once the prey is inside, *Deepstaria* contracts a sort of living "drawstring" around its mouth, trapping the prey. It seems that the jellyfish is trying to do just that with *Alvin!* But big as the jellyfish is, *Alvin* is much bigger. The creature bumps up against the sub, letting the crew get another good look at it, before it undulates away into the mysterious emptiness. The biologist is a little unsettled by this experience, but it also makes him very, very curious. Are there other jellyfish this large out there? Larger? He would love to capture one of them and study it. But, aside from the difficulty of getting any of these delicate animals to the surface alive, there's nothing on *Alvin* large enough to hold it.

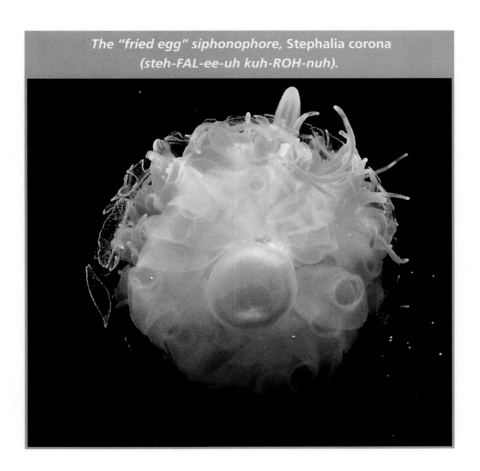

The "fried egg" siphonophore, *Stephalia corona* (steh-FAL-ee-uh kuh-ROH-nuh).

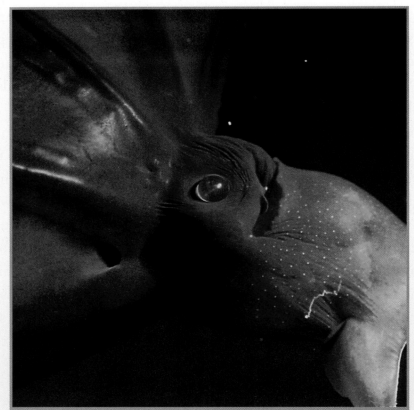

With its spiked tentacles flipped over its head (below), this tiny squid has a strong defense against predators.

Dive-time is almost up. The biologist keeps staring out the porthole, hoping to see at least one more unusual animal before the sub resurfaces. And what he sees is a squid that's only recently been seen alive. Tipped off to its presence by its tiny glowing tentacle tips, the pilot positions the sub so its lights reflect off the black-skinned relative of the octopus. The biologist has just enough time to get a photograph of the 4-inch- (10-centimeter-) long creature.

The sub's time near the seafloor is at an end. The pilot turns off the lights and prepares to resurface. After five hours of total concentration, the scientists are very tired. As the sub surfaces, they review their notes, try to relax, try to stay warm, and don't try too hard to stay awake.

As deep as *Alvin* can dive, the deepest portions of the sea remain beyond its reach. But advances in undersea technology continue to be made. The Japanese research submersible *Shinkai 6500* can dive deeper, as far as 19,500 feet (6,500 meters), and has already begun to explore the seafloor at great depths that are unreachable by all other research subs. *Jason*, a remotely operated vehicle that can be controlled from a ship's deck, can dive for days on end, far longer than any submersible with a human crew. New self-propelled subs not connected to a research ship by a tether will be able to patrol the seafloor for days, weeks, even years at a time, while capturing video images and sending many different kinds of measurements to scientists on land. They will also be able to perform experiments and deliver the results. Who knows what creatures they will discover at these unfathomable depths?

Think About the Selection

1. Why is it important for scientists to concentrate hard while they are in *Alvin*?

2. Prove or disprove this statement with examples from the selection: The deep sea is a cold, unchanging environment.

3. The ctenophore in the photograph on page 602 has not yet been named. What would you name it? Why?

4. What are the advantages and disadvantages of using a remotely operated vehicle such as *Jason* instead of a submersible with a human crew?

5. Choose one of the creatures described in the selection and explain how it has adapted to live in the deep ocean.

6. Would you accept an invitation to join the crew on board *Alvin*? Why or why not?

7. **Connecting/Comparing** How are the scientists aboard *Alvin* like the astronauts who travel into space? How are they different?

Write an Adventure Story

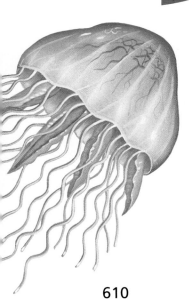

Rewrite the scene in which *Alvin* encounters the giant jellyfish as an adventure story. Include characters, a dangerous challenge to overcome, and an interesting ending.

Tips

- **Decide whether to tell the story in the first person ("I") or third person ("he" or "she").**
- **Begin with a short description of the setting.**
- **Use active verbs.**

Science

Record a Scientist's Observations

Each scientist on the *Alvin* has a tape recorder to record observations. With a partner, record what you might see through one of *Alvin*'s portholes if you were there. Begin each observation with the ocean depth and time.

Bonus Find out more about one of the animals you would observe. Add that information to your recording. Play your recording for the class.

Viewing

Make Comparisons

The authors compare the unusual life forms of the deep sea with familiar objects such as trashbags and fried eggs. With a partner, look again at the photographs of the creatures. Discuss what each reminds you of. Make a list of the creatures and next to each name, write the name of an object you would compare it to in order to help someone visualize it. (Choose comparisons that are different from the authors'.)

Tips

- Read the text for clues about the size of the animal.
- Think of familiar, everyday objects for your comparison.

Internet

Play a Trivia Game

Are you ready for a challenge? Show what you learned from reading *Beneath Blue Waters*. Play an online trivia game at Education Place.

www.eduplace.com/kids

Skill: How to Adjust Your Rate of Reading

Before you read . . .

Identify the **purpose** of your reading. For example, are you studying for a test? Are you reading for pleasure? Your purpose will determine your reading rate.

As you read . . .

- Keep in mind the purpose of your reading.
- Stop occasionally to **monitor** your understanding. Ask yourself **questions** about your reading. If you don't understand the material, slow down. If the material is easy to understand, speed up your rate.
- Remember that it often helps to read nonfiction more slowly than fiction.

SHARKS UNDER ICE

Text and Photographs by Nick Caloyianis

As I floated in the frigid Arctic Ocean, an 11-foot-long shark started swimming toward me.

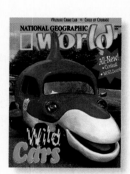

As an underwater photographer, I'd photographed many sharks but never before in such freezing conditions. My assignment for the National Geographic Society: Dive beneath the thick Arctic ice to find and photograph the rarely seen Greenland shark. *Brrrrr!*

Greenland sharks generally live far deeper than humans can dive, so we know little about them. I knew just enough to respect the shark's enormous jaws and razor-sharp teeth.

As I traveled to the seas surrounding Baffin Island in Canada — one of the shallower areas where Greenland sharks are found — I tried not to think of the hardships that lay ahead. The water here is barely above freezing. For each dive, I'd have to wear thick rubber gloves, an insulated hood, layers of long underwear, and a waterproof suit. Even with all this protection, I'd be lucky not to freeze after two hours in the icy water. Would I have time to get my photos?

On one of my first dives, I saw a shark swimming my way. At a distance, I could barely make out its stubby fins and strange tail. But as the shark drew nearer, I could almost count the many rows of teeth in its mouth.

Lucky for me, this particular shark was interested only in my bag of shark bait floating nearby. It opened its cavernous mouth and, like a huge vacuum cleaner, sucked up the entire bag. Then it turned and gave *me* the eye.

I quickly aimed my camera, focused, and clicked off two shots — all that my half-frozen equipment could manage after almost two hours beneath the sea. Mission accomplished, I hurried to the surface and emerged from a hole in the ice with my prize — the first photos ever taken of a live Greenland shark in the Arctic Ocean.

I returned a year later to photograph the sharks again. I was hooked on these mysterious fish!

UNIQUE PHOTOS REVEAL SHARK SECRETS

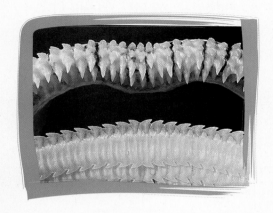

◀ The Greenland shark's upper teeth pierce and grip prey such as fish and seals. Bands of razor-sharp teeth lining the lower jaw are perfect for slicing.

◀ Oxygen-rich water flows through a row of five gill slits on each side of the Greenland shark's head. Its gill slits are smaller than those of most sharks. Scientists think the smaller slits might allow more powerful suction as the sharks suck in prey.

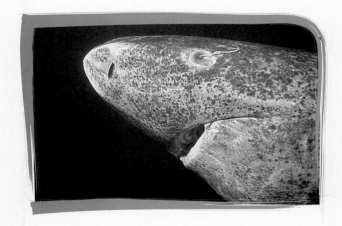

◀ Tiny parasites called copepods hang from the Greenland shark's eyes, damaging the animal's vision or even causing blindness. The parasites may also help the shark find food by acting as lures for fish and other prey.

▲ Sharks As Stars
Photographer Nick Caloyianis approaches a Greenland shark during a return trip to Baffin Island. "We took movies of the sharks as they fed," he recalls. "The films show the sharks sucking in food from a distance of three feet."

◄ Fierce Storms and Frigid Seas
Life on Baffin Island, the fifth largest island in the world, is a challenge for all but the hardiest people. Arctic Bay was Caloyianis's home base while he photographed Greenland sharks.
Map by Martin Walz

SHARKS IN TROUBLE

Sharks have been around for more than 400 million years. A growing demand for shark meat, fins, skin, and organs for food, medicines, and other products has placed in danger many of the approximately 370 shark species that live in Earth's oceans. Whether sharks will be around in the future is largely up to us. Even the elusive Greenland shark has been overfished. Its liver oil was used as a lubricant for airplane engines during World War II. Today the sharks are caught for dog food.

Recently a few of the 125 countries that buy or sell sharks have taken steps to control shark fishing. Perhaps more will follow their lead in limiting the number of sharks that can be caught each year.

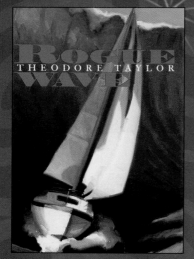

THEODORE TAYLOR
ROGUE WAVE

Out There

Read to find the meanings of these words.

e • Glossary

afterdeck

buoy

discount

inquiries

visibility

A HIDDEN AND UNKNOWN WORLD

The more scientists explore Earth's oceans, the more they realize that they don't know a lot about this watery frontier. They have studied only about one percent of the ocean's floor. Billions of unknown animals live there. Some are tiny, barely visible to the human eye. But some of them might be huge.

A common eel

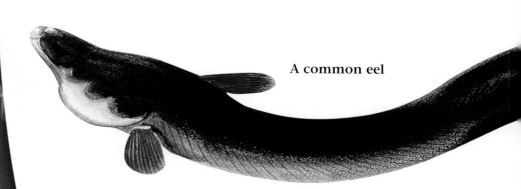

Dolphins playing are a common sight at sea. However, under poor visibility in rough weather, they occasionally have been mistaken for mysterious and threatening creatures.

Sailors often tell stories about strange creatures they have seen at sea. The Coast Guard also has stories of unusual sightings and of incidents that have no clear explanation. When **visibility** is poor or when passengers are bored, what might they see as they stand on the **afterdeck** of a boat? Was that just a dark **buoy**, rocking back and forth in the fog? Or was it *something else* swimming past the boat's stern?

Would you **discount** a story about a sea monster, or would you believe it? Would you make **inquiries**, seeking information until you learned the truth? Find out what Danny Aldo did in Theodore Taylor's story "Out There."

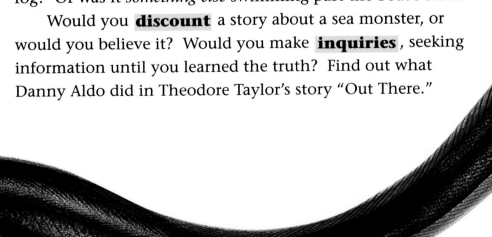

Theodore Taylor

BORN: June 23, 1921, in Statesville, North Carolina

CHILDHOOD: Spent much of his childhood exploring fields, creeks, old buildings, and the shipyard where his father worked

FIRST WRITING JOB: Sports writer for a local newspaper at the age of thirteen

SAILING EXPERIENCE: Served in the U.S. Merchant Marines and the U.S. Naval Reserve in the 1940s

Rob Bolster

CHILDHOOD: Every summer in Point Judith, Rhode Island, Rob Bolster nourished his love for the outdoors, especially the ocean.

HOBBIES: Fly-fishing, carpentry work, building and flying radio-controlled aircraft

FAVORITE ILLUSTRATOR: Chris Van Allsburg, who was one of Bolster's instructors at the Rhode Island School of Design

To discover more about Theodore Taylor and Rob Bolster, visit Education Place. **www.eduplace.com/kids**

618

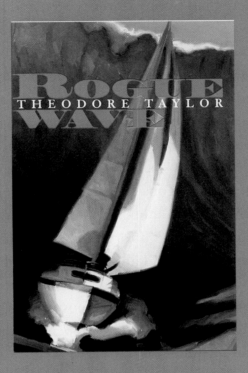

ROGUE WAVE
THEODORE TAYLOR

Out There

by Theodore Taylor

illustrated by Rob Bolster

Strategy Focus

Some fishing expeditions are pretty unusual, as Danny Aldo is about to discover. As you read, stop every few pages to **predict** what will happen next.

Not five minutes after I cleared the Dana Harbor jetty in the *Spanker*, a sixteen-foot boat, dense fog rolled in and I cut the outboard to almost steerage way, two knots, groping along. Thick, wet mist takes away your sight but sharpens your hearing, fine-tunes your nerves.

Visibility was no more than twenty or thirty feet, and I crept south for about a quarter mile toward the red buoy that marked the harbor channel. I had planned to drift-fish about two miles offshore, let the boat ride the current and drag the bait along the bottom; if I had been lucky I would have caught a nice halibut or a big sand bass. But it was too risky out there in the fog. A large boat might have run me down accidentally. Instead I decided to drop anchor and fish by the buoy until the fog lifted. Sometimes in shallow water — if you didn't get tangled in kelp — croakers or calicos, sand bass will bite.

Before launching the boat I'd gone to Dana Wharf Sportsfishing for a plastic bag of frozen anchovies and another of squid. My dad always bought a half scoop of live bait but I couldn't afford the fifteen dollars the bait barge charged. Now I cut an anchovy in half and hooked the tail end, tossing the bait and sinker into the water, which I knew was about twelve feet deep in this spot. I'd fished these waters since I was a kid, mostly with a school friend, Buck Crowder, or my father. I settled back and opened a thermos of hot chocolate. My watch said the time was 6:40 A.M.

The foghorn on the jetty was bleating, and in the distance, more than a mile away on shore, the air horn on the San Diego–Los Angeles train kept breaking the early-morning peace.

I waited for almost another hour in the ghostly silence, small fish or perhaps crabs tapping the bait or stealing it. Then the fog began to slowly withdraw toward the west, leaving patches. A big cruiser, probably with radar, twin diesels boiling, passed not far away, barely visible; and the wake rocked the *Spanker*, tossing me back and forth on the stern seat.

In the middle of a toss, something, *something*, in the water toward shore startled me. I'm sure my mouth opened, and I know my heart drummed, for the *something* looked like a huge gray-green eel slowly moving on the gray surface, its blunt but serpentlike head awash, dark eyes the size of salad plates. Whatever it was, it must have measured twenty feet because, in my judgment, it was longer than the *Spanker*. I couldn't believe what I was seeing.

Barely breathing, I watched it disappear into a patch of low-lying fog. Only then did I realize I'd had a strike and the reel was screaming. Watching for the *thing* to reappear, I halfheartedly jerked back on the rod, hooking whatever had struck, not even bothering to heave in. For a moment, I wondered if I'd seen something that really wasn't there. Then I decided that I hadn't just imagined it. I'd seen a huge eel, or something that resembled an eel. It hadn't had fins or flippers, so it wasn't a fish or a whale. I held the twitching rod as if in a trance, more amazed than afraid.

I kept looking toward where the *thing* seemed to have disappeared, and then my attention was drawn to the other side. Coming out of the fog was a boat headed straight for the *Spanker*, but seemingly without power; adrift. A derelict, a sea ghost.

Jamming the rod butt beneath the seat, I began yelling, thinking that the owner of the boat was asleep or down below. It was a small white cabin cruiser. On it slowly came, and in a moment it bumped the *Spanker* on the port side. Scrambling to grab it by the bow chain, I kept yelling for the owner.

No answer, and I tied off to *Spanker*. Boat owners had no business sleeping while under way, powered or not.

Still no answer, and I decided to board the *Lotta Fun*, suddenly worried about what I might find. What else could happen this foggy morning? Was the owner just asleep, or had something else happened? I stepped aboard, noticing what I thought might be blood on the railing at the stern of the boat. It had a sheen and didn't look dried. Was it just fish blood or was it human blood? There was a small pool of it.

Cautiously I ducked into the tiny cabin, again asking for someone to respond. No one was home but I noticed a red light on the battery-powered coffeepot and felt it. Hot! So someone had been aboard within the last few hours. I unhooked the pot and became aware of a smell in the boat that I hadn't noticed on boarding, a burnt-rubber odor.

I looked closer around the cabin and the interior deck but didn't see any more blood or any signs of a fight. On the counter near the small galley stove was an old battered tin lunch box. Someone had been getting ready to eat. Except for what was at the stern, it all looked normal.

Between sighting the huge eel and getting bumped by the derelict with the fresh blood on it, a core of fright was now lodged in my belly. I quickly reboarded the *Spanker* and noticed the rod tip still bobbing. Trying to think of what to do next, I dislodged the rod butt from beneath the seat and reeled in. A small blue shark, tail whipping, came out of the water. I popped it loose.

Tow the *Lotta Fun* in and turn it over to Harbor Patrol, I finally decided. I led the boat around to my stern, flipped a line over its port bow cleat, and made it fast, then let out ten feet or so, just enough to control an easy haul. The sea was still calm, the fog still patchy.

I got under way, thinking that maybe there was some kind of connection between that giant eel, or whatever it was, and whoever had been aboard the *Lotta Fun*.

Dana Harbor Patrol is in a two-story building on a narrow island at the head of twin channels that are waterways leading to hundreds of boat berths, home to million-dollar yachts as well as humbler boats, fifteen-foot sailing types. The *Spanker* had a berth at the north end.

Harbor Patrol is a function of the Orange County Sheriff-Coroner Department. Fish and Game also operate out of the sheriff spaces. In back of the building are spaces for the patrol and rescue craft. Coming back through the jetties, where pelicans and gulls perch on gigantic rocks, I steered to the county berthing area, rehearsing what I was going to say.

I brought the *Lotta Fun* alongside the *Spanker*, then maneuvered both boats into an empty stall, jumped out on the dock, and tied them off fore and aft on cleats.

In a moment I was climbing the steps to the second-story patrol office and at the desk told the brown-uniformed duty sergeant that I'd just brought a drifting boat in; no one on it. "I tied it up at your dock. Name is *Lotta Fun*." Let them find the blood themselves.

I turned to leave, but Sergeant Lamont, who looked like he was midforties, a big man with a graying mustache, said, "Whoa! Let me get a report." He walked back to his desk, then returned to the counter with a form.

"OK, name, age, address . . ."

"Danny Aldo. I live at Seventy-two Trumpeter Way, Laguna Beach. I'm seventeen."

The sergeant wrote slowly, frowning. "You by yourself out there?"

"Yes, sir."

"Isn't seventeen a little young to be alone out in the ocean, even in clear weather? Your parents know?"

"My dad does. He owns the boat." He always says it's really "our" boat.

Lamont nodded. "Name of your boat and number?"

"*Spanker*. Sixteen-foot." I dug out my wallet. "Charley-Fox, three-nine-zero-five, Jake-Zebra . . ."

"OK, what were you doing out there, and where were you?"

"I was fishing near the red buoy, had the anchor down, waiting for the fog to lift."

"And the *Lotta Fun* bumped into you?"

"Yes, sir, with no warning."

"What time?"

"About a half hour ago."

"You hear any voices, anyone calling for help before it hit you?"

"No, sir."

"You see anyone in the water?"

"No, sir."

"Anything at all unusual before it hit you?"

I hesitated, wondering whether or not I should tell Sergeant Lamont about the huge eel I saw just before the *Lotta Fun* showed up. Fish stories often made people laugh. But this was true and might have something to do with the *Lotta Fun* and its owner.

I took a deep breath and said, "Just before it bumped me, I saw a big green-gray eel come by about fifty feet away. It was longer than the *Spanker* and bigger around than a telephone pole."

Lamont's eyes rolled back in his head. "An eel longer than sixteen feet, bigger than a phone pole?"

"Yes, sir."

He made a face. "You sure you saw that?"

"Yes, sir."

"OK, I'll write it all down. And you were alone on your boat? The sixteen-foot eel comes by, then the *Lotta Fun* shows up, owner missing. I'm sure gonna get a call from Santa Ana on this one. Loch Ness Monster off Dana Point?"

I remained silent, thinking I shouldn't have told him about the eel.

"Anything else?"

I hesitated again. "One more thing. When you go down to look at the *Lotta Fun* you'll see what I think is blood on the stern railing, portside. I don't know whether it's fish blood or human blood."

"Whoops," said Sergeant Lamont. "Why don't you just take a seat over there on that bench? I'll be back in a moment. I have to call investigators."

I sat down on the bench, now wishing I'd heaved up my anchor, started the motor, and left all the trouble behind when I'd first seen the *Lotta Fun* coming. But my father had always taught me to render help to anyone who needed it at sea.

I had the feeling that my fishing day might be over.

About an hour later, the men from Santa Ana showed up. They read the sergeant's report, then approached me.

"Danny, I'm Deputy Roper, Orange County Sheriff's Department, and this is Deputy Cooper. Sergeant Lamont asked us to come down here and talk to you about that boat you brought in with the blood on it. Don't be frightened. Just relax. You're not being charged with anything."

I was finding it hard to relax. "Yes, sir."

"Where is your father today?"

"In Washington, D.C., on business. He's a lawyer. I live with him. My mother lives in Denver. They're divorced."

"And he approves of you going out alone? That's the truth?"

"Yes, sir. I'm a good sailor." My dad first took me fishing when I was three or four. These days, I always handle the boat when we go out.

"I bet you're a good sailor. Mind if I tape this interview?"

"No, sir."

Deputy Cooper said, "First things first. Sergeant Lamont has written here that you saw something unusual in the water before the *Lotta Fun* came along."

"A huge eel of some kind, I think. One eighteen or twenty feet long. It was this big around." I made an oval of my arms.

Cooper said, "Pardon me for laughing, but seals are never eighteen or twenty feet long."

"It wasn't a seal, sir. I've seen plenty of seals — there's a bell buoy about four miles north and they sleep and bark on top of it all the time. What I saw wasn't a seal. It wasn't a fish, either. It didn't have fins. It was longer than our boat. I think it was an eel."

Cooper shook his head, laughing again. "You sure you didn't have a bad dream out there, Danny? Like a sea serpent dream?" I disliked him immediately.

"I wasn't dreaming. I saw it."

"You expect us to believe you saw a sea monster? Well, I have to tell you, Danny boy, they don't exist."

"I didn't say I saw a sea monster, sir. Not a sea monster. It looked to me like a huge eel." I was sweating.

Roper sighed and said, "As a matter of fact, Phil, no one knows. Like UFOs, no one knows. But that's not what we're here to talk about. Let's get to the subject — that abandoned boat . . ."

Cooper asked, "OK, Danny, why didn't you radio in to Harbor Patrol and ask them to come out and check before you towed it in?"

"My dad put the radio on the boat just for me. But it's out of whack."

"You shouldn't have gone aboard, Danny," Cooper said. "If a crime has been committed, you contaminated the crime scene. Shoeprints, fingerprints — how do you know someone wasn't murdered?"

"I didn't even think about that, sir." Yes, I did. The blood!

"Our crime lab people are down there right now, and they'll make tests," Deputy Roper said. He added, "Sergeant Lamont checked the boat registration number with the Coast Guard. The *Lotta Fun* belongs to Jack Stokes, who lives here in Dana Point. Old guy, seventy-four. We've got people, including the local police, looking for him." Roper was the younger of the two. The nicer, too. Both wore civilian clothes.

"Do you think that big eel, or whatever it was, had anything to do with what happened on the *Lotta Fun*?" I asked.

"I doubt that very much," Roper replied.

"But the boat did drift up not long after I spotted whatever it was. Could that thing have knocked Mr. Stokes overboard, then swum up beside me?"

"Not likely," Roper answered.

"Pardon me for laughing again," Cooper said. "If Stokes fell overboard, it wasn't because of any sea monster."

I looked over at him. I hadn't said it was a sea monster.

"How do you account for the blood, Phil?" Roper asked.

"Fishermen cut themselves all the time. He cut himself, fainted, and fell overboard. No sea monster stuck its head up and grabbed old Jack . . ."

Buck Crowder called me the next morning about eight. "Hey, Danny, you made the paper. And they mentioned you on channel nine."

"I know." I had read the story quoting seventeen-year-old Danny Aldo as saying that the "sea monster" and the missing senior citizen might be somehow connected. It also quoted Deputy Phil Cooper as saying, "That kid gets A-plus for imagination. Sea monsters don't exist. Jack Stokes is the problem here."

The newspaper said that inquiries at Dana Wharf Sportsfishing had drawn laughter. "That boy ought to have his eyes examined," one veteran fisherman said.

"I swear, Buck, I saw that thing, whatever it was."

"Yeah, but 'sea monster'?"

"Buck, I never did call it a sea monster. I keep saying that. Nobody listens. All I said was 'a big eel.' I don't even want to talk about it anymore."

"You're telling the truth?"

"I swear it."

"I wish I'd been out there with you. Man, I missed somethin'. That lousy dentist appointment."

We usually had fun. Fishing, laughing, talking. We both worked nights at the ice-cream and yogurt place fronting the inner harbor.

"Well, an eel twenty feet long, Danny. That's a very big eel," Buck said.

Yes, it was a very big eel.

"I faxed the newspaper story to my dad in Washington. He called me about an hour ago and laughed, then asked, 'Did it really happen that way?' I said it did. He said, 'I believe you; shame I wasn't there to be your witness. Keep me posted about Jack Stokes.' Maybe only my dad believes me."

Buck said, "OK, I believe you." But his voice was hollow.

"Yeah, you do . . ."

I took the jeep and went for a hamburger, using phone order, then drove home again. On the drive back and forth, I got what I thought was a bright idea — use my dad's PC. As I ate, I logged onto our on-line service, and checked to see what their reference sources had on sea serpents/sea monsters/giant eels.

Up came:

In Greek mythology, Perseus, the son of Zeus and Danäe, encountered Andromeda, whom he saved from a fearful sea monster . . .

There were a half dozen other entries on sightings dated back to A.D. 300 and of no use whatsoever. It was all treated as mythology, anyway.

So I went on to the Internet, accessing the Library of Congress. Here I found more what I was looking for.

Just after noon, October 19, 1898, the sixty-five-foot wooden trawler Eva Maria *was about eighty-five miles off Cape Blanco, Oregon, when the master, Alfonso Pombal, sighted something in the water off his starboard bow. It was swimming on the surface and he estimated it to be seventy or eighty feet long. With binoculars he determined it was not a whale. He called sleeping crewmen to the wheelhouse. The head was estimated to be at least twelve feet long. Pombal and his crewmen agreed it was some type of giant snake.*

"I'm convinced we saw a sea serpent," said Captain Rober Faircloth, of the pollock fisher Savoonga, *off the Aleutians in remarkably calm weather. A crewman mending a net saw a serpentlike creature at least twenty-five feet in length. He called Faircloth and soon the other crewmen joined them as witnesses. The creature kept pace with the* Savoonga *for at least three miles and seemed to be watching the boat. Incident was reported to the Coast Guard upon arrival at Dutch Harbor, June 23, 1926.*

There were dozens of other cases, in both the Atlantic and the Pacific, as well as in foreign seas. One report said there'd been "thousands of such incidents," dating back to sailing-ship days. It was estimated that many other sightings were not reported by sailors because of fear of being laughed at. I could sympathize. The latest incident, one that caused me to slam the desk in triumph, had occurred not long ago. August 3, 1991: Having departed San Francisco en route to Los Angeles and Acapulco, the cruise liner *Pacific Empress* was about twenty miles off Point Concepcion, off the California coast, when:

Captain Thomas Judy said, "I couldn't believe what I was seeing after the third mate called me to the bridge. I'd been at sea forty-five

years, thirty-one as a master, and here was this huge sea-snake, maybe
thirty feet long, off the port side, moving as fast as we were. The third
mate ran to get his camera but by the time he was back on the bridge, the
monster had disappeared. I can tell you it wasn't a whale, or a seal or a
giant squid. It was a sea serpent, something I'd sworn never existed."

Point Concepcion wasn't all that far north of Dana Point.

I called Buck to come by and take a look at what the printer had spewed
out. Buck read it and said, "You weren't imagining things after all."

"Nope, I wasn't."

"Now, look at this one from the National Oceanographic Data Center,
Washington, D.C., 1989."

Although we discount the fabled sea monsters, such as the kraken
which could swallow vessels whole, we have not yet explored the ocean
thoroughly enough to say with absolute certainty that there are no mon-
sters in the deep. Scientific observations and records note that giant
squid with tentacles forty feet long live at 1500 feet and that sizable
objects have been detected by echo sounding at even greater depths.
Oarfish forty to fifty feet long have been observed by scientists. In
recent years, Danish scientists have studied large eel larvae that will
grow to ninety feet if their growth rate is the same as other eel species.

A day later I got a call from a Captain Patrick Carroll, who owned the
swordfisher *Time of Joy.* I had watched her going out or coming in, sometimes
flying the catch flag that meant she'd nailed one. I knew she tied up in front of
Proud Mary's at the wharf. Carroll said he wanted to talk about what I'd seen,
so I stopped by on my way to work.

The *Time of Joy* was about thirty feet in length, with a beam of nine or ten
feet. She had a "pulpit," a harpooning platform that was drawn up while in
harbor, and a crow's nest to look for swordfish.

I thought Carroll was about fifty, but no grizzled old seadog that you
might find at the wharf in late afternoon. Though deep-tanned, he looked
more like an insurance agent than a swordfisher. I had heard he'd been a college professor but discovered fishing was more fun than teaching.

Carroll said, "Have a seat." We were on the afterdeck. "Want coffee,
cola?"

"Cola'll be fine," I said, sitting on top of the engine box.

Carroll went into his combination wheelhouse, cookhouse, and bunkhouse and came back with two frosty cans. He put his bottom against the rail and said, "Get used to being called a liar. Long after they've found and forgotten Jack Stokes somebody around here will remember Danny Aldo and his sea monster. But I believe you. Sixteen years ago I saw something out there bigger than what you saw. Ever since, they've laughed about Pat Carroll and his sea monster. But I saw it . . ."

I frowned. Imagine being called a liar for sixteen years, almost the whole time I'd been on earth.

"Not only did I see it but I photographed it."

"And they still called you a liar."

He laughed and nodded. "Forty feet was my guess, and it looked like what you described to the sheriff's department."

"But how can we ever prove it?" I asked.

"Most scientists scoff at reports of strange giant sea creatures. They say 'Prove it,' and I say, 'Look at the *National Geographic* photos of fish at six thousand feet with big fanged heads and luminous eyes. No one can name the species. Plant life ceases to grow at six hundred feet and what's below, in darkness, is basically unknown. So-called sea monsters have washed ashore and scientists are embarrassed, calling them 'unknown species.'

"I've taken pictures. Even so, the first reaction is that you somehow faked the picture. People claimed I made a clay model, photographed it, then rephotographed it against water. Soon they've made a laughingstock out of you. Now I have a raft to throw overboard just for scale."

"You believe in sea monsters?"

Carroll shook his head. "I believe there are creatures that only a few people have seen. The oceans and seas are the most mysterious places on earth and billions of things exist that are smaller than pinheads and as large as blue whales. Every so often we get lucky and meet a new one."

I said, "Do you have that photo, the one you shot?"

Carroll nodded and went forward. I followed. He ducked into the wheelhouse, and there on the port bulkhead was a framed black-and-white picture, faded with age.

Staring at it, I said, "The one I saw was smaller but it looks like the same thing."

Carroll smiled. "Does it look like a clay model to you?"

"No."

"Guess where I shot that picture."

"Somewhere off here?"

The swordfisher nodded. "Two miles south, three miles west. Now let me show you a clipping from the fisherman's trade journal, last month's edition."

SEA SOUND MYSTIFIES RESEARCH SCIENTISTS
A massive heartbeatlike thumping sound has been recorded by professional divers in waters off Dana Point, California, mystifying scientists from the Naval Undersea Research Institute. They admit, "We hear the signal, and we're staring at it and listening to it, trying to figure out what it is. We know it's alive . . ."

Carroll had a gleam in his eyes. "It's out there. *Out there!* So hang in, Danny. Someday we'll both be proved not to be liars."

The fish-nibbled body of Jack Stokes was recovered the next day: It had drifted north about ten miles. Preliminary tests on the blood found on the *Lotta Fun* indicated it did not belong to Jack Stokes. The paper reported that according to the medical examiner's office, it wasn't human blood.

Not human blood? Another mystery of the sea was added to the ageless list.

A day later, one so clear that the low mountains to the east could be seen, Buck and I went past the Dana Point jetties, outbound. In the *Spanker* locker was my dad's camcorder and my camera. Both had full loads of film. A rubber raft was also aboard for scale purposes.

We were outbound to drift-fish for sand bass and halibut, and to see what we could see.

Responding

Out There

Think About the Selection

1. What kind of person is Danny? Give examples from the selection to support your answer.

2. Do you think Danny makes the right decision when he tells Sergeant Lamont about the giant eel? Why or why not?

3. Do you think there is a connection between the giant eel and the disappearance of Jack Stokes? Explain your answer.

4. What does it mean that Captain Carroll carries a raft "to throw overboard just for scale"?

5. Have you ever had an experience when people did not believe you? What happened? Why didn't they believe you?

6. How might the story have been different if Danny's father had been with him on the boat?

7. **Connecting/Comparing** Captain Carroll says, "What's below, in darkness, is basically unknown." How does the information in *Beneath Blue Waters* support this statement?

Creating

Write an Interview Script

Prepare a set of interview questions that you would like to ask Danny about his experience. Then write the answers that you think Danny would give.

Tips

- Ask questions that require more than "yes" or "no" for an answer.
- Base Danny's answers on what you have learned about his character.

634

Art

Make an Illustrated Chart

Look again at the different ocean creatures in *Beneath Blue Waters*. Note the size of each creature. In "Out There," reread Danny's description of the creature he sees. With a partner, create an illustrated chart that shows all these creatures, including a giant eel, arranged by size.

Bonus
Make the drawings in your chart to scale.

Listening and Speaking

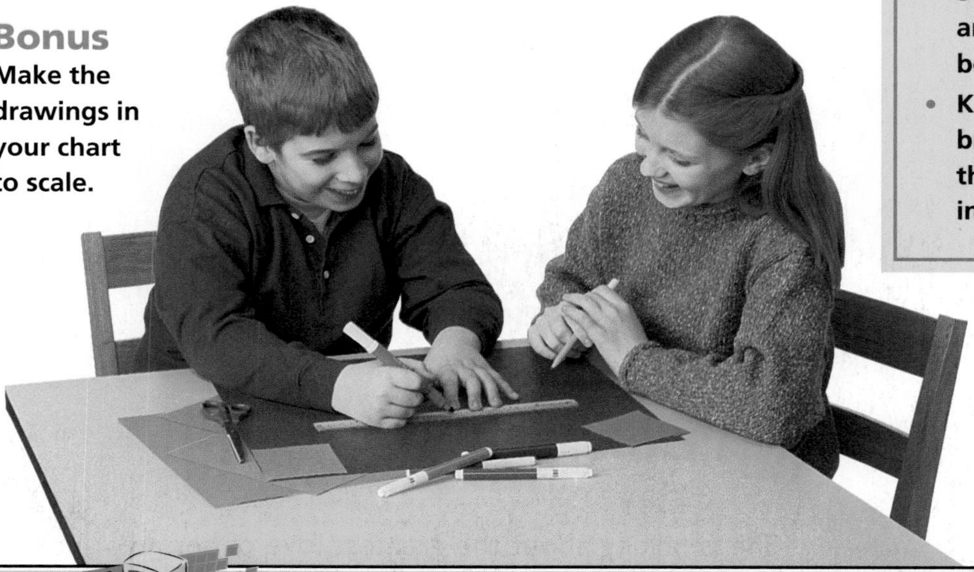

Give a Radio Message

Role-play a situation in which Danny sends a radio message from his boat. Prepare and deliver a message in which he explains the sighting of the giant eel and his encounter with the *Lotta Fun*. Include details from the story in the message.

Tips

- **State Danny's name and the name of his boat clearly.**
- **Keep your message brief, and include only the most important information.**

Internet

Post a Review

Would you recommend "Out There" to a friend? Why or why not? Write a review of the story. Post your review on Education Place.

www.eduplace.com/kids

Career Link

Skill: How to Use the SQP3R Strategy

Use the SQP3R Strategy to help you organize and remember facts in many nonfiction articles.

As you read . . .

S **Survey** the article by reading the title, looking at the pictures, and noting words that seem important.

Q Read the first heading and turn it into a **question**.

P **Predict** what the answer will be.

R **Read** the section that follows the heading to find the answer.

R **Recite** the answer from memory.

R **Review** each heading and recall the answer to each question.

Exploring the DEEP

by Roger Rosenblatt

"You have to love it before you are moved to save it," says world-famous marine biologist Sylvia Earle.

She is talking about the greatest love of her life — the ocean. And if anyone in the world knows what it will take to save the millions of species that live in our oceans, it's Earle.

The oceans define the earth. They cover almost 75% of the planet and hold 97% of its water. Nearly half of the world's population lives within 60 miles of the sea. Scientists say that 10 million to 30 million species of sea life may still be undiscovered.

Under the Sea

Earle, 63, takes fish personally. She has gone on at least 50 diving expeditions and spent more than 6,000 hours under the sea. After one dive she rejoiced that she had met an 18-inch-long shark with glowing green eyes. She claims she once bumped into "a grouper with attitude."

In 1970 she was captain of the first team of women to live beneath the ocean's surface. The five "aquanauts" spent two weeks in an underwater laboratory — a small structure — off the U.S. Virgin Islands.

Since 1979, when she walked freely on the ocean floor 1,250 feet beneath the water's surface, Earle has been known as Her Deepness. She holds the world record for the deepest dive by any human outside a submarine.

Now Earle has a new job: explorer-in-residence for the National Geographic Society. As the leader of a five-year project, Earle will use a zippy new submarine to study the waters of the twelve national marine sanctuaries — underwater areas similar to national parks that are protected by the U.S. government.

Earle feels personal responsibility for the ocean's future and safety. She believes human beings are the first species to be able to have an impact on the entire world.

Sylvia Earle, here at Big Sur in California, sees many threats to the world's oceans.

Noted oceanographer Dr. Sylvia Earle, left, and an unidentified diver as they examine fish reference charts in the Florida Keys.

Threats to the Ocean

Earle is terribly concerned that people are polluting and overfishing the ocean. Fishing methods that use trawlers to dredge the ocean floor also destroy underwater habitats. Earle calls the trawlers "bulldozers."

Another threat comes from man-made fertilizers, which wash off fields into streams and eventually into the ocean. This encourages the harmful over-growth of algae and the spread of toxic germs that can kill fish and cause human health problems. Billions of fish died along the Middle and Southern Atlantic coast of the U.S. in recent years, and pollution is the main suspect.

Earle offers several solutions to these problems. She urges people to take action, to volunteer to clean a beach. She also hopes people will learn as much as they can about how the ocean keeps all of us alive. "Far and away the greatest threat to the ocean, and thus to ourselves, is ignorance," she says. "But we can do something about that."

Earle sits on a rock and stares out at her beloved sea. She claims the key to the earth's future is not to be found among the stars. "The future is here," she says. "This aquatic planet blessed with an ocean."

Career File

Marine Biologist

Are you interested in exploring the ocean professionally? You'll need a four-year college degree in biology or environmental science. And it helps if you enjoy:

- Swimming, snorkeling, and scuba diving
- Observing marine animals in their natural habitat
- Communicating your discoveries with others

To learn more, contact your local aquarium about school programs and about becoming a volunteer.

Theme Wrap-Up

Check Your Progress

Your reading has taken you from the deep ocean depths in a submersible to the rocky surface of Mars with Sojourner. Now you will have a chance to look back at the selections, compare two new ones, and polish your test-taking skills.

Take a moment to look back at pages 544–546. When Eugenie Clark writes that she "felt like Genie in Wonderland" on her first SCUBA dive, she is expressing how strange and wonderful she felt. What selections in the theme so far do you think have captured this feeling?

You will read about people who are curious about the stars and the sea in the two new selections that follow. Think about how their curiosity leads to new discoveries. Compare these explorations with each other and with the other selections in this theme.

Read and Compare

The Night of the Pomegranate

by Tim Wynne-Jones

Read a short story about a girl whose love of Mars rescues her school project.

Try these strategies:
Predict and Infer
Summarize

by Ellen R. Butts & Joyce R. Schwartz

Learn more about Eugenie Clark, the pioneering shark researcher and scientist.

Try these strategies:
Question
Evaluate

Strategies in Action *Keep in mind all your reading strategies while you read.*

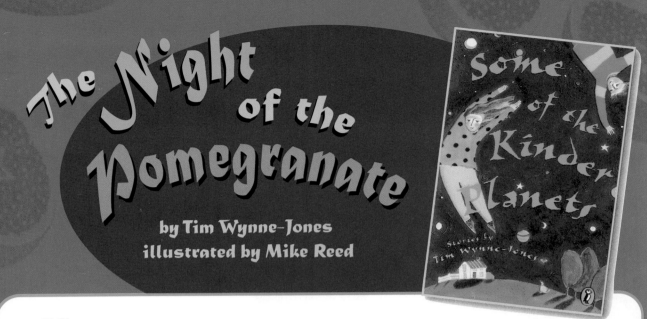

The Night of the Pomegranate

by Tim Wynne-Jones
illustrated by Mike Reed

HARRIET'S solar system was a mess. She had made it — the sun and its nine planets — out of rolled-up balls of the morning newspaper. It was mounted on a sheet of green bristol board. The bristol board had a project about Austria on the other side. Harriet wished the background were black. Green was all wrong.

Everything about her project was wrong. The crumpled paper was coming undone. Because she had used the last of the Scotch tape on Saturn's rings, the three remaining planets had nothing to keep them scrunched up. Tiny Pluto was already bigger than Jupiter and growing by the minute. She had also run out of glue, so part of her solar system was stuck together with grape chewing gum.

Harriet's big brother, Tom, was annoyed at her because Mom had made him drive her to school early with her stupid project. Dad was annoyed at her for using part of the business section. Mostly she had stuck to the want ads, but then an advertisement printed in red ink in the business section caught her eye, and she just had to have it for Mars. Harriet had a crush on Mars; that's what Tom said. She didn't even mind his saying it.

Mars was near the earth this month. The nights had been November cold but clear as glass, and Harriet had been out to see Mars every night, which was why she hadn't gotten her solar system finished, why she was so tired, why Mom made Tom drive her to school. It was all Mars's fault.

She was using the tape on Ms. Krensky's desk when Clayton Beemer arrived with his dad. His solar system came from the hobby store. The planets were Styrofoam balls, all different sizes and painted the right colors. Saturn's rings were clear plastic painted over as delicately as insect wings.

Harriet looked at her own Saturn. Her rings were drooping despite all the tape. They looked like a limp skirt on a . . . on a ball of scrunched-up newspaper.

Harriet sighed. The wires that supported Clayton's planets in their black box were almost invisible. The planets seemed to float.

"What d'ya think?" Clayton asked. He beamed. Mr. Beemer beamed. Harriet guessed that *he* had made the black box with its glittery smears of stars.

She had rolled up her own project protectively when Clayton entered the classroom. Suddenly one of the planets came unstuck and fell on the floor. Clayton and Mr. Beemer looked at it.

"What's that?" asked Clayton.

"Pluto, I think," said Harriet, picking it up. She popped it in her mouth. It tasted of grape gum. "Yes, Pluto," she said. Clayton and Mr. Beemer walked away to find the best place to show off their project.

Darjit arrived next. "Hi, Harriet," she said. The project under her arm had the planets' names done in bold gold lettering. Harriet's heart sank. Pluto tasted stale and cold.

But last night Harriet had tasted pomegranates. Old Mrs. Pond had given her one while she busied herself putting on layer after layer of warm clothing and gathering the things they would need for their Mars watch.

Mrs. Pond lived in the country. She lived on the edge of the woods by a meadow that sloped down to a marsh through rough frost-licked grass and prickly ash and juniper. It was so much darker than town; good for stargazing.

By 11:00 P.M. Mars was directly above the marsh, which was where Harriet and Mrs. Pond set themselves up for their vigil. They found it just where they had left it the night before: in the constellation Taurus between the Pleiades and the Hyades. But you didn't need a map to find Mars these nights. It shone like rust, neither trembling nor twinkling as the fragile stars did.

Mrs. Pond smiled and handed Harriet two folding chairs. "Ready?" she asked.

"Ready, class?" said Ms. Krensky. Everyone took their seats. Harriet placed the green bristol board universe in front of her. It was an even worse mess than it had been when she arrived. Her solar system was ravaged.

It had started off with Pluto and then, as a joke to make Darjit laugh, she had eaten Neptune. Then Karen had come in, and Jodi and Nick and Scott.

"The planet taste test," Harriet had said, ripping off a bit of Mercury. "Umm, very spicy." By the time the bell rang, there wasn't much of her project left.

Kevin started. He stood at the back of the classroom holding a green and blue marble.

"If this was Earth," he said, "then the sun would be this big —." He put the earth in his pocket and pulled out a fat squishy yellow beach ball from a garbage bag. Everybody hooted and clapped. "And it would be at the crosswalk," he added. Everyone looked confused, so Ms. Krensky helped Kevin explain the relative distance between the earth and the sun. "And Pluto would be fifty miles away from here," said Kevin. But then he wasn't sure about that, so Ms. Krensky worked it out at the board with him.

Meanwhile, using Kevin's example, the class was supposed to figure out where other planets in the solar system would be relative to the green and blue marble in Kevin's pocket. Harriet sighed.

Until last night, Harriet had never seen the inside of a pomegranate before. As she opened the hard rind, she marveled at the bright red seeds in their cream-colored fleshy pouches.

"It's like a little secret universe all folded in on itself," said Mrs. Pond.

Harriet tasted it. With her tongue, she popped a little red bud against the roof of her mouth. The taste startled her, made her laugh.

"Tonight," Mrs. Pond said, "Mars is only forty-five million miles away." They drank a cocoa toast to that. Then she told Harriet about another time when Mars had been even closer on its orbit around the sun. She had been a girl then, and had heard on the radio the famous broadcast of *The War of the Worlds*. An actor named Orson Welles had made a radio drama based on a story about Martians attacking the world, but he had presented it in a series of news bulletins and reports, and a lot of people had believed it was true.

Harriet listened to Mrs. Pond and sipped her cocoa and stared at the earth's closest neighbor and felt deliciously chilly and warm at the same time. Mars was wonderfully clear in the telescope, but even with the naked eye she could imagine canals and raging storms. She knew there weren't really Martians, but she allowed herself to imagine them, anyway. She imagined one of them preparing for his invasion of the earth, packing his laser gun, a thermos of cocoa, and a folding chair.

"What in heaven's name is this?" Ms. Krensky was standing at Harriet's chair, staring down at the green bristol board. There was only one planet left. "Harriet says it's Mars." Darjit started giggling.

"And how big is Mars?" asked Ms. Krensky. Her eyes said Unsatisfactory.

"Compared to Kevin's marble earth, Mars would be the size of a pomegranate seed, including the juicy red pulp," said Harriet. Ms. Krensky walked to the front of the class. She turned at her desk. Was there the hint of a smile on her face?

"And where is it?" she asked, raising an eyebrow.

Harriet looked at the calculations she had done on a corner of the green bristol board. "If the sun was at the crosswalk," said Harriet, "then Mars would be much closer. Over there." She pointed out the window at the slide in the kindergarten playground. Some of the class actually looked out the window to see if they could see it.

"You *can* see Mars," said Harriet. "Sometimes." Now she was sure she saw Ms. Krensky smile.

"How many of you have seen Mars?" the teacher asked. Only Harriet and Randy Pilcher put up their hands. But Randy had only seen it on the movie *Total Recall*.

"Last night was a special night, I believe," said Ms. Krensky, crossing her arms and leaning against her desk. Harriet nodded. "Tell us about it, Harriet," said the teacher.

So Harriet did. She told them all about Mrs. Pond and the Mars watch. She started with the pomegranate.

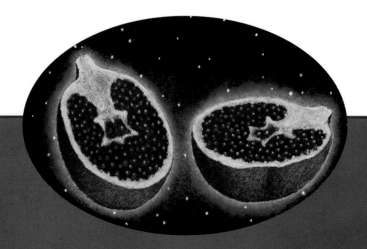

Eugenie Clark
Adventures of a Shark Scientist
by Ellen R. Butts and Joyce R. Schwartz

Dr. Eugenie Clark

At the age of nine, Genie Clark discovered her love of fish while visiting the New York Aquarium. The gift of a fish tank from her mother started Genie raising fish; later she earned a zoology degree in college. After founding the Cape Haze Marine Laboratory in Florida, Dr. Clark established herself as a shark expert. Her research took her to many countries, including Mexico, where she investigated the mysterious "sleeping sharks" of the Yucatan Peninsula.

During the 1970s, Genie became famous for her work on the mysterious "sleeping" sharks and the Moses sole, a type of sandfish. Later, much of her research focused on other sandfish like the sand tilefish and the sandperch. She even co-authored a children's book about them called *The Desert Beneath the Sea*.

Genie Clark swims next to a "sleeping" hooked bull shark.

In 1972, a friend of Genie's, who was a diver and underwater photographer, sent her some pictures of sharks taken in caves off Mexico's Yucatan Peninsula. These large fast-swimming sharks were behaving in a very strange way — they were crowded into the caves and appeared to be sleeping. Usually, fast-swimming sharks need to keep moving in order to "breathe" by pushing oxygen-rich water over their gills. Mexican divers reported seeing several species "sleeping" in the caves — lemon, ridge-backed, and bull sharks. All of these are normally fast swimmers that can be dangerous to human beings. Yet as long as they stayed in the caves, they remained in a trance-like state and didn't even react when divers handled them.

Genie was curious to see these "sleeping" sharks for herself. With funding from private grants and the Mexican government, she was able to make several trips to the Yucatan Peninsula. She first saw the sharks in 1973, when she, her student Anita, and her daughter Aya swam into a cave where they found sharks lying on the floor in a dazed state. Their eyes were open and they watched the divers, but they didn't react. One female, Genie noticed, "stood still as if for inspection. . . . Her eyes were open. . . . Her mouth opened and closed rhythmically." What was the explanation for this strange behavior?

Genie eventually made ninety-nine dives to visit sharks in three different caves. She and her assistants discovered several interesting features of the caves. Fresh water apparently seeped into them from the mainland. The seepage caused the cave water to be less salty than sea water and changed the *electromagnetic field* inside the caves. Cave water also contained higher amounts of both oxygen and carbon dioxide than did sea water.

Dr. Clark observes a remora attached to a hooked shark.

Genie noticed that remoras, tiny fish that travel with sharks and eat parasites on their skin and gills, were giving the sharks a careful cleaning in the caves. From her experience raising fish as a child, she remembered that a salt-water bath helped remove parasites from her fresh-water fish. Since sharks live in salt water, the fresh water in the caves probably helped weaken and loosen the parasites from their skin, making them easier for the remoras to remove. Genie thought the sharks might be smart enough to use the caves as "cleaning stations." Some of her assistants wondered if changes in the electromagnetic field in the caves caused the sharks to become euphoric, which felt good, or if the increased amount of carbon dioxide acted as an anesthetic and made them relax. "Sleeping" sharks were later found in caves off the coast of Japan. Genie was so intrigued by the sharks' behavior that she made many trips to both Mexico and Japan to study them. But the mystery of the "sleeping" sharks is still unsolved.

Genie first saw the Moses sole in 1960 when she traveled to the Red Sea to study garden eels. The sole is a flatfish, related to flounders. According to legend, the Moses sole was created when Moses parted the Red Sea. A fish was cut in half. Each half became a new fish — a Moses sole. With its speckled top and white underside, it lies camouflaged on the sandy bottom of the Red Sea, hidden from its enemies. But it has another defense against predators. The first time Genie touched a Moses sole, she noticed a milky, slippery fluid oozing from pores along its fins. The fluid made her fingers feel tingly and numb, and Genie wondered what other effects it might have. A scientific report from 1871 had described the milky fluid, but she didn't have a chance to investigate further until 1972, 100 years later.

When Genie tested the fluid on sea urchins, sea stars, and reef fishes, she found that small doses killed these creatures quickly. Then she tried baiting a line with a live Moses sole and placing it in a tank with several sharks. The sharks rushed toward the little fish with their mouths opened wide, but stopped a few feet away. Their jaws seemed frozen open and they

Dr. Clark and an assistant catch a sole in the Red Sea.

jerked quickly away, shaking their heads frantically from side to side. Genie also tried the same experiment in the open sea on free-swimming sharks. She baited an eighty-foot shark line with several kinds of fish, including a Moses sole. As she and her assistants snorkeled nearby and watched, hungry sharks devoured all the fish except the sole. Then Genie wiped the skin of the Moses sole with alcohol to remove the poison and threw the fish back into the water. It was instantly swallowed by a shark.

During her years at Cape Haze, Genie was often approached by people who claimed to have invented a shark repellent, but none of them

Dr. Clark examines a Moses sole.

actually worked. She once tested an electrical repellent designed by a group of engineers. When she hung the gadget in the shark pen at the Lab and turned it on, all of the sharks were attracted and came over to investigate the strange box! The poison of the Moses sole, however, turned out to be a powerful shark repellent. Genie found that a tiny amount kept sharks away for more than a day. She originally hoped to turn the poison into an effective commercial shark repellent, but it had a drawback: The chemical compound broke down quickly at room temperature. The poison could not be sold for general use. Later, Genie decided there was no need to develop a shark repellent, since people are much more dangerous to sharks than sharks are to people.

Besides poison, the Moses sole makes another chemical that interests scientists. A student of Genie's discovered that the sole protects itself from its own poison by making an *antidote*. In tests, the antidote also worked against scorpion, bee, and snake venom. But it couldn't be used to protect humans because to be effective, it needed to be injected into the blood at the same time as the poison. Later, Genie discovered that the peacock sole, which lives far from the Red Sea near southern Japan, makes a similar poison and antidote.

Dr. Clark poses inside the jawbone of a
great white shark (British Museum, London).

In addition to her research with sharks, Dr. Clark has
studied various kinds of fish and their behaviors. She is also
an accomplished deep-sea diver and a spokesperson for ocean
conservation. Although she has retired from her university
post, she remains active in her research and encourages
young people, especially girls, to study science.

Think and Compare

The Night of the Pomegranate

by Tim Wynne-Jones

Eugenie Clark

by Ellen R. Butts & Joyce R. Schwartz

Franklin R. Chang-Díaz

Out There

by Theodore Taylor
illustrated by Rob Bolster

1. How is Harriet's love of Mars similar to Eugenie Clark's interest in fish? In what ways are their interests unusual?

2. What traits do Franklin Chang-Diaz and Eugenie Clark have in common? Which traits do you think are most important to becoming an explorer of new frontiers?

3. How are the environments described in *The Adventures of Sojourner* and *Beneath Blue Waters* similar? Which frontier do you think will be easier to explore? Why?

4. Compare Harriet to Danny in "Out There." In what ways are the characters in the two selections alike and different?

5. How have the two new selections added to your feelings about the new frontiers? About people exploring the oceans and space?

Strategies in Action Tell about two or three different reading strategies you used to help you understand your reading during this theme.

Explaining

Write an Explanation

How would you explain the importance of the exploration of the oceans and space to someone who doesn't know much about it? Write a brief explanation, using information you have learned in this theme.

Tips

• **Start with a heading that clearly states your purpose.**

• **Support your explanation with a sincere and polite tone.**

Writing a Persuasive Essay

You may take a test that asks you to persuade a particular audience to agree with you about a specific topic. Read this sample test prompt. Then use the steps when you write a persuasive essay.

> Write an essay to persuade people to support scientific efforts to explore the ocean.

1 Read the prompt.

Find the key words that tell the topic and the kind of writing. Restate in your own words what you need to do. Decide what to write about.

2 Explore and plan.

Brainstorm reasons and details to support your goal. Organize your reasons and details in a chart.

Here is a good example of a planning chart.

Goal: People should support scientific efforts to explore the ocean.	
Reasons	**Facts and Examples**
1. last frontier on Earth	1. so much ocean left to explore
2. new discoveries	2. Alvin finds life in unexpected places
3. expensive	3. each mission needs many people, preparation, expensive machines

③ Write your paper.

Draft your persuasive essay. Follow the chart you made. Revise your paper. Look for places to add exact words and details. Proofread your essay to correct errors.

Let's Explore the Ocean

Do you want to learn about animals that no one has ever seen? Do you want to see places that no one has ever seen? If so, you should support scientific efforts to explore the oceans. Oceans are the last frontier on Earth. With all the things we can do, we still can't explore the deepest parts of the ocean. I wonder what is down there. Do you?

Glossary

Visit www.eduplace.com for
e • Glossary and *e* • Word Game.

This glossary contains meanings and pronunciations for some of the words in this book. The Full Pronunciation Key shows how to pronounce each consonant and vowel in a special spelling. At the bottom of the glossary pages is a shortened form of the full key.

Full Pronunciation Key

Consonant Sounds

b	**bib**, ca**bb**age	kw	**ch**oir, **qu**ick	t	**t**igh**t**, stopp**ed**
ch	**ch**ur**ch**, sti**tch**	l	**l**id, need**l**e, ta**ll**	th	ba**th**, **th**in
d	**d**ee**d**, mail**ed**, pu**dd**le	m	a**m**, **m**an, du**mb**	*th*	ba**the**, **th**is
		n	**n**o, sudd**en**	v	ca**v**e, val**v**e, **v**ine
f	**f**ast, **f**i**f**e, o**ff**, **ph**rase, rou**gh**	ng	thi**ng**, i**n**k	w	**w**ith, **w**olf
		p	**p**op, ha**pp**y	y	**y**es, **y**olk, on**i**on
g	**g**a**g**, **g**et, fin**g**er	r	**r**oa**r**, **rh**yme	z	ro**s**e, si**z**e, **x**ylophone, **z**ebra
h	**h**at, **wh**o	s	mi**ss**, **s**au**c**e, **sc**ene, **s**ee	zh	gara**g**e, plea**s**ure, vi**s**ion
hw	**wh**ich, **wh**ere				
j	**j**ud**g**e, **g**em	sh	di**sh**, **sh**ip, **s**ugar, ti**ss**ue		
k	**c**at, **k**i**ck**, s**ch**ool				

Vowel Sounds

ă	p**a**t, l**au**gh	ŏ	h**o**rrible, p**o**t	ŭ	c**u**t, fl**oo**d, r**ou**gh, s**o**me
ā	**a**pe, **ai**d, p**ay**	ō	g**o**, r**ow**, t**oe**, th**ough**	û	c**i**rcle, f**u**r, h**ear**d, t**er**m, t**u**rn, **u**rge, w**or**d
â	**ai**r, c**a**re, w**ea**r	ô	**a**ll, c**augh**t, f**or**, p**aw**		
ä	f**a**ther, k**o**ala, y**a**rd	oi	b**oy**, n**oi**se, **oi**l		
ĕ	p**e**t, pl**ea**sure, **a**ny	ou	c**ow**, **ou**t	yo͝o	c**u**re
ē	b**e**, b**ee**, **ea**sy, p**ia**no	o͝o	f**u**ll, b**oo**k, w**o**lf	yo͞o	ab**u**se, **u**se
ĭ	**i**f, p**i**t, b**u**sy	o͞o	b**oo**t, r**u**de, fr**ui**t, fl**ew**	ə	**a**go, sil**e**nt, penc**i**l, lem**o**n, circ**u**s
ī	r**i**de, b**y**, p**ie**, h**igh**				
î	d**ear**, d**eer**, f**ie**rce, m**ere**				

Stress Marks

Primary Stress ´: bi·ol·o·gy [bī **ŏl´** ə jē]
Secondary Stress ´: bi·o·log·i·cal [bī´ ə **lŏj´** ĭ kəl]

Pronunciation key and definitions © 1998 by Houghton Mifflin Company. Adapted and reprinted by permission from *The American Heritage Children's Dictionary*.

A

a·ban·doned (ə **băn´** dənd) *adj.* Permanently left behind; deserted. *A colony of squirrels is living in the abandoned house.*

ab·stract (ăb **străkt´**, ăb´ străkt´) *adj.* Not representing a recognizable image. *People enjoy abstract art for its colors and forms.*

ac·ces·si·ble (ăk **sĕs´** ə bəl) *adj.* Affordable; easy to get. *The silver bowls are very expensive, but the stainless steel ones are accessible to most customers.*

ac·com·plish (ə **kŏm´** plĭsh) *v.* To succeed in doing something. *Her education will help her accomplish great things.*

ac·count·ant (ə **koun´** tənt) *n.* Someone trained to keep the financial records of a business. *The accountant figured out how much money the company owed in taxes.*

ac·count·ing (ə **kount´** ĭng) *n.* A detailed narrative; a record of events. *For several days, the newspaper gave a detailed accounting of destruction from the hurricane.*

a·dorn (ə **dôrn´**) *v.* To decorate. *The Hawaiians adorned their visitors with garlands of beautiful flowers.*

aer·o·nau·tics (âr´ ə **nô´** tĭks) *n.* The design and construction of aircraft. *The person in charge of our rocket experiments has vast knowledge of aeronautics.*

af·ter·deck (**ăf´** tər dĕk´) *n.* The part of a ship's deck near the rear. *The passengers stood on the afterdeck, watching the island disappear.*

a·nal·y·sis (ə **năl´** ĭ sĭs) *n., pl.* **analyses** (ə **năl´** ĭ sēs) The separation of a substance into its parts in order to study each part. *A high-powered microscope was used for an analysis of the virus.*

ap·pli·cant (**ăp´** lĭ kənt) *n.* A person who requests employment or acceptance. *There were six applicants for the shipping clerk job.*

as·cent (ə **sĕnt´**) *n.* An upward climb. *The ascent to the mountain's summit took two days.*

as·tro·naut (**ăs´** trə nôt´) *n.* A person trained to fly in a spacecraft. *Sally Ride was the first American female astronaut in space.*

at·ten·tion (ə **tĕn´** shən) *n.* Close or careful observing or listening. *The tour guide asked the group to give her their full attention.*

a·vi·a·tion (ā´ vē **ā´** shən, ăv´ ē **ā´** shən) *n.* The operation of aircraft. *The history of aviation goes back to the days of hot air balloons.*

awk·ward (**ôk´** wərd) *adj.* Uncomfortable. *Roger felt awkward when he realized that everyone else had worn nice clothes to the party.*

astronaut

aviation
French speakers in the nineteenth century created a word for the operation of aircraft from the Latin word *avis,* which means "bird."

ōo b**oo**t / ou **ou**t / ŭ c**u**t / û f**u**r / hw **wh**ich / th **th**in / *th* **th**is / zh vi**si**on / ə **a**go, sil**e**nt, penc**i**l, lem**o**n, circ**u**s

B

bartering
Our modern meaning for the word *barter* comes from the old French word *barater*, which means both "to exchange" and "to deceive."

buoy

bar·ter·ing (bär´ tər ĭng) *n.* The trading of goods without the exchange of money. *By clever **bartering**, the milkmaid got two geese in exchange for the butter.*

be·lay (bĭ lā´) *v.* To secure by means of a rope, in mountain climbing. *To protect themselves, the mountain climbers will **belay** as they climb.* —*adj.* Secured by a rope. *He waited in the **belay** position while the others caught up with him.*

brag (brăg) *v.* To boast. *Nella **bragged** that she was the best basketball player in her class.*

brisk·ly (brĭsk´ lē) *adv.* Quickly, energetically. *The pilot strode **briskly** through the airport to the plane.*

bulk·head (bŭlk´ hĕd´) *n.* One of the walls that divides the cabin of a ship into compartments. *A sailing chart was pinned on the **bulkhead** by the cabin door.*

buoy (bōō´ ē, boi) *n.* An anchored float, often with a bell or light, used on a lake or ocean to mark safe passage or to warn of danger. *Swimmers are told not to swim beyond the harbor **buoy**.*

C

can·vas (kăn´ vəs) *n.* The stiff, heavy fabric on which an artist paints. *Before painting, Emma stretched the **canvas** tightly over a wooden frame.*

car·a·bi·ner (kăr´ ə bē´ nər) *n.* In mountain climbing, an oval ring that attaches to a piton. *The **carabiners** allow ropes to run freely through them.*

car·a·van (kăr´ ə văn´) *n.* A file of vehicles or pack animals traveling together. *Twenty camels led the **caravan** of spice traders across the desert.*

cause·way (kôz´ wā´) *n.* A raised roadway across water or marshland. *The farmers built **causeways** crossing the fields that flooded in the spring.*

cer·ti·fy (sûr´ tə fī´) *v., pl.* **certifies** Official recognition of a particular skill or function. *Medical technicians are **certified** to provide help in an emergency.*

cheap (chēp) *adj.* Costing very little. *Because she had very little money, Randi bought a **cheap** rubber ball instead of a real baseball.*

com·mon room (kŏm´ ən rōōm) *n.* A large room where people gather to eat or share other activities. *The storyteller drew a crowd in the **common room** after dinner.*

ă rat / ā **pay** / â **care** / ä **father** / ĕ **pet** / ē be / ĭ **pit** / ī **pie** / î **fierce** / ŏ **pot** / ō **go** / ô **paw, for** / oi **oil** / ōō **book**

D

com·mute (kə myo͞ot´) *v.* To travel back and forth regularly. *My aunt and uncle commute from Gilroy to Sunnyvale every day.*

con·cep·tu·al (kən sĕp´ cho͞o əl) *adj.* Having to do with ideas. *A conceptual artist uses a variety of media to communicate an idea.*

con·di·tion·ing (kən dĭsh´ ə nĭng) *adj.* Contributing to the process of becoming physically fit. *The track coach stressed the importance of conditioning drills.*

con·quered (kŏng´ kərd) *adj.* Defeated in battle. *The conquered peoples gave up their treasures to their victorious enemy.*

con·sol·ing (kən sōl´ ĭng) *adj.* Comforting. *Marcia's father gave her a consoling hug after she wrecked her bike.*

con·ver·sa·tion (kŏn´ vər sā´ shən) *n.* A spoken sharing of thoughts between two or more people. *Alexa knows so much about sports that our conversations are always interesting.*

crafts·man (krăfts´ mən) *n., pl.* **craftsmen** A skilled worker. *The work of colonial craftsmen is highly valued today.*

crus·ta·cean (krŭ stā´ shən) *n.* One of a large group of hard-shelled animals that have jointed parts and live mostly in the water. *The lobster is a well-known crustacean.*

day·dream (dā´ drēm´) *v.* To think in a dreamy way, often about things one wishes would come true. *Because Cho was daydreaming, he did not hear my question.*

de·ci·sion (dĭ sĭzh´ ən) *n.* A choice that involves judgment. *Alex's decision was to quit the team.*

dem·on·strate (dĕm´ ən strāt´) *v.* To show clearly. *Mike demonstrates that he has what it takes to become a great pitcher.*

de·pot (dē´ pō, dĕp´ ō) *n.* A railroad station. *Brent arrived at the depot just as the train from Baltimore was pulling in.*

der·e·lict (dĕr´ ə lĭkt´) *n.* A piece of property, usually a ship at sea, that has been deserted by its owner. *A derelict was blown in by the storm and smashed on the rocks.*

des·o·late (dĕs´ ə lĭt, dĕz´ ə lĭt) *adj.* Having few or no inhabitants; deserted. *The car ran out of gas on a desolate stretch of highway.*

des·per·ate (dĕs´ pər ĭt) *adj.* Feeling full of despair, hopeless. *The girl made a desperate plea for someone to save the cat.*

de·ter·mi·na·tion (dĭ tûr´ mə nā´ shən) *n.* The firm intention to accomplish a goal. *The combination of talent and determination enabled Alf to win a medal.*

depot

---

o͞o b**oo**t / ou **ou**t / ŭ c**u**t / û f**u**r / hw **wh**ich / th **th**in / th **th**is / zh vi**si**on / ə **a**go, sil**e**nt, penc**i**l, lem**o**n, circ**u**s

E

dip·lo·mat (dĭp′ lə măt′) *n.* One who is appointed to represent his or her government in its relations with other governments. *Rachel's mother was sent as a diplomat to Brazil.*

dis·ap·pear·ance (dĭs′ ə pîr′ əns) *n.* The state of having vanished. *Lydia was saddened by the disappearance of her pet mouse.*

dis·count (dĭs′ kount, dĭs kount′) *v.* To doubt the truth of something or regard it as a wild exaggeration. *Reference books discount myths about dragons and sea serpents.*

dis·cour·aged (dĭ skûr′ ĭjd, dĭ skŭr′ ĭjd) *adj.* Disheartened; in a low mood because of a disappointment. *Having never won a baseball game, Nathan felt very discouraged.*

do·main (dō mān′) *n.* The territory ruled by a government. *Spain was included in the domain of ancient Rome.*

du·ra·ble (door′ ə bəl, dyoor′ ə bəl) *adj.* Sturdy and long-lasting. *Stone fences are more durable than wooden fences.*

dy·nas·ty (dī′ nə stē) *n., pl.* **dynasties** A line of rulers from one family. *China's ancient Ming dynasty held power for about 300 years.*

em·pire (ĕm′ pīr) *n.* A large area made up of many territories under one government. *The ancient Roman empire once included parts of Great Britain.*

en·cour·age (ĕn kûr′ ĭj, ĕn kŭr′ ĭj) *v.* To give support or confidence. *Effective coaches encourage their players during a game.*

en·deav·or (ĕn dĕv′ ər) *v.* To attempt. *She endeavored to keep her balance on the rocking deck of the ship.*

en·dur·ance (ĕn door′ əns, ĕn dyoor′ əns) *n.* The ability to keep going without giving in to stress or tiredness. *A marathon runner must have exceptional endurance.*

en·gi·neer (ĕn′ jə nîr′) *n.* A person specially trained to design and build machines and systems. *The engineers designed a complex landing system for the spacecraft.*

en·tan·gled (ĕn tăng′ gəld) *adj.* Twisted together. *The kitten's paws became entangled in the yarn.*

en·tou·rage (ŏn′ too räzh′) *n.* A group of followers. *The queen's entourage included both servants and people of high rank.*

e·ro·sion (ĭ rō′ zhən) *n.* All the natural processes that wear away earth and rock. *The erosion of the hillside was caused by heavy rains and wind.*

erosion

ă rat / ā pay / â care / ä father / ĕ pet / ē be / ĭ pit / ī pie / î fierce / ŏ pot / ō go / ô paw, for / oi oil / oo book

F

ev·i·dence (ĕv´ ĭ dəns) *n.* The data used to draw a conclusion. *Scientists studying dinosaurs look at the evidence found in prehistoric bones.*

ex·ca·va·tion (ĕk´ skə vā´ shən) *n.* The process of finding something by digging for it. *A later excavation of the site turned up more fossils.*

ex·clude (ĭk sklōōd´) *v.* To keep someone or something out. *The boys angered the girls by excluding them from the basketball game.*

ex·hi·bi·tion (ĕk´ sə bĭsh´ ən) *n.* A show of an artist's work. *A traveling exhibition of Winslow Homer's work has come to our museum.*

ex·press (ĭk sprĕs´) *v.* To put into words; to communicate. *Toddlers express their feelings through words, noises, and actions.*

ex·tinct (ĭk stĭngkt´) *adj.* No longer living on the earth; having died out. *The passenger pigeon became extinct at the beginning of the twentieth century.*

ex·trav·a·gance (ĭk străv´ ə gəns) *n.* Careless, wasteful spending on luxuries. *Luke's extravagance put him deeply into debt.*

fa·tigue (fə tēg´) *n.* Extreme tiredness. *Her fatigue was so great she wanted to sleep for days.*

fig·u·rine (fĭg´ yə rēn´) *n.* A small molded or sculpted figure. *China figurines of children and dogs were lined up on the windowsill.*

flour·ish·ing (flûr´ ĭsh ĭng, flŭr´ ĭsh ĭng) *adj.* Growing energetically. *After the railroad was built, Greensville became a flourishing community.*

foot·hold (fŏŏt´ hōld´) *n.* A place that gives firm support for a foot while climbing. *The crumbling ledge could not provide a safe foothold.*

fos·sil (fŏs´ əl) *n.* The hardened skeleton or other remains of a creature of prehistoric times. *Dinosaur fossils have been found in many parts of the world.*

frus·tra·tion (frŭ strā´ shən) *n.* The discouragement and irritation that comes from not being able to achieve one's goal. *She felt frustration at not being able to solve the math problem.*

func·tion (fŭngk´ shən) *v.* To fill a particular purpose or role. *The knife functioned as a screwdriver to take the screws out of the clock.*

excavation
For ancient Latin speakers, *excavare* meant to hollow something out. Thus, an excavation is the hollowing out of a space by digging. The English word *cave* is from the same Latin verb.

flourishing
The Latin verb *florere*, meaning "to flower," is the origin of both *flourish* and *flower*.

fossil
Our word *fossil* came from the Latin adjective *fossilis*, meaning "dug up."

ōō b**oo**t / ou **ou**t / ŭ c**u**t / û f**u**r / hw **wh**ich / th **th**in / *th* **th**is / zh vi**si**on / ə **a**go, sil**e**nt, penc**i**l, lem**o**n, circ**u**s

G

humble

Humble has its origins in the Latin word *humus*, meaning "ground."

hatchet

ge·lat·i·nous (jə **lăt´** n əs) *adj.* Like gelatin; thick and slow to flow. *Tapioca pudding has a lumpy, gelatinous texture.*

ge·ol·o·gist (jē **ŏl´** ə jĭst) *n.* A scientist who studies the earth's crust and the rocks it is made of. *Rocks can tell geologists a lot about how the earth changed in a particular place.*

goods (gŏŏdz) *n.* Items for sale. *The small store sold fabric, boots, farm tools, and other useful goods.*

gov·ern·ment (**gŭv´** ərn mənt) *n.* The body or organization that manages a nation. *Our government sent representatives to Australia to discuss trade regulations.*

H

hatch·et (**hăch´** ĭt) *n.* A small, short-handled ax, to be used with only one hand. *A hatchet is useful for cutting firewood.*

hearth (härth) *n.* The floor of a fireplace, which usually extends into a room. *Julia sat by the wide brick hearth and warmed her hands.*

hov·er (**hŭv´** ər, **hŏv´** ər) *v.* To remain close by. *Helicopters hovered above the freeways so reporters could check the traffic conditions.*

hum·ble (**hŭm´** bəl) *adj.* Not rich or important. *The humble workers could not afford luxury items.*

hy·per·re·al·is·tic (hī´ pər rē ə **lĭs´** tĭk) *adj.* Extremely real-looking. *Many hyperrealistic paintings look exactly like photographs.*

hy·poth·e·sis (hī **pŏth´** ĭ sĭs´) *n., pl.* **hypotheses** (hī **pŏth´** ĭ sēz´) A scientific suggestion based on what is known so far. *Ideas remain hypotheses until evidence proves that they are true.*

I

ice ax (īs ăks) *n.* An ax used by mountain climbers to cut into the ice. *Jennifer hacked at the cliff with her ice ax.*

im·pro·vise (**ĭm´** prə vīz´) *v.* To make something from available materials. *When it began to rain, the hikers improvised a tent out of plastic garbage bags.*

in·quir·y (ĭn **kwĭr´** ē, **ĭn´** kwə rē) *n., pl.* **inquiries** A request for information. *The park ranger received many inquiries about campsites.*

in·spi·ra·tion (ĭn´ spə **rā´** shən) *n.* A positive example that encourages others to attempt to reach their goals. *Her success in college is an inspiration to her younger sisters.*

ă rat / ā pay / â care / ä father / ĕ pet / ē be / ĭ pit / ī pie / î fierce / ŏ pot / ō go / ô paw, for / oi oil / ŏŏ book

in·ter·fer·ing (ĭn´ tər **fîr´** ĭng) *adj.* Intruding in the business of other people; meddling. *Kara did not ask why her brother was crying, because she didn't want to seem to be **interfering**.*

in·ter·pret (ĭn **tûr´** prĭt) *v.* To determine or explain the meaning of something. *She **interpreted** the lab data to draw conclusions about the experiment.*

in·tri·cate (**ĭn´** trĭ kĭt) *adj.* Complicated; made up of many details. *The bracelet has an **intricate** design.*

J

jour·nal (**jûr´** nəl) *n.* A personal record of events; a diary. *Angela wrote about her vacation in her **journal**.*

K

kay·ak (**kī´** ăk´) *n.* A lightweight canoe, propelled by a double-bladed paddle, with a small opening for one or two people. *The girls paddled the **kayak** across the bay.*

kin·dling (**kĭnd´** lĭng) *n.* Small pieces of wood or other material used for starting fires. *A big log won't catch fire unless **kindling** is burning below it.*

L

lab·o·ra·to·ry (**lăb´** rə tôr´ ē, **lăb´** rə tōr´ ē) *n., pl.* **laboratories** A room or building equipped for scientific research or experiments. *She works in a **laboratory** where blood cells are analyzed.*

la·bor·er (**lā´** bər ər) *n.* A worker who does tasks that do not require special skills. *The managers of the mines hired many **laborers**.*

ledg·er (**lĕj´** ər) *n.* A book in which financial records are kept. *The **ledgers** show how much the business has paid its employees.*

M

main·land (**mān´** lănd´, **mān´** lənd) *n.* The large land mass of a country or continent that does not include its islands. *Hawaiians refer to the rest of the United States as the **mainland**.*

make·shift (**māk´** shĭft´) *adj.* Used as a substitute for something. *The pioneer mother used a bureau drawer as a **makeshift** crib for the new baby.*

man·age (**măn´** ĭj) *v.* To succeed in doing something with difficulty. *Rolf **managed** to finish the race even though he turned his ankle near the end.*

kayak

ōō b**oo**t / ou **ou**t / ŭ **cu**t / û f**u**r / hw **wh**ich / th **th**in / *th* **th**is / zh vi**si**on / ə **a**go, sil**e**nt, penc**i**l, lem**o**n, circ**u**s

meticulous
Perhaps Latin speakers of long ago lived in fear of making mistakes, for this adjective comes from the Latin word *meticulosus*, meaning "fearful."

metropolis
The ancient Greeks combined their words for *mother* and *city* to form *metropolis*, a word they used to describe the first settlement in a colony.

navigation, navigator
The Latin word *navis*, meaning "ship," and the word *agere*, meaning "to drive," were combined to form the Latin verb *navigare*, "to navigate."

ma·neu·ver (mə noo´ vər, mə nyoo´ vər) *n.* A controlled change in the movement or direction of a vehicle. *Beginning drivers practice maneuvers for getting into tight parking spaces.*

mas·sive (măs´ ĭv) *adj.* Large and solid. *Redwoods are massive trees.*

me·nag·er·ie (mə năj´ ə rē, mə năzh´ ə rē) *n.* A collection of wild animals. *The veterinarian attended to a menagerie of wounded animals at the wildlife shelter.*

me·thod·i·cal·ly (mə thŏd´ ĭ kə lē, mə thŏd´ ĭk lē´) *adv.* In a careful, orderly way. *She methodically searched through her books for the facts she needed.*

me·tic·u·lous (mĭ tĭk´ yə ləs) *adj.* Extremely careful and exact. *His meticulous lettering made the poster easy to read.*

me·trop·o·lis (mĭ trŏp´ ə lĭs) *n.* A major city; a center of culture. *Being a transportation center has made Chicago a great metropolis.*

mon·i·tor (mŏn´ ĭ tər) *v.* To supervise; to keep watch over. *The fire chief monitored the rescue operation.*

N

nav·i·ga·tion (năv´ ĭ gā´ shən) *n.* The practice of planning and controlling the course of a craft. *The captain's skill at navigation brought the ship safely through the storm.*

nav·i·ga·tor (năv´ ĭ gā´ tər) *n.* Someone who plans, records, and controls the course of a ship or plane. *The navigator plotted a course across the Pacific Ocean.*

no·mad·ic (nō măd´ ĭk) *adj.* Moving from place to place. *Nomadic shepherds often move their sheep to new grazing lands.*

no·tice (nō´ tĭs) *v.* To become aware of. *People will notice the colorful balloons tied to the stair railing.*

O

o·a·sis (ō ā´ sĭs) *n., pl.* **oases** (ō ā´ sēz) A green spot in a desert, where water can be found. *The travelers rested at the oasis and watered their camels at its spring.*

ob·sta·cle (ŏb´ stə kəl) *n.* Something that makes it difficult to continue. *His sisters' loud music and his lack of privacy were obstacles to serious studying.*

o·cean·og·ra·pher (ō´ shə nŏg´ rə fər) *n.* A scientist who specializes in the study of the sea. *Both oceanographers are interested in undersea volcanoes.*

ă rat / ā pay / â care / ä father / ĕ pet / ē be / ĭ pit / ī pie / î fierce / ŏ pot / ō go / ô paw, for / oi oil / oo book

op·ti·cal·ly (ŏp´ tĭk ə lē, ŏp´ tĭk lē) *adv.* Having to do with vision. *As I stared at the painting, the colors blended **optically** into a vivid swirl.*

o·ver·come (ō´ vər kŭm´) *v.* To conquer. *She has **overcome** her fear of heights.*

P

pains·tak·ing (pānz´ tā´ kĭng) *adj.* Requiring great and careful effort. *Repairing watches is **painstaking** work.*

pa·le·on·tol·o·gist (pā´ lē ŏn tŏl´ ə jĭst) *n.* A scientist who studies prehistoric life. *A **paleontologist** compares the bones of dinosaurs to those of modern animals.*

pal·ette (păl´ ĭt) *n.* A board on which an artist mixes colors. *Austin squeezed dabs of white and blue paint onto his **palette**.*

per·mis·sion (pər mĭsh´ ən) *n.* Necessary approval to do some-thing. *The travelers need official **permission** to cross the border.*

per·mit·ted (pər mĭt´ əd) *adj.* Allowed. *Swimming is **permitted** from sunrise to sunset at Howe's Beach.* —*n.* A person who is allowed to do something. *Only **permitteds** can go past the gate.*

phase (fāz) *n.* One of the changes in appearance that the moon or a planet goes through each month. *The moon looks like a half circle in one of its **phases**.*

phys·ics (fĭz´ ĭks) *n.* The science of matter and energy and of how they relate to one another. *You can use simple **physics** to predict how soon a falling object will hit the ground.*

pi·ton (pē´ tŏn´) *n.* A metal spike, used in mountain climbing, with an eye or ring at one end. *The mountain climber's standard gear includes **pitons**.*

pix·el (pĭk´ səl, pĭk sĕl´) *n.* One of the tiny elements that make up an image on a TV or computer screen. *In computer drawing programs, widths of lines are measured in **pixels**.*

por·trait (pôr´ trĭt, pôr´ trāt) *n.* A drawing, painting, or photograph of a person. *A **portrait** of the first mayor of Centervale hangs in the lobby of the town hall.*

port (pôrt´) *n.* The left side of a ship as one faces forward. *A small rowboat pulled up on the **port** side of the ship.*

pre·vi·ous (prē´ vē əs) *adj.* Occurring before something else in time or order. *The professor had explained the rule in a **previous** lecture.*

pri·mar·y (prī´ mĕr´ ē, prī´ mə rē) *adj.* Main; basic. *The club's **primary** purpose is to welcome new students.*

palette

palette
In Old French, *pale* was the word for a shovel or spade. A palette, then, was a small shovel.

pixel
The word *pixel* was created around 1969 by combining the word *pix* (short for *pictures*) and the first syllable of the word *elements*.

---

o͞o b**oo**t / ou **ou**t / ŭ c**u**t / û f**u**r / hw **wh**ich / th **th**in / *th* **th**is / zh vi**si**on / ə **a**go, sil**e**nt, penc**i**l, lem**o**n, circ**u**s

651

pro·vi·sions (prə **vĭzh´** ənz) *n.* Necessary supplies, especially food. *The hikers had enough* **provisions** *for only one more day of camping.*

Q

qual·i·fi·ca·tion (kwŏl´ ə fĭ **kā´** shən) *n.* A skill or other trait that suits a person for a particular job or activity. *What* **qualifications** *are needed to join the Peace Corps?*

quill (kwĭl) *n.* One of a collection of sharp, hollow spines on the back of a porcupine. *It isn't true that porcupines can shoot their* **quills** *at their attackers.*

quills

quill

R

rat·line (**răt´** līn) *n.* One of the small ropes, fastened horizontally to ropes supporting a ship's mast, which together form a ladder. *A large seabird perched on one of the* **ratlines** *of the ship.*

ref·u·gee (rĕf´ yoo **jē´**) *n.* A person who flees his or her home in order to escape harm. *Many* **refugees** *escaped from Cuba in small boats.*

rel·e·gate (**rĕl´** ĭ gāt´) *v.* To put in a less important place. *Her least favorite clothes were* **relegated** *to the back of the closet.*

re·lieve (rĭ **lēv´**) *v.* To aid, to help. *A cool washcloth might* **relieve** *the pain of your headache.*

re·set·tling (rē´ **sĕt´** əl ĭng) *n.* The process of moving to a new place. *I have been watching the raccoon family's recent* **resettling** *in the tree next door.*

rig·ging (**rĭg´** ĭng) *n.* The system of ropes, chains, and other gear used to control a ship's sails. *A good sailor had to be able to climb the* **rigging** *like a rat.*

rock·et·ry (**rŏk´** ĭ trē) *n.* The science of designing, building, and flying rockets. *His knowledge of* **rocketry** *led to a job in the NASA space program.*

rov·er (**rō´** vər) *n.* A vehicle designed to explore the surface of a planet. *The* **rover** *rolled down the ramp of the spacecraft and onto the Martian soil.*

run·way (**rŭn´** wā´) *n.* A strip of level ground where airplanes take off and land. *The plane sped down the* **runway** *and rose into the air.*

S

sea·soned (**sē´** zənd) *adj.* Experienced. *After four months at sea, Mario felt like a* **seasoned** *sailor.*

rover

The Middle English verb *roven* meant "to shoot arrows at a mark." From this origin came the English verb *rove,* meaning "to roam or wander."

ă **rat** / ā **pay** / â **care** / ä **father** / ĕ **pet** / ē **be** / ĭ **pit** / ī **pie** / î **fierce** / ŏ **pot** / ō **go** / ô **paw, for** / oi **oil** / oo **book**

sen·sor (sĕn´ sər, sĕn´ sôr) *n.* A sensitive device that responds to changes in the environment. *The toy's electronic **sensors** kept it from bumping into the wall.*

ses·sion (sĕsh´ ən) *n.* A gathering held for a special purpose. *The cheerleaders hold their practice **sessions** after school.*

shel·ter (shĕl´ tər) *n.* A place that provides protection from the weather. *They found a cave to use for a **shelter**.*

sim·u·late (sĭm´ yə lāt´) *v.* To pretend in an imitation of something. *The computer program lets users **simulate** driving on a real highway.*

site (sīt) *n.* The place where things were, are, or will be located. *Diggers have turned up old pottery at several **sites**.*

slith·er·ing (slĭth´ ər ĭng) *n.* A sliding, slipping movement. *The rustling noise was made by the **slithering** of a snake. —adj.* Slipping and sliding. *A **slithering** movement in the grass caught his attention.*

sod (sŏd) *n.* A chunk of grassy soil held together by matted roots. *Pioneers sometimes built their houses out of **sod** where trees were scarce.*

spar·kling (spär´ klĭng) *adj.* Giving off flashes of light. ***Sparkling** fireflies darted across the dark lawn.*

spec·i·men (spĕs´ ə mən) *n.* A sample taken for scientific study. *The **specimens** of pond water were full of tiny creatures.*

sprint (sprĭnt) *n.* A short race run at top speed. *Runners don't have to pace themselves when they run **sprints**.*

squad (skwŏd) *n.* A small group of people organized for an activity. *Antonio hopes to become a member of the football **squad**.*

steppe (stĕp) *n.* A vast dry, grassy plain. *Very little rain falls on a **steppe**.*

ster·e·o·scop·ic (stĕr´ ē ə skŏp´ ĭk, stîr´ ē ə skŏp´ ĭk) *adj.* Seeing objects in three dimensions. *Human beings have **stereoscopic** vision.*

stoop (sto͞op) *n.* A small porch, staircase, or platform leading to the entrance of a house or building. *Our family sits on the **stoop** of our building on warm nights.*

sub·mers·i·ble (səb mûr´ sə bəl) *n.* A craft that operates underwater. *The **submersible** carried a camera into the depths of the ocean.*

sub·tle (sŭt´ l) *adj.* Not obvious; hard to detect. *The waiter's gesture was so **subtle** that none of the diners noticed it.*

su·pe·ri·or (so͞o pîr´ ē ər) *n.* One who has higher rank and more authority. *The worker took orders from his **superiors**.*

slithering
A shift in pronunciation over the centuries turned the Old English word *slidrian* ("to slide" or "to slip") into *slither*.

sparkling
In the thirteenth century, to say that something was sparkling was to say that it gave off sparks.

specimen
The word *specimen* comes from the Latin word *specere*, which means "to look at."

squad
A Latin slang word for "square" may have inspired the medieval Italians to use the word *squadra* to refer to a group of soldiers marching in square formation.

o͞o b**oo**t / ou **ou**t / ŭ c**u**t / û f**u**r / hw **wh**ich / th **th**in / th **th**is / zh vi**si**on / ə **a**go, sil**e**nt, penc**i**l, lem**o**n, circ**u**s

sur·viv·al (sər **vī**´ vəl) *n.* The preservation of one's life; the continuing of life. *An injury lessens an animal's chance of* **survival***.*

sus·pi·cious (sə **spĭsh**´ əs) *adj.* Having the feeling that something unusual or wrong is going on. *The long silence in the children's room made their mother* **suspicious***.*

T

tax·i (**tăk**´ sē) *v.* To move slowly on the ground before taking off or after landing. *The plane* **taxied** *to a halt at the end of the runway.*

ten·ta·cle (**tĕn**´ tə kəl) *n.* One of the long, elastic, narrow limbs of an animal, used to feel, grasp, or move. *An octopus uses its* **tenta-cles** *to hold its prey.*

ter·rain (tə **rān**´) *n.* The physical features of an area of land. *The rugged* **terrain** *of the desert discourages travelers.*

ter·ri·fy (**tĕr**´ ə fī´) *v.* To frighten. *The howls of the mountain lion* **terrified** *the camper.*

the·o·ry (**thē**´ ə rē, **thîr**´ ē) *n., pl.* **theories** An idea that is based on evidence but that cannot be stated as fact. *In the 1860s, Joseph Lister published his* **theory** *that unseen germs cause infections.*

trans·mis·sion (trăns **mĭsh**´ ən, trănz **mĭsh**´ ən) *n.* A message sent by radio. *The tornado interrupted the* **transmission** *from the research station.*

treach·er·ous (**trĕch**´ ər əs) *adj.* Marked by unpredictable dangers. *A narrow ledge provided a* **treacherous** *path up the mountainside.*

trib·ute (**trĭb**´ yo͞ot) *n.* A gift given to those in power by people who have been defeated or who want protection. *Each year* **tributes** *of gold and spices were sent to the capital city from all over the kingdom.*

trin·ket (**trĭng**´ kĭt) *n.* A small item of little value. *For her son's sixth birthday party, Ana decorated the room with strings of beads, toy horns, and other* **trinkets***.*

U

un·con·ven·tion·al (ŭn´ kən **vĕn**´ shə nəl) *adj.* Out of the ordinary. *Nowadays, wearing an old-fashioned top hat is* **unconventional***.*

un·du·late (**ŭn**´ jə lāt´, **ŭn**´ dyə lāt´) *v.* To move in a smooth, wavy motion. *Tall grass* **undulates** *when a breeze blows over it.*

un·fath·om·a·ble (ŭn **făth**´ ə mə bəl) *adj.* Impossible to measure. *In mid-ocean the sea floor lies at* **unfathomable** *depths.*

tentacle

treacherous
This adjective comes from the Old French verb *trichier,* meaning "to trick." If something is treacherous, or marked by unpredictable dangers, it may also be said to be tricky.

ă rat / ā pay / â care / ä father / ĕ pet / ē be / ĭ pit / ī pie / î fierce / ŏ pot / ō go / ô paw, for / oi oil / o͞o book

654

ur·gen·cy (ûr´ jən sē) *n., pl.*
urgencies The need to do something quickly. *When Vikash
asked for a ride to the hospital,
there was a sense of **urgency** to
his voice.*

V

vi·cin·i·ty (vĭ sĭn´ ĭ tē) *n., pl.*
vicinities The region within
close range of a particular place.
*The middle school is in the **vicinity** of Lincoln Park.*

vil·lage (vĭl´ ĭj) *n.* A small settlement. *There are thirty houses in
the mountain **village**.*

vi·sa (vē´ zə) *n., pl.* **visas** A
document that gives a person
approval to travel through a specific country. *Most tourists need
visas as well as passports to travel through Russia.*

vis·i·bil·i·ty (vĭz´ ə bĭl´ ĭ tē) *n., pl.*
visibilities The greatest distance
over which it is possible to see.
*When the fog rolled in, **visibility**
was limited to a few yards.*

vol·un·teer (vŏl´ ən tîr´) *n.* A
person who freely offers to do
something. *Our clubhouse was
built by **volunteers**.*

W

ware (wâr) *n.* An item for sale.
*The rug merchants displayed
their **wares** at the street fair.*

village

visa

ōō b**oo**t / ou **ou**t / ŭ c**u**t / û f**u**r / hw **wh**ich / th **th**in / *th* **th**is / zh vi**si**on / ə **a**go,
sil**e**nt, penc**i**l, lem**o**n, circ**u**s

Acknowledgments

Main Literature Selections

Selection from *The Adventures of Sojourner: The Mission to Mars That Thrilled the World,* by Susi Trautmann Wunsch. Copyright © 1998 by Susi Trautmann Wunsch. Reprinted by permission of the publisher, Mikaya Press Inc.

Selection from *Amelia Earhart: First Lady of Flight,* by Jan Parr. Copyright © 1997 by Jan Parr. Reprinted by permission of Franklin Watts, a division of Grolier Publishing.

Selection from *Beneath Blue Waters: Meetings with Remarkable Deep-Sea Creatures,* by Deborah Kovacs and Kate Madin, principal photographs by Larry Madin. Copyright © 1996 by Deborah Kovacs and Kate Madin. Reprinted by permission of Viking Children's Books, a division of Penguin Putnam Inc.

Selections from *The Buried City of Pompeii,* a Hyperion/ Madison Press Book by Shelley Tanaka, diagrams by Jack McMaster. Copyright © 1997 by Madison Press Limited. Reprinted by permission of Madison Press Limited.

"The Challenge" from *Local News,* by Gary Soto. Copyright © 1993 by Gary Soto. Reprinted with permission of Harcourt Inc.

Selection from *Chuck Close Up Close,* by Jan Greenberg and Sandra Jordan. Copyright © 1998 by Jan Greenberg and Sandra Jordan. Reprinted by permission of Dorling Kindersley Publishing, Inc.

Selection from *Climb or Die,* by Edward Myers. Copyright © 1996 by Edward Myers. Reprinted by permission of Hyperion Books for Children.

Selection from *Dinosaur Ghosts: The Mystery of Coelophysis,* by J. Lynett Gillette, illustrated by Doug Henderson. Text copyright © 1997 by J. Lynett Gillette. Illustrations copyright © 1997 by Douglas Henderson. Reprinted by permission of Dial Books for Young Readers, a division of Penguin Putnam Inc.

Excerpt from *Eugenie Clark: Adventures of a Shark Scientist,* by Ellen R. Butts and Joyce R. Schwartz. Copyright © 2000 by Ellen R. Butts and Joyce R. Schwartz. Reprinted by permission of Linnet Book, an imprint of The Shoe String Press, Inc., North Haven, CT.

"Franklin R. Chang-Díaz" from *Standing Tall: The Stories of Ten Hispanic Americans,* by Argentina Palacios. Copyright © 1994 by Argentina Palacios. Reproduced by permission of Scholastic Inc.

The Girl Who Married the Moon: Tales from Native North America. Text copyright © 1994 by Joseph Bruchac and Gayle Ross. Published by BridgeWater Books, an imprint and trademark of Troll Communications, LLC. Reprinted by permission of Troll Communications LLC.

Selection from *The Great Pyramid,* by Elizabeth Mann, illustrations by Laura Lo Turco. Copyright © Mikaya Press. Reprinted by permission of Mikaya Press.

Selection from *The Great Wall,* by Elizabeth Mann, with illustrations by Alan Witschonke. Copyright © 1997 Mikaya Press. Original illustrations copyright © by Alan Witschonke. Reprinted by permission of Mikaya Press Inc.

Selection from *Hatchet,* by Gary Paulsen. Jacket painting by Neil Waldman. Copyright © 1987 by Gary Paulsen. Jacket copyright © 1987 by Bradbury Press. Reprinted by permission of Simon & Schuster Books for Young Readers, an imprint of Simon & Schuster Children's Publishing Division.

Selection from *The Ink-Keeper's Apprentice,* by Allen Say. Text copyright © 1979 by Allen Say. Reprinted by permission of Houghton Mifflin Company. All rights reserved.

"Jerry Pinkney: My Story," published in the book *Talking with Artists* © 1992, compiled and edited by Pat Cummings, published by Bradbury Press, a division of Macmillan Publishing Company. Copyright © 1992 by Jerry Pinkney. Reprinted by permission of the author and the Sheldon Fogelman Agency, Inc. The watercolor painting "Boy with a Wagon" Jerry Pinkney. Copyright © 1946 by Jerry Pinkney. Reprinted by permission of the author and the Sheldon Fogelman Agency, Inc. The illustration from *Black Cowboy, Wild Horses: A True Story,* by Julius Lester, illustrated by Jerry Pinkney. Illustration copyright © 1998 by Jerry Pinkney. Reprinted by permission of Dial Books for Young Readers, a division of Penguin Young Readers Group, a member of Penguin Group (USA) Inc. The illustration from *Aesop's Fables,* illustrated by Jerry Pinkney, published by Sea Star Books, a division of North-South Books Inc. Copyright © 2000 by Jerry Pinkney. Reprinted by permission of the publisher. Cover and one-page spread from *The Adventures of Spider,* by Joyce Cooper Arkhurst, illustrated by Jerry Pinkney. Text copyright © 1964 by Joyce Cooper Arkhurst. Illustration copyright © 1964 by Barker/Black Studio, Inc. Reprinted by permission of Little, Brown and Company, (Inc.). All rights reserved.

Selection from *A Kind of Grace,* by Jackie Joyner-Kersee. Copyright © 1997 by Jackie Joyner-Kersee. Reprinted by permission of Warner Books Inc.

Selection from *Last Summer with Maizon,* by Jacqueline Woodson. Copyright © 1990 by Jacqueline Woodson. Reprinted by permission of Random House Children's Books, a division of Random House Inc.

"The Lord of the Nile" from *Egyptian Myths,* by Jacqueline Morley, published by Peter Bedrick Books. Copyright © 1999 by Jacqueline Morley. Reprinted by permission of The McGraw-Hill Companies.

Selection from *Lost Temple of the Aztecs,* by Shelley Tanaka, illustrated by Greg Ruhl. Copyright © 1998 by The Madison Press Ltd. Illustrations © by Greg Ruhl. Reprinted by permission of Hyperion Books for Children.

"The Night of the Pomegranate" from *Some of the Kinder Planets,* by Tim Wynne-Jones, published by Orchard Books, an imprint of Scholastic Inc. Copyright © 1993 by Tim Wynne-Jones. Reprinted by permission of Scholastic Inc., and Groundwood Books/Douglas & McIntyre Ltd., Toronto, Canada.

"Out There" from *Rogue Wave and Other Red-Blooded Sea Stories,* by Theodore Taylor. Copyright © 1996 by Theodore Taylor. Reprinted by permission of Harcourt Inc.

Passage to Freedom, by Ken Mochizuki, illustrated by Dom Lee. Text copyright © 1997 by Ken Mochizuki. Illustrations copyright © 1997 by Dom Lee. Reprinted by permission of Lee & Low Books, Inc.

Selection from *Rosa Parks: My Story,* by Rosa Parks with Jim Haskins. Copyright © 1992 by Rosa Parks. Published by arrangement with Dial Books for Young Readers, a member of Penguin Putnam Inc.

Selection from *The Royal Kingdoms of Ghana, Mali, and Songhay,* by Patricia and Fredrick McKissack. Copyright © 1994 by Patricia and Fredrick McKissack. Reprinted by permission of Henry Holt and Company, LLC.

Selection from *The True Confessions of Charlotte Doyle,* by Avi. Copyright © 1990 by Avi. Reprinted by permission of Orchard Books, New York.

Selection from *Under the Royal Palms,* by Alma Flor Ada. Copyright © 1998 by Alma Flor Ada. Reprinted with the permission of Atheneum Books for Young Readers, an imprint of Simon & Schuster Children's Publishing Division. Cover photograph copyright © 1998 by Alma Flor Ada. Photograph used with permission of the Author and Bookstop Literary Agency. All rights reserved.

"*Brazilian Moon Tale,*" by Jane Yolen was first published in *What Rhymes with Moon?* published by Philomel Books. Copyright © 1993 by Jane Yolen. Reprinted by permission of Curtis Brown, Ltd.

"*Build and Launch a Paper Rocket!*" was adapted from *NASA's Rockets: Physical Science Teacher's Guide with Activities.*

"*Courage in the News*" from an article entitled "Boy Wonder" published in the October 4, 1995 issue of the *St. Louis Post-Dispatch.* Copyright © by the *St. Louis Post-Dispatch.* Reprinted by permission of the publisher.

"*Daily Life in Ancient Greece*" from *Ancient Greece,* by Robert Nicholson. Text copyright © 1994 by Two-Can Publishing Ltd. Reprinted by permission of Chelsea House Publishers.

"*Different Strokes,*" by Samantha Bonar from *American Girl,* May/June 1999 issue. Copyright © 1999 by Pleasant Company. Artwork © Alexandra Nechita. Reprinted by permission of Alexandra Nechita and Pleasant Company.

"*Doctor Dinosaur,*" by Carolyn Duckworth. Copyright © 1997 by Carolyn Duckworth. Reprinted by permission of the author.

"*Half Moon,*" by Federico Garcia Lorca © Herederos de Federico Garcia Lorca from *Obras Completas* (Galaxia Gutenberg, 1996 edition). Translation by W.S. Merwin copyright © Herederos de Federico Garcia Lorca and W.S. Merwin. All rights reserved. For information regarding rights and permissions, contact lorca@artslaw.co.uk or William Peter Kosmas, Esq., 8 Franklin Square, London W14 9UU, England. Translation reprinted by permission of New Directions Publishing Corp.

"*Help Wanted: Groups Seek Kid Volunteers to Change the World, No Experience Necessary*" by Anna Prokos, from the December 1997 issue of 3-2-1 *Contact* magazine. Copyright © 1997 by Children's Television Workshop. Reprinted by permission of Children's Television Workshop.

"*Home-Grown Butterflies*" from the May 1998 issue of *Ranger Rick* magazine with the permission of the National Wildlife Federation. Copyright © 1998 by the National Wildlife Federation.

"*How to Be a Good Sport*" from *Current Health* 1®, Vol. 22, No. 4, December 1998. Copyright © 1998 by Weekly Reader Corporation. All rights reserved. Reprinted by permission of the publisher.

"*Little Brother, Big Idea,*" by Ethan Herberman, from *Current Science* magazine, December 1998. Copyright © 1998 by the Weekly Reader Corporation. Reprinted by permission of the publisher.

"*Moon*" from *Sky Songs,* by Myra Cohn Livingston (Holiday House, New York). Copyright © 1984 by Myra Cohn Livingston. Reprinted by permission of Marian Reiner.

"*A Poem for Langston Hughes*" from *The Selected Poems of Nikki Giovanni,* by Nikki Giovanni. Copyright © 1996 by Nikki Giovanni. Reprinted by permission of HarperCollins Publishers.

"*Poetic Power*" by Ariel Eason, Julia Peters-Axtell and Rebecca Owen. Copyright © 1996 by New Moon Publishing. Reprinted with permission from *New Moon*®: *The Magazine for Girls and Their Dreams,* New Moon Publishing, Duluth, MN.

"*Puppy Love*" adapted from *American Girl,* Vol. 3, No. 2. Copyright © 1995 by Pleasant Company. Reprinted by permission of Pleasant Company.

"*Raising Royal Treasures*" from the November 13, 1998 issue of *Time for Kids.* Copyright © 1998 by Time Inc. Reprinted by permission of the publisher.

"*A Real Jazzy Kid!*" from the March 1994 issue of *U.S. Kids.* Copyright © 1994 by Children's Better Health Institute, Benjamin Franklin Literary & Medical Society, Inc., Indianapolis, IN. Reprinted by permission.

"*Sharks Under Ice*" from the February 1999 issue of *National Geographic World.* Copyright © 1999 by the National Geographic Society. Reprinted by permission of the publisher.

"*Summer Full Moon,*" by James Kirkup. Copyright © 1992 by James Kirkup. Reprinted by permission of the author.

"*Sylvia Earle*" from *"Exploring the Deep"* in the Winter 1999 issue of *Time for Kids.* Copyright © 1999 by Time Inc. Reprinted by permission of the publisher.

"*Winter Moon*" from *Collected Poems,* by Langston Hughes. Copyright © 1994 by the Estate of Langston Hughes. Reprinted by permission of Alfred A. Knopf, a division of Random House, Inc.

"*Youth*" from *Collected Poems,* by Langston Hughes. Copyright © 1994 by the Estate of Langston Hughes. Reprinted by permission of Alfred A. Knopf, a division of Random House Inc.

Special thanks to the following teachers whose students' compositions appear as Student Writing Models.

Writing Models

Cindy Cheatwood, Florida; Diana Davis, North Carolina; Kathy Driscoll, Massachusetts; Linda Evers, Florida; Heidi Harrison, Michigan; Eileen Hoffman, Massachusetts; Julia Kraftsow, Florida; Bonnie Lewison, Florida; Kanetha McCord, Michigan

Credits

Photography

3 (t)© Jules Frazier/Photodisc Green/Getty Images. (m) Hemera Technologies Inc. (b) © Rick Fischer/Masterfile. **5** © Jules Frazier/Photodisc Green/Getty Images. **6** (l) © PhotoDisc/Getty Images. (r) © Chris Jones/Corbis. **8** Hemera Technologies Inc. **11** Hemera Technologies Inc. **13** © Bowers Museum of Cultural Art/Corbis. **16** Hemera Technologies Inc. **17** (t) property of the American Library Association. (l) The Granger Collection, New York. (r) Corbis/Bettmann. **19** © Rick Fischer/Masterfile. **20–1** (bkgd) © Jim Cummins/Taxi/Getty Images. **21** (m) Jules Frazier/Photodisc Green/Getty Images. **22** (tr) Ed Lallo Index Stock Imagery, (mr) Courtesy of Avi, (ml) © Siede Preis/PhotoDisc/PictureQuest. **23** Vince Streano Stone/Getty Images. **24** (t) Michael Newman/PhotoEdit (bl) Myrleen Ferguson Cate/PhotoEdit, (br) David Young–Wolff/PhotoEdit. **26** (t) © Neil Rabinowitz. (b) © Art Wolfe. **27** (tl) (tr) (bl) Art Wolfe. **27** (br) © David A. Northcott/CORBIS. **28–9** (bkgd) © Paul A. Souders/Corbis. **28** (t) Craig Virden. (b) Michael Justice/Mercury Pictures. **47** St. Louis Post Dispatch. **48–9** (bkgd) Corbis Royalty Free. **50** (bkgd) © PhotoDisc/Getty Images. **50–1** (bkgd) PhotoSpin. **50** ©Sovfoto/Eastfoto. **51** Visas for Life Foundation. **52–3** (bkgd) © E.O. Hoppé/Corbis. **65** (t) Jeff Reinking/Mercury Pictures. (b) Courtesy Dom Lee. **68–71.** Monique Goodrich. **69** (frame) Image Farm. **71** (frame) Image Farm. **72** (l) Terje Rakke/The Image Bank/PictureQuest. **72–3** © Chris Rainier/CORBIS. **73** (t) © Phil Schermeister/CORBIS. (r) © Galen Rowell/CORBIS. (b) TR Youngstrom/Outside Images/PictureQuest. **74–5** (bkgd) Steve Casimiro/Allsport Concepts/Getty Images. **87** (t) Courtesy Ed Myers. (b) Courtesy Bill Farnsworth. **90–1** © Michael Lewis/CORBIS. **92–3** (bkgd) © Wild Country/CORBIS. **92** (t) Royal Geographic Society. **93** (b) Royal Geographic Society. **96–7** (bkgd) John Lawlor/Stone/Getty Images. **96** (t) Eric Bakke/Mercury Pictures. (b) Lorraine Parow/Mercury Pictures. **115** (t) James Sugar/Black Star. (b) AP/Wide World. **120** Chris Jones/Corbis. **116–6A** (bkgd) © Stephen Simpson/Taxi/Getty Images. **116** (b) Jules Frazier/Photodisc Green/Getty Images.

658

Ada. (b) Courtesy Stephanie Garcia. **490** Ashbee/Christie's Images/PictureQuest. **491** (l) © PhotoDisc/Getty Images. **493** Courtesy 321 Contact Magazine. **494** Courtesy 321 Contact Magazine. **495** Courtesy 321 Contact Magazine; **497** (tl) National Gallery of Art, Washington. Andrew W. Mellon Collection. Photo by Richard Carafelli. (tr) Art Resource, New York; (bl) © 2001 Estate of Pablo Picasso/Artists Rights Society (ARS), New York. Photograph courtesy of PaceWildenstein. (br) © Chuck Close. Photograph by Maggie L. Kundt, courtesy of PaceWildenstein. **498–9** (bkgd) © Richard Schulman/Corbis. **498** (t) Courtesy Jan Greenberg. (b) Courtesy Candlewick Press. **500** Chuck Close, *John II*, 1993, oil on canvas, 72 x 60", detail. Photographs by Bill Jacobson, courtesy of PaceWildenstein. **501** Photograph by Ellen Page Wilson. Photograph courtesy of PaceWildenstein. **502** Oliver/Hoffman Family collection, Naperville, Illinois. Photographs courtesy of PaceWildenstein. **503** (tr) (tml) (tm) (tmr) Photograph courtesy of PaceWildenstein (tr) Beatrice C. Mayer Collection, Chicago. Photograph courtesy of PaceWildenstein. (b) Hiroshima City Museum of Contemporary Art, Japan. Photograph courtesy of PaceWildenstein. **504** National Gallery of Art, Washington, DC. Lila Acheson Wallace Fund. **505** Collection of John and Mary Shirley. Photograph courtesy of PaceWildenstein. **506** Chuck Close, *John*, 1992, oil on canvas, 100 x 84" Photograph by Bill Jacobson, courtesy of PaceWildenstein. **507** Chuck Close, *John*, 1992, oil on canvas, 100 x 84" work in progress. Photographs by Bill Jacobson, courtesy ofPaceWildenstein **508** Private Collection. Photograph by Bill Jacobson, courtesy of PaceWildenstein. **509** Photograph by Ellen Page Wilson. Photograph courtesy of PaceWildenstein. **510** Photograph by Ellen Page Wilson. Photograph courtesy of PaceWildenstein. **511** (inset) The Eli and Edythe L. Broad Collection. Photograph by Ellen Page Wilson. Photograph courtesy of PaceWildenstein. (bkgd) Chuck Close, John II, 1993, oil on canvas, 72 x 60", detail. Photographs by Bill Jacobson, courtesy of PaceWildenstein. **512** © PhotoDisc/Getty Images. **513** © PhotoDisc/Getty Images. **514–6** Olivier Laude Photography. **517** (t) © Allugra. (b) Olivier Laude Photography. **518–8A** (bkgd) © Peter Cade/STONE/Getty Images. **518** (b) Hemera Technologies Inc. **522** The Granger Collection, New York. **523** The Granger Collection, New York. **524** CORBIS. **526** (l) Michael S. Yamashita/CORBIS. (r) Kevin R. Morris/CORBIS. **529** property of the American Library Association. **530–1** Ray Lincoln Literary Agency. **534** (t) Atlan/Sygma. (b) Lee Snider/CORBIS. **535** CORBIS/Bettmann. **537** The Granger Collection, New York. **538** CORBIS/Bettmann. **539** Archive Photos/PictureQuest. **540** (bkgd) Bob Daemmrich/Stock Boston/PictureQuest. (l) Tony Freeman/PhotoEdit/PictureQuest. (r) © PhotoDisc/Getty Images. **542–3** (bkgd)© Jeff Hunter/The Image Bank/Getty Images. **543** (m) © Rick Fischer/Masterfile. **544** (tr) Courtesy of Eugenie Clark, (t) Gray Hardel/Corbis. **545** (tr) Corbis, (b) Japack Company/Corbis. **546** (b) Stephen Frink/Corbis,(tl) Shirley Vanderbilt/Index Stock Imagery, (tr) Nasa/Index Stock Imagery. **547** Ian Cartwright/Getty Images. **549** Caltech/JPL/NASA. **550–1** (bkgd) James Porto/Taxi/Getty Images. **552** NASA. **563** Michael Tamborrino/Mercury Pictures. **564** © PhotoDisc/Getty Images. **565** © PhotoDisc/Getty Images. **567** (l) Caltech/JPL/NASA. (r) NASA. **568** Caltech/JPL/NASA. **569** Iris Schneider/LA Times. **570** © PhotoDisc/Getty Images. **572** NASA. **573** NASA. **574–5** (bkgd) © 1996 Corbis; Original image courtesy of NASA/Corbis. **576** (tl) (tr) The Granger Collection, New York. (m) Blank Archives/Archive Photos. (bl) (br) Archive Photos. **579** NASA. **583** (t) Art On File/CORBIS. (b) NASA. **585** NASA.

586 NASA. **587** (l) Michael Tamborrino/Mercury Pictures. (r) © PhotoDisc/Getty Images. **588** Archive Photos. **589** (t) Archive Photos. (b) Sovfoto/Eastfoto/PictureQuest. **596–7** (bkgd) Brian Skerry/National Geographic/Getty Images. **596** (t) Jesse Nemerofsky/Mercury Pictures. (b) Courtesy Kate Madin. **612–3** Nick Caloyianis/NGS Image Collection. **613** (t) Nikolas Konstantinou. **614** (t) George Benz & Todd Stailey. (m) (b) Nick Caloyianis/NGS Image Collection. **615** (t) Nick Caloyianis/NGS Image Collection. (b) Martin Walz/NGS Image Collection. **616** (t) Culver Pictures/PictureQuest. **616–7** The Academy of Natural Sciences of Philadelphia/CORBIS. **617** (t) © VCG 1998/FPG International/Getty Images. **618–9** (bkgd) Anne B. Keiser/National Geographic/Getty Images. **618** (t) Courtesy Theodore Taylor. (m) © PhotoDisc/Getty Images. (b) Richard Benjamin/Mercury Pictures. **634** © PhotoDisc/Getty Images. **636** Doug Frazier. **637–8** © Macduff Everton. **640–0A** (bkgd) © Adastra/Taxi/Getty Images. **640** (b) © Rick Fischer/Masterfile. **640G–K** David Doubilet. **640G** (bkgd) PhotoDisc. **643** © PhotoDisc/Getty Images. **644** Bob Krist/CORBIS. **645** Jan Butchofsky-Houser/CORBIS. **646** Galen Rowell/CORBIS. **648** Tria Giovan/CORBIS. **649** Neil Rabinowitz/CORBIS. **651** W. Cody/CORBIS. **652** © PhotoDisc/Getty Images. **654** Jeffrey L. Rotman/CORBIS. **655** (t) Corbis Royalty Free.

Assignment Photography

44, 45 (r), **89, 111, 159, 164–7, 183, 209, 216–7, 227, 229, 231, 233, 234, 274** (r), **293, 384–6** © HMCo./Joel Benjamin, **347** © HMCo./Kim Holcombe, **117, 215, 353, 429, 519, 641** © HMCo./Michael Indresano Photography. **240** (b), **241** (br), **425, 491** (r), **591–3, 611, 635** © HMCo./Ken Karp. **299** © HMCo./Allan Landau.

Illustration

22 Tom Barrett. **30–44, 45** (r) Copyright, 2001 by Michael Steirnagle. **52** (inset) **53–64, 67** (r) Dom Lee. **74** (i) **75–86** Bill Farnsworth. **94** (i), **97–110** Scott McKowen. **94–95, 409** Luigi Galante. **112, 114** Bryn Barnard. **116H–L** Robert Rodriguez. **118–119** Leonid Gore. **171** (i) **172–181** Lisa Desimini. **184–187** Copyright © 2001 by Nicholas Wilton. **190** (inset) **195, 196–206** Douglas Henderson. **214B–F** Blue Turrell. **240** Nancy Freeman. **246** (inset) **247–264** Joel Spector. **278–291** Eric Velasquez. **298, 300, 301–313** David Díaz. **322–346** Kevin Beilfuss. **352I, 352K, 352L, 352N** Jerry Pinkney. **352C, 352E** Allen Say. **356–358** Frank Riccio. **404–407** Philip Argent. **411–423** Rob Wood. **419** (I) Nenad Jakesevic. **426–427** Andrew Wheatcroft. **428B–F** Micheal Jaroszko. **432–436** Emma Chichester Clark. **437–444** Bee Willey. **481** (tl) John Gampert. **481–489** Copyright 2001 by Stephanie Garcia. **518C, 518E, 581F** Colin Backhouse. **518H, 518I, 518J** Tricia Tusa. **518G–J** (border) Megan Halsey. **520–521** Michael McCurdy. **549, 594–595** Paul Lee. **619** (i), **620–633** Rob Bolster. **640B–F** Mike Reed.